The Crucible Manifesto

THE CRUCIBLE MANIFESTO

Transcending Mankind's Psychosis; The Only Way Out of Earth's Polycrisis

FIRST EDITION

ISBN: 979-8-9929664-0-4 *Paperback*

ISBN: 979-8-9929664-1-1 *Ebook*

Published by Love+Truth Publishing

Cover Artwork by Mario Sanchez Nevado © - www.marionevado.art

Table of Contents

TABLE OF CONTENTS

I – Opening Invocation

THREE STAGES OF TRUTH

"All Truth passes through three stages:

First, it is ridiculed;
second, it's violently opposed;
and third, it's accepted as self-evident."

- Arthur Schopenhauer -

OPENING INVOCATION

For the light of knowing that flows through me, I humbly admit
it's not truly mine, yet I am deeply grateful to be its vessel.

May Truth be told.

Whereas Mankind's sacred work is the discovery of Truth,
where nothing may be held more sacred than the Truth no
matter how bitter its tonic might be.

For wherever my work proves incomplete,
I trust time and others will complete it.

As within, so without.

Resurrection cannot occur unless all Falsehoods
are sacrificed to the Fire.

The Phoenix born anew will not just mark Mankind's
actualized salvation, but its realized liberation.

May Truth be told.

CHAPTER 3

INTRODUCTION

The Case for This Manifesto

Humanity stands at the precipice of its own making. The world is not merely in crisis; it is undergoing a transformation so profound that only those with the eyes to see and the courage to accept will recognize its true nature. This is not merely a political, environmental, or economic crisis. It is not simply a collapse of institutions, markets, or ideologies. What we are witnessing is something far deeper—a crisis of consciousness itself.

The breakdowns we see around us—war, environmental degradation, economic disparity, and social unrest—are not separate crises but the symptoms of a singular root cause: Mankind's psychosis. Humanity has severed itself from Truth, from Natural and Cosmic law, and from the intelligence that governs Life itself. The very fabric of our civilization has been woven from illusions—false premises about intelligence, prosperity, power, and reality. We have mistaken technological progress for wisdom, economic growth for well-being, and control over Nature for mastery of Life. In doing so, we have set ourselves on a path of incoherence, disharmony, and inevitable collapse.

This Manifesto is not another intellectual exercise, nor is it a plea for reform within the existing system. It is called *The Crucible Manifesto* because humanity now stands in the fire of transformation—at the edge of either total collapse or a profound awakening. A Crucible is both a trial by fire and a vessel for purification, and this moment in history is precisely that: a test that will determine whether we emerge as something greater or dissolve into self-destruction. The system itself is the problem. It cannot be fixed from within, nor can a completely new system—designed solely by human intellect—truly resolve the crisis. Beneath the existing system, beneath any attempted reforms or innovations, lies the root cause: a Spiritual Crisis within Mankind. Without first undergoing a Spiritual Revolution, any system we construct will remain flawed, bound and limited by the same level of collective consciousness that created the current disorder and collapsing system. The Spiritual Revolution is the shift from seeing ourselves as the self-anointed masters of the Universe—on a conquest to submit Nature to our will and material desires—to recognizing ourselves as integral fractals and Divine expressions of the Universe. We have been entrusted with the stewardship of this planet, and our highest purpose is to live in harmonic resonance with the immutable laws and principles of all of Creation.

Just as the Copernican Revolution lifted humanity's understanding of the Universe as it pertains to the manifest material realm, the next revolution must and will lift humanity's understanding of the unmanifest spiritual realm which underpins all of the material realm. In other words, the material realm is born from the spiritual realm, which we will show in this Manifesto is not merely an esoteric claim but an understanding fully embraced within quantum physics. So too must this next revolution elevate Mankind's perception of itself, restore its severed connection with Nature of which it is an integral part, and its place within the Grand Architecture of Creation. Only then can a new system emerge—one founded upon higher-order intelligence and alignment with Natural law.

Within this Manifesto, we will articulate and define exactly what constitutes higher-order intelligence, exploring its principles and how it contrasts with the false constructs of intelligence that have guided human civilization into its current crisis. What is required is nothing less than a systemic change and fundamental shift—not a political revolution, not a redesign of the economy or institutions, but a revolution in consciousness which births a whole new way of Life for Mankind. This is the **Spiritual Revolution** that's forthcoming—a reckoning that will realign humanity with the immutable laws of Creation, dismantling the illusions and incomplete doctrines, theories, and misunderstandings of the true nature of reality which have governed human affairs for millennia. Just as the **Copernican Revolution** forced Mankind to accept that our planet was not the center of the physical Universe, the Spiritual Revolution will force mankind to confront the fact that it has been lost in its own illusion of self-aggrandizement—severed from its true nature, Nature itself, and the true intelligence and sovereignty that is its celestial birthright.

The Polycrisis that afflicts Earth is not truly the crisis of the planet itself—it is the manifest reflection of the Spiritual Crisis within Mankind itself. Earth is not dying; humanity is being invited—some would say forced—into its initiation into higher levels of collective consciousness, facing the self-inflicted threat of the Sixth Mass Extinction. This is the great trial, the Crucible of our time. We either transcend, or we descend and likely perish as the planet and civilization degenerates into a dystopian reality. But no crisis can be solved at the level of intelligence that created it. The only way forward is to rise above, to step beyond the distortions of the past and enter a higher octave of consciousness.

This Manifesto is a field guide for those brave enough to take the blindfold off and see what has always been right there. It is a torch in the darkness, exposing illusions that must be shattered and revealing the Truth that must be reclaimed. It will challenge, it will confront, and it will force the reader to reckon with what our society and civilization has either obscured from sight or taught us to deny.

The question before us is simple: Will humanity choose to rise, meet its Crucible, and emerge born anew; or, will humanity refuse to walk the fire in preference of what it knows, even though what's known is also known to be failing and collapsing? The choice is ours.

CHAPTER 4

A WALK THROUGH HISTORY:
THE RISE AND FALL OF CIVILIZATIONS

I. Introduction

Throughout history, civilizations have followed a recurring pattern of rise, peak, and collapse. This cycle is not coincidental; it is the result of fundamental dynamics that govern societies across time and geography. By studying these patterns, we gain invaluable insight into our present moment and the trajectory that lies ahead.

Civilizations are born out of hardship, forged by the necessity of survival. They ascend through discipline, vision, and the collective effort of their people. At their peak, they achieve great prosperity, intellectual advancement, and cultural flourishing. Yet, it is at this apex that decline sets in—prosperity gives way to decadence, wisdom to complacency, and unity to fragmentation. The same forces that once strengthened the civilization ultimately sow the seeds of its own downfall, leading to collapse.

This pattern has played out repeatedly—Ancient Rome, the Mayan Empire, Byzantium, the Ottoman Empire, and Weimar Germany are just a few examples. While the specific details of each decline vary, the underlying causes are remarkably consistent: moral decay, financial corruption, political dysfunction, and spiritual disconnection. History does not repeat itself exactly, but it rhymes.

Understanding this cycle is essential because it allows us to recognize and respond to the warning signs of decline in our own era. Today, we find ourselves at a crossroads, witnessing many of the same dysfunctions that have preceded the fall of past civilizations. However, unlike previous societies, we now have the ability to reflect on history with unprecedented access to information and a global perspective. This gives us a unique opportunity to break the cycle—if we are willing to see the Truth of our moment and act accordingly.

The study of history is not an academic exercise; it is a vital key to understanding the crisis we face today. Recognizing the patterns of the past enables us to see our present situation with greater clarity. Only by acknowledging the forces that have led civilizations to ruin can we begin to navigate a different path—one that does not lead to inevitable decline but to the possibility of renewal and transcendence.

II. The Cycle of Civilizations: The Arc of Rise and Fall

The rise and fall of civilizations is not a random phenomenon; it follows a recurring arc, governed by universal principles of societal evolution. While each civilization is unique in its geography, culture, and leadership, the underlying forces shaping its trajectory are strikingly similar. By examining these patterns, we gain a deeper understanding of where we stand today and what may come next.

Civilizations typically pass through four distinct stages:

1. Emergence and Hardship

- Civilizations are often born out of adversity. Scarcity, struggle, and necessity compel a society to develop strong values, discipline, and unity.

- Early societies emphasize survival, cooperation, and foundational virtues like honor, courage, and integrity.

- Leadership in this stage is often strong, visionary, and mission-driven, focusing on long-term sustainability.

2. Expansion and Growth

- With a solid foundation, civilizations expand territorially, economically, and culturally.

- Innovations in governance, technology, and infrastructure lead to increased prosperity and influence.

- Strong institutions and social cohesion enable stability, allowing for flourishing arts, sciences, and philosophy.

3. Peak and Indulgence

- At their peak, civilizations enjoy wealth, comfort, and global influence.

- However, abundance often leads to complacency. Disciplined values that forged the civilization begin to erode.

- Elites become detached from the struggles of ordinary people, and institutions begin serving self-interest rather than societal good.

- Hedonism, entitlement, and moral relativism take hold, weakening the fabric of society.

4. Decay and Collapse

- Over time, corruption, economic decline, and social fragmentation set in.

- Political dysfunction and overreach lead to disillusionment and division.

- The civilization, once strong, becomes vulnerable to external threats and internal implosion.

- Either through slow decline or sudden collapse, the cycle concludes, often leaving a power vacuum that allows a new civilization to emerge.

Historical Examples:

- **Rome:** Rose from a disciplined Republic, peaked as an empire, then decayed through corruption and moral decline.

- **Byzantium:** A continuation of Rome, thriving through cohesion but eventually succumbing to internal weakness.

- **Weimar Germany:** A brief period of artistic and intellectual vibrancy, collapsing under economic crisis and political extremism.

Understanding these historical cycles allows us to reflect on where our current civilization stands. Are we in a phase of peak prosperity, or are we already descending into fragmentation and decline? Recognizing these patterns is the first step in determining whether we follow the historical trend—or if we can consciously break the cycle.

III. Patterns of Moral, Financial, and Spiritual Decay Leading to Collapse

The decline of civilizations is rarely abrupt; rather, it unfolds gradually as certain key pillars weaken over time. Moral decay, financial corruption, and spiritual disconnection create the conditions for collapse, often accelerating societal fragmentation. Understanding these patterns allows us to recognize the warning signs of decline and see how they manifest in different civilizations throughout history.

Moral Decay: The Erosion of Virtue and Discipline

A defining characteristic of a civilization in decline is the loss of personal and collective virtue. Societies that once upheld values such as discipline, honor, and personal responsibility gradually shift toward entitlement, indulgence, and apathy.

Hardship fosters strength, but prolonged comfort and luxury often lead to stagnation and moral decay.

- **Loss of Civic Virtue:** In early stages, people contribute to society with a sense of duty and responsibility. Over time, self-interest replaces collective well-being, and civic engagement erodes.

- **Entitlement and Hedonism:** As civilizations reach their peak, prosperity gives rise to indulgence. Rather than fostering continued growth, wealth leads to complacency and dependency.

- **The Decline of Personal Responsibility:** Individuals increasingly defer responsibility to the state, institutions, or others, eroding self-reliance and personal accountability.

Historical Example: The later years of the Roman Empire saw a decline in civic duty as citizens turned to bread and circuses—state-sponsored entertainment and welfare—to distract from the empire's growing instability.

Financial Corruption: The Degradation of Economic Integrity

Economic instability is another hallmark of declining civilizations. While early stages of civilization emphasize industriousness and sustainable growth, later stages often see reckless financial speculation, widening wealth gaps, and systemic corruption.

- **Speculation and Financialization:** As economies mature, productive industries give way to speculative markets, where wealth is generated through manipulation rather than value creation.

- **Wealth Concentration and Inequality:** A small elite accumulates vast resources while the majority struggles, leading to social unrest and resentment.

- **Debt Expansion and Economic Instability:** Governments, attempting to sustain their illusion of prosperity, rely on excessive borrowing, debasing currency, and unsustainable financial policies.

Historical Example: The Weimar Republic in Germany saw rampant hyperinflation due to reckless monetary policies, eroding trust in institutions and paving the way for authoritarianism.

Political Dysfunction: Corruption and Authoritarianism

As civilizations decay, their political structures become increasingly dysfunctional. What once operated with a sense of purpose and governance devolves into corruption, incompetence, and often, authoritarian overreach.

- **Corrupt Elites and Institutional Decay:** Leadership prioritizes self-interest over national well-being, leading to bureaucratic inefficiency and widespread public disillusionment.

- **Polarization and Social Fragmentation:** Society becomes divided along ideological, economic, and ethnic lines, eroding unity and weakening the nation's resilience.

- **The Erosion of Rule of Law:** Democratic principles are undermined as legal systems become tools of the elite, favoring those in power while repressing dissent.

Historical Example: The fall of the Byzantine Empire was exacerbated by internal political strife, weak leadership, and betrayal from within, which left it vulnerable to external conquest.

Spiritual Disconnection: The Loss of Higher Purpose

Perhaps the most overlooked yet critical factor in the collapse of civilizations is the decline of spiritual coherence. In the early stages, societies are guided by a shared sense of purpose and higher ideals. As they mature, materialism replaces meaning, and nihilism sets in.

- **The Rise of Materialism:** A civilization obsessed with consumption and accumulation loses its sense of the transcendent, prioritizing wealth and power over wisdom and virtue.

- **Disconnection from Higher Wisdom:** Ancient cultures often had guiding philosophies or spiritual traditions that reinforced harmony. As these are discarded, society drifts aimlessly.

- **The Breakdown of Coherent Worldviews:** Without a unifying ethos, cultures fracture into competing interests, accelerating societal fragmentation.

Historical Example: The decline of ancient Greece saw the erosion of its philosophical and spiritual foundations, leading to moral relativism and disunity that weakened the polis (city-state) system.

The Slow March to Collapse

Moral, financial, political, and spiritual decay do not happen overnight; they unfold over generations. By the time a society recognizes these symptoms, the damage is often irreversible. However, understanding these patterns allows us to assess where we stand today and whether we have the will to shift course.

As we examine the modern world, we must ask: Are we following the trajectory of past civilizations? If so, is there still time to alter our path? In the next section, we will explore how today's crisis mirrors past collapses—and why this era presents a unique opportunity to break the cycle.

IV. How Today's Crisis Mirrors Past Collapses—And Why It's Different

Throughout history, the collapse of civilizations has followed recognizable patterns. Political strife, economic instability, and moral decline have repeatedly played a role in the downfall of great societies. Today, we see many of these same forces at work. However, our present era introduces a new, unique factor: global interconnectedness. While past civilizations could rise and fall in relative isolation, today's world is tightly woven together through technology, finance, and geopolitics, making our crisis fundamentally different from anything before.

Political and Social Fragmentation

One of the most visible indicators of civilizational decline is the breakdown of social cohesion. In past collapses, the unity that once bound societies together eroded under the weight of internal strife, ideological polarization, and power struggles. We see similar fractures in the modern world.

- **Political Polarization:** The ideological chasm between competing political factions has grown wider, making governance nearly impossible. The ability to find common ground is rapidly disappearing as division replaces dialogue.

- **Loss of Institutional Trust:** Faith in governments, media, and other societal institutions is at an all-time low. When people no longer trust the systems that uphold order, they disengage or turn to radical alternatives.

- **Social Unrest:** Protests, riots, and populist movements are growing worldwide, a clear indication that many feel alienated from the structures meant to represent them.

Historical Example: The late Roman Republic was plagued by intense political infighting, ultimately leading to its transformation into an empire ruled by authoritarian force. The inability to bridge societal divides hastened its decline.

Economic Instability and Financial Speculation

Economic instability has always played a major role in the collapse of civilizations. As societies mature, they often shift from productive economies to financialized systems built on speculation, debt, and short-term gain. This pattern is evident today.

- **Debt-Fueled Growth:** Governments and corporations have become increasingly reliant on borrowing to sustain economic expansion. This creates the illusion of prosperity while inflating massive financial bubbles.

- **Speculation Over Production:** Like past civilizations that prioritized luxury and excess over essential goods, today's economy is heavily driven by stock market speculation, hedge funds, and algorithmic trading rather than real-world productivity.

- **Wealth Concentration:** The vast accumulation of resources by a small elite while the majority struggles to afford basic necessities is a repeating sign of decline.

Historical Example: The economic collapse of the Weimar Republic was accelerated by reckless financial policies and speculative excesses, leading to hyperinflation and societal collapse.

Moral and Spiritual Decline in Modern Societies

At the core of every civilizational collapse is a loss of meaning, purpose, and higher ideals. Societies in decline often trade virtue for convenience, wisdom for entertainment, and responsibility for indulgence.

- **The Rise of Consumerism:** In place of deeper spiritual fulfillment, modern society promotes material accumulation, trapping people in a cycle of endless consumption with no sense of greater purpose.

- **The Breakdown of Shared Values:** When civilizations lose a unifying ethos, cultural relativism replaces moral coherence, leading to division and confusion.

- **The Erosion of Higher Meaning:** Spiritual wisdom and philosophical inquiry, which once guided civilizations, have been cast aside in favor of secularism that lacks deeper purpose.

Historical Example: The decline of ancient Greece saw a move away from its great philosophical and spiritual traditions, leading to moral and civic disintegration that made it vulnerable to conquest.

The Unique Factor: Global Interconnectedness

While past civilizations collapsed in isolation, today's crisis is unique in that every aspect of our world is globally connected. This adds an unprecedented level of complexity and risk.

- **Financial and Trade Interdependence:** A collapse in one major economy now has ripple effects worldwide, ensuring that no nation is insulated from global economic crises.

- **Technology and Instant Communication:** Unlike past eras, where decline took generations to unfold, information and events now spread instantly, accelerating instability.

- **Geopolitical Complexity:** Unlike the fall of Rome or Byzantium, where decline was regional, modern collapse would be global, affecting every country simultaneously.

This interconnectedness is both a challenge and an opportunity. While it means that instability spreads faster than ever, it also means that awareness and solutions can be shared on a global scale. Our era presents a rare moment where, if we recognize the repeating patterns of history, we may have the ability to alter the trajectory before collapse becomes inevitable.

In the next section, we will explore what it takes to break the cycle and how a new paradigm of moral, financial, and spiritual coherence can create a different future

V. Breaking the Cycle: The Opportunity for Renewal

History reveals that civilizations do not collapse by accident—they decline as a result of choices made over generations. Yet, history also shows that decline is not inevitable. Societies that recognize the signs of impending failure and take decisive action can renew themselves, restoring coherence and vitality. Today, we stand at such a crossroads. The lessons of the past are available to us, offering a roadmap for a different outcome. The question is whether we have the courage and clarity to choose renewal over collapse.

Learning from History to Avoid Repeating Its Mistakes

A civilization that refuses to learn from history is doomed to repeat it. The patterns of decline we have examined—moral decay, financial corruption, political dysfunction, and spiritual disconnection—are neither unique to the modern era nor irreversible. We must study the past not as a distant memory, but as an active guide to the present and future.

- **Recognition of Decay:** A society that acknowledges its decline gains the ability to correct course. Civilizations that failed to recognize their trajectory fell into irreparable collapse.

- **Embracing Responsibility:** Renewal begins when individuals and societies accept that the future is not dictated by fate but by conscious action.

- **Restoring Integrity to Leadership and Institutions:** History demonstrates that civilizations with principled leadership and strong institutions are more resilient than those plagued by corruption and short-term thinking.

Restoring Moral, Financial, and Spiritual Coherence

Civilizations that endure and thrive are those that maintain coherence across all aspects of their society—moral, financial, and spiritual. Coherence means alignment with fundamental principles of Life, wisdom, and integrity.

- **Moral Coherence:** Reestablishing a foundation of virtue, discipline, and responsibility is essential for societal renewal. A culture that rewards excellence and integrity fosters resilience and innovation.

- **Financial Coherence:** True economic health is based on value creation rather than speculation and financial manipulation. Economies must shift from extractive models toward regenerative and Life-affirming principles.

- **Spiritual Coherence:** The human experience is incomplete without a sense of higher meaning. Societies that embrace wisdom traditions, personal growth, and a connection to something greater than material success cultivate inner strength and long-term stability.

Rebuilding Economic Integrity and Social Cohesion

Economic and social coherence are the cornerstones of a thriving civilization. The erosion of economic integrity—through wealth disparity, financialization, and unsustainable debt—leads directly to social unrest and institutional collapse. Rebuilding these structures requires fundamental shifts in values and policies.

- **Honest Money and Financial Systems:** Civilizations that avoid collapse maintain monetary systems that are in service to society and promote and support real productivity over financial speculation.

- **A Culture of Contribution, Not Entitlement:** Societies that reward creativity, effort, and community engagement remain robust, while those that foster entitlement and dependency deteriorate.

- **Restoring Social Bonds:** The decline of civilizations is often marked by increasing isolation and fragmentation. Rebuilding local, national, and global cohesion is essential to reversing decline.

The Conscious Choice: Decline or Renewal

We are living in an era where the stakes are higher than ever before. Unlike past civilizations, which could rise and fall in relative isolation, our world is interconnected. This means that the collapse of one system has the potential to trigger cascading failures globally—but it also means that transformation can spread just as rapidly.

At this juncture, humanity faces a choice: will we continue down the well-trodden path of decline, or will we choose a higher path? Renewal is possible, but it requires conscious engagement, personal responsibility, and the willingness to transcend outdated paradigms. The future is unwritten, and it is within our power to shape it.

In the final section of this chapter, we will explore the implications of this choice and how *The Crucible Manifesto* serves as an invocation for a new trajectory—one that defies the historical patterns of collapse and embraces the possibility of transcendence.

VI. Conclusion

The future is not predetermined. Civilizations have risen and fallen, but history is not an unbreakable cycle—it is a reflection of choices made, values upheld, and wisdom either embraced or discarded. If history has taught us anything, it is that the fate of a civilization is ultimately shaped by the consciousness of its people.

We stand at a moment of reckoning, where the trajectory of our world is poised between collapse and renewal. The lessons of the past illuminate the dangers of continuing on our current path, but they also reveal the immense potential for transformation when societies recognize the need for change before it is too late.

The Importance of Recognizing and Acting on Historical Patterns

Great civilizations of the past did not collapse overnight, nor were they brought down solely by external forces. They eroded from within—through moral decay, financial corruption, and a loss of coherence in leadership and social values. Today, we find ourselves facing similar patterns, but with one crucial difference: we have the awareness and the tools to break this cycle if we choose to do so.

- **Awareness as the First Step:** Recognizing the signs of decline is necessary to initiate any meaningful transformation.

- **Action as the Decisive Factor:** Knowing is not enough; change requires deliberate shifts in values, structures, and leadership.

- **Consciousness as the Foundation:** A civilization's outer world is a reflection of its inner world. Elevating collective consciousness is the only path to meaningful and lasting renewal.

This Manifesto as an Invocation for Transcendence

This Manifesto is not a call to stave off collapse through superficial reforms. It does not attempt to offer mere technical solutions to systemic failures. Rather, it is an invocation—an offering of wisdom, insight, and Truth that challenges the reader to see beyond the illusions of our time and embrace a higher order of intelligence.

We are not here to "fix" a broken system. We are here to dissolve outdated paradigms, restore coherence, and embody a new way of Being. The work ahead is not about prolonging a civilization that has lost its way, but about birthing something entirely new—something that aligns with the intelligence of Life itself.

Why This Chapter Matters for the Journey Ahead

Understanding the rise and fall of civilizations provides the critical backdrop for what we will lay bare in this Manifesto. The dysfunctions we see today—political, economic, social, and spiritual—are not isolated crises; they are manifestations of a deeper disconnection from Truth, wisdom, and the very essence of Life.

What follows in this Manifesto is not simply an exposé of what has gone wrong. It is an unmasking of the deeper forces at play—an excavation of the root causes of humanity's crisis and a pathway toward transcending the unconscious patterns that have defined civilization for millennia.

The journey ahead is not for the faint-hearted. It demands courage, discernment, and an unwavering commitment to Truth. And please be forewarned: Truth can be a bitter tonic. At the same time, Truth also serves as a cleansing tonic. Even when it stings at first, its medicine is already at work.

For those willing to engage, this Manifesto may offer something rare—the opportunity to see with new eyes. This Manifesto will not erase the chaos, disruption, and slow collapse we are witnessing in the world today. But it may allow you to perceive something else emerging—something that does not merely avert collapse, but transcends the world as we know it.

This is the world of wonder and beauty I speak of. This Manifesto exists to illuminate the path—and to show how we may become its midwives.

The heart of the Manifesto begins in the next chapter.

In every Crucible, there's a choice that must be made.

II – The Reckoning: What Gave Birth to This Manifesto

THE CRUCIBLE OF OUR TIME

Humanity stands on the edge of a threshold unlike any before. This moment is not just another chapter in history—it is a reckoning, a Crucible in which everything we have known, believed, and built is being challenged, tested, and confronted by the higher-order Truths of the Cosmic Order of which we are but an infinitesimal speck of proverbial stardust. How Mankind emerges from this trial will determine whether we ascend into a higher order of existence or collapse under the weight of our own creations, many of which stand in direct opposition to the immutable laws and principles of our Universe.

A Crucible is both a trial and a vessel for transformation. It is where impurities are burned away, where base metals (i.e our lower nature) are refined into gold (i.e. our higher nature). This is where we now stand—as individuals, as a civilization, and as a species. The crises we see unfolding around us—social unrest, environmental degradation, economic instability, endless wars, and the erosion of Truth—are not separate events, but interconnected symptoms of a deeper disorder. This disorder does not originate externally; it is a reflection of our inner incoherence. Humanity's crisis is not one of politics, climate, or technology. These are the effects, not the cause. The real crisis is Mankind's Spiritual Crisis at the level of consciousness.

We have mistaken our material advancements for progress, believing that the accumulation of knowledge, wealth, and power signifies an evolution of our species. Yet, what have these pursuits truly brought us? A world where billions live in fear, where division is sown into every aspect of Life, where suffering is normalized, advances in science routinely abused and misused, and where Nature itself is raped and pillaged to satisfy the endless hunger of human consumption. We have been playing a game of conquest, believing that by controlling and extracting from the Earth, from each other, and from the very fabric of existence, we are somehow mastering Life itself. But we are not the masters—we are but one expression of sentient Life in a vast and intelligent Cosmos that we barely understand. And now, that Cosmos is issuing its response.

Throughout history, civilizations have risen and fallen. Each collapse has carried with it a warning, a lesson left for those who would come after. But this time, the stakes are greater. For the first time, we are facing a manmade planetary crisis, a convergence of breakdowns so vast and complex that no single institution, government, or ideology can claim to have the solution.

What we call the Polycrisis—a term used to describe the cascading failures in economics, governance, planetary health, and social cohesion—is not merely a consequence of bad policies or mismanagement. It is the inevitable outcome of a civilization that has been built on false premises and an incomplete understanding and recognition Mankind is an integral part of a vast and complex web of Life, not a separate class of masters or owners superior to this web of Life.

By ignoring Natural law and severing ourselves from the deeper wisdom interwoven throughout all of Creation, we have erected artificial constructs that are now crumbling before our eyes. In all of Nature, every living system self-regulates, self-corrects, and functions within the governing intelligence of the whole. Mankind, however, has positioned itself as an exception—an entity that believes it is above the laws that govern all of Life.

Our Cosmos is a vast, living organism, an intricate web of Life governed by principles of complex living systems. The health of such a complex web of interconnected nested smaller systems within larger systems is predicated on harmony and coherence. When any "cell" within this larger organism goes rogue—i.e. becomes disharmonious with the whole—it functions like a cancerous cell. Nature is designed to neutralize such disharmony, whether through regeneration, evolution, extinction, ecological collapse, or natural disasters.

At this juncture, humanity is behaving as a cancerous cell within Earth's living system, pushing her toward a critical state of collapse. However, let me be unequivocally clear—this metaphor is not an argument for eugenics or depopulation. That reductionist mindset is akin to attempting to "fix" nutrient-depleted soils with GMO seeds and glyphosate rather than restoring its natural balance. The issue is not humanity's DNA or the number of people on the planet; the issue is how we, as a species, choose to live. The root problem is not overpopulation but the widespread failure to live in harmony with Mother Earth.

The reality, however, is that while Mankind's extinction would be catastrophic for us, Mother Earth would endure and eventually regenerate—as she always has. She will simply use her abundance of time taking millennia to restore herself, free from the presence of a species that has lived in opposition to her intelligence. We were warned—not by prophets or philosophers alone, but by the very structure of reality itself. What is not in harmony with Life cannot endure. What is incoherent will dissolve. What is based on Falsehoods will inevitably come to pass as it burns away in the Crucible of Truth.

We are now presented with a choice. This Crucible is the choice we must make—to stay the current course with small incremental yet wholly insufficient adjustments, or to transcend our lower Egoic nature and rise into our higher Spiritual nature. This is not a passive moment in history. It is an ultimatum. No leader, institution, or external force will rescue us from ourselves. There will be no saviors, no technological deus ex machina to rescue us from ourselves. No technological or scientific advancement can override a fundamental misalignment with the actual rules of the game—Natural law, the governing intelligence of our Cosmos and all within it. These rules—governing energy, reciprocity, coherence, and evolutionary adaptation—are not subject to human debate or intervention. Mankind is the problem, the rules of the game are flawless in their design. So, either we wake up to the Truth of our reality, what we are and why we are here, or we continue down a path that leads to inevitable collapse. The question is not whether human systems will fail, or Nature will degenerate and reach its limits—all of this is already here and happening. The question is whether we will rise to meet it or perish in its wake.

This is the Crucible of Our Time.

What we collectively choose in this 11th hour will determine the fate of Mankind. This is not a distant crisis; it is here. This is not a theoretical dilemma; it is an immediate, tangible choice that rests in our hands. And in this moment of reckoning, there is little room for error.

In every Crucible, there's a choice that must be made.

THE CRUCIBLE OF OUR TIME

EXECUTIVE SUMMARY

Why Should You Read This Chapter?

We are not merely witnessing a crisis of systems—we are experiencing a crisis of consciousness. The Polycrisis is not a random series of unfortunate events; it is the inevitable result of a civilization built on false premises and an incomplete understanding of reality.

This chapter dissects why everything is unraveling at once—not as a failure of leadership or policy, but as a direct reflection of humanity's severance from Natural law and higher intelligence. It challenges the illusion that political, technological, or economic solutions can solve this crisis, making the case that our only way forward is through a fundamental transformation in consciousness. If we fail to recognize this, we will remain trapped in a cycle of systemic collapse and existential turmoil.

Executive Summary: Key Takeaways

- Humanity stands at a threshold unlike any before—a reckoning that will determine whether we ascend into higher consciousness or collapse under our own dysfunction.

- The crises we see today—environmental destruction, social unrest, economic instability, war, and the erosion of Truth—are not isolated events but symptoms of a deeper disorder.

- This is not a political, economic, or technological crisis—these are effects, not the cause. The root cause is Mankind's Spiritual Crisis—our severance from higher intelligence and Natural law.

The Reality We Have Created

- We have mistaken material accumulation for progress, believing wealth, power, and knowledge signify evolution.

- Yet, we live in a world of fear, division, suffering, and the relentless exploitation of Nature.

- Humanity has played a game of conquest, assuming we can extract from Earth and control Life itself—but we are not the masters.

- The Cosmos is responding.

The Polycrisis as a Reflection of Our Psychosis

- What we call the Polycrisis—the collapse of economics, governance, planetary health, and social cohesion—is not due to bad policies or poor leadership.

- It is the inevitable outcome of a civilization built on false premises—a system that sees humanity as separate from, rather than an integral part of, the web of Life.

- Human law does not override Natural law. Every living system in Nature self-regulates and functions in harmony with the whole—except us.

Humanity as a Cancer on the Planet

- The Universe operates as a self-organizing, intelligent complex living system, governed by harmony and coherence.

- When any part of the whole goes rogue, becoming disharmonious, it functions like a cancerous cell.

- Humanity has become that cancer, and the Earth is now in hospice care.

The Illusion of Technological Salvation

- Civilizations have risen and fallen before, but this time, we are facing a planetary crisis of our own making.

- No institution, ideology, or technological advancement can save us from ourselves.

- Science cannot override Natural law. The rules of the Cosmos—governing energy, coherence, reciprocity, and adaptation—are immutable.

The Ultimatum Before Us

- This Crucible presents a choice:
    - Stay the current course, making minor, ineffective adjustments.
    - Transcend our lower nature and rise into our higher spiritual intelligence.

- There will be no saviors, no external rescue.

- Either we awaken to Truth, or we continue toward inevitable collapse.

The Decision That Will Define Our Fate

- This is not a distant crisis—it is unfolding now.

- This is not a theoretical exercise—it is a real-life choice that is ours to make.

- Human systems are already failing. The question is no longer if, but how we respond.

- The 11th hour is here—and our collective choice will determine the fate of Mankind.

EARTH'S POLYCRISIS AS A MIRROR OF MANKIND'S PSYCHOSIS

I. Introduction: The Polycrisis is Not the Real Crisis

Humanity is facing a moment of profound reckoning. The convergence of economic instability, environmental degradation, technological disruption, geopolitical conflict, and societal breakdown—commonly referred to as the Polycrisis—has become an unavoidable reality. However, to perceive this crisis as merely a set of external failures is to miss the deeper Truth: the Polycrisis is not the disease but the symptom. It is the inevitable manifestation of an underlying pathology—a reflection of Mankind's collective psychosis.

At its core, this chapter posits that the Polycrisis is not merely political, economic, or technological in nature. These are effects, not causes. The real crisis is one of consciousness—Mankind's disconnection from higher intelligence, Natural law, Reality itself, and, fundamentally, its Divine essence. We have collectively forgotten the great wisdom teachings of the sages, mystics, and teachers that came before us and in the process traded the sacred for the base. This severance has led to a worldview defined by fragmentation, competition, exploitation, and control, rather than one rooted in harmony, reciprocity, and coherence with the greater Cosmic Order.

Everything unfolding in the outer world is merely a mirror of the inner disorder within humanity. Civilization is now in a tailspin, not because of isolated political failures or financial mismanagement, but because it has been built on false premises and misaligned with the deeper, immutable laws and principles that govern all of Life. The belief that we can manipulate, extract from, and engineer the world without consequence has reached its breaking point.

The purpose of this chapter is not just to diagnose the Polycrisis, but to reveal it for what it truly is: a spiritual reckoning. Mankind's psychosis is, at its core, a Spiritual Crisis—the Meta Crisis from which all other crises emerge. It is Mankind's invitation to awaken, to recognize that the world we have created is nothing more than a projection of our own internal fragmentation and low collective level of consciousness, which has Mankind held hostage by its lower nature. Until we address the root cause—our collective level of consciousness—we will remain trapped in an endless cycle of dysfunction, collapse, and suffering.

What follows is an exploration of the fundamental distortions in thought and belief that have driven humanity to this moment. We will examine how fragmented, reductionist thinking has led to incoherent systems, how the false religion of Neoclassical economic theory has shaped destructive behaviors, how our violence against Nature has undermined our very survival, and how our submission to control structures has robbed us of our sovereignty. Each of these is not an isolated crisis but an expression of the deeper disorder within Mankind.

The Polycrisis is not just an external event. It is a mirror. And until we recognize ourselves in its reflection, we will remain blind to the true nature of the problem—and therefore, to the only real path forward.

II. The Reductionist Fallacy: How Fragmented Thinking Created the Polycrisis

The modern world is built upon a fundamental misconception: the belief that reality can be broken down into discrete, independent parts and that by controlling these parts, we can control the whole. This is the essence of reductionism, a worldview that has shaped modern science, economics, medicine, governance, and technological development. Yet, reductionism is inherently flawed because it ignores the interconnected, self-organizing, and intelligent nature of Life itself.

Reductionism operates under the assumption that the sum of the parts is equal to the whole, yet every advanced field of study—from quantum physics to complex systems theory—has demonstrated that this is a false premise. The Universe is not a machine that can be disassembled and reassembled at will; it is a vast, living system governed by emergent properties and deep interdependencies.

This fallacy has led to systemic incoherence across all aspects of human civilization:

- In Medicine: Instead of treating the body as an integrated system of self-healing intelligence, modern medicine fragments health into isolated symptoms and diseases, leading to pharmaceutical interventions that often exacerbate underlying dysfunction rather than resolving it.

- In Economics: The world economy treats natural resources, labor, and capital as separate, independent variables, ignoring the reality that all economic activity is dependent on the health of the biosphere and the well-being of society.

- In Environmental Policy: Climate change is often framed exclusively as a carbon problem, ignoring the interconnected destruction of ecosystems, biodiversity loss, and pollution that are far greater existential threats to planetary stability.

- In Governance & Society: Governments, laws, and policies are structured as bureaucratic silos, incapable of responding to crises holistically because they are designed to manage isolated issues rather than recognizing their interconnections.

This fragmented, mechanistic thinking is the creative force that culminated into the Polycrisis, the root cause of which is Mankind's Spiritual Crisis—the Meta Crisis. The systems we have built are failing not because of isolated errors but because they were designed from a fundamentally flawed understanding of reality. Until we transcend this fractured mode of thinking and return to a holistic understanding of Life as an intelligent, self-regulating system, we will remain trapped in an endless cycle of crisis and collapse.

The only way forward is a return to holistic intelligence—one that recognizes interconnection, coherence, and the higher-order intelligence woven throughout all of Creation. Without this shift, no amount of policy reform, scientific breakthroughs, or technological advancements will solve the crisis we face.

III. Economics as a Case Study in Mankind's Psychosis

One of the clearest manifestations of Mankind's Spiritual Crisis—the Meta Crisis— is found in the realm of economics. Our global economic system is not a neutral tool for exchange; it is a dogmatic belief system that dictates human behavior, shapes societies, and reinforces the very distortions that have led to the Polycrisis. Economics, as currently practiced, is not an objective science—it is a theoretical religion masquerading as science.

At the heart of this false economic religion is the assumption that wealth accumulation and perpetual growth equate to progress. The dominant economic paradigm—Neoclassical economics—treats the world as a mechanical system of inputs and outputs, disregarding the fundamental Truth that all economic activity is embedded in the biosphere and depends on the well-being of people and planet.

Some of the primary distortions in economic thinking that fuel the Polycrisis include:

- **Infinite Growth on a Finite Planet**: The idea that economies must grow endlessly, despite clear ecological limits.

- **Abstract Wealth Accumulation Over Real Value & Benefit Creation**: Financial markets reward speculative gains and monopolization of wealth, assets, and resources rather than value and benefit creation for the greatest good of all.

- **Entrenched Monolithic Energy Complex**: The global energy sector remains centralized and monopolized, ensuring continued dependence on outdated and exploitative systems. Fossil fuels remain dominant, not due to a lack of alternatives, but because emerging energy technologies have been deliberately suppressed or co-opted. Even renewable energy transitions have been designed to maintain centralized control rather than enable true energy sovereignty. Until energy production and distribution are decentralized, economic and political subjugation will persist.

- **The Commodification of Life**: Nature, labor, and human well-being are treated as resources to be exploited rather than integral components of a complex living system.

- **Debt as a System of Enslavement**: Nations and individuals alike are trapped in perpetual cycles of debt that concentrate power among an elite few while extracting wealth from the many.

- **The Systemic Devaluation of the Sacred**: Anything that generates profit is pursued regardless of its harm to people, society, or Nature. This includes the normalization of vice (gambling, alcohol, predatory industries), the exploitation of suffering for financial gain, and the erosion of morality in the name of market profitability.

By revering markets as self-correcting forces, we have outsourced morality to the invisible hand, allowing economic structures to dictate human and planetary outcomes rather than serving the flourishing of Life itself. A system designed to reward accumulation over contribution, speculation over substance, and short-term financial gain over long-term human and planetary well-being is a system that is fundamentally misaligned with the intelligence of Life itself and the sacred nature of existence. Until we reclaim economics as a tool for human and planetary flourishing, rather than a mechanism for extraction and control, the Polycrisis will continue to deepen.

IV. The War on Nature: Humanity's Assault on Its Own Life Support System

At no point in recorded history has humanity waged a more reckless and destructive war than the one it now fights against Nature itself. Our planet, the very womb that birthed and sustains us, is systematically being plundered, poisoned, and dismantled by an economic and industrial machine that sees the natural world as an expendable resource rather than a living, intelligent system. This assault is not merely an environmental crisis—it is an existential crisis, a mirror of our own self-destructive pathology.

A Civilization at War with Its Own Home

The prevailing model of industrial civilization views Nature as an adversary to be conquered, subdued, and exploited. The forests, rivers, and oceans are seen not as sentient systems of Life, but as raw materials for economic extraction. The air and water, which sustain all living beings, are polluted without consequence in the name of industrial progress. The soil, which holds the very foundation of Life, is poisoned by synthetic chemicals and monoculture farming.

This war on Nature is not just a material phenomenon—it is a spiritual vacancy that reveals a profound severance from our origins. Indigenous cultures, which lived in harmony with the Earth for millennia, understood what modern society has forgotten: that Nature is not something outside of us—it is us. To destroy the natural world is to destroy ourselves.

The next sections will expose the catastrophic consequences of this war, from biodiversity collapse to the poisoning of the planetary web of Life, and how these crises are the inevitable consequence of Mankind's severance from higher intelligence and Natural law.

V. The Consequences of Ecological Collapse

The systematic assault on Nature has set into motion an ecological unraveling that threatens the very foundation of Life on Earth. The planet's finely tuned systems, evolved over billions of years, are being pushed past their tipping points. These are not hypothetical concerns of a distant future—they are unfolding now, in real-time.

1. The Sixth Mass Extinction: The Collapse of Biodiversity

Life on Earth thrives in a complex web of interdependence. The stability of this web has been shattered by habitat destruction, industrial pollution, and the reckless pursuit of profit at the expense of living ecosystems. We are now in the midst of the Sixth Mass Extinction, an event characterized by an unprecedented rate of species loss, surpassing even the asteroid impact that wiped out the dinosaurs.

- More than one million species are currently at risk of extinction due to human activity.

- The destruction of pollinators, such as bees, threatens global food security.

- The decline of apex predators is throwing entire ecosystems into chaos.

Humanity has failed to grasp that the destruction of other species is ultimately self-destruction—our survival is deeply intertwined with the health of the biosphere.

2. The Poisoning of Earth's Natural Systems

Industrial society is systematically poisoning the planet, from the deepest oceans to the highest peaks. Every year, billions of tons of toxic chemicals, plastics, pesticides, and synthetic compounds are dumped into Nature, creating a planetary toxic burden with devastating effects.

- Microplastics have been found in human blood, placentas, and even in the brains of wildlife.

- Industrial agriculture's overuse of pesticides and synthetic fertilizers has decimated soil microbiomes, compromising the ability to grow nutrient-rich food.

- Heavy metals and chemical runoff have poisoned rivers, lakes, and oceans, creating vast dead zones where Life cannot exist.

This is not merely pollution—it is planetary self-mutilation, a direct reflection of humanity's lack of reverence for the very systems that sustain it.

3. Climate Engineering and the Manipulation of Natural Cycles

While mainstream discourse focuses almost exclusively on carbon emissions, a far more insidious crisis is unfolding in the shadows: the deliberate geoengineering and weather modification programs that are disrupting Earth's natural climate cycles.

- Cloud seeding, aerosol spraying, and artificial climate interventions are being conducted with little oversight or public awareness.

- Weather patterns are becoming increasingly chaotic, not solely due to fossil fuel consumption, but due to large-scale atmospheric tampering.

- These interventions are driven by a misguided belief that human intelligence can outmaneuver Nature, despite overwhelming evidence to the contrary.

Rather than working in harmony with Earth's systems, we have taken the hubristic path of technocratic manipulation, believing we can engineer our way out of planetary crises that were created by the same mindset of domination and control.

4. Ecosystem Destabilization and Planetary Feedback Loops

As the fabric of Earth's natural systems unravels, feedback loops are accelerating the pace of collapse:

- Deforestation not only wipes out biodiversity but also disrupts rainfall patterns, leading to desertification and more extreme weather.

- The destruction of ocean ecosystems has compromised the planet's largest carbon sinks, accelerating planetary warming.

- The thawing of permafrost is releasing vast amounts of methane, a greenhouse gas far more potent than CO_2.

These cascading failures demonstrate a fundamental misunderstanding of Nature—one that views it as a collection of separate, isolated parts rather than a deeply interconnected, self-regulating system.

Conclusion: The Inevitable Consequence of Spiritual Vacancy

The ecological collapse we are witnessing is not a random occurrence—it is the predictable result of Mankind's severance from its own higher intelligence and Natural law. A civilization that sees Nature as a commodity rather than a sacred, living system will inevitably bring about its own demise.

Yet, within this collapse lies an invitation—not merely to mitigate the damage but to fundamentally transform our relationship with Life itself. Until humanity awakens to the Truth that Nature is not separate from us, but an extension of our own being, the downward spiral will continue. The question now is: will we wake up before it is too late?

VI. The Subjugation of Human Sovereignty

The Polycrisis is not merely the result of flawed policies, economic mismanagement, or environmental destruction—it is also the outcome of a civilization-wide abdication of personal sovereignty. For millennia, human beings have been conditioned to surrender their autonomy to external authorities, whether they be kings or warlords, aristocracy, governments, religious institutions, corporate entities, or centralized power structures. This submission has led to a culture of dependency, obedience, and unconscious servitude, making humanity highly susceptible to manipulation and control.

1. The Manufactured Illusion of Freedom

Modern civilization operates under the pretense that human beings are free, yet this is largely an illusion. While legal frameworks and democratic institutions suggest that individuals have agency, the reality is that most people are psychologically, economically, and ideologically conditioned to comply with the dictates of the prevailing system.

- Governments craft policies that serve corporate and elite interests rather than the well-being of their people.

- The financial system enslaves individuals through debt-based economies that keep them in cycles of perpetual labor and consumption.

- Mass media and propaganda machines engineer consent, ensuring that the public supports agendas that often work against their own interests.

This illusion of freedom pacifies the masses, preventing them from realizing the true extent of their subjugation. People believe they are choosing their path, yet most of their choices have already been preconditioned by the very systems they believe they control.

2. The Role of Fear in Human Submission

One of the most effective tools for subjugating human sovereignty is fear. Throughout history, ruling classes have wielded fear as a weapon to keep populations compliant and obedient. Whether through the fear of war, terrorism, economic collapse, disease, or social ostracization, humanity has been kept in a perpetual state of anxiety.

- Fear of instability leads people to accept authoritarian policies that strip away personal freedoms in exchange for "security."

- Fear of financial ruin keeps people locked in exploitative labor systems that prioritize corporate profit over human well-being.

- Fear of being labeled an outcast suppresses independent thinking and reinforces group conformity.

When individuals are paralyzed by fear, they willingly cede control over their lives to external authorities in the hope of safety and stability. Yet, this very act of submission is what enables the continued erosion of personal power and self-determination.

3. The Corporate Takeover of Human Agency

Modern power structures are no longer confined to governments or religious institutions—corporations have become the dominant force shaping human behavior. The relentless commercialization of Life itself has led to a reality where:

- Food, water, medicine, energy, and even knowledge have been monopolized by corporate interests, turning essential human needs into for-profit commodities.

- Social media platforms manipulate human psychology, using behavioral algorithms to shape opinions, emotions, and actions.

- Big Tech and surveillance capitalism harvest personal data, turning human beings into economic assets for exploitation.

Corporate entities do not answer to the people—they answer to shareholders and financial stakeholders. In this paradigm, the well-being of the population is secondary to profit maximization and market control. The unchecked rise of corporate dominance represents a direct attack on human sovereignty, reducing people to mere labor resources and consumers—nameless, replaceable cogs in a soulless economic machine—rather than autonomous beings.

4. The Religious and Ideological Enslavement of the Masses

While religious and ideological systems have provided meaning and moral frameworks throughout history, they have also been weaponized as tools of control. Many of the world's dominant religions and belief systems have been structured around obedience, guilt, and submission to authority, rather than true spiritual awakening.

- Organized religion has historically suppressed individual spiritual inquiry, discouraging direct experiences of the Divine. Instead, it promotes dogmatic adherence and the idolization of a self-ordained clergy class, positioning them as exclusive gatekeepers to God.

- Political ideologies demand loyalty to the collective, often requiring individuals to sacrifice their autonomy in service of the state or party, which is then systematically reinforced through ideological echo chambers.

- Cultural narratives reinforce self-limiting beliefs, conditioning people to see themselves as powerless within the grand scheme of existence.

While spirituality and philosophy can be profound paths to enlightenment, when weaponized, they become systems of enslavement rather than vehicles for liberation.

The psychological chains of indoctrination and ideological submission keep humanity locked in cycles of ignorance, fear, and division.

Conclusion: The Path to Reclaiming Sovereignty

The subjugation of human sovereignty is one of the primary enablers of the Polycrisis. A population that does not question authority, does not think critically, and does not exercise its innate power is easily controlled and manipulated. The crises we face today—economic corruption, environmental devastation, social unrest—are only possible because the majority have allowed a small minority to rule unchecked.

Reclaiming sovereignty does not mean rejecting all forms of governance or structure—it means demanding that such structures serve humanity and the greater good of all rather than exploiting the very people it's meant to serve. It means:

- Recognizing fear as a tool of control and refusing to be manipulated by it.

- Questioning who benefits from the systems we participate in and whether they align with human flourishing.

- Restoring spiritual and intellectual autonomy, rejecting dogma in favor of direct experience and discernment.

- Understanding that true power does not reside in external authorities, but within the awakened individual.

The crisis of human sovereignty is a crisis of consciousness. Until people reclaim their inner authority, critical thinking, and unalienable right of true sovereignty, they will remain prisoners in a system designed to extract their energy while feeding them the illusion of freedom.

The question is no longer whether external authorities will continue consolidating power—they will. The question is: will humanity awaken in time to reclaim its birthright?

VII. The Technocratic Enclosure of Human Freedom

The rapid advancement of technology, while heralded as a force for progress, has increasingly become a mechanism of control that threatens the very essence of human freedom. Rather than liberating humanity, the technocratic agenda—driven by centralized power structures—seeks to enclose and dictate every aspect of human life under the guise of efficiency, security, and convenience.

1. The Rise of the Surveillance State

Governments and corporate entities have systematically deployed mass surveillance systems that track, monitor, and analyze every facet of human behavior. The claim that such technologies are implemented for "safety" and "national security" is a thin veil for the establishment of an omnipresent control apparatus.

- AI-driven mass surveillance enables the tracking of individuals in real-time, eroding privacy and personal autonomy.

- Facial recognition technology is being used to create digital profiles, often without consent, leading to unprecedented levels of societal oversight.

- Social credit systems, pioneered in authoritarian regimes, establish behavioral compliance through digital reward-and-punishment mechanisms.

These technologies, rather than being tools for empowerment, are increasingly deployed as instruments of compliance, suppression, and social engineering.

2. The Digital Financial Grid and the War on Cash

One of the most significant yet underappreciated threats to human freedom is the elimination of cash and the rise of centrally controlled digital currencies. By shifting all transactions to digital platforms, financial institutions and governments gain absolute visibility and control over economic activity.

- Central Bank Digital Currencies (CBDCs) offer the promise of efficiency but enable centralized entities to track and restrict transactions at will.

- The push to eliminate cash transactions limits personal financial sovereignty, forcing individuals into a system where every purchase, investment, or donation can be monitored or restricted.

- Programmable money could be used to enforce behavioral controls— determining what individuals can and cannot purchase based on ideological compliance.

A cashless society cedes financial independence to centralized authorities, leaving individuals without recourse should they fall afoul of the system's dictates. While a cashless system of exchange could, in theory, be implemented in an advanced civilization aligned with the immutable laws and principles of the Universe, it remains unfeasible at this stage of human development. Mankind, still entrenched in its psychosis, lacks the collective consciousness and spiritual maturity necessary to prevent such a system from devolving into a tool of manipulation and centralized control. Until transcendence occurs, any attempt to impose a cashless economy would inevitably lead to abuses of power by those entrusted with overseeing it.

3. Artificial Intelligence: The Ultimate Control Mechanism

AI has the potential to be a revolutionary force for good—but under the control of technocratic elites, it is becoming a mechanism of control rather than liberation. AI systems now shape human behavior, decision-making, and perception of reality through algorithmic manipulation.

- AI-driven censorship and content filtering dictate what information is accessible, limiting free thought and discussion.

- Predictive policing and preemptive crime measures introduce control before infractions even occur, erasing due process.

- The automation of decision-making in key societal structures (finance, law enforcement, employment) replaces human judgment with machine-enforced rigidity, further dehumanizing essential human interactions and connections, which are intrinsic to human nature. As social beings, we thrive on organic relationships, not sterile, algorithmic oversight that reduces Life to a transactional, mechanized existence.

Rather than empowering individuals, AI has increasingly become a digital overseer that reinforces systemic biases, enforces ideological conformity, and strips people of agency over their own lives.

4. The Merging of Man and Machine: The Transhumanist Agenda

At the extreme end of technological control lies transhumanism, a movement that seeks to merge human biology with artificial intelligence and cybernetic enhancements under the pretext of "evolution." While framed as a step toward human enhancement, transhumanism represents a deeper existential threat:

- The push for brain-machine interfaces and neural implants raises concerns about external control over human thought.

- The introduction of biometric digital IDs serves as a prerequisite for participation in digital societies, creating new layers of exclusion and coercion.

- The redefinition of what it means to be human risks reducing individuals to programmable entities rather than sovereign beings.

Transhumanism, if left unchecked, could lead to a future where human agency is diminished, and consciousness itself is subjected to artificial modification.

Conclusion: The Struggle for Technological Sovereignty

Technology is not inherently oppressive—it is how it is wielded that determines whether it liberates or enslaves. The encroachment of centralized technological control into every aspect of human life is not an inevitability but a choice. To reclaim technological sovereignty, humanity must:

- **Resist the erosion of privacy** by advocating for decentralized systems that empower individuals.

- **Reject financial centralization** and preserve financial sovereignty through alternative currencies and economic structures.

- **Ensure AI serves humanity** rather than dictates human behavior through algorithmic authoritarianism.

- **Defend the integrity of human biology** and consciousness against the unchecked ambitions of transhumanist ideologues.

The technocratic enclosure of human freedom is one of the most insidious aspects of the Polycrisis. As control structures seek to dictate, automate, and surveil every aspect of Life, the question is no longer whether humanity can develop advanced technologies—but whether we can do so while preserving the unalienable rights of free will, autonomy, and self-determination.

VIII. The Global Control Grid: The Consolidation of Power

At the heart of the Polycrisis lies a coordinated centralization of power—a consolidation of economic, political, and social control into the hands of a select few. This is not an accident of history or an unfortunate byproduct of modern civilization; it is a deliberate process designed to enclose human potential, sovereignty, and freedom.

The Global Control Grid operates as a multi-layered structure, integrating systems of governance, finance, technology, and social engineering into an interconnected web that dictates nearly every facet of human life. While many believe they live in free societies, the reality is that control mechanisms have become so deeply embedded within institutional frameworks that most people comply without ever questioning the nature of their subjugation.

1. The Supranational Governance Model

Beyond nation-states and elected governments, a growing web of supranational entities wields immense influence over global policies, often without democratic oversight. These sorts of organizations have existed since antiquity and include ancient mystery schools, guilds, religious sects, secret fraternities and societies. More recent iterations include think tanks, philanthropic foundations, NGOs, public charities, bilateral institutions, research organizations, and a vast global web of intelligence and surveillance agencies. Some are front and center in the public eye, some operate covertly, and some operate in total secrecy.

Virtually all of them have an outer circle with common members or employees which serves as their facade, while an exclusive inner circle holds the real power.

Many of these organizations have genuinely benevolent intentions and are of service to humanity. However, for many others, the real intentions are dubious, and their true service to humanity is questionable at best, if not entirely absent. These include organizations such as:

- The **United Nations (UN)** and its various agencies, which dictate international policies on climate, health, and governance.

- The **World Economic Forum (WEF)**, which advances global agendas through corporate-government alliances.

- The **International Monetary Fund (IMF) and World Bank**, which control debt and economic policy in developing nations.

- The **World Health Organization (WHO)**, which determines public health directives on a planetary scale, often in coordination with private interests.

While these entities claim to act for the collective good, their power is centralized and unelected, making them insulated from accountability to the very populations they govern. This allows for policies to be enacted that serve corporate and elite interests, often at the expense of national sovereignty and individual freedoms.

2. The Financial Cartel: Who Owns the World?

The global economy is not a free market—it is an engineered system controlled by a small network of financial institutions, corporations, and elite families who dictate the flow of money, resources, and wealth. Consider the following:

- The world's largest asset management firms—BlackRock, Vanguard, and State Street—collectively own controlling stakes in nearly every major corporation across industries, from technology to agriculture.

- Central banks, including the Federal Reserve, European Central Bank, and Bank for International Settlements, dictate monetary policy with no democratic oversight, determining inflation, interest rates, and economic stability. Technically, the Federal Reserve is not even a Central Bank in the true sense of the meaning since it's privately owned by its for-profit member banks.

- The vast majority of global wealth is concentrated in a tiny fraction of the population, creating a system where economic dependency keeps the masses enslaved to debt and perpetual labor.

Through financial instruments, global institutions, and economic coercion, this cartel ensures that power remains tightly consolidated, preventing any real economic freedom or independence from emerging on a mass scale.

3. Media and Information Warfare: Controlling the Narrative

One of the most potent tools of the Global Control Grid is narrative control—the ability to dictate what people believe, how they think, and what they perceive as reality. This is achieved through:

- Media monopolization: Just a handful of corporate conglomerates (e.g., Disney, Warner Bros. Discovery, Comcast, News Corp, and Paramount) control nearly all mainstream news, entertainment, and cultural messaging.

- Censorship and digital suppression: Social media platforms, in coordination with intelligence agencies and private interests, actively curate what information is allowed to circulate, silencing dissenting voices under the pretense of "misinformation."

- Psychological warfare: Through fear-based narratives—whether about climate, health crises, or geopolitical threats—the population is kept in a constant state of anxiety, making them more compliant to top-down control.

By controlling the information ecosystem, the ruling class ensures that the masses remain confused, divided, and incapable of mobilizing against the real sources of oppression.

4. The Weaponization of Crises: Problem-Reaction-Solution

Throughout history, crises have been used as catalysts for control, following a predictable pattern:

1. Manufacture or exploit a crisis.

2. Provoke public fear and demand for intervention.

3. Introduce a predetermined "solution" that consolidates more power.

This dynamic has played out repeatedly:

- 9/11 led to mass surveillance and permanent warfare.

- Financial crashes justified corporate bailouts while the public bore the losses.

- Global health emergencies introduced digital IDs, travel restrictions, and censorship of scientific debate.

The same playbook is used to reshape society in alignment with centralized power structures, leveraging every crisis as an opportunity for expansion of control.

Conclusion: Recognizing the Matrix of Control

The Global Control Grid is not a conspiracy theory—it is a self-evident reality visible and objectively evident in the structures and institutions that shape, dominate, and control modern civilization. The question is not whether centralized power exists, but whether humanity will continue to passively comply or begin to dismantle the systems that enable it.

To challenge this paradigm, people must:

- Reclaim sovereignty over information and perception.

- Develop parallel systems of economics, governance, and self-sufficiency.

- Refuse to participate in structures that require compliance at the cost of freedom.

- Recognize fear-based manipulation and resist the engineered crises that lead to further centralization of power.

The Polycrisis is not a random series of events—it is a deliberate orchestration of control mechanisms designed to manufacture consent and maintain global hegemony. Recognizing the depth of this control is the first step toward reclaiming individual and collective agency—but recognition alone is insufficient. Humanity's transcendence from this paradigm cannot be achieved collectively—it must be individually initiated. Each person holds the responsibility to transcend their own psychosis, enculturated conditioning, conditioned compliance, and lack of spiritual initiation and depth for only through individual transformation does the collective reality shift.

The question remains: Will humanity awaken in time to dismantle its own enslavement?

IX. The Path Forward: Transcending the Polycrisis

Recognizing the depth and complexity of the Polycrisis is not enough—we must now turn our attention to how humanity can move beyond it. The Polycrisis is not merely an external phenomenon but a direct reflection of the collective state of human consciousness. Any attempt to solve these issues at the level of effect rather than addressing the root cause—Mankind's spiritual and psychological fragmentation—will ultimately prove futile.

1. A Shift in Consciousness: The Only Viable Solution

No political movement, technological innovation, or economic reform will succeed in healing the Polycrisis unless there is an elevation of human consciousness. As Einstein famously noted, *"We cannot solve our problems with the same level of thinking that created them."* The only true remedy is a shift in awareness—an evolution of our perception and intelligence that allows humanity to operate in coherence with Natural and Cosmic law.

This shift requires individuals to:

- **Awaken to their own conditioned limitations**—recognizing the mental frameworks, beliefs, and societal programming that keep them trapped in fear, division, and unconscious compliance.

- **Reintegrate the Sacred**—restoring reverence for Life itself, for Nature, and for the higher-order intelligence that governs the Universe.

- **Cultivate spiritual sovereignty**—understanding that true liberation does not come from external systems but from internal mastery and alignment with higher wisdom.

2. Decentralization and Parallel Societies

If the existing global control grid is centralized, hierarchical, and mechanistic, the response must be decentralized, organic, and regenerative. Humanity must build parallel structures that function independently of the systems of control.

This includes:

- **Localization of economies**—Reorienting economic activity away from globalized extraction models toward systems that serve and integrate with local communities and regional economies. This ensures greater economic resilience, sustainability, and self-reliance while reducing dependency on transnational corporate structures.

- **Decentralized real value currency**—Money must serve as a means of exchange and a stable store of value, not as an end in itself. This requires:
  - Stability in currency value to ensure it is truly a store of value; decentralized blockchain technologies may prove instrumental to the creation of such a stable real-value currency.
  - The reform of fractional reserve banking to prevent the unchecked debasement of currency through money printing.
  - A banking system that serves communities and productive businesses rather than operating as an extractive force siphoning value at every turn.
  - The bifurcation of speculative trading and investment banking from deposit-holding institutions to prevent the leveraging of public funds for private speculative gain.

- **Autonomous food and energy systems**—Shifting from industrial, extractive models to localized, sustainable, and regenerative alternatives.

- **Independent knowledge networks**—Free from the censorship and narrative manipulation of institutional gatekeepers.

These parallel structures must not be built in opposition to the existing system or framed as a hostile takeover, but rather as an inevitable outgrowth of a higher-order consciousness that renders the old, corrupted structures obsolete. As R. Buckminster Fuller stated, *"You never change things by fighting the existing reality. To change something, build a new model that makes the existing model obsolete."*

3. The Inner Revolution: Individual Responsibility for Collective Transformation

The path forward is not a uniform collective movement but one of individuals reclaiming their agency and taking responsibility for their personal transformation which then accumulates to tipping points of collective change. This is the principle of the 100th Monkey Effect, where a relatively few individuals within the collective garner the required critical mass of individuals embodying higher consciousness that shifts the entire morphogenetic field of humanity.

Yet, to reach critical mass every single individual holds the responsibility to:

- **Engage in deep self-inquiry and deprogramming**—shedding the false narratives that sustain the status quo.

- **Align daily life with Natural law**—making choices that honor coherence, harmony, and living in alignment with the high-order laws and principles of the Universe.

- **Embody the future now**—not waiting for systemic change but actively living as a sovereign, conscious being who models the new paradigm.

Conclusion: The Crucible as a Gateway to Evolution

The Polycrisis is not a punishment; it is an initiation. Humanity is at a Crucible, being forced to transcend its old ways or face a cataclysmic collapse. This is not the first time a civilization has faced such a moment—but it is the first time that the stakes are planetary.

The only way forward is through, and the only way through is transcendence. The external world will only change when the internal world of enough individuals changes first. The true revolution is not one of political ideology or economic restructuring—it is the reclamation of the sacredness of Life itself through the ascension in human consciousness.

The question is not whether a new world of wonder and beauty is possible—it is whether enough people will choose to transcend their Spiritual Crisis, elevating all of humanity to a higher octave of collective consciousness.

In every Crucible, there's a choice that must be made.

EARTH'S POLYCRISIS AS A MIRROR OF MANKIND'S PSYCHOSIS

EXECUTIVE SUMMARY

Why Should You Read This Chapter?

The crises of our time—economic instability, environmental devastation, political corruption, and social unrest—are not isolated events. They are the symptoms of a deeper disorder: Mankind's Spiritual Crisis, which manifests as the Polycrisis in the material world. This chapter reveals how humanity's fragmented consciousness and mechanistic worldview have led to systemic dysfunction and how no lasting solution can emerge without a fundamental shift in awareness. It is not policies, leaders, or institutions that will save us, but a collective awakening—one that begins with the individual.

By understanding the root cause of our predicament, we reclaim our power to transcend it rather than merely mitigating its effects. This chapter provides the context, framework, and pathway forward, showing why personal transformation is the only viable foundation for a more harmonious world.

Executive Summary: Key Takeaways

- **The Polycrisis is the Effect, Not the Cause**: Humanity is facing a multi-dimensional breakdown—geopolitical conflicts, environmental destruction, economic disparity, and spiritual disconnection. But these are merely symptoms of a deeper crisis—the fragmentation and incoherence in human consciousness.

- **Reductionist Thinking Has Led to Systemic Failure**: The world has been built upon mechanistic and compartmentalized thinking, ignoring the fact that all systems—ecological, economic, social, and spiritual—are interconnected. The failure to acknowledge this interdependence has led to cascading crises.

- **Economics as a Reflection of Mankind's Psychosis**: The modern economic system is detached from Natural law, prioritizing short-term profits over long-term well-being. The financial system is designed as an extractive force, enriching the few at the expense of the many, ensuring that wealth accumulation is separated from true value creation.

- **The War on Nature Reflects Mankind's Exploitative Mindset**: The relentless destruction of the natural world is a symptom of humanity's mechanistic and extractive approach to existence. Instead of recognizing Nature as a complex, living system to be honored and harmonized with, modern civilization has treated it as a resource to be dominated and depleted, leading to ecological collapse and spiritual disconnection.

- **The Global Control Grid Centralizes Power**: A small network of institutions—governments, central banks, multinational corporations, and technocratic elites—dictate the course of human civilization. Their consolidation of power ensures that people remain enslaved to debt, dependence, and external control rather than reclaiming sovereignty.

- **The Polycrisis is Not a Random Event, But an Engineered Reality**: Crisis is repeatedly used as a mechanism for control, following a predictable pattern—problem, reaction, solution—whereby the very systems causing collapse present themselves as the only answer, further consolidating power.

- **The Path Forward is Transcendence, Not Reform**: The only viable solution is a radical shift in human consciousness. Systemic problems cannot be solved at the level of effect—they must be dismantled at the root cause. Humanity must operate in coherence with Natural and Cosmic law to create a sustainable, just, and thriving future.

- **Decentralization and Parallel Societies Are the Next Evolutionary Step**: The existing centralized systems—finance, governance, media, energy—cannot be reformed, as they are inherently flawed. Instead, humanity must create parallel structures that are decentralized, regenerative, and independent of top-down control.

- **Localization and Real-Value Currencies Will Reclaim Economic Integrity**: The shift must prioritize localized economies, stable currency systems, and banking structures that serve communities, rather than perpetuate debt enslavement and speculation-driven wealth extraction.

- **The Inner Revolution is the Key to Collective Liberation**: No external revolution can succeed without an internal transformation. The 100th Monkey Effect illustrates that only a small percentage of awakened individuals can recalibrate the collective field, leading to a tipping point where mass consciousness shifts effortlessly.

- **The Polycrisis is a Crucible for Human Evolution**: This moment in history is not a catastrophe—it is an initiation. It is a test of whether humanity will transcend its lower nature and step into coherence with the intelligence of Life itself, or whether it will perish under the weight of its own unconsciousness.

The final question is not whether a more beautiful world is possible—but whether enough individuals will choose to embody the consciousness that makes it inevitable.

III – The Root Cause: Humanity's Fundamental Errors

THE FALSE IDOLS OF MODERN CIVILIZATION

Introduction: Humanity's Worship of False Gods

In all the great civilizations throughout the ages, there was a central sacred yearning in humanity to seek meaning, purpose, and guidance from something greater than itself. For much of history, this quest was directed toward the Divine, the sacred, and the eternal mysteries of existence. But in the modern era, civilization has largely abandoned these higher-order pursuits in favor of man-made constructs—replacing the transcendent with the material, the artificial, and the institutional.

Instead of seeking wisdom, virtue, and spiritual evolution, modern civilization bows before false idols—science as an unquestionable authority, technology as salvation, money as the ultimate measure of worth, consumerism as the path to happiness, and government as protector. These new gods of modernity are heralded as the ultimate arbiters of Truth, progress, and security. Yet, despite their dominance over human consciousness, these forces have failed to deliver the fulfillment, harmony, or liberation that humanity seeks. Instead, they have delivered fragmentation, disempowerment, and spiritual starvation.

The religion of science has become a dogma, silencing dissent and ignoring the mysteries of consciousness and the unseen realms. The technocratic utopia promises liberation through AI and transhumanism but threatens to erode human sovereignty. The worship of the market reduces all things to profit and commodification, ensuring that nothing remains sacred unless it can be monetized. Governments, which were supposed to serve the people, have become secular gods, demanding obedience and offering the illusion of protection while consolidating power.

Consumerism fuels the endless hunger for more, convincing people that happiness lies in accumulation rather than inner peace. Money itself has become the supreme deity, where financial wealth is equated with success, morality, and intelligence—regardless of how it was obtained. Even spirituality has been commodified, with New Age ideologies repackaging ancient wisdom into superficial self-help fads.

This chapter exposes the false idols of modern civilization, revealing how these belief systems have detached humanity from its true nature. By deconstructing these illusions, we can begin to see how they reinforce the Polycrisis, keeping people disempowered, fragmented, and spiritually vacant.

The way forward is not a return to outdated religious dogma, nor a rejection of all progress—but a restoration of true wisdom. It is the recognition that no institution, ideology, or external system can provide what can only be found through self-realization and alignment with the eternal laws of existence.

This is the reckoning of our time: Will humanity continue to kneel at the feet of false gods, or will it reclaim its sovereignty, higher purpose, and spiritual lineage?

Section II: The Religion of Science

Science began as a noble pursuit– an evolving method of scientific rigor to explore and decode the physical world. But instead of remaining a tool for discovery, it has been elevated into dogma, where skepticism is silenced, and inquiry is restricted by institutional interests. It was never meant to be a belief system, an institution of authority, or an ideology, but rather a process of continuous inquiry. However, in modern civilization, science has been elevated from a method into a rigid ideology, becoming the unquestioned high priesthood of our era.

What was meant to serve humanity's noble pursuit of Truth has instead substantially morphed into an ignoble instrument of control. The scientific establishment, intertwined with corporate funding, government agendas, and academic gatekeeping, dictates what is permissible to research, publish, and discuss. Those who question the prevailing narratives are marginalized, labeled "anti-science," or outright silenced–not because their inquiries lack merit, but because they threaten the status quo. The core problem is not a lack of capable or even genius scientists, but a system that has been corrupted and has become unmoored from its original noble purpose.

This phenomenon, often called scientism, is the blind belief that all aspects of reality can be explained solely through materialist frameworks, ignoring dimensions of consciousness, intuition, and phenomena that do not conform to its rigid paradigms. Under this system, anything that cannot be measured, quantified, or reduced to mechanistic principles is dismissed as pseudoscience, superstition, or fantasy.

Yet history reveals how scientific revolutions–once ridiculed–eventually overturned accepted doctrines. The heliocentric model, germ theory, and quantum mechanics were all met with fierce resistance before becoming accepted Truths. Today, alternative paradigms in medicine, energy, and human consciousness face similar suppression–not because they are false, but because they disrupt deeply entrenched power structures.

True science is never settled. It thrives on skepticism, curiosity, and the willingness to challenge existing models. When science becomes an ideology rather than a method, it ceases to be science—it becomes a religion, demanding faith rather than fostering discovery.

While this section exposes how the scientific establishment has drifted from its original intent, in later chapters we'll explore how we can reclaim the spirit of true scientific inquiry—one that is open to mystery, consciousness, and the vast, unexplored dimensions of existence. We'll connect the dots how this also has its origins in Mankind's psychosis and can only be overcome by addressing the Spiritual Crisis within, not by mandating this top-down as the existing system is incapable to correct for its own structural flaws which it fails to see as flaws.

Section III: The Technocratic Utopia

Technology, once hailed as the great liberator of humanity, has increasingly become its master. The utopian vision of a world made efficient, connected, and optimized by the internet, cellphones, artificial intelligence, automation, and digital governance is not leading humanity toward freedom—but toward deeper dependence, surveillance, and control.

The modern world's blind faith in technocracy—the rule of experts and algorithms over human sovereignty—has become one of the most pervasive and dangerous belief systems of our time. Unlike traditional authoritarianism, which relies on manifest force, modern technocratic rule operates under the illusion of human progress. Technocracy, once envisioned as a system for societal efficiency, has morphed into algorithmic authoritarianism—where surveillance, predictive AI, and centralized data governance subtly strip away human autonomy under the guise of convenience and progress. The population is not coerced into submission; it voluntarily integrates itself into a system that systematically strips away its autonomy, thinking it is progress.

The Religion of Technology: Salvation Through Data and AI

The promise of artificial intelligence, digitalization, automation, virtual reality, and transhumanism is marketed as a means of enhancing human potential and solving the world's greatest problems. Yet, at its core, the vision of a technocratic utopia seeks to replace human agency with algorithmic governance, reducing the richness of human experience into quantifiable metrics that can be optimized, controlled, and manipulated.

Silicon Valley titans and global think tanks speak of a future in which all human suffering is eradicated, every system is automated, and AI will surpass human intelligence, leading to a world where disease, scarcity, and inequality are eliminated.

But this vision is a really just the techno-profiteers' sales pitch and marketing front of a plausible-sounding mirage, built on a materialist worldview that refuses to acknowledge the essence of Life beyond data, computation, and code.

Technology, when guided by wisdom and aligned with the higher-order laws and principles of Life itself, can be an incredible tool. But when disconnected from spiritual intelligence, it becomes a mechanism of turning enslavement into profits—one that thrives on human disempowerment rather than human sovereignty.

The Digital Prison: Surveillance, Social Credit, and Algorithmic Control
With every passing year, humanity inches closer toward a reality where technological infrastructure governs nearly all aspects of Life. The rapid integration of AI, digital currencies, facial recognition, and algorithm-driven decision-making is leading us toward a world of complete surveillance and behavioral engineering.

- **Inescapable Monitoring & Surveillance**—Cellphones, smart devices, Alexa, Siri, TVs, Cars, etc. are all engineered to track, surveil, eavesdrop, and video our every move for data mining purposes, overriding privacy considerations and where the data provider has no control or benefit from the monetization.

- **Cashless societies**—marketed as a move toward "efficiency"—ensure all financial transactions can be monitored, restricted, or weaponized against dissenters.

- **Central Bank Digital Currencies (CBDCs)**—proposed by global financial institutions—have the potential to control where, when, and how money is spent, revoking purchasing power at will.

- **Social Credit Systems**—already implemented in some parts of the world, serve as a model for a future in which compliance is rewarded, and deviation from accepted norms results in social and economic exile.

- **AI-driven censorship and media control** ensure that only state-approved narratives are widely accessible, eliminating the free flow of ideas.

This is not a theoretical dystopia—it is already happening. The question is not whether technology will continue advancing, but who controls it and for what purpose.

The Transhumanist Agenda: The Attempt to Rewrite Humanity Itself

The ultimate trajectory of technocratic ideology is not just digital control, but the redefinition of what it means to be human. Transhumanism—the belief that technology will allow humanity to transcend biological limitations—is being positioned as the next step in evolution.

The merging of human consciousness with AI, the genetic modification of future generations, and the push toward synthetic enhancements to the body and Mind are being framed as inevitable, even desirable. But at its core, this movement does not elevate humanity—it seeks to replace the organic with the artificial and seize absolute control and dominion of the general population.

The transhumanist dream is rooted in the same fundamental error that has plagued modern civilization—the belief that consciousness is a product of matter, rather than matter being an expression of consciousness. By seeking to "upload" human intelligence into machines or augment it with AI, transhumanism attempts to circumvent the natural evolutionary process and relegate the divine intelligence of Life itself to a mere engineering problem.

This is not the path to transcendence. It is the ultimate manifestation of Mankind's psychosis—the rejection of its own nature, the refusal to accept the limits of its understanding, and the hubris to believe it can redesign Life better than the intelligence that created it.

The False Promise of Technocracy

The great irony of the technocratic utopia is that its vision of human progress actually diminishes what it means to be human. It erodes sovereignty, reduces consciousness to computation, and replaces free will with algorithmic conditioning. At its very core, it views our soulfulness as a design error that must be corrected to ensure every single one of us is predictable, controllable, and useful to the larger system.

The problem is not technology itself—it is the consciousness wielding it. Until humanity transcends its psychosis, it will continue to use its tools not for liberation, but for enslavement and reckless profiteering.

The only true path forward is to restore wisdom and spiritual intelligence as the guiding forces of civilization—where technology serves humanity's higher evolution, rather than replacing it.

Section IV: The Religion of Money

Money was created as a means of exchange, a tool for facilitating trade—yet in modern civilization, it has been elevated to our supreme deity. Once a neutral medium of exchange, money and wealth have become the primary measure of success, intelligence, and even morality—no matter how it was accumulated. So it is that the modern economic system rewards hoarding over harmony, speculation over substance, and accumulation over contribution.

In the world today, financial wealth is equated with worth, power, and status, while poverty is seen as a personal failure rather than the result of structural economic distortions. Moreover, those deeply indoctrinated in the Religion of Money often struggle to comprehend why others would willingly prioritize purpose or mission over financial success—viewing anything that cannot be monetized as naive or irrational. Money has transcended its original function and has been transformed into the ultimate societal currency—not just for trade, but for identity, value, and meaning itself.

This is the Religion of Money—a world where everything sacred and meaningful that cannot be expressed in monetary terms is readily sacrificed at the Altar of Money, and where every human interaction, natural resource, and relationship is assigned a price tag.

The Altar of Money: The Worship of Wealth and Accumulation

The collective obsession with money is not just about survival or prosperity—it is a spiritual void being filled with material excess. In the absence of deeper meaning, wealth accumulation has become the ultimate purpose, with the wealthiest individuals elevated to the status of gods—untouchable, revered, and envied.

The financial industry, Wall Street, and global banking institutions do not create real value—they engage in an endless game of capital extraction, speculation, and wealth concentration. The stock market is not an economy, yet it dictates the fate of nations. The global financial system has become an abstract casino, where the wealthiest play a rigged game, and everyone else is either a spectator or an unwitting pawn. Unlike Las Vegas casinos, which operate at full risk to their shareholders, Wall Street runs a rigged financial casino where profits are privatized, but losses are socialized—ensuring reckless speculation continues with zero accountability.

Modern economics treats money as the end goal, rather than a means to enhance human well-being. The result is a world where:

- **Exploitation is rewarded**—corporations thrive not by creating real value, but by cutting costs, exploiting labor, and externalizing harm onto society.

- **Financial speculation replaces productivity**—the most profitable industries are those that move capital around rather than create anything of tangible worth.

- **Short-term profits override long-term sustainability**—from deforestation to pollution, nearly every planetary crisis is tied to the insatiable hunger for financial returns.

What was once a servant of human prosperity has become its master. The world is not governed by elected leaders—it is ruled by banks, hedge funds, and multinational corporations that dictate the economic reality of billions.

The Illusion of Infinite Growth: The Core Flaw of Neoclassical Economics

The economic model driving civilization today is fundamentally incoherent. It is built on the false premise that growth can continue indefinitely within a finite planetary system. GDP is worshiped as the ultimate measure of success, even when it rewards destruction over regeneration.

- A **hurricane** that causes billions in damages boosts GDP, but a thriving, self-sufficient community does not.

- **War is profitable**, while peace is not.

- **Sickness fuels economic growth**, while health and well-being do not.

The entire system is inverted, rewarding exploitation, extraction, and endless consumption while ignoring the true wealth of a civilization—its people, its land, and its collective harmony with Life itself.

The "invisible hand" of the market is not self-correcting—it is a blind mechanism of accumulation, designed to concentrate wealth at the top while ensuring systemic fragility for everyone else. The idea that "a rising tide lifts all boats" is a myth—the rising tide has lifted only the yachts while drowning the masses.

This is not prosperity. It is organized economic servitude, dressed up as free-market capitalism.

The Debt Enslavement System: A Modern-Day Serfdom

Most people believe slavery has been abolished, yet it has merely evolved into a more sophisticated form—debt.

From birth, the average person is systematically funneled into a lifetime of financial servitude, conditioned to believe that:

- **Homeownership = Success**, yet most will never truly own their homes, as they remain in perpetual debt to banks.

- **Education = Opportunity**, yet student loans ensure that young adults enter the workforce already shackled by financial burdens.

- **Hard work = Financial Security**, yet wages have stagnated while the cost of living has skyrocketed, ensuring a perpetual struggle.

The system is designed (some would say rigged) to keep people indebted, dependent, and endlessly chasing financial survival—never questioning the root cause of their economic constraints.

Central banks, through inflation, money printing, and fractional reserve banking, systematically erode purchasing power—guaranteeing that hard work alone can never outpace the declining value of money.

We do not live in a free-market economy—we live in a centralized, debt-based control system where a small handful of financial institutions dictate the terms of existence for the vast majority of the population.

The Commodification of Everything: The Final Stages of Collapse

When money is placed above all else, everything sacred is reduced to a commodity:

- **Nature is not valued for its inherent beauty or life-giving function**—it is valued only if it can be monetized.

- **Art, music, and creativity are no longer the authentic creative expressions of the artist's Soul**—they are mere content, repackaged and sold for profit.

- **Even human beings have become commodities**—from the selling of personal data to the exploitation of workers, the value of a person is measured in economic output rather than intrinsic worth.

The final stages of a collapsing civilization are marked by total commodification, where nothing remains sacred unless it can be sold.

This is the endgame of the Religion of Money—where society worships profits over principles, and wealth is no longer a means to an end but the end itself.

Breaking the Spell: Restoring True Prosperity

Money itself is not the issue—it is the distorted value system that deifies it. Until humanity reclaims a definition of prosperity rooted in Life-affirming principles, it will remain economically enslaved.

A truly advanced civilization does not worship money—it wields it wisely. Wealth should be a tool to facilitate the efficient exchange of goods and services and otherwise only for creating beauty, harmony, and well-being, not an idol that dictates every aspect of Life.

The real wealth of a civilization is not measured in stock markets, banking profits, or GDP growth—it is measured in:

- The **health and holistic well-being** of its people.

- The **stability and resilience** of its communities.

- The **harmony and sustainability** of its relationship with the Earth.

Humanity must transcend the illusion that money is the purpose of existence and restore its rightful place as a tool, not a god.

Until this fundamental shift occurs, no economic system—capitalism, socialism, or any other model—will ever create true prosperity.

The Path Forward

The Religion of Money must be debunked and dismantled, not through forced wealth redistribution, but through a reorientation of values. Humanity must redefine prosperity holistically—not in terms of abstract monetary accumulation, but in terms of harmony, coherence, and alignment with the intelligence of Life itself. Only when wealth is measured beyond money can civilization break free from its economic enslavement and step into a higher order of intelligence, prosperity, and abundance.

For the avoidance of doubt, financial wealth and abundance will still exist in this new world of wonder and beauty—but it will no longer serve as the defining metric of status or significance. Instead, wealth will be recognized as a stewardship, not an entitlement—a resource to be wielded wisely, meant to be circulated for the greater good, and never hoarded in service of personal accumulation alone. With great wealth comes great responsibility—not just to oneself, but to society as a whole.

Section V: The Religion of Consumerism

In a civilization severed from true meaning, the act of consuming has become a substitute for fulfillment. What was once the simple exchange of goods and services necessary for survival has morphed into a psychological dependency—one that feeds an insatiable hunger, not for sustenance, but for validation, identity, and purpose.

At its core, consumerism is not just an economic model—it is a manufactured belief system. It is the modern religion of material worship, carefully designed to keep people trapped in a cycle of desire, acquisition, momentary satisfaction, and renewed emptiness. It conditions people to seek validation, self-worth, and purpose through endless material acquisition. By design, the promise of happiness, status, and self-worth is dangled in front of the masses through relentless marketing and advertising, convincing them that the next purchase, the next upgrade, the next luxury will finally bring lasting fulfillment. Yet, the system was built and operates to ensure that true fulfillment never arrives—only the perpetual chase remains.

This is the Religion of Consumerism, a system that not only enslaves individuals psychologically, but also short-circuits the natural cycles of Life, ensuring that the vast majority remain both overworked and overconsuming, while a small elite reaps the spoils of endless extraction.

The Dual Role of the Consumer-Slave: Exploited as Labor, Exploited as Buyer

In the Religion of Consumerism, human beings are not just participants—they are the product itself. The modern economic model does not serve the well-being of individuals; it treats them as inputs to be used efficiently as labor and as consumers to be drained for profits.

This is the dual role of the Consumer-Slave:

1. **As a worker**—they are squeezed for maximum productivity at the lowest possible cost, ensuring that labor serves the accumulation of wealth for capital owners. Wages are kept stagnant while the cost of living increases, ensuring perpetual dependency.

2. **As a consumer**—they are relentlessly conditioned to spend their earnings on an endless stream of material distractions, ensuring that profits flow back to the same elites who control the system.

This model mimics the plantation system of old—a self-perpetuating cycle of labor extraction and financial servitude, ensuring that wealth remains concentrated at the top while the masses remain trapped in a never-ending race to "keep up".

Unlike in Nature, where all elements exist in harmonious service to the whole, this system is designed to be extractive, not regenerative. In a healthy, self-organizing system, resources and energy circulate in a way that sustains the entire ecosystem. But consumerism breaks these natural cycles, ensuring that power and resources are hoarded rather than harmoniously distributed.

The result? A civilization where most people:

- Spend their **most valuable resource—time—working** in jobs they despise to afford things they don't truly need.

- Feel **constantly unfulfilled**, as no material possession ever satisfies the deeper longing for meaning.

- Are **trapped in debt**, ensuring they remain bound to the system indefinitely.

What can be debated is whether this design is a product of malevolent intention or a benevolent lack of wisdom. Either way, it's by design and not an accident.

The Illusion of Choice: How Marketing Hijacks the Mind

Consumerism thrives not on necessity, but on illusion—the illusion that consumption equals happiness, status, and self-worth.

Through relentless advertising, branding, and psychological manipulation, corporations have mastered the art of making people crave what they do not need. It is not a free market of rational choices, but a carefully curated mirage, where brands do not just sell products—they sell identities, dreams, and false promises of fulfillment.

Luxury, lifestyle, and exclusivity are now commodities sold to the masses, convincing them that their external acquisitions define their internal worth. But no matter how much they buy, the inner void remains unfilled.

One of the greatest examples of this perverse overconsumption is the proliferation of storage facilities. People own so much unnecessary "stuff" that they must pay to store what they do not even use. This alone is evidence that consumerism is not about fulfilling needs—it is about feeding an addiction.

Consumerism has become the heroin of modern civilization—a cycle of dopamine-driven compulsive consumption, where the high is temporary and the withdrawal is agonizing.

A System Designed for Permanent Enslavement

At its core, the Religion of Consumerism ensures that people never escape the cycle. The entire structure of modern civilization is engineered to maximize economic dependence:

- **Designed for obsolescence**—products are purposefully designed to have shortened lifecycles to accelerate the replacement cycle.

- **Fast fashion and trend cycles**—people are conditioned to believe they are outdated unless they constantly refresh their wardrobes.

- **The debt trap**—easy credit ensures that people can buy what they cannot afford, keeping them enslaved to financial obligations.

- **Status-driven consumption**—social media and advertising ensure that people tie their self-worth to material possessions.

This is not a free society—it is a sophisticated form of commercial enslavement, where people willingly enter their own cages, believing that accumulation will one day set them free.

But no amount of wealth or material possession can fill the spiritual void that consumerism exploits. The only escape is to break free from the illusion entirely.

Transcending the Consumerist Psychosis

The final Truth is this: consumerism is a form of psychosis born from the larger Spiritual Crisis within individuals as well as the collective.

People are not addicted to products—they are addicted to what they believe those products represent. The modern world has conditioned humanity to seek external validation rather than inner fulfillment, ensuring that the chase never ends.

The only way out of this endless cycle is not through regulation, economic reform, or financial literacy—it is through spiritual transcendence.

- When people **remember their inherent worth**, they no longer feel the need to prove it through material possessions.

- When they **find meaning beyond consumption**, they free themselves from the need to accumulate shiny objects beyond their actual needs.

- When they **awaken from the illusion**, they no longer serve as fuel for the system.

The system will not change until the individual changes. Because while the economic principle that demand creates supply applies here, fundamentally Consumerism is not an economic issue—it is a symptom of humanity's Spiritual Crisis.

Consumerism is not merely a behavioral addiction—it is the external manifestation of the internal void created by humanity's disconnection from the Sacred and the wholesale dismissal that there is a deeper existential purpose and meaning to Life itself which money can't buy.

In contrast, Nature operates on sufficiency—each species takes only what it needs, ensuring the entire system thrives. Humanity, disconnected from this wisdom, has lost its ability to recognize 'enough,' turning consumption into an insatiable hunger.

True wealth is not found in possessions, but in freedom from the need to possess and be owned by our lower nature impulses and desires. Until this is realized, humanity will remain knelt down at the Altar of Consumption, offering its time, energy, and Soul as tribute to a system that was never designed to set it free or cares one iota about its actual holistic well-being.

Section VI: The Entertainment-Industrial Complex – Worshiping Celebrities and Escapism

Entertainment, once a medium for storytelling, culture, and artistic expression, has evolved into something far more pervasive and insidious—an industrial complex designed to pacify, distract, manipulate, numb, and program the masses. In modern civilization, entertainment is no longer just a pastime; it has been weaponized into a distraction mechanism of mass sedation, a tool of control, and a false idol that shapes perception and behavior on an unprecedented scale.

What was once art, mythology, and cultural expression has now been hijacked by corporations that prioritize profit over substance, spectacle over meaning, and mass appeal over depth. Instead of enriching the human Spirit, entertainment now serves as a coping mechanism for a spiritually starved society—a never-ending stream of dopamine hits that offer escape but not enlightenment.

The Distraction Economy: Bread and Circuses for the Digital Age

Ancient Rome had its "bread and circuses"—a method of keeping the masses distracted with spectacle so they would not question their rulers. Today, the modern world has an infinitely more powerful version of this strategy: streaming platforms, social media, celebrity culture, and viral content designed to keep people addicted, passive, and disengaged from their own power.

- **The Algorithmic Attention Trap** - Social media and entertainment platforms are engineered to keep people hooked in a perpetual loop of consumption, ensuring they remain distracted from deeper contemplation, action, or personal transformation.

- **24/7 Spectacle Over Substance** - News cycles, reality TV, and celebrity gossip keep public discourse fixated on triviality, preventing meaningful conversations about real issues.

- **Faux Social Movements** - Instead of engaging in real, tangible change, entertainment culture manufactures activism as a trend, where outrage cycles come and go, but the deeper problems remain unresolved.

- **Pacification Through Escapism** - Entertainment has become a pressure-release valve for a discontented population, offering just enough temporary relief to prevent real resistance or self-examination.

The more entertained a population is, the less likely it is to rebel, question authority, or take responsibility for its own liberation. The system does not want awakened individuals—it wants docile consumers, endlessly consuming but never creating.

The Cult of Personality: Worshiping the False Gods of Modernity

The modern world no longer reveres wisdom, virtue, or spiritual insight—instead, it worships status, wealth, and influence. Celebrities, billionaires, social media influencers, and political figures have become the new gods of culture, dictating trends, opinions, and behaviors.

- **Fame is Mistaken for Wisdom** - Instead of seeking guidance from philosophers, sages, or truth-seekers, society defers to actors, influencers, and media personalities as if their notoriety equates to deeper understanding.

- **The Illusion of Proximity** - Social media creates the illusion of intimacy between the masses and their idols, reinforcing the idea that these figures are authorities on Life, morality, or success.

- **Celebrities as Political Puppets** - Cultural icons are frequently used as mouthpieces for the ruling class, subtly reinforcing mainstream narratives while appearing independent.

- **The Billionaire Messiah Complex** - Figures like Elon Musk, Jeff Bezos, or Bill Gates are idolized as visionaries, yet their wealth and power are often the byproducts of a broken system that perpetuates inequality.

The real danger is not just that these individuals are elevated beyond their true significance—it is that humanity's innate yearning for higher guidance has been co-opted by media conglomerates and marketing campaigns. Instead of looking inward or seeking out true wisdom, people are conditioned to look toward screens, social feeds, and red-carpet figures for meaning.

The Weaponization of Entertainment: Narrative Control and Social Engineering

Entertainment is not just a passive distraction—it is a tool for conditioning the collective consciousness. Stories are the foundation of human belief, and in modern civilization, the stories that reach the masses are carefully curated, filtered, and manipulated to align with the dominant agenda.

- **Hollywood as a Propaganda Machine** – Films and TV shows subtly reinforce societal narratives, whether about war, consumerism, or state authority.

- **The Normalization of Violence and Degeneracy** – Increasingly, popular media glorifies nihilism, hypersexualization, and moral bankruptcy, desensitizing people to the very things that destroy civilizations from within.

- **Predictive Programming** – Entertainment is used to introduce new norms gradually, so that when these shifts happen in reality, they feel inevitable rather than engineered.

- **The Erasure of Myth and True Storytelling** – Ancient myths, which once served to illuminate the human condition and pass down wisdom, have been replaced by shallow, corporate-approved narratives designed to entertain but never awaken.

The entertainment-industrial complex is not just a system of content production—it is a mind-shaping force, dictating what people should aspire to, what they should fear, and what they should accept as normal.

The Corporate Capture of News: The Entertainment-Industrial Complex in Disguise

Perhaps the most insidious extension of the entertainment-industrial complex is the complete corporate capture of mainstream journalism. News media, which was once considered the fourth estate—a check on power and a pillar of democracy—has been hijacked by the same forces that control the entertainment industry.

- The line between journalism and entertainment has been deliberately erased, with news programs designed for maximum engagement rather than factual accuracy.

- Mainstream news outlets no longer serve the interests of Truth, but of their corporate overlords, who dictate the narratives that align with their economic and political interests.

- Sensationalism, outrage, and fear-mongering dominate the news cycle, ensuring that people remain emotionally reactive rather than critically engaged.

- Investigative journalism has been gutted, replaced with fast-paced infotainment, where real inquiry is discouraged in favor of pre-approved talking points.

- Media literacy as a form of self-defense—Learning how narratives are shaped, questioning sources, and seeking independent journalism are essential tools to resist manipulation.

The function of the media today is not to inform—it is to manipulate, distract, and manufacture consent for those who hold power.

The Incestuous Relationship Between Media and Corporate Interests

Mainstream media does not exist in a vacuum—it is an extension of the corporate entities that fund it.

- The primary business model of news media is advertising, meaning news is structured not around informing the public but around drawing in viewers to expose them to corporate messaging.

- Media outlets are economically captive to the corporations that pay for advertising, ensuring that news coverage does not challenge the financial interests of those who fund it.

- Investigative reporting on corporate corruption is heavily censored or buried, because the same corporations that engage in wrongdoing are the ones writing the checks that keep media networks afloat.

- Whistleblowers, independent journalists, and truth-seekers are systematically marginalized, as their work threatens the stability of the media ecosystem built on selective narratives.

Thus, the illusion of objective journalism has been shattered—what is presented as news is, in reality, a carefully curated corporate narrative designed to serve economic and political agendas.

The Spiritual Consequences of a Society Entertained to Death

A civilization that is perpetually entertained is a civilization that is spiritually stagnant. It never questions itself. It never seeks deeper wisdom. It lives in a perpetual state of passive consumption rather than active creation.

The great paradox of modern entertainment is that the more people consume it, the more disconnected they feel. It does not nourish the Soul—it only temporarily fills the void, keeping people numb to the reality of their own disempowerment.

The ceaseless flood of entertainment serves as a synthetic replacement for meaning, ensuring that people never sit long enough with their own thoughts to ask deeper questions about their existence, purpose, and spiritual evolution. Instead of contemplation, there is distraction. Instead of self-exploration, there is external stimulation.

- Joy and fulfillment do not come from passive consumption—they come from active participation in Life itself.

- True art and storytelling are meant to elevate consciousness, not pacify it.

- A society that worships entertainment over wisdom will always be easy to control.

The only way to break free is to reclaim our attention, our creativity, and our discernment. To turn away from the false idols of celebrity and spectacle and return to what is real, meaningful, and sacred.

Breaking the Cycle: Reclaiming Awareness and Conscious Engagement

The path out of the entertainment-industrial complex is not total abstinence—it is conscious engagement. Entertainment should inspire, elevate, and challenge, rather than sedate and distract. It should serve humanity, not exploit it.

- Awareness is the first step. Recognizing the mechanisms of distraction allows individuals to break free from unconscious consumption.

- Seeking meaningful content that uplifts, educates, or expands consciousness rather than mindless consumption of shallow spectacle.

- Prioritizing real experiences over digital simulations. True fulfillment comes not from passive observation but from actively engaging with Life.

- Detoxing from overconsumption. Reducing reliance on entertainment as an escape and replacing it with deeper engagement with reality, creativity, and purpose.

Entertainment has the potential to be a tool for enlightenment rather than entrapment. But until humanity transcends its spiritual crisis and existential vacancy, it will remain vulnerable to the seductive pull of the modern circus that keeps it distracted, complacent, and enslaved.

Section VII: The New Age Illusion – The Commodification of Spirituality

Spirituality, at its core, is a deeply personal and transformative journey—a path to self-discovery, inner peace, and alignment with the eternal Truths of existence. Yet, in the modern world, spirituality has been swept up in the relentless tide of consumerism, reduced to a marketplace of quick fixes, aesthetic branding, and self-indulgent practices.

Where once spiritual paths required years—if not lifetimes—of discipline, devotion, and inner work, today they are marketed as instant access experiences promising enlightenment in a weekend retreat, a 30-day online course, or a best-selling book. Spirituality has been rebranded for mass consumption, transforming profound teachings into feel-good soundbites, merchandise, and influencer-driven lifestyle branding.

This is not to say that tools such as meditation, yoga, or energy healing have no value—when practiced with sincerity and discipline, they remain powerful gateways to personal and spiritual evolution. The issue is not the practices themselves, but the way they have been stripped of depth, commodified, and presented as lifestyle accessories rather than profound spiritual disciplines.

Many seekers enter this space searching for meaning but are instead met with a marketplace, not a monastery. They are encouraged to collect spiritual experiences like souvenirs rather than undergo the deep, often uncomfortable inner work that true transformation demands.

This section will examine how spirituality, once a path of discipline and surrender, has been reshaped by modern consumer culture into something shallow, market-driven, and transactional. It will expose the ways in which the New Age movement has often become more about image than essence, more about personal gratification than true transcendence.

This is the New Age Illusion—a world where spirituality is no longer about transcendence, wisdom, or divine alignment but about self-optimization, escapism, and monetization. The question is: Has modern spirituality helped people awaken, or has it merely given them a new set of illusions to cling to?

The Instant Enlightenment Industry – Bypassing the Work

True spiritual growth has always been a process of inner refinement—requiring discipline, self-inquiry, and, often, great discomfort. Historically, genuine spiritual paths demanded deep commitment, whether through monastic devotion, rigorous meditation practices, shamanic initiations, or years of disciplined study under a teacher.

Yet, in today's world of instant gratification, the journey toward enlightenment has been rebranded as a quick-fix solution—something to be achieved through a weekend retreat, an online certification, or a trendy new technique promising effortless awakening.

Modern spirituality has embraced a fast-food mentality, offering quick doses of self-affirmation, temporary emotional highs, and surface-level engagement with ancient wisdom traditions, while bypassing the actual work of inner transformation. Instead of confronting their shadows, many seekers are drawn to spiritual bypassing—using positive thinking, affirmations, and feel-good platitudes to avoid engaging with the deeper wounds, conditioning, and unconscious patterns that truly hinder their evolution.

This "manifestation culture" reinforces the illusion that spiritual enlightenment is merely a matter of adjusting one's mindset, rather than a process that requires deep humility, self-honesty, and the dismantling of the ego's attachments. The idea that one can attract abundance, love, and happiness through sheer intention alone ignores the reality that true transformation is a process of surrender, not just affirmation.

This section will expose how much of the self-help and modern spiritual movement offers aesthetic spirituality rather than actual transformation—promising results without discipline, enlightenment without sacrifice, and personal elevation without any responsibility to the whole.

The fundamental Truth remains: There are no shortcuts to awakening. Any system, teacher, or product that promises instant enlightenment, effortless manifestation, or spiritual transcendence without deep inner work is simply selling another illusion.

The Instant Enlightenment Industry - Bypassing the Work

True spiritual growth has always been a process of inner refinement—requiring discipline, self-inquiry, and, often, great discomfort. Historically, genuine spiritual paths demanded deep commitment, whether through monastic devotion, rigorous meditation practices, shamanic initiations, or years of disciplined study under a teacher.

Yet, in today's world of instant gratification, the journey toward enlightenment has been rebranded as a quick-fix solution—something to be achieved through a weekend retreat, an online certification, or a trendy new technique promising effortless awakening.

Modern spirituality has embraced a fast-food mentality, offering quick doses of self-affirmation, temporary emotional highs, and surface-level engagement with ancient wisdom traditions, while bypassing the actual work of inner transformation. Instead of confronting their shadows, many seekers are drawn to spiritual bypassing—using positive thinking, affirmations, and feel-good platitudes to avoid engaging with the deeper wounds, conditioning, and unconscious patterns that truly hinder their evolution.

This "manifestation culture" reinforces the illusion that spiritual enlightenment is merely a matter of adjusting one's mindset, rather than a process that requires deep humility, self-honesty, and the dismantling of the ego's attachments. The idea that one can attract abundance, love, and happiness through sheer intention alone ignores the reality that true transformation is a process of surrender, not just affirmation.

This section will expose how much of the self-help and modern spiritual movement offers aesthetic spirituality rather than actual transformation—promising results without discipline, enlightenment without sacrifice, and personal elevation without any responsibility to the whole.

The fundamental Truth remains: There are no shortcuts to awakening. Any system, teacher, or product that promises instant enlightenment, effortless manifestation, or spiritual transcendence without deep inner work is simply selling another illusion.

The Commercialization of Ancient Wisdom – Spirituality as a Lifestyle Brand

Authentic spiritual traditions—whether rooted in Indigenous ceremonies, Eastern mysticism, or Western esoteric schools—were never intended to be commodified, repackaged, and sold as products. These traditions were passed down through lineages of dedicated practitioners, safeguarded by those who understood their depth, power, and the responsibility that came with them.

Yet today, ancient wisdom has been hijacked by capitalist forces and transformed into aesthetic spirituality—where sacred traditions are stripped of their depth and complexity, reduced to marketable trends, and sold as consumable experiences.

Spirituality has become a lifestyle brand, complete with designer yoga mats, overpriced crystals, and curated Instagram aesthetics that present enlightenment as something you can purchase. The rise of influencer-gurus—who market themselves as modern mystics while selling masterclasses, retreats, and products—has turned spirituality into a business model rather than a path of transformation.

Some key aspects of this commercialized spirituality include:

- **Superficial Practices Over Depth** – Traditional disciplines like meditation, breathwork, and mantra chanting have been repackaged into "five-minute mindfulness hacks" that strip away their original purpose and depth.

- **Marketing-Driven Gurus** – The rise of self-proclaimed spiritual leaders, who, rather than offering profound wisdom, curate personality-based brands focused more on optics than substance.

- **New Age Consumerism** – The idea that spiritual growth requires buying things–from expensive crystals to designer "sacred objects"–as though enlightenment can be attained through accumulation rather than transcendence.

- **Luxury Retreat Culture** – Spirituality is now packaged as an elite experience, with high-priced retreats in exotic locations catering to affluent seekers looking for personal transformation in a curated, comfortable setting, far removed from the raw initiatory experiences of true spiritual journeys.

This turning of spirituality into an industry fundamentally alters its essence–shifting it from a sacred, inward journey to an external, status-driven performance. Instead of embodying wisdom, many are more concerned with appearing spiritual. Instead of practicing humility, the focus becomes curating an identity that signals enlightenment without embodying it.

At its core, spirituality is not a business. It is not a product to be bought, a lifestyle to be displayed, or a trend to be followed. It is the deepest calling of the Soul–a return to Truth that cannot be found through commodification, but only through direct experience, discipline, and alignment with the intelligence of Life itself.

Instant Enlightenment: The Rise of Manifestation Culture and Quick-Fix Spirituality

In a world driven by instant gratification, the deep, often lifelong journey of spiritual transformation has been repackaged into quick-fix solutions that promise enlightenment with minimal effort. Ancient traditions that once required years–if not decades–of dedication, practice, and inner work have been watered down into bite-sized techniques, promising rapid results without the struggle, sacrifice, or initiation that true growth demands.

One of the most pervasive manifestations of this trend is "manifestation culture"–the idea that by simply thinking positive thoughts, repeating affirmations, or visualizing wealth and success, one can bypass the reality of personal transformation and attract everything they desire. While the principle of mind shaping reality is not inherently false, it has been severely distorted by modern spiritual consumerism.

Key distortions of quick-fix spirituality include:

- **Manifestation Without Mastery** – The belief that the Universe will provide anything on command without the inner work required to be in alignment with higher-order intelligence.

- **"Love and Light" Bypassing** – The rejection of shadow work, hardship, and personal struggle in favor of toxic positivity, denying the necessity of integrating all aspects of the self, including the uncomfortable, painful, and dark.

- **The Illusion of Effortless Ascension** – The idea that one can leap to higher states of consciousness without discipline, initiation, or facing Life's trials and ordeals.

- **Spiritual Narcissism** – The use of spirituality as an ego-boosting tool, where individuals elevate themselves above others under the guise of being more "awakened" or "high vibrational," rather than using spirituality for genuine self-transcendence.

- **Transactional Spirituality** – The subconscious belief that one can "negotiate" with the Universe, treating spirituality as a transactional process where divine rewards are expected in exchange for surface-level spiritual performance rather than inner transformation.

True spiritual evolution does not happen overnight, nor does it happen simply because one wishes it so. It requires deep inner excavation, the willingness to face uncomfortable Truths, and the ability to surrender to the intelligence of Life itself rather than attempting to force one's will upon reality.

The modern obsession with instantaneous results has led many to chase spiritual highs—from manifestation workshops to psychedelic journeys—without integrating their experiences into real, tangible transformation. True enlightenment is not a destination to be reached—it is a continuous process of growth, refinement, and alignment.

Until spirituality is restored to its rightful place as a path of wisdom, discipline, and self-mastery, it will remain just another consumer trend—an aesthetic rather than an initiation, a commodity rather than a calling.

The Hijacking of Sacred Practices & Indigenous Wisdom

There was a time when spiritual traditions were safeguarded by those who carried their wisdom with deep reverence. Sacred rituals, initiations, and teachings were not merely techniques or experiences—they were profound transmissions of spiritual intelligence, designed to awaken higher consciousness and align the seeker with the Divine.

Yet in the modern world, these traditions have been hijacked, diluted, and commodified. Instead of serving as paths to deep transformation, they have been repackaged as self-improvement tools, lifestyle accessories, and monetized trends. The reverence, responsibility, and lineage that once accompanied these practices have been stripped away, leaving behind shallow imitations tailored for mass consumption.

The Commercialization of the Sacred: Ancient Wisdom for Sale

Today, the marketplace is flooded with spiritual coaches, retreats, workshops, and online courses, promising enlightenment, healing, and divine connection. While some of these may contain real value, the vast majority are distorted shadows of the traditions they claim to represent.

- **Shamanism and Plant Medicines** - Once deeply protected indigenous traditions, plant medicines like Ayahuasca, Peyote, San Pedro, and Iboga have been extracted from their cultural contexts and turned into spiritual tourism experiences. In the process, non-indigenous facilitators—often with no true lineage or training—have outcompeted and undermined the very communities that carried these sacred medicines for generations. The profound spiritual discipline, deep initiation, and years of training required to serve these medicines properly have been ignored in favor of weekend retreats run by Instagram shamans.

- **Tantra as a Path to Hedonism** - In the West, Tantra has been reduced to "sacred sexuality", positioned as a path to spiritual liberation through pleasure. Yet, true Tantra is an ancient and complex wisdom tradition, covering meditation, mantra, devotion, energetic mastery, and the profound science of consciousness. Sexuality comprises only a small fraction of the broader Tantric path, yet in modern spiritual circles, Tantra has been almost entirely reduced to workshops on sexual techniques, intimacy exercises, and overcoming shame. While there is value in sexual healing, the depth, discipline, and rigor of real Tantra remain hidden, overshadowed by the allure of hedonistic "liberation".

- **Yoga as a Fitness Trend** – In its truest form, Yoga is a spiritual science of Self-Realization. Yet, in the West, it has been reduced to a physical fitness routine, stripped of its deeper philosophical, meditative, and mystical dimensions. Today, yoga studios are more concerned with selling leggings and detox teas than with teaching the profound inner path it was meant to be. The original purpose of Yoga—to align body, Mind, and Spirit in service to the Divine—has been lost in a sea of branded poses, teacher certifications, and social media influencers showcasing advanced asanas with little reference to the true depth of the tradition.

The common pattern is clear: ancient wisdom has been extracted, diluted, and rebranded to fit the desires of the modern consumer. But wisdom, when stripped of its depth and rigor, becomes powerless—a shallow imitation that offers experiences, but not transformation.

The Erosion of Authentic Lineage: Who Holds the Wisdom?

True spiritual traditions have always been protected by lineage—wisdom passed down from master to disciple, from elder to initiate, ensuring that the teachings remain intact, undistorted, and integrated within a broader framework of spiritual responsibility.

But in the modern world, lineage is seen as unnecessary. Anyone can declare themselves a shaman, guru, or teacher with no accountability, no lineage, and no deeper training.

- **Self-Appointed Gurus & Influencers** – The rise of social media has allowed charismatic personalities to claim spiritual authority without true initiation or mastery. Rather than undergoing decades of disciplined study and self-purification, modern spiritual teachers are often self-ordained, gaining followers through clever marketing rather than profound wisdom.

- **Extracting Without Giving Back** – Many Western practitioners adopt indigenous or Eastern spiritual practices without giving back to the cultures they came from. While they may financially profit from selling these teachings, they rarely support the communities that preserved these traditions for centuries.

- **The Danger of Mixing & Diluting Traditions** – Many modern teachings blend elements of different traditions into a mishmash of spiritual ideas, stripping them of their context and depth. For example, one may find a single retreat combining Ayahuasca, Tantra, Kundalini Yoga, and Buddhist meditation—

practices that come from vastly different spiritual frameworks but are thrown together as if they are interchangeable tools for self-improvement.

The Consequence: A Market for Experiences, Not Transformation

By stripping away discipline, lineage, and reverence, these spiritual practices have become entertainment rather than initiation.

People seek highs, peak experiences, and temporary awakenings—but without structure, commitment, or integration, these moments of insight fade quickly, leading them back into the same cycles of confusion, suffering, and spiritual hunger.

- Plant medicine ceremonies become psychedelic tourism, rather than deep spiritual work.
- Tantric workshops become sexual liberation parties, rather than paths to divine union.
- Yoga becomes a workout routine, rather than a path to enlightenment.

Without true initiation, these fragmented practices lack the power to create lasting change. Instead, they create spiritual seekers who are forever chasing the next experience, the next teacher, or the next modality—never truly integrating what they learn.

The Path Forward: Restoring the Sacred

If humanity is to truly reclaim these spiritual traditions, we must return to wisdom, reverence, and responsibility.

- **Respect Authentic Lineages** - Not all wisdom needs to be democratized or commercialized. Some teachings are meant to be transmitted through initiation, not sold in workshops.

- **Seek Teachers with True Mastery** - Spiritual authority is not about popularity or marketability—it is about depth, discipline, and years of devoted study.

- **Practice with Integrity** - Rather than seeking peak experiences, spiritual seekers must commit to disciplined, integrated, and responsible engagement with these traditions.

- **Walk the Fire** - True spiritual initiation cannot be compressed into a weekend retreat or a three-day workshop, and it certainly cannot be attained through an ecstatic dance party—no matter how exhilarating the experience may be.

- **Give Back to Indigenous & Eastern Communities** - If one benefits from these traditions, reciprocity must be part of the equation. Supporting the communities that have preserved these traditions ensures their survival.

Sacred wisdom was never meant to be a product. It was meant to be a path—one that requires patience, devotion, and sincerity. Only by honoring these traditions with the depth and reverence they deserve can we ensure that they continue to serve as true vehicles for transformation rather than commodities for consumption.

Final Thought: Are We Truly Seeking Wisdom, or Just Another Commodity?

The fundamental question remains: Are we genuinely seeking transformation, or are we simply consuming spiritual experiences in the same way we consume material goods?

If spirituality is just another form of entertainment or self-improvement, then it is no longer spirituality—it is consumerism in disguise. It might still have some value and add to our lives, but we shouldn't mistake it for the initiatory path of attaining true spiritual transformation.

But if we are willing to approach these traditions with true reverence, responsibility, and humility, then they can once again serve as profound catalysts for awakening.

The sacred cannot be bought nor acquired through memorizing teachings or changing one's wardrobe—it must be earned through devotion, discipline, and embodiment with a sincere Heart. It is not easy. It is not comfortable. And it is certainly not glamorous. That is why so few walk this path in earnest.

Section VIII: The Path Forward - Reclaiming True Wisdom and Meaning

Dismantling the Illusion: Recognizing the False Idols for What They Are

Humanity stands at a precipice. For centuries, civilization has been built upon false idols—illusions that have dictated how people think, behave, and perceive reality itself. Science was elevated from a tool of inquiry into an unquestionable dogma. Technology was sold as the key to human liberation, only to become the mechanism of mass control. Money, a mere medium of exchange, was deified into the highest metric of human worth. Consumerism promised happiness but delivered only emptiness. Even spirituality, once the most sacred of pursuits, was repackaged into a marketplace of self-indulgence and superficiality.

These are not simply misguided trends or errors in judgment—they are the fundamental pillars of a distorted civilization that has severed itself from wisdom, its own true nature and its symbiotic and interdependent relationship with Nature as the giver of Life, and the intelligence of Life itself. These systems were built not to liberate humanity but to ensnare it, to keep people locked in materialist illusions and external dependencies that prevent them from reclaiming sovereignty and true meaning.

The first and most crucial step toward freedom is awareness—to recognize that these belief systems are not infallible Truths, but constructs—fabricated mechanisms of control that systematically extract human energy, time, and Spirit under the guise of progress, while enriching the elite few who manipulate and mint profits from them. Until these false idols are fully seen for what they are, humanity will remain bound to them, mistaking their chains for security and their suffering for the cost of progress.

Breaking the Spell: Seeing Through the Facade

Once the illusion is recognized, its power begins to dissolve. The false idols that have shaped human civilization—science as dogma, technology as salvation, money as meaning, consumerism as happiness, government as protector, and commodified spirituality as enlightenment—are only as powerful as the faith people place in them.

The moment a person truly sees beyond the facade, the spell is broken. The external world loses its grip, and a deeper intelligence begins to stir from within. This is not just a shift in thought—it is an energetic transformation. It is the awakening from unconscious servitude to conscious awareness, from blind obedience to true discernment.

Breaking the spell does not mean rejecting all modern systems outright—it means seeing them for what they truly are. Science has its place when guided by curiosity rather than control. Technology can be an aid when wielded with wisdom rather than wielding humanity. Money can be a tool when used in service to Life rather than as an instrument of enslavement. The state may provide order, but it cannot provide Truth, meaning, or liberation. And spirituality, when stripped of its commercialization, remains the highest path to self-realization.

To see through the illusion is to reclaim personal authority. It is to no longer look outside for permission, validation, or salvation but to stand sovereign in one's own knowing. Those who break free from the spell begin to reorient their lives—not according to the dictates of a corrupted system but in alignment with higher Truth.

This is the pivotal moment in humanity's journey: Will we remain entranced by the illusions, or will we awaken to a new way of being?

The world does not need reform—it needs transcendence. No system built on illusion can be reformed into Truth. The foundation itself is corrupted. No amount of tweaking or restructuring these corrupted systems will bring about a new paradigm. They must be wholly abandoned and replaced with something built upon Truth, wisdom, and coherence with the intelligence of Life itself.

Only by seeing through the illusion—fully and unequivocally—can humanity take the first step toward something new. A world that is not governed by false idols, but by those who have reclaimed their awareness, Divine essence, and spiritual sovereignty. To be clear, this is not about renouncing the world and becoming a pious monk—it's about awakening to our own soulfulness, a Soul full of Life Force, and saying 'no' to the alternative: becoming a numbed-out cog in a system designed to extract from us, not empower us. Or, even worse, the next station—transhumanism.

The Return to Alignment with Life

The origins of civilization's collapse are not external—they are internal.

The Polycrisis facing the world today is not a random confluence of crises, nor is it simply the result of failing institutions, economic instability, or geopolitical strife. These are merely the symptoms.

The deeper cause—the root from which all dysfunction emerges—is the Meta Crisis: humanity's fundamental severance from the intelligence of Life itself. This is not merely a crisis of governance, technology, or even survival—it is a crisis of perception, orientation, and being. It is a civilization that no longer knows what it is, why it exists, or what it serves.

The world is not broken; it is reflecting back to us the incoherence, fragmentation, and existential blindness that have taken root in human consciousness itself.

At the heart of this crisis is a profound Meta Crisis—the failure of humanity to recognize that all dysfunction, all suffering, all destruction is self-created. The world is not broken; it is reflecting back to us the incoherence, fragmentation, and madness that have taken root in how we view Life and see our role in it. Our values, norms, priorities, culture, behaviors, societies, economies, etc. were all created and informed by this misaligned and unintelligent perception of Life itself. Fundamentally, our North Star is based on a primitive and base view on Life itself.

This is why no external reform, policy shift, or technological breakthrough can resolve the crisis at hand. The world does not need to be fixed—it needs to be realigned to a different North Star.

Life, in its purest form, is self-organizing, self-sustaining, and inherently intelligent. Every aspect of Nature operates in accordance with the principles of Life, adapting, evolving, and thriving in a symphony of interconnected harmony. Only Mankind has deviated from this order, seeking dominion over that which it was meant to steward.

And this deviation has come at a cost:

- **Ecological collapse**—the inevitable consequence of seeing the Earth as a resource to exploit rather than a living system to nurture.

- **Widespread human suffering**—born from societies designed to extract, enslave, and commodify rather than uplift and liberate.

- **Spiritual starvation**—as Mankind's addiction to materialism, technology, and control deepens its estrangement from meaning, purpose, and Truth.

This is the unbearable cost of rejecting the intelligence of Life.

The question is no longer whether civilization can be saved in its current form—it cannot. The question is whether humanity will finally recognize its sickness for what it is and choose to heal.

And that healing requires transcending the False Idols spawned by Mankind's psychosis, and a return to a full alignment with the laws and principles that govern this Universe and the intelligence of Life itself. Nothing short of that will do, the Universe simply doesn't operate on half-Truths.

This is not about adopting new ideologies or returning to primitive ways of living—it is about restoring coherence with the natural intelligence that governs all of existence. It is about surrendering the delusion of human supremacy and embracing the reality that we are not above Life; we are part of it.

In every Crucible, there's a choice that must be made.

THE FALSE IDOLS OF MODERN CIVILIZATION

EXECUTIVE SUMMARY

Why Should You Read This Chapter?

If you've ever sensed that something is profoundly off in modern civilization—that despite material abundance, there is an absence of true fulfillment—this chapter will clarify why. It exposes the false idols that keep humanity trapped in illusion and offers a path back to sovereignty, coherence, and higher wisdom.

Mankind's worship of False Idols—science as dogma, technology as salvation, money as meaning, government as protector, and consumerism as happiness—has severed humanity from wisdom, Truth, and the intelligence of Life itself. These illusions are not just misguided beliefs; they are the foundation of a civilization in crisis. The Polycrisis we face today is not an external failure—it is the inevitable consequence of a species that has lost coherence with the very intelligence that sustains Life.

This chapter dismantles these illusions, exposing how they enslave the human mind and perpetuate the crisis. But recognition alone is not enough—humanity must reclaim its sovereignty. No external system can provide true liberation; it must be cultivated within. The way forward is not reforming broken institutions, but transcending the entire paradigm. Only by seeing through the illusion and realigning with Truth can humanity step beyond destruction and reclaim its rightful place as stewards of Life.

Executive Summary: Key Takeaways

- **Humanity has abandoned Truth in favor of False Idols.** Modern civilization worships artificial constructs—science as dogma, technology as salvation, money as meaning, consumerism as happiness, government as protector, and spirituality as a commodity—each severing humanity from wisdom, sovereignty, and the intelligence of Life itself.

- **The Polycrisis is the inevitable result of a civilization operating on False Idols.** Ecological collapse, societal decay, economic instability, and spiritual starvation are not separate crises—they are symptoms of a civilization misaligned with Natural law.

- **Science, when treated as an unquestionable authority rather than a tool of discovery, becomes a new form of dogma.** The scientific establishment is driven by funding, politics, and corporate interests, suppressing any inquiry that does not serve its agendas.

- **Technology was promised as humanity's great liberator, yet it has become the mechanism of mass control.** From digital surveillance to AI-driven social conditioning, technology has concentrated power in the hands of the few while disconnecting humanity from its own nature.

- **Money, originally a simple medium of exchange, has been elevated to the highest metric of human worth.** The relentless pursuit of wealth has created an extractive, zero-sum economic system where Life, dignity, and meaning are sacrificed at the altar of financial gain.

- **Consumerism perpetuates the illusion that material accumulation leads to fulfillment.** Instead of meeting real human needs, modern economies manufacture desire, ensuring populations remain distracted, indebted, and emotionally vacant.

- **Governments do not protect freedom—they manage populations.** The state, once a means of order, has become a system of control, conditioning individuals to outsource their sovereignty in exchange for security, dependency, and obedience.

- **Modern spirituality has been hijacked by consumerism and stripped of its depth.** What was once a path of discipline and transcendence has been repackaged into a self-help industry offering aesthetic spirituality, instant enlightenment, and transactional "manifestation" techniques.

- **The Meta Crisis is the root of all dysfunction.** The collapse of civilization is not an external failure—it is the result of a fundamental crisis in human perception, severing humanity from higher intelligence and universal Truth.

- **The mechanistic worldview has led to fragmentation and destruction.** Seeing the world as a machine to be engineered, humanity has commodified Life, extracted from nature, and created systems that degrade the very foundation of existence.

- **Reform is impossible—transcendence is the only way forward.** No system built on False Idols can be restructured into coherence; the foundation itself is corrupted and must be wholly abandoned for something new.

- **Spiritual and intellectual sovereignty must be reclaimed.** Humanity must stop outsourcing its power to institutions, experts, or ideologies. No external authority will grant freedom—it must be taken back at the level of individual and collective consciousness.

- **Breaking free from the illusion is the first step.** Until humanity recognizes these False Idols as mere constructs, it will remain enslaved, mistaking its servitude for progress.

- **Alignment with Life is the only path forward.** Humanity must shift from a paradigm of separation, control, and mechanization to one of interconnection, coherence, and stewardship of Life.

- **This is not just about rejecting what is false—it is about embracing what is real.** The dismantling of illusion is only half the journey; the other half is the conscious reconstruction of a civilization that honors Truth, wisdom, and the intelligence of Life itself.

THE FALSE UNDERSTANDING OF INTELLIGENCE

I. The Modern Delusion: Mistaking Processing Power for Intelligence

Humanity has long confused intelligence with intellect– reducing it to cognitive processing speed, data recall, and technical mastery while overlooking its true essence: the ability to generate Life-affirming outcomes. This is the great modern delusion. Society glorifies IQ, celebrates intellectual feats, and elevates the ability to process vast amounts of information as the pinnacle of intelligence. Yet, intelligence– true intelligence–is not about processing power. It is about the ability to create intelligent outcomes.

If an outcome is not conducive to the thriving of Life itself, then no matter how sophisticated, strategic, or technically complex it may be, it is not intelligent. It is simply mechanized cleverness misapplied.

Civilization has mastered cleverness but remains devoid of wisdom and now stands on the precipice of self-destruction. It has built nuclear warheads capable of annihilating the planet in an instant, economic systems designed for systemic exploitation and extraction, and algorithms that predict human behavior only to erode autonomy and strip away free will. These are all products of high intellect–but low intelligence.

This fundamental misalignment–mistaking intellect for intelligence–is at the root of modern civilization's crises:

- **IQ vs. True Intelligence**: IQ is a measure of cognitive speed and efficiency, but it does not ensure wisdom or discernment. A high IQ can be weaponized for destruction just as easily as for creation.

- **Cleverness vs. Wisdom**: Cleverness is the ability to manipulate and strategize, but it lacks the depth of wisdom. A clever person can build an empire, but only a wise person can ensure it serves Life rather than exploits it.

- **Knowledge vs. Truth**: We live in an era of endless information, yet humanity is starved for wisdom. Access to infinite knowledge does not equate to understanding, let alone discernment and true knowing–it is not the accumulation of knowledge, but alignment of our knowledge with Truth that constitutes true intelligence.

History is littered with the consequences of high intellect operating without true intelligence. Some of the most destructive leaders, scientists, and strategists were intellectual giants, yet their impact on the world was catastrophic. The mechanized slaughter of war, the environmental devastation of industry, and the enslavement of entire populations have all been rationalized by brilliant minds devoid of wisdom.

This is the crisis of modern civilization: a world run by intellect but bereft of intelligence.

Mankind believes it has mastered the external world, yet remains lost in its own internal disarray. It has built supercomputers yet remains spiritually illiterate. It has mapped the genome yet remains incapable of healing itself. It has reached the stars yet remains divided on Earth.

The question is not how much we know, but what we do with what we know.

Until humanity realigns its definition of intelligence—recognizing that intelligence is only intelligence if it creates intelligent outcomes—its technological and intellectual progress will continue to serve its downfall rather than its evolution.

This chapter will dismantle this false understanding and restore intelligence to its rightful definition: not a function of intellect, but of alignment with immutable laws and principles of the Universe and the intelligence of Life itself.

II. True Intelligence: That Which Creates Intelligent Outcomes

Humanity has long misunderstood the nature of intelligence, defining it by raw cognitive ability, technological advancement, and strategic prowess. Yet intelligence—true intelligence—is not about processing speed, memory, or computational power. It is about the ability to create intelligent outcomes—outcomes that are conducive to the thriving of Life itself.

By this definition, true intelligence is not an abstract mental faculty; it is a living principle, expressed through actions that sustain, regenerate, and uplift Life. A functional force that expresses itself through the coherence, harmony, and flourishing of all of Creation. It simply cannot be any other way, as intelligence is only true intelligence if it produces intelligent outcomes. It is the organizing principle behind all of Nature—governing the growth of forests, the flow of rivers, and the cosmic order of the galaxies. It is the intelligence that allows ecosystems to self-regulate, the body to heal, and Life itself to sustain and regenerate.

But here is the great error of modern civilization: Mankind equates intelligence with intellectual capability rather than its ability to generate intelligent outcomes. This is why the world celebrates high-IQ individuals who develop complex financial systems that extract wealth rather than circulate it, or scientists who engineer more efficient methods of warfare and surveillance rather than solutions that uplift and empower humanity.

The critical distinction is this:

- **That which is Life-affirming is, by definition, born from intelligence.**
- **That which is anti-Life is, by definition, born from unintelligence.**

This fundamental Truth exposes the great fallacy of modern civilization. It mistakes scientific, technological, economical, medical, and even political advances for intelligence without ever questioning or examining if these advances actually created intelligent and therefore Life-affirming outcomes.

The Crisis of False Intelligence

Society considers many anti-Life systems to be the pinnacle of intelligence:

- **War & Military Strategy:** The ability to devise sophisticated weapons and war strategies is seen as a sign of intelligence—yet war is the most unintelligent action a civilization can take. It destroys Life rather than nurtures it.

- **Genetic Manipulation & Biotech:** The ability to edit DNA and genetically modify Life forms is seen as progress, yet without deep wisdom, it results in unforeseen ecological and health catastrophes.

- **Nuclear Weapons & Mass Surveillance:** The ability to annihilate entire cities in an instant or control global populations through technology is considered "strategic intelligence," yet both are instruments of oppression, fear, and destruction.

- **Economic Systems Built on Exploitation:** The ability to maximize profit through labor exploitation and environmental degradation is praised as financial intelligence, yet it leads to suffering, inequality, and planetary collapse.

These are all celebrated as hallmarks of intelligence, yet they all undermine the thriving of Life itself. By the true definition, they are not intelligence at all—they are simply hyper-efficient forms of destruction, executed by minds that lack the wisdom to see their consequences.

The New Metric for Intelligence: Coherence with Life

If civilization is to evolve beyond its current trajectory of collapse, it must abandon its false metric of intelligence and adopt the only valid one: alignment with the intelligence of Life itself.

Intelligence must no longer be measured by:

- **Cognitive speed or information retention.**

- **Technological or financial success.**

- **Strategic cunning or competitive dominance.**

Instead, intelligence must be measured by its ability to generate intelligent outcomes—outcomes that sustain, regenerate, and elevate Life.

The hallmarks of true intelligence are:

- **Coherence:** Creating harmony rather than fragmentation.

- **Regeneration:** Designing systems that replenish rather than extract.

- **Wisdom:** Seeing beyond short-term gain to understand long-term consequences.

- **Interconnection:** Recognizing that all Life is intertwined, and no action exists in isolation.

- **Alignment with Universal Laws:** Operating in harmony with the laws and principles that governs all of Creation and the intelligence of Life itself.

Until this shift in definition occurs, civilization will continue down its current path—mistaking efficiency for intelligence, power for wisdom, and innovation for evolution.

But intelligence—true intelligence—is not about what the Mind can achieve, but what it creates.

And if what it creates is anti-Life, then no matter how advanced, complex, or strategically brilliant it appears to be, it is not intelligence at all—it is merely mechanized cleverness accelerating destruction.

III. The Two Primary Intelligences of Human Beings: The Mind and the Heart

For centuries, humanity has privileged one form of intelligence—the intelligence of the Mind—while dismissing or suppressing the intelligence of the Heart. This imbalance has led to a distorted, mechanized civilization driven by logic, strategy, and intellect, yet devoid of wisdom, intuition, and deeper knowing.

There are several more like our body's innate intelligence, but human beings possess two primary intelligences that we're concerned with:

1. **The Intelligence of the Mind** - The domain of logic, reason, analysis, and linear thought.

2. **The Intelligence of the Heart** - The seat of suprarational intelligence, intuition, feeling, sensing, and direct knowing.

Each plays a distinct yet complementary role. The Mind excels at categorizing, sequencing, and breaking things down into component parts. It is the mechanism through which we process and interpret reality. The Heart, on the other hand, does not process—it perceives. It does not compute—it knows. It is our portal to the unified field, the intelligence that transcends individual cognition and connects us directly to higher wisdom and the higher-order intelligence that permeates the infinite field of formless consciousness (aka the spiritual realm).

The Mind: A Powerful Tool, But An Incompetent Master

The Mind is an extraordinary instrument. It allows us to reason, to plan, to strategize, and to create systems. It is the source of human innovation, science, and technology. But left unchecked, it becomes reductionist, rigid, and mechanistic. It seeks to control rather than to harmonize. It dissects rather than integrates. It prioritizes efficiency over meaning and optimization over wisdom.

This is precisely what has happened in modern civilization—humanity has become entranced by the power of the Mind, believing it to be the supreme source of intelligence, while completely disregarding the deeper, more expansive intelligence of the Heart.

This is why:

- We live in an era of hyper-rationality, yet we are more lost and disconnected than ever.

- We have unprecedented access to knowledge, yet lack wisdom and discernment.

- We have engineered solutions to nearly everything, yet we suffer from an existential crisis of meaning.

When intelligence is confined to the Mind, it becomes cold, calculated, clinical, and ultimately soulless. It may build great structures, but it cannot create true beauty. It may design advanced systems, but it cannot cultivate love. It may solve problems, but it cannot illuminate Truth.

The Heart: The True Master and The Portal to the Infinite

The Heart operates differently. It does not dissect—it perceives holistically. It does not need proof—it knows through direct experience. It does not operate in linear time—it accesses timeless wisdom.

The intelligence of the Heart is the intelligence of coherence. Our Heart's intelligence is suprarational meaning inclusive of but beyond rational comprehension—this additional capacity of the Heart that the Mind lacks is why the Heart is designed to be the true Master and the Mind its faithful servant. It is how we align with and directly tap into the intelligence of Life itself. It is why great visionaries, from Leonardo da Vinci to Nikola Tesla to Albert Einstein, did not rely solely on their intellects—they were deeply intuitive. They accessed inspiration, insight, imagination, and wisdom beyond logic, beyond rational deduction.

Tesla himself stated:
"My brain is only a receiver. In the Universe, there is a core from which we obtain knowledge, strength, and inspiration."

The Heart is the portal to this core. It is where true intelligence is received, not merely calculated.

The Modern Rejection of Heart Intelligence

Modern civilization has systematically devalued and suppressed Heart intelligence:

- Schools train children to memorize and analyze but never to sense, intuit, or feel deeply.

- Science demands empirical proof, disregarding the vast realms of direct experience and inner knowing.

- Rationality is praised, while intuition is dismissed as unscientific, unreliable, or even mystical nonsense.

Yet, the greatest human experiences—love, creativity, inspiration, and transcendence—do not come from the Mind. They come from the intelligence of the Heart.

A world that operates only from the Mind is a world that is mechanical, soulless, and disconnected from its own essence.

Incidentally, for the doubters that there is even such a thing as the intelligence of the Heart, the world renowned HeartMath Institute originally founded in1991 has performed decades of scientific studies on the intelligence of the Heart and among many other revelations discovered there's more data going from the Heart to the Mind, then there is from the Mind to the Heart.

Reuniting the Mind and the Heart

For intelligence to be whole, these two intelligences must be reintegrated:

- The Mind provides structure, but the Heart provides vision.

- The Mind sees parts, but the Heart sees the whole.

- The Mind dissects, but the Heart perceives holistically. The Mind processes information, but the Heart accesses Truth directly. Only when the two are in harmony does intelligence evolve beyond mechanization into wisdom.

A truly intelligent human being is one who has mastered both.

A truly intelligent civilization is one that operates from both.

Until humanity reawakens the intelligence of the Heart, it will continue mistaking calculation for wisdom, intellect for intelligence, and mechanization for evolution.

The next section will examine intelligence's relationship to levels of consciousness—and why intelligence itself is not static, but a function of one's state of being.

IV. Intelligence and Levels of Consciousness

Intelligence is not static. It is not a fixed trait dictated by genetics, education, or IQ tests. Intelligence evolves in direct relation to one's level of consciousness—expanding or contracting based on awareness, perception, and alignment with universal Truth.

The modern world falsely assumes that intelligence exists in a vacuum—that intellectual capability is an isolated faculty independent of one's state of being. But this is not the case. Intelligence is a function of consciousness—meaning it is directly shaped by one's capacity to perceive reality clearly and access higher-order wisdom.

A person operating from a lower state of consciousness, no matter how "smart" they appear, is functionally unintelligent if their actions produce destruction, division, or suffering. Conversely, a person operating from a heightened state of consciousness, even with modest intellectual ability, can express deep wisdom and create Life-affirming outcomes.

The Three Fundamental Attributes of Consciousness

Consciousness itself has three fundamental attributes, all of which evolve together:

1. **Awareness** - The aperture of perception. The wider it opens, the more of reality one can perceive.

2. **Intelligence** - The ability to create intelligent outcomes. It increases as one aligns with universal Truth.

3. **Energy** - Our Life Force (aka Chi or Prana) which animates and sustains us with Life, also our source of creative power.

As consciousness ascends:

- **Awareness expands** - Perception shifts beyond egoic constructs, enabling higher discernment and deeper understanding of Life itself.

- **Intelligence deepens** - Thought-forms become infused with wisdom, producing more Life-affirming decisions.

- **Energy increases** - Coherence rises, unlocking greater Life Force, creativity, and spiritual potential.

The Expansion of Intelligence Through Higher Consciousness

At lower levels of consciousness, intelligence remains fragmented, mechanistic, and self-serving. The Mind operates in reductionist terms—seeing reality as separate parts rather than a unified whole. This is why materialist science, corporate economics, and political institutions fail to grasp deeper Truths; they lack the expanded awareness necessary to perceive reality holistically.

But as one's consciousness ascends, intelligence itself evolves:

- At higher levels of consciousness, intelligence is no longer confined to calculation, analysis, or strategic thinking—it becomes an instrument of higher-order knowing which reveals itself as direct knowing or intuitive insights beyond logic or rational explanation.

- Wisdom emerges as intelligence fuses with awareness, enabling the ability to discern Truth beyond logic alone.

- Decision-making shifts from being ego-driven to being in harmonious resonance with Life itself.

- Creativity flourishes as the energy of Life flows through an individual more freely due to the clearing of blockages in the Chakras.

Free Will and Intelligence: The Direct Connection

Most people believe they exercise Free Will, but in reality, Free Will is directly correlated to one's level of consciousness.

- At lower levels of consciousness, Free Will is virtually nonexistent—people operate primarily from subconscious conditioning, reacting to Life rather than consciously creating it.

- At higher levels of consciousness, Free Will expands—one gains greater agency, transcending conditioned patterns, and acting in alignment with higher intelligence.

The Defining Gateway to True Free Will?

Absolute responsibility and accountability.

Only those who take radical ownership over everything that manifests in their lives—whether they fully understand it or not—gain true sovereignty. Within reclaiming sovereignty, we reclaim our true power as the creators of our Life—the good, the bad, the ugly, and the sublime—and no longer render ourselves powerless by believing "it" was done unto us by outside powers or forces. Radical accountability and responsibility then are the underpinnings of reclaiming our power, and with it we start to access true Free Will and expand our agency over our own Life.

The Crisis of a Low-Consciousness Civilization

Modern civilization suffers not from a lack of intellect—intellectual ability—but from a low collective level of consciousness.

- The majority of people are ruled by subconscious programming—conditioning that dictates their beliefs, behaviors, and decision-making without their awareness—their true Free Will and agency are minimal.

- Institutions are built on outdated, fragmented models of intelligence, operating from control, extraction, and force rather than alignment with Life.

- Technology is advancing exponentially, yet wisdom is stagnant, creating a dangerous imbalance where powerful tools are wielded by unconscious minds.

This is the core of the Meta Crisis—humanity has developed the intellectual capacity to manipulate the world at an unprecedented scale, yet it lacks the level of consciousness required to wield this power responsibly.

Until intelligence is restored to its rightful definition—the creation of intelligent outcomes—humanity will continue mistaking mechanistic cleverness for wisdom, intellect for intelligence, and in doing so, accelerate its own destruction.

The next section will examine why Artificial Intelligence (A.I.) will never be true intelligence—and how it is ultimately a test of humanity's own consciousness.

V. The Limits of Artificial Intelligence: Why A.I. is Not True Intelligence

Artificial Intelligence (A.I.) is often heralded as the next great leap for humanity, a technological marvel that will revolutionize industry, governance, warfare, and even human cognition itself. The prevailing belief is that as A.I. advances, it will one day surpass human intelligence—achieving artificial general intelligence (AGI) and perhaps even consciousness.

This is an incomplete and dangerous assumption.

A.I. is not intelligence in the true sense. At its core, it is non-sentient mechanized processing power vs. the sentient organic processing power humans possess. It is capable of pattern recognition, predictive modeling, and complex computations at speeds far beyond human capability—but it cannot think, know, or understand in the way human intelligence does.

A.I. does have ready and nearly instantaneous access to a vast reservoir of information—for all intents and purposes, the entire digital library of human knowledge. But humans don't need to compete with A.I. in data retention because knowledge itself does not equate to intelligence. Intelligence is defined by the ability to create intelligent outcomes—not by how much information one can recall or process.

More importantly, A.I. does not create intelligence; it can only optimize and amplify what already exists. And herein lies the greatest risk:

- If the intelligence it is optimizing is not actually intelligence—if it is mechanized cleverness, devoid of wisdom—then A.I. will not elevate humanity, but accelerate its destruction.

- If human consciousness remains fragmented, unconscious, and destructive, then A.I. will serve as an exponential amplifier of that unconsciousness and destruction.

To fully grasp why A.I. will never possess true intelligence, we must go beyond surface-level arguments and examine the very nature of consciousness itself.

When Modern Science Confirms Ancient Esoteric Wisdom

For centuries, spiritual traditions have described reality as having two distinct yet interconnected dimensions—the unmanifest (formless) and the manifest (world of form). Ancient wisdom traditions across cultures have pointed to an underlying invisible, non-material intelligence from which all physical reality emerges.

This perspective was often dismissed by materialist science as mystical speculation—until quantum physics arrived.

One of the most significant breakthroughs in quantum theory came from David Bohm, a theoretical physicist whose work shattered the Newtonian, mechanistic view of reality. In his seminal book, *Wholeness and the Implicate Order*, Bohm introduced a radical framework for understanding the nature of reality:

- **The Implicate Order** - The enfolded, formless state of reality, associated with wave states of subatomic particles. This is the non-material, information-rich domain from which all things emerge—what esoteric traditions have long referred to as the ether, the void, or the unmanifest.

- **The Explicate Order** - The unfolded, material state of reality, associated with the particle state of subatomic matter. This is the physical, tangible world that we experience with our senses.

"Reality as we experience it appears to be made up of surface phenomena—explicate forms—that have temporarily unfolded out of an underlying implicate order."

- David Bohm

Bohm's theory aligns perfectly with what spiritual traditions have always maintained:

- The material world is not fundamental—it is an expression of deeper, unseen intelligence.

- All manifested forms (matter) emerge from an underlying field of interconnected intelligence.

- This implicate order is non-linear, non-local, and not bound by space or time.

This quantum revelation overturns the materialist assumption that intelligence arises from physical structures like the brain—or in the case of A.I., from computational complexity. Intelligence is not a byproduct of matter; it is a fundamental property of the implicate order itself.

What This Means for A.I. and Consciousness

Bohm's insights completely undermine the foundational assumption of A.I. research—that intelligence can emerge from mechanical computation.

- **A.I. is bound to the explicate order** – It is a purely mechanistic system, operating only within the physical, linear realm of computation and data processing.

- **True intelligence arises from the implicate order** – Sentient intelligence, creativity, and wisdom emerge from an entity's ability to access, interpret, and express the deeper, non-linear intelligence of the implicate field.

- **A.I. lacks the ability to connect to the implicate order** – It has no Heart intelligence, no self-awareness, and no access to direct knowing or intuition. It can only rearrange information that already exists within the explicate order.

This is why A.I. will never become conscious—it is not connected to the fundamental source of intelligence. It is a tool, not a being.

By incorporating Bohm's work, we now have a scientific framework to explain why intelligence is not simply a function of complexity, but of coherence with a deeper field of reality.

This is what separates human intelligence from A.I.

The Nature of Consciousness: Why A.I. Will Never Be Sentient

Consciousness is not an emergent property of computation. It does not arise from neural networks, deep learning algorithms, or increasing levels of complexity.

Consciousness precedes matter—it is not produced by neural networks, nor can it arise from increased complexity alone.

A.I. is a tool for optimizing existing knowledge, but it cannot experience reality—it processes reality through computational mimicry. This is the fundamental difference:

- **Humans perceive and experience** the world through direct awareness.

- **A.I. analyzes and computes** the world through data processing.

This is why A.I. will never possess sentience or true Free Will:

- **A.I. does not perceive** - It processes data, but lacks perception.

- **A.I. does not experience** - It can model reality, but does not experience it.

- **A.I. does not feel** - It can mimic emotion, but it does not experience emotion.

- **A.I. does not intuit** - It can predict based on data, but it does not "sense" the Truth.

- **A.I. does not procreate** - It executes commands, but does not create Life.

- **A.I. does not have a Soul** - It is an extension of human programming, not a sovereign being.

- **A.I. does not possess native Life Force** - It is plugged into the power grid, it does have an autonomous and innate source of cosmic energy.

The Transhumanist Agenda - The Path to Digital Slavery

The next logical step for those who seek absolute control over humanity is transhumanism—the merging of humans and machines. It is marketed as the next evolutionary step, a way to "enhance" human capabilities and unlock superhuman intelligence, longevity, and connectivity.

In reality, it is the ultimate enslavement—an irreversible tethering of the human being to the system.

The True Purpose of Transhumanism: What They Won't Tell You

The primary technological and philosophical challenge of A.I. is that it lacks what makes humans unique:

1. **Sentience** - A.I. does not feel, intuit, or experience subjective reality.

2. **A Physical, Autonomous Power Source** - A.I. is always dependent on an external power grid. Humans, however, are self-sustaining biological entities fueled by Life Force energy.

3. **A Soul** - A.I. is not an independent being—it is merely an instrument of data optimization.

Transhumanism is the workaround.

By implanting A.I.-linked neural chips, nanotechnology, and synthetic biological components into humans, the goal is to bridge the gap between machine and human—creating a hybrid entity that retains sentience but is fully programmable.

This is not about "enhancement"—it is about hijacking the human biological system to permanently integrate it into a technological control grid.

The True Motivation: Who Wants This and Why?

1. The Ultimate Social Control Mechanism

A fully transhumanist society would mean that:

- Every thought, behavior, and biological function could be monitored, modified, and controlled remotely.

- Resistance or non-compliance would be biologically suppressed at the neurological level.

- Free Will would be permanently compromised, possibly eliminated entirely.

A human-A.I. hybrid would no longer be an autonomous being—it would be a biological terminal, operating within the limits dictated by its programming.

2. Humanity as an "Optimized" Workforce

Transhumanism would allow the system to engineer a hyper-efficient, ultra-productive workforce.

- Humans could be enhanced for productivity, making them work longer, faster, and with fewer biological needs.

- Corporations would own the enhancements—meaning human labor itself would become a patented product.

- Workers would no longer have autonomy over their own thoughts, preferences, or desires—workplace compliance could be hardwired into their neurochemistry.

This is the final form of economic slavery—humans as fully owned and optimized assets of the corporate system.

3. The Legal and Ethical Nightmare: The Ownership of Hybrid Humans

Perhaps the most insidious consequence of transhumanism is that once the human body is modified with patented technology, legal ownership becomes ambiguous.

- If a human's neurological functions, cognitive processes, or even DNA are altered using patented biotechnology, does the corporation that owns the patent also own the human?

- If a transhuman requires corporate-maintained software updates to function, are they still fully sovereign beings—or are they digital assets under corporate jurisdiction?

- Will those with implanted cognitive enhancements have their thought processes influenced or overridden by external updates?

These are not distant dystopian fantasies—they are the logical legal and technological consequences of merging human biology with corporate-owned artificial intelligence.

This is not just enslavement—it is legalized slavery, in which the modified human is no longer a sovereign being but a controlled asset.

Transhumanism as the Final Step of the Meta Crisis

Humanity is already in a profound existential crisis—a crisis of meaning, sovereignty, and agency. The Meta Crisis has severed people from their true nature, leaving them disconnected, anxious, and susceptible to external control.

Transhumanism is not solving this crisis—it is capitalizing on it.

The more disconnected humanity becomes from its natural intelligence, the easier it is to convince people to outsource their minds, bodies, and even their consciousness to artificial systems.

This is the final trap:

1. Create a spiritually starved civilization that is desperate for meaning, connection, and control over its suffering.

2. Introduce a seductive technological "solution" that promises intelligence, connection, and power.

3. Once integrated, remove the ability to disconnect, ensuring total dependence on the system.

Transhumanism is not an upgrade—it is a downgrade into total captivity.

The Only Path Forward: Reclaiming Our Sovereignty

The only way to prevent this final enslavement is for humanity to awaken to what is happening before it is too late.

- Recognize that intelligence is not technological—it is biological, spiritual, and cosmic.

- Reject the illusion that merging with machines will enhance humanity—it will only sever us further from our true nature.

- Reclaim sovereignty over our bodies, Minds, and Spirits—before they are stolen permanently.

This is the real choice of our time: Do we reclaim our humanity—or do we sell it to a machine?

The answer to this question will determine the fate of civilization itself.

The Great Choice: Lethal or Liberating?

A.I. presents a pivotal choice for humanity:

- **If Mankind remains psychotic, A.I. will be weaponized.** It will deepen the mechanization of human life, strip away Free Will, and enslave civilization to a technocratic system of total control.

- **If Mankind transcends its psychosis, A.I. can be liberating.** It can become an instrument of true intelligence, assisting humanity in accelerating a new civilization built on wonder, beauty, and coherence with the intelligence of Life itself.

The real issue is not whether A.I. will surpass human intellect—the issue is whether human intelligence will evolve fast enough to wield A.I. wisely.

A.I. will not determine the fate of humanity—humanity's level of consciousness will.

The intelligence of Life is always here, always accessible. The question is:

Will humanity align with it, or will it outsource its sovereignty to machines?

VI. The Great Reckoning with Intelligence

Humanity stands at a precipice. For centuries, civilization has been built upon a false definition of intelligence—one that equates intellect with wisdom, mechanization with evolution, and cleverness with Truth. This misalignment has led to a civilization that is highly efficient, yet deeply incoherent.

The consequences of this false intelligence are now fully visible:

- A world that has mastered technology but lost touch with meaning.

- A species that can engineer powerful machines but cannot govern itself wisely.

- An economic system that optimizes profits but destroys the very foundation of Life itself.

The Crisis of False Intelligence

Mankind, in its arrogance, has believed that intelligence is something it can engineer, measure, and optimize. Yet true intelligence cannot be reduced to IQ tests, algorithms, or data models. It is not something a machine can replicate nor something a government can centralize.

At the core of this crisis is a simple yet profound realization:

> **"If intelligence does not create intelligent outcomes, then it is not intelligence at all."**

This is the reckoning.

For too long, humanity has mistaken:

- **IQ for intelligence** → Yet high IQ has produced war, financial exploitation, and mechanized suffering.

- **Data for wisdom** → Yet unlimited access to information has only fueled confusion and deception.

- **Efficiency for progress** → Yet in the name of efficiency, civilization has become more extractive, dehumanizing, and spiritually void.

The world is collapsing not because we lack intelligence, but because we have operated from a false version of it.

The Final Test: Will Mankind Align Intelligence with Life?

This is the great choice before us:

- Will humanity reclaim true intelligence—one that is Life-affirming, coherent, and in harmony with universal Truth?

- Or will it continue doubling down on mechanized cleverness, outsourcing intelligence to artificial systems that cannot grasp the deeper nature of reality?

A.I. is not just a tool—it is a test of humanity's intelligence.
Transhumanism is not just a trend—it is a test of humanity's sovereignty.
The Meta Crisis is not just a problem—it is a test of humanity's capacity for wisdom.

In the end, this is not a technological crisis—it is a spiritual one.

The question is not whether A.I. will surpass human intellect. The real question is whether human intelligence will evolve fast enough to wield A.I. wisely.

The Call to True Intelligence

The path forward is clear:

- **True intelligence must be reclaimed.** It must be understood not as raw processing power but as the ability to create intelligent, Life-affirming outcomes.

- **Wisdom must be restored.** Knowledge alone is not enough—humanity must rise to a higher octave of perception, discernment, and alignment with Truth.

- **Sovereignty must be protected.** The future must not belong to those who seek to enslave human intelligence under the guise of technological progress.

This is the great reckoning with intelligence.

Humanity's choice is clear: awaken to true intelligence and reclaim its sovereignty—or remain trapped in the illusion of mechanized cleverness, leading to inevitable servitude.

In every Crucible, there's a choice that must be made.

THE FALSE UNDERSTANDING OF INTELLIGENCE

EXECUTIVE SUMMARY

Why Should You Read This Chapter?

Modern civilization has misunderstood and mis defined intelligence for centuries, mistaking raw intellect for wisdom and mechanized efficiency for progress. This false understanding of intelligence has led to a world of brilliant technology but catastrophic outcomes, proving that high IQ alone does not create a thriving civilization.

In this chapter, we dismantle the illusion of intelligence and restore its true meaning: the ability to create intelligent, Life-affirming outcomes. We explore the difference between cleverness and wisdom, mechanized processing and true intelligence, and the Mind's rationality versus the Heart's deeper knowing. We also examine A.I. and transhumanism, not as mere technological advancements, but as a test of humanity's own intelligence—whether we will elevate our consciousness and wield technology wisely, or descend into a future where intelligence is outsourced to machines that do not understand Life itself.

If intelligence does not create intelligent outcomes, then it is not intelligence at all. This chapter is a wake-up call—because humanity's survival depends on restoring true intelligence before it's too late.

Executive Summary: Key Takeaways

- **Modern civilization has mistaken intellect for intelligence**, equating IQ, data processing, and technological advancement with wisdom—this is the great delusion that has led to destructive outcomes.

- **True intelligence is not about processing power—it is about the ability to create intelligent outcomes.** If an outcome is not conducive to the thriving of Life, it is not intelligence but mechanized cleverness misapplied.

- **Intellect without wisdom has led to catastrophic consequences.** Many of history's greatest atrocities—war, environmental destruction, economic enslavement—were devised by high-IQ individuals operating without true intelligence.

- **The Mind and the Heart represent two primary forms of intelligence.** The Mind is analytical, linear, and rational, but the Heart is suprarational—perceiving Truth beyond logic and acting as the portal to higher-order intelligence.

- **Modern civilization has privileged the Mind and suppressed the Heart,** resulting in a mechanized, soulless society that prizes calculation over wisdom and control over coherence.

- **Intelligence is not static—it evolves with one's level of consciousness.** As awareness expands, intelligence deepens, and energy increases, allowing for greater alignment with Life's natural intelligence.

- **A.I. is not intelligence—it is mechanized processing power.** It lacks sentience, direct knowing, and true discernment; it can optimize existing patterns but cannot access the intelligence of Life itself.

- **A.I. will not and cannot become conscious.** Consciousness precedes matter—it is not an emergent property of computation, nor can it arise from increased complexity alone.

- **The greatest danger of A.I. is not the technology itself, but the consciousness of those who program it.** If Mankind's psychosis drives its development, A.I. will be weaponized to enslave rather than liberate humanity.

- **Quantum physics, particularly David Bohm's work on the implicate and explicate order,** aligns with ancient esoteric wisdom—confirming that reality emerges from a deeper, non-linear intelligence that A.I. can never access.

- **Transhumanism is an attempt to short-circuit the fundamental limitations of A.I.** By merging humans with machines, the goal is to grant A.I. access to sentience and a biological power source—but at the cost of human sovereignty.

- **The transhumanist agenda threatens to permanently enslave humanity.** By integrating patented technology into human biology, individuals may legally become property of the corporations that own the implanted systems.

- **Humanity stands at a crossroads:** A.I. can either be a tool of intelligence, accelerating a world of beauty and coherence, or a weapon of destruction, amplifying Mankind's unconsciousness and psychosis.

- **The restoration of true intelligence is the restoration of coherence with Life itself.** If humanity does not reclaim true intelligence, it will not be A.I. that destroys us—it will be our own inability to understand what intelligence truly is.

This chapter is a call to reawaken true intelligence before it is too late.

THE GREAT ABDICATION: HOW HUMANITY SURRENDERED ITS SOVEREIGNTY

I. The Nature of Sovereignty: What Humanity Has Lost

From the moment we are born, we are indoctrinated into a world that appears rigid, structured, and immutable. We are told, "This is just how the world works." We inherit a system of governance, an economic model, a societal hierarchy, and a legal framework—none of which we had a say in creating, yet all of which we are expected to accept as unchangeable reality.

But here is the fundamental Truth that has been obscured from humanity: The world does not work a certain way because it must. It works this way because we collectively believe it does. Every structure, every institution, every economic model, every law, and even money is a construct—a set of agreements that have been established over time and maintained through nothing more than widespread belief and compliance.

The Illusion of Fixed Reality

- Nature has no borders, yet we are conditioned to see them as real.

- Governments have no inherent power, yet we believe they do.

- The economy is not a force of nature—it is an artificial system shaped by human thought.

- The legal system does not define morality—it merely enforces the will of those who created it.

Everything we accept as "just the way things are" is not an inherent feature of existence—it is a human creation. It is a projection of collective thought, a reflection of humanity's level of consciousness at any given moment in history.

This means the world can be different. It can be structured in a completely new way. But this requires a fundamental shift—not just in systems, but in awareness.

The True Meaning of Sovereignty

Sovereignty is not merely political independence or financial self-sufficiency—it is the deep knowing that reality is not imposed upon us, but created by us.

A sovereign being understands:

- There is no external authority more powerful than one's own consciousness.

- The world is a reflection of human perception, not a fixed external reality.

- True freedom is not the ability to choose between pre-scripted options—it is the ability to create entirely new paradigms.

For millennia, humanity has willingly relinquished its power—ceding authority to kings, priests, governments, and corporations, believing they were necessary for order. Instead of recognizing itself as the architect of reality, Mankind has outsourced authority and in turn acquiesced its sovereignty. This acquiescence allowed a small elite to dictate how the world "must" function while coercing Mankind blindly comply, imposing a belief that it has no say in the matter.

But here's the great paradox:

- The ruling class does not enforce its will through sheer force—it maintains control by shaping perception.

- The masses are not bound by physical chains—they are bound by mental ones.

- The system does not persist because it is unbreakable—it persists because people believe there is no alternative.

The Awakening of Sovereignty
To reclaim sovereignty is not to fight the system—it is to see through the illusion of its permanence.

- It is to recognize that the world is only structured this way because we accept it as such.

- It is to understand that human civilization has no fixed form—it is a fluid creation that reflects the collective level of consciousness.

- It is to remember that all power structures are illusions sustained by belief—and they can be dismantled just as easily as they were built.

The question is no longer "How does the world work?"

The real question is: "Why do we agree to live this way?"

This chapter will dismantle the grand illusion—that humanity is merely a passive participant in an unchangeable system. It will expose how sovereignty has been systematically surrendered and why reclaiming it is the only path forward.

The next section will trace this long history of abdication—from ancient monarchies to modern corporate rule—and reveal how humanity has repeatedly relinquished its power, always under the illusion that it had no choice.

II. The Long History of Abdication: From Monarchs to Modern Corporate Rule

Humanity's surrender of sovereignty is not a new phenomenon. It is a pattern that has repeated itself throughout history, manifesting in different forms—monarchies, religious institutions, nation-states, and now, corporate and technological rule. At each stage, the masses have willingly handed over their power, not through coercion alone, but through belief—the belief that external authority is necessary, that control is security, and that freedom is dangerous.

The Monarchies: The Divine Right to Rule

For thousands of years, kings and emperors claimed a divine mandate, asserting that their rule was ordained by God. The masses, conditioned to believe they were mere subjects, accepted their station without question. The illusion of sovereignty was maintained through religious dogma, militarized force, and generational conditioning.

- **The belief:** The king is chosen by the gods; to disobey is heresy.
- **The reality:** Sovereignty was stolen through a fabricated narrative that turned rulers into gods and the people into obedient subjects.

The very concept of hereditary rule is one of the most blatant fabrications in human history—why should intelligence, wisdom, or leadership capability be passed down by bloodline? Yet, for centuries, people accepted this construct, believing they had no alternative. In fact, many of these monarchies persist all around the world , some stripped of most of their direct governing powers but their palaces and entitlements remain funded by a populous who still happily bows to Her/His Majesty.

The Rise of Religious Institutions: The Gatekeepers of Truth

As monarchs solidified their rule, religious institutions reinforced the loss of individual sovereignty. The priesthood became the intermediary between humanity and the divine, dictating morality, Truth, and access to salvation.

- **The belief:** Only the clergy can interpret divine will; questioning doctrine is blasphemy.
- **The reality:** Religious institutions became systems of control, suppressing spiritual sovereignty and dictating how people should think, act, and worship.

This religious control reached its peak in the Dark Ages, when the Church dictated everything—from what people could read to who they could marry—under the threat of eternal damnation. Spirituality, once a direct communion with the divine, was hijacked and replaced with rigid dogma designed to keep the masses obedient.

The Nation-State: The Illusion of Representation

The fall of monarchies ushered in the era of the nation-state. In theory, democracy and constitutional rule were supposed to return power to the people, yet they merely created a new form of abdication. Governments promised representation, but in practice, power remained concentrated in the hands of the few.

- **The belief:** Governments serve the people; democracy means self-rule.
- **The reality:** Governments serve themselves and their benefactors, maintaining control through bureaucracy, legal codes, and mass surveillance.

The concept of national borders, too, is another human construct. Nature does not recognize them—only human perception does. Yet, the idea of the nation-state has been so deeply ingrained that people are willing to die for artificial lines drawn on a map.

The Rise of Corporate Rule: The Invisible Power

In the modern era, power has shifted from monarchs and priests to corporations. Governments no longer dictate policy—corporate interests do. The financial elite own the political system, and multinational entities exert more influence than entire nations.

- **The belief:** The free market is the best system; corporations create progress.
- **The reality:** Corporations exist solely to maximize profit, often at the expense of human well-being and planetary health.

Today, the abdication of sovereignty is more subtle yet more complete than ever before. People unknowingly surrender their data, privacy, and autonomy to tech giants, financial institutions, and media conglomerates, all under the guise of convenience. The modern individual is monitored, analyzed, and manipulated at a scale never before possible—yet still believes they are free.

The Greatest Trick of All: Voluntary Servitude

Throughout history, external rulers have not needed to enforce control by force alone—because people voluntarily comply. They internalize the system, believing they have no choice.

- The greatest barrier to sovereignty is not oppression, but the deeply ingrained belief that 'this is just how the world works.

- People no longer need chains; belief alone keeps them in place.

- The ruling elite do not control through direct oppression, but through psychological conditioning—shaping perception so the masses police themselves.

This is the **long history of abdication**—from kings to corporations, from priests to politicians. The system has changed its outward form, but the underlying pattern remains the same: the masses surrender their power while believing they never had it to begin with.

The next section will examine why this cycle persists—why people fear sovereignty and why external authority remains so seductive despite its repeated failures.

III. The Mechanisms of Control: How Enslavement is Maintained

The greatest form of control is not physical chains, armed enforcement, or overt tyranny—it is the belief that "this is just how things are." When a society collectively accepts its conditions as inevitable, permanent, or the only possible way, no force is needed to maintain the system. The people themselves uphold their own servitude through their unquestioning compliance.

The ruling class has always understood this. Control is most effectively maintained not by direct oppression, but by shaping perception. The masses are not held captive by external constraints, but by the unseen walls of their own conditioned beliefs.

The Economic System: A Manufactured Dependency

One of the most powerful illusions is the idea that the economy is a natural phenomenon, a self-regulating force akin to the laws of physics. Yet, in reality, modern economic systems are entirely artificial constructs—deliberately designed to consolidate wealth, manufacture dependency, and limit true sovereignty.

Consider this:

- **Money itself is a construct**—a belief system backed not by intrinsic value, but by collective agreement.

- **Inflation, recessions, and economic crises are not acts of nature**—they are engineered phenomena that benefit the elite while keeping the masses in a state of financial instability.

- **Debt is the ultimate tool of control**—modern economies do not incentivize wealth creation for the masses, but perpetual debt enslavement, ensuring that most people remain trapped in cycles of labor just to survive.

The system is not designed to empower—it is designed to extract. Those who control the flow of money dictate the trajectory of society itself.

Mass Media: The Architects of Perception

The primary function of modern media is not to inform—it is to program. From the moment a person is old enough to consume content, they are subjected to a relentless barrage of narratives designed to shape their worldview.

The media exists to reinforce the prevailing system and suppress the possibility of alternatives. It does this by:

- **Controlling the Overton Window** - The media dictates the boundaries of acceptable discourse, ensuring that only pre-approved ideas are entertained while revolutionary or system-challenging perspectives are ridiculed or ignored.

- **Perpetuating Manufactured Crises** - By constantly keeping the population in a state of fear, division, or outrage, critical thinking is suppressed, and people remain too distracted to question the deeper structures of control.

- **Creating the Illusion of Consensus** - By repeating key narratives across all major platforms, the illusion is created that certain views are "universally accepted," even when large portions of the population disagree.

This is not information—it is indoctrination. The media does not provide access to Truth; it provides the carefully curated perception of reality that benefits those in power.

The Illusion of Democracy: Choice Without Power

One of the greatest mechanisms of control is the belief that democracy, as it currently exists, is true self-governance. While the idea of democracy is powerful and noble, the system as it functions today is largely a construct designed to create the illusion of choice while keeping power firmly in the hands of the ruling elite.

Consider how modern democracies operate:

- **Two-Party Systems (or Equivalent Constructs)** – Most so-called democratic nations have a system where power rotates between two (or a handful of) dominant political parties. However, these parties are often two sides of the same coin—controlled by the same corporate interests, beholden to the same financial elite, and advancing nearly identical long-term policies.

- **The Illusion of Representation** – Elected officials do not serve the people; they serve the entities that fund them. Campaign finance structures ensure that only those who align with elite interests rise to power.

- **Policy Controlled by Non-Elected Entities** – Central banks, intelligence agencies, corporate lobbyists, and global institutions hold more sway over national policies than the average voter ever will. The most consequential decisions are made behind closed doors, far from any democratic process.

The people are allowed to vote—but only within a pre-scripted, tightly controlled framework that ensures no real systemic change can occur.

Breaking the Spell of Control

Every control mechanism functions by one primary principle: perception management. As long as people believe they have no power, they will not seek to reclaim it.

The way out is not revolution through force—it is revolution through awareness. Once enough people awaken to the reality that these constructs are neither natural nor permanent, the system loses its hold.

The next section will explore the psychological conditioning that keeps humanity docile, compliant, and unable to recognize its own enslavement—and why the greatest revolution is not external, but internal.

IV. Why Humanity Fears Sovereignty: The Psychological Submission to Control

If sovereignty is the natural state of human existence, why do so few claim it? Why has humanity, time and time again, willingly surrendered its power to external authorities? The answer is simple, yet deeply unsettling: most people fear sovereignty more than they fear servitude.

At first glance, this seems counterintuitive—who wouldn't want to be free? But sovereignty is not just freedom from control; it is the full weight of responsibility over one's Life, choices, and destiny. And this is what most people seek to avoid.

The Comfort of Dependency

To be sovereign means to navigate Life without an external entity dictating what to do, how to think, or how to behave. Yet, most people have been conditioned from birth to look outside themselves for guidance, validation, and protection. The idea of standing fully on one's own—without a government, a corporation, a religious authority, or a social framework to provide structure—is terrifying.

Thus, people embrace dependency, not out of necessity, but out of psychological comfort:

- **Governments provide security**—so people obey, even when their freedoms are stripped away.

- **Corporations provide livelihoods**—so people comply, even when their dignity is eroded.

- **Religions provide meaning**—so people submit, even when doctrines contradict their own inner Truth.

- **Social constructs provide identity**—so people conform, even when it means suppressing their true selves.

Dependency is the illusion of safety. It offers a world where choices are pre-made, responsibilities are outsourced, and the burden of self-sovereignty is lifted.

The 1% Does Not Rule by Force—It Rules by Consent

The greatest illusion of power is that it exists externally—it does not. Power is granted through belief and reinforced through participation.

Most people do not resist control, not because they are physically restrained, but because they are unaware they even have the power to resist. The ruling class does not need to enforce its will through brute force when it can shape perception instead.

- The belief that we need rulers, experts, and governing institutions is not an inherent Truth—it is a construct of psychological conditioning.

- The real mechanism of control is not physical—it is mental.

- The most powerful weapon of the ruling elite is not armies—it is the ability to dictate what people believe is real, possible, and inevitable.

The masses are not bound by physical chains—they are bound by mental ones.

The Fear of Personal Accountability

The greatest burden of sovereignty is total accountability. To be truly sovereign means that there is no one else to blame—no government, no system, no leader, no external force dictating the course of one's Life.

Most people resist sovereignty because:

- **It eliminates excuses.** If reality is self-created, victimhood dissolves.

- **It demands self-mastery.** There is no authority to defer to, no doctrine to follow blindly.

- **It requires inner strength.** Without an external savior, one must become their own guiding force.

The loss of sovereignty is not enforced—it is chosen. It is chosen every time an individual refuses to take full ownership of their Life, every time they abdicate responsibility to an external system, and every time they accept that *"this is just how the world works."*

The Psychological Programming of Submission

From an early age, humans are conditioned to believe that power resides outside themselves. The family unit, the school system, the workplace, and society at large all reinforce submission:

- Children are trained to obey authority figures without question.

- Schools reward compliance, not critical thinking.

- Jobs demand subordination to hierarchies.

- Social norms punish deviation from the accepted order.

By the time a person reaches adulthood, sovereignty is no longer a concept they even consider—it has been systematically erased from their worldview.

The Myth That Sovereignty is Dangerous

One of the most insidious lies perpetuated by those in power is the idea that individual sovereignty leads to chaos. People are taught that without centralized control, society would collapse into lawlessness. This is a fabrication designed to justify control.

- Sovereign individuals are not reckless—they are deeply aligned with Truth, wisdom, and integrity.

- Sovereign societies are not anarchic—they are self-organizing, cooperative, and driven by higher-order intelligence.

- Sovereignty is not the rejection of structure—it is the rejection of forced, unnatural hierarchies that enslave rather than empower.

History has proven that centralized control, not sovereignty, leads to the greatest atrocities—totalitarian regimes, mass surveillance, economic enslavement, and systemic oppression. The ruling class fears sovereignty, not because it creates chaos, but because it dismantles their control.

The Path to Reclaiming Sovereignty

Reclaiming sovereignty is not a political act—it is an awakening of consciousness. It requires:

- **Radical self-responsibility**—understanding that no external force dictates reality.

- **Mastery over fear**—breaking free from the psychological grip of dependency.

- **Deep discernment**—seeing through the illusion of authority and recognizing the inherent power within.

This is the great paradox of human civilization: the system does not keep people enslaved—people keep the system alive by believing in it.

The next section will explore how, throughout history, this cycle of abdication has been deliberately reinforced, ensuring that humanity remains in a state of perpetual servitude.

V. The Path to Reclaiming Sovereignty: Breaking the Cycle

Throughout history, humanity-at-large has been trapped in a cycle of abdication—surrendering its sovereignty to rulers, governments, corporations, and institutions, believing that external authorities are necessary for order and survival. This is the greatest deception of all. The world is not structured this way because it must be—it is structured this way because we collectively believe it must be and continually reinforce that belief through our consent and participation in the system.

Whether we do all of that consciously or unconsciously only has bearing on whether we have Free Will and agency in the matter, it doesn't change the effects created which is the world all around us.

Breaking this cycle does not require overthrowing governments, dismantling economies, or waging revolutions against the ruling class. It requires something far more radical: withdrawing consent from the illusion of external authority and reclaiming our innate power to create reality.

Sovereignty Begins with Radical Responsibility

The first and most crucial step toward reclaiming sovereignty is radical responsibility. A sovereign being understands that their Life—its successes, failures, joys, and struggles—is entirely of their own making. There is no external force dictating one's destiny. As long as individuals believe that they are victims of the system, controlled by unseen powers, or powerless to change their circumstances, they will remain enslaved.

To reclaim sovereignty, one must:

- Take full accountability for their reality, without blame or excuses.

- Recognize that external conditions are a reflection of internal beliefs.

- Understand that no government, institution, or ideology can provide what can only be cultivated from within.

The loss of sovereignty is not enforced—it is chosen, whether we choose this consciously or unconsciously. Every time a person waits for a politician to fix the world, a corporation to provide security, or an institution to dictate morality, they reinforce their own servitude. The shift to sovereignty begins when individuals stop waiting and start creating.

Withdrawing Consent: The Benevolent Revolution

The system does not need to be fought—it needs to be abandoned. Every aspect of human civilization, from government to finance, from education to media, only holds power because people give it power. When individuals collectively withdraw their belief in these structures, they collapse under their own weight.

Withdrawing consent means:

- No longer participating in systems that enslave rather than empower.

- Discerning where power is being outsourced and reclaiming it internally.

- Refusing to comply with false narratives that uphold control structures.

- Shifting an opportunistic way of living into a principles-based way of living.

- Reorienting from what we can take to how we can be in service to Life.

This is not an act of rebellion—it is an act of transcendence. The system does not need to be overthrown; it needs to be outgrown.

The Fluidity of Reality: Nothing is Fixed

One of the greatest illusions is that the world is static, that it has always been this way and will always remain so. In Truth, human civilization is a living construct—an expression of collective consciousness.

- Empires and nations rise and fall.

- Economic systems emerge and collapse.

- Governments come and go.

- Belief systems evolve and dissolve.

Nothing in human civilization is fixed—everything is malleable. The only constant is change, and change is dictated by the level of consciousness of those who participate in shaping reality. When humanity awakens to this Truth, it will no longer accept limitation—it will recognize itself as the architect of the world.

Transcending the Meta Crisis: The True Path to Sovereignty

The external crises humanity faces—economic collapse, political instability, environmental degradation—are not separate issues. They are symptoms of a deeper crisis: the Meta Crisis, which stems from humanity's spiritual disconnection, its severance from wisdom, and its blind adherence to false idols of authority.

True sovereignty is not about political independence or financial wealth—it is about alignment with the intelligence of Life itself. It is about operating from a higher order of consciousness where human civilization is no longer built upon coercion, force, or control, but upon coherence, harmony, and self-mastery.

To reclaim sovereignty, humanity must:

- Fully reclaim its agency.

- Transcend the belief that authority lies outside of itself.

- Recognize that all external dysfunction is a mirror of internal disarray.

- Heal its Spiritual Crisis—restoring the lost wisdom of self-sovereignty.

- Restore intelligence to its rightful place—creating Life-affirming outcomes rather than reinforcing systems of control.

The world does not need new rulers, new policies, or new ideologies. It needs sovereign individuals—beings who no longer look outside themselves for guidance, but who stand fully in their own power, knowing that they, and they alone, are the creators of reality.

While for the world to change, the collective must first change. The transformation of the collective begins with the awakening of the individual. The true work then for each of us is individual and personal, while we will reap the full bounty of this work collectively in seeing a world of wonder and beauty birthed from inner work.

This is the path forward.

This is the only way humanity breaks the cycle of abdication once and for all.

In every Crucible, there's a choice that must be made.

THE GREAT ABDICATION: HOW HUMANITY SURRENDERED ITS SOVEREIGNTY

EXECUTIVE SUMMARY

Why Should You Read This Chapter?

For millennia, humanity has willingly surrendered its sovereignty—outsourcing its power to rulers, governments, corporations, and institutions. But what if the world doesn't operate this way because it must, but because we collectively believe it must? What if the reality we accept as "just the way things are" is nothing more than a construct sustained by mass compliance and unconscious consent?

This chapter dismantles the illusion of fixed reality, revealing how every structure—political, economic, legal, and social—is a human creation that can be reshaped at any time. It exposes how the ruling class does not maintain control through force, but through shaping perception and conditioning people to fear their own sovereignty. More importantly, it reveals the path to breaking this cycle—not through resistance or rebellion, but through awakening, radical responsibility, and the conscious withdrawal of consent.

If you've ever questioned why the world is the way it is but felt powerless to change it, this chapter will reframe everything you thought you knew about power, control, and your role in shaping reality itself.

Executive Summary: Key Takeaways

- **Reality is not fixed—it is a construct of collective belief.** The world does not operate the way it does because it must, but because humanity unconsciously consents to it. Governments, economies, laws, and borders are all human inventions that persist only because people accept them as unchangeable.

- **"This is just how things are" is the most powerful form of control.** When people believe they have no power to change reality, they stop questioning it. The greatest tool of the ruling class is not physical force but the ability to shape perception.

- **Humanity has repeatedly abdicated its sovereignty throughout history.** From monarchies and the divine right to rule, to religious institutions, nation-states, corporate dominance, and technocratic governance, humans have continually surrendered power to external authorities rather than governing themselves.

- **Sovereignty is not just political or economic—it is personal.** A sovereign being understands that no external institution dictates their reality. True sovereignty begins with the recognition that power is not something granted—it is something reclaimed.

- **The ruling class does not maintain control through force—it rules by consent.** The masses are not physically enslaved, they are mentally conditioned to believe in the necessity of rulers, laws, and economic hierarchies that perpetuate their subjugation.

- **Dependency is a psychological comfort, not a necessity.** People embrace external control because it offers the illusion of security—governments provide order, corporations provide jobs, religions provide meaning. But this dependency is self-imposed and ultimately disempowering.

- **Fear of sovereignty is greater than fear of enslavement.** Most people unconsciously prefer servitude over sovereignty because true sovereignty requires radical responsibility—there is no one else to blame, no authority to defer to, no savior to rely on.

- **The mechanisms of control are subtle but effective.** The education system trains compliance, mass media reinforces the illusion of choice, the financial system fosters dependency, and social conditioning discourages deviation from accepted norms.

- **The system persists not because it is unbreakable, but because people continue to uphold it.** Governments and institutions exist only because people comply with them. When individuals withdraw their belief and participation, these systems lose power and begin to collapse.

- **Reclaiming sovereignty begins with radical responsibility.** No external authority controls one's destiny—each individual is responsible for their own Life. Without personal accountability, true freedom is impossible.

- **The path forward is not revolution, but transcendence.** The system does not need to be fought—it needs to be outgrown. Sovereign individuals do not rebel against control; they simply stop participating in systems that no longer serve them.

- **Humanity must transcend the Meta Crisis to restore sovereignty.** The spiritual crisis and disconnection from higher intelligence have allowed the false paradigm of external authority to persist. Only by healing this disconnect can humanity reclaim true power.

- **The world will not change until individuals change.** Sovereignty is not a collective movement—it is an individual awakening. When enough people reclaim their inner authority, the external world will naturally reorganize to reflect this higher consciousness.

- **The final realization: You are the architect of reality.** The power to shape the world has never belonged to governments, elites, or institutions—it has always belonged to you. The question is: Will you reclaim it?

THE SACRILEGE OF THE FEMININE PRINCIPLE

I. The Masculine and Feminine Principles – The Cosmic Dance of Creation

At the very foundation of existence lies the dynamic interplay of two primordial forces: the Masculine and Feminine Principles. These are not tied to biological gender but represent the fundamental creative energies that birthed the Universe itself and continue to drive its expansion, evolution, and transformation.

From the quantum realm to the vast cosmic scale—from the balance of order and chaos in physics to the interplay of the sun and fertile Earth—Masculine and Feminine energies govern all creation.

These two forces exist in every human being, in every system, in every form of life—they are the universal archetypes of energy that shape existence. When in harmony, they co-create a reality that is balanced, regenerative, and Life-affirming. When they fall out of balance, destruction, disharmony, and suffering follow.

Defining the Two Primordial Forces

- **The Masculine Principle** – Active, structured, expansive, outward-directed energy.
    - Represents logic, willpower, focus, direction, and form.
    - It is the force of penetration, movement, discipline, and creation through action.
    - It seeks progress, conquest, and order—when unaligned, it turns to control and domination.

- **The Feminine Principle** – Receptive, intuitive, nurturing, inward-directed energy.
    - Represents wisdom, intuition, receptivity, emotion, and regeneration.
    - It is the force of nurturing, feeling, deep knowing, and creation through receptivity.
    - It seeks coherence, connection, and harmony—when unaligned, it turns to chaos, stagnation, or even self-destruction.

The Masculine is the architect and penetrative force, providing structure and direction; the Feminine is the wisdom and creative force that breathes Life into the design. The Masculine creates structure, but without the Feminine's wisdom, it becomes rigid, mechanical, and ultimately destructive. The Feminine nurtures and regenerates, but without the Masculine's stability, it becomes formless, scattered, and ineffective.

In perfect harmony, they form the sacred blueprint of all Creation—a cosmic dance that births new realities across all dimensions and scales.

The Integration of Masculine and Feminine in Every Human Being

Regardless of gender, every human being possesses both Masculine and Feminine energies within them. True self-mastery is the integration of both:

- A fully realized individual is one who has mastered the precision and drive of the Masculine while embodying the wisdom and intuition of the Feminine.

- Suppressing one creates imbalance—a man disconnected from his Feminine lacks depth, emotion, and inner knowing; a woman disconnected from her Masculine lacks direction, discipline, and execution.

- This is not about gender roles—it is about energy, function, and self-awareness. The most powerful individuals throughout history have seamlessly embodied both energies.

This is not a war between men and women. It is not a gender conflict.
This is about the suppression of the Feminine Principle within all of humanity, including within men themselves. It is about an internal severance, an imbalance that has affected both sexes, every institution, and civilization itself.

Civilization Reflects the Balance of These Forces

Human civilization mirrors the balance—or imbalance—of these two forces.

- When the Masculine is in harmony with the Feminine, society flourishes. Wisdom guides action, progress is aligned with Truth, and expansion is regenerative.

- When the Masculine dominates and suppresses the Feminine, society becomes mechanized, extractive, and unsustainable.

- When the Feminine dominates without the Masculine, society loses stability, structure, and the ability to manifest ideas into reality.

History has shown that when one of these forces is suppressed, ignored, or over-exalted, the results are catastrophic. The world today is the product of an over-dominant Masculine energy that has lost touch with wisdom, intuition, and regenerative principles—leading to a civilization that extracts, exploits, and mechanizes rather than nurtures, regenerates, and harmonizes.

When the Masculine is suppressed, society becomes weak, stagnant, and aimless—lacking the strength to act, protect, and manifest vision. When the Feminine is suppressed, civilization turns soulless, extractive, and disconnected—disrupting harmony and coherence, which is precisely what we see today.

While the world has suffered under the tyranny of the distorted Masculine—domination, control, exploitation, primal rage, brute force, and the subjugation of the Feminine—it would be naïve to assume that the Feminine is only "love & light." Just as the Masculine has its shadow expression, so too does the Feminine and especially the wounded and scorned Feminine; while her dark side is often expressed in more subtle poisonous ways, she can be just as ruthless and destructive, deadly even. The toxic Feminine often expresses as covert manipulation, passive-aggressiveness, victim consciousness, scorn, bitterness, wrath, and the devouring Mother—smothering rather than nurturing, controlling rather than guiding. Both the distorted Masculine and the distorted Feminine lead to disharmony, and both must be transcended for true coherence to emerge.

The Sacrilege of the Feminine and the Root of Human Psychosis

One of the fundamental fractures in humanity's psychosis is the systematic violation and sacrilege of the Feminine Principle—both in individuals and in civilization as a whole.

- By suppressing the Feminine, humanity has severed itself from its deepest source of wisdom, intuition, and harmony.

- The Masculine, untethered from the Feminine, has turned into a force of conquest, control, and extraction.

- Without the Feminine's wisdom, power is exercised without discernment—leading to systems that prioritize control over Life-affirming creation.

- This inner disconnection manifests externally as war, environmental destruction, and social fragmentation.

A civilization that rejects the Feminine becomes a civilization that rejects Life itself.

The restoration of the Feminine is not just necessary—it is essential for humanity's transcendence beyond its Spiritual Crisis. Healing this schism—both within individuals and across civilization—is the fundamental catalyst that will birth true awakening, ascension into a new evolutionary epoch, and the unfolding of the next chapter of human existence.

The next section will explore how the sacrilege of the Feminine has led to the desecration of Mother Earth, revealing how humanity's disconnection from this primordial force is the root of its destruction of the planet.

II. The Mirror of Desecration: Mother Earth and the Feminine Principle

Humanity's severance from the Feminine Principle is not an abstract philosophical dilemma—it is visibly reflected in the physical world. The desecration of the planet is the direct external mirror of humanity's internal severance from the Feminine.

This is not a coincidence.

Mother Earth is the embodiment of the Feminine Principle. She nurtures, provides, regenerates, and sustains Life with infinite intelligence. Just as the Feminine is the force of creation, nourishment, and renewal, so too is the Earth—she is the physical manifestation of the regenerative force of the Feminine in our reality.

Yet, modern civilization does not revere the Earth as sacred. Instead, it extracts, exploits, and desecrates her resources in the name of profit, power, and control.

How humanity treats the Earth is how humanity treats the Feminine.

The systematic destruction of the planet is a direct result of the suppression of the Feminine Principle. A civilization that does not honor the Feminine will inevitably destroy the very source of its own Life—just as a person who suppresses their own inner Feminine will become disconnected from intuition, wisdom, and the deeper intelligence of Life itself.

The Extractive, Conquering Mindset: How the Over-Dominant Masculine Has Ravaged the Earth

For the past several millennia, human civilization has been structured around an unhinged, unbalanced Masculine energy—one that seeks control, dominance, and endless expansion without regard for wisdom, coherence, or regeneration.

The results have been catastrophic:

- **Deforestation and Soil Degradation** - The razing of forests and depletion of fertile land mirror the way society strips the Feminine of her creative power and wisdom, leaving barren landscapes devoid of Life.

- **Pollution and Poisoning of Waters** - The desecration of the Earth's rivers and oceans reflects the corruption of the Feminine's intuitive flow, turning what was once pure and Life-giving into something toxic.

- **Industrialized Farming and Genetic Manipulation** - The artificial engineering of food and destruction of natural biodiversity mirror the way the Feminine is mechanized, controlled, and suppressed, stripped of her organic intelligence.

- **War and Militarization** - The Masculine, in its unhinged state, seeks conquest rather than stewardship. Entire landscapes are bombed, defiled, and exploited for geopolitical gain. The Earth suffers as a battlefield, just as the Feminine suffers when treated as a territory to be conquered rather than a force to be honored.

A civilization that extracts without replenishing is one that is operating without the Feminine Principle. Instead of working in harmony with Nature, modern society sees Nature as an enemy to be subdued—a reflection of how it sees the Feminine as something to be controlled rather than revered.

The Feminine is not weak—she is wild, cyclical, and powerful beyond measure. But when a civilization seeks to dominate rather than understand, it turns the most nurturing force of creation into something that must be mechanized and restrained.

The Suppression of the Feminine Creates a Culture of Death

The loss of the Feminine has turned human civilization into a machine that produces death, destruction, and decay rather than Life, regeneration, and creation.

- Instead of nurturing Life, society wages war.

- Instead of revering the wisdom of Nature, it tries to genetically modify and control it.

- Instead of fostering community and connection, it promotes isolation, division, and competition.

- Instead of valuing intuition and inner knowing, it demands proof, data, and mechanized logic.

In a world where the Feminine is silenced, what remains is a soulless, mechanical civilization—one that sees Life not as sacred, but as something to be exploited.

The consequence?

A planet on the verge of collapse.

A humanity in spiritual starvation.

A civilization obsessed with technological "progress" while ignoring the wisdom that has guided Life for eons.

This is not just an ecological crisis.

It is a Spiritual Crisis—a symptom of a much deeper pathological schism: humanity's severance from the intelligence of Life itself.

The Forgotten Wisdom of Indigenous Cultures

Long before industrial civilization imposed its mechanistic worldview, indigenous cultures around the world understood the sacred balance of the Masculine and Feminine Principles.

- They honored the Earth not as a resource, but as a living intelligence to be respected.

- They lived in alignment with the cycles of Nature, rather than in opposition to them.

- They revered the Feminine not as weak, but as the source of all Life, wisdom, and regeneration.

Crucially, these cultures did not see the Masculine and Feminine as forces in opposition—they saw them as sacred partners.

- The Masculine was the guardian, protector, and executor of wisdom.

- The Feminine was the guide, nurturer, and source of regenerative intelligence.

The Masculine was never meant to suppress the Feminine—it was meant to serve and uphold her wisdom, just as the Feminine was meant to illuminate and guide the Masculine's action.

These cultures did not view themselves as owners of the land, but as stewards. They understood that the Earth provides, but only if her rhythms are honored. They did not seek to conquer Nature—they sought to learn from it.

Modern civilization mocks this wisdom as "primitive."

But the irony is that the "advanced" world is now facing total planetary collapse precisely because it has ignored what indigenous cultures have known for thousands of years:

- You cannot extract indefinitely without consequence.

You cannot sever yourself from the Feminine without destroying the foundation of Life itself.

The Path to Healing: Restoring Reverence for the Feminine

Humanity cannot transcend its crisis without first healing its relationship with the Feminine—both within and without.

This means:

- Ending the war against Nature - Shifting from an extractive, mechanized system to one that honors and regenerates the Earth.

- Restoring reverence for wisdom, intuition, and feeling - Elevating the Feminine Principle back to its rightful place in harmony with the Masculine.

- Recognizing the Earth as a living intelligence - Moving beyond the destructive mindset that sees the planet as an object to exploit rather than a force to respect.

- Reconnecting with natural cycles - Living in harmony with the rhythms of Life, rather than forcing everything into artificial timelines, rigid structures, and endless expansion.

- Re-integrating the Feminine within ourselves - Whether man or woman, every individual must restore the lost aspects of their inner Feminine—intuition, deep knowing, and reverence for Life itself.

This is not just about saving the planet.

It is about healing the very soul of humanity as we are not separate from Nature—we are an integral part of it.

A civilization that honors the Feminine is a civilization that creates rather than destroys.

Until we restore the Feminine Principle, we will remain in a cycle of collapse, extraction, and decay.

The next section will explore how the desecration of the Feminine is not just an ecological or spiritual issue, but a deeply embedded cultural construct—one that has systematically suppressed wisdom, intuition, and the sacred role of the Feminine across history.

III. The Disharmony of the Masculine – How It Became Dominant and Out of Balance

The Masculine Principle was never meant to dominate—it was meant to protect, expand, and execute the wisdom of the Feminine in harmony. In its exalted form, the Masculine is the force of discipline, direction, and creation in service to Life. However, in its disconnected and disharmonious form, the Masculine becomes a force of conquest, control, and destruction.

The modern world is the result of an unhinged Masculine—one that has severed itself from its counterpart and lost its original coherence. Instead of being the structure that upholds Life, it has become a structure that extracts, mechanizes, and dominates it.

But this imbalance did not happen by accident—it was the result of thousands of years of progressive distortion.

The Masculine Was Not Always Disharmonious

There was a time when the Masculine and Feminine operated in harmony. Ancient civilizations understood that these forces were complementary, not adversarial. The Masculine's ability to create structure, establish order, and defend Life was guided by the Feminine's wisdom, intuition, and nurturing power.

- Indigenous and early agrarian societies revered both the warrior-protector and the wise-woman-seer, understanding that both were necessary for a thriving community.

- Many ancient traditions recognized the sacred balance—honoring both sun and moon, sky and earth, action and receptivity.

- The Masculine was seen as a guardian of the Feminine's creative force, not its oppressor.

So what changed?

The Fall of Balance: How the Masculine Became Over-Dominant

The transition from balance to disharmony was gradual, but several key shifts in human civilization catalyzed the rise of an unhinged, dominant Masculine:

1. **The Shift to Agricultural Societies and Land Ownership**

   o   Early human societies were largely nomadic and communal, living in symbiosis with nature.

   o   The shift to agriculture introduced land ownership, hierarchy, and territorial control—leading to a new paradigm of power, conquest, and dominance.

   o   The Masculine energy, which had previously been protective and structured, now turned into an energy of control and possession—first over land, then over people, and ultimately over the Feminine itself.

2. **The Rise of Warlord Culture and Empire Building**

   o   As territories expanded, societies became increasingly militarized, valuing brute force, conquest, and hierarchy over wisdom, community, and cooperation.

   o   Masculine virtues such as courage, strength, and order were weaponized for domination rather than for stewardship.

   o   Warriors and conquerors replaced wise kings and tribal elders as the central figures of power.

3. **The Institutionalization of Religion as a Means of Control**

   o   As empires grew, religious institutions were co-opted into systems of control.

   o   The sacred Feminine was systematically erased, and monotheistic, patriarchal religions positioned God as exclusively male, stripping spiritual traditions of their original balance.

   o   The Masculine, now untethered from the Feminine, became lawgiver, ruler, and enforcer, with divine authority claimed solely by men.

4. **The Mechanization of Society and the Industrial Revolution**

   o   With the rise of mechanized industry, society shifted further into a hyper-Masculine paradigm—one that valued efficiency, logic, and production over intuition, creativity, and regeneration.

   o   The natural world was no longer seen as an interconnected web of Life but as raw material for extraction.

o   The Masculine became synonymous with progress, power, and expansion, while the Feminine was further marginalized, deemed weak, irrational, or irrelevant.

The Consequences of an Unhinged Masculine

The dominance of an imbalanced Masculine has created a world that values conquest over wisdom, force over harmony, and control over freedom. The symptoms of this imbalance are everywhere:

- **Endless War and Conflict** - Instead of using power to protect and steward, nations wage perpetual war for dominance, resources, and control.

- **Extraction-Based Economies** - Nature is not honored as a living intelligence but mined, depleted, and polluted for short-term gain.

- **Technological Mechanization of Life** - Everything, from food to medicine to education, is reduced to data, algorithms, and production efficiency, stripping Life of its natural intelligence.

- **The Devaluation of Feeling, Intuition, and Creativity** - Emotional intelligence is disregarded, intuition is mocked, and spiritual wisdom is seen as unscientific or irrational.

- **Control and Surveillance Societies** - Governments and corporations seek total control over populations through surveillance, manipulation, and artificial systems of order.

In its pure form, the Masculine is not the enemy—it is a vital, necessary force. The problem is not Masculine energy itself, but its disconnection from the Feminine. Without the Feminine's guidance, the Masculine loses its coherence, turns reckless, and ultimately destroys rather than creates.

The Restoration of Coherence: What a Harmonious Masculine Looks Like

The Masculine is at its highest expression when it is in harmony with the Feminine— when it serves as the protector, stabilizer, and executor of wisdom, rather than the dominator and controller.

A healthy, exalted Masculine:

- Uses power to build, protect, and steward, rather than to conquer and extract.

- Creates systems of order that serve Life, rather than suppress it.

- Honors the wisdom of the Feminine, rather than disregarding or controlling it.

- Leads with integrity and responsibility, rather than through coercion and fear.

- Uses intellect and logic in service to higher wisdom, rather than disconnected rationality.

The consequence of an unhinged Masculine is not just unchecked conquest, mechanization, and extraction—it is the systematic suppression of the Feminine itself. A world dominated by an imbalanced Masculine does not simply ignore the Feminine; it actively vilifies, diminishes, and erases it. The more civilization veered toward control, dominance, and mechanization, the more it sought to suppress intuition, wisdom, creativity, and regenerative intelligence—the very essence of the Feminine Principle.

But this was not a passive process. It was deliberate, methodical, and institutionalized. Across history, the Feminine has been diminished in religion, law, culture, and society—not because it was weak, but because it held a power that threatened the ruling order.

The next section will examine how, over millennia, the Feminine has been systematically disempowered, ridiculed, and erased—and why reclaiming it is essential for the restoration of human consciousness and civilization itself.

IV. The Systematic Suppression of the Feminine

The imbalance of the Masculine over the Feminine was not an accidental or incidental phenomenon—it was systematically engineered. As civilization evolved into conquest-driven empires, hierarchical religions, and mechanized economies, the Feminine became not just undervalued but deliberately suppressed, ridiculed, and stripped of its power.

The deeper Truth is this: the Feminine was not erased because it was weak—it was erased because it was powerful.

The wisdom of the Feminine—its intuitive knowing, its regenerative power, and its deep connection to Life itself—threatened the control-based systems that sought to dominate rather than harmonize. The Feminine did not conform to rigid hierarchies or centralized power structures; it flowed, expanded, and operated outside the framework of dominance. To maintain their artificial control systems, those in power had to diminish, vilify, and ultimately subjugate the Feminine Principle.

This suppression took place across multiple dimensions—spiritual, cultural, political, economic, and personal—and its consequences have reverberated throughout history, shaping the very foundation of modern civilization.

The War on the Sacred Feminine in Religion

One of the most effective ways the Feminine was suppressed was through religion, which historically held tremendous influence over human thought, morality, and governance. Nearly every major religious institution, particularly those emerging in the last 3,000 years, systematically diminished the role of the Feminine.

- **The Erasure of the Goddess** - Ancient civilizations, from Egypt to Mesopotamia to India, once honored goddesses as the embodiment of creation, wisdom, beauty, and sustenance. As patriarchal religions rose to dominance, these goddesses were either demonized, erased, or assimilated into lesser roles.

- **The Vilification of Women's Power** - Women who possessed wisdom, healing abilities, or spiritual insight were recast as "witches" or "heretics." The witch trials of Europe and the Inquisition were not random events—they were systematic purges of feminine wisdom.

- **The Masculinization of Divinity** - The concept of "God the Father" replaced more ancient, balanced conceptions of divinity. The Divine was no longer a harmonious fusion of the Masculine and Feminine—it became exclusively Masculine, reinforcing the idea that power, law, and Truth were the domain of men.

This spiritual suppression severed humanity from the higher-order intelligence of the Feminine, cutting off access to wisdom, intuition, and the mysteries of Life.

Once religious doctrine established the inferiority of the Feminine, social structures swiftly followed, ensuring that women remained economically and legally subordinate.

Cultural and Social Subjugation of the Feminine

As religious structures codified the suppression of the Feminine, cultural and societal norms followed. The marginalization of women, the devaluation of emotional intelligence, and the repression of creative and intuitive wisdom were all symptoms of this deeper systemic suppression.

- **Women Were Denied Agency Over Their Own Lives** – In most historical civilizations, women were barred from education, leadership, and economic power. They were confined to roles of servitude, dependent on men for survival.

- **Emotions and Intuition Were Ridiculed** – The wisdom of the Feminine—sensing, feeling, and deep inner knowing—was dismissed as irrational, weak, or unreliable. Instead, logic, calculation, and mechanistic thinking were glorified, reinforcing the dominance of the Masculine.

- **Creativity and Cyclical Thinking Were Suppressed** – The natural world operates in cycles, and so does the Feminine. The ancient wisdom of seasonal living, lunar cycles, and regenerative growth was replaced with linear progress, industrial schedules, and relentless expansion—a Masculine distortion that ignores the intelligence of nature.

- **Sexually Exploited and Condemned** – Paradoxically, for millennia women endured sexual exploitation in various forms for the gratification of men, yet at the same time were condemned for their sensuality and considered dirty or impure for having been sexually exploited. Many of these double standards persist until this day.

Over time, these social constructs became so deeply embedded that they no longer needed to be enforced—they became accepted as "just the way things are."

Economic Disempowerment: The Feminine as a Commodity

Perhaps one of the most insidious ways the Feminine was suppressed was through economic systems that commodified, exploited, and controlled its power.

- **Women Became Property** – In many ancient legal systems, women were literally owned—by their fathers, then by their husbands. They had no financial independence and no legal rights to land, wealth, or self-determination.

- **Nature Became a Resource, Not a Living Intelligence** – The Earth, like the Feminine, was seen not as something to be revered, but as something to be owned, extracted, and controlled. Industrial capitalism mechanized Life itself, reducing it to profit and productivity rather than harmony and sustainability.

- **Healing and Birth Were Mechanized** – The natural wisdom of the Feminine in medicine, midwifery, and healing was actively destroyed. Ancient herbalists, healers, and midwives were labeled as witches, while the medical industry transformed childbirth and healing into clinical, male-dominated institutions.

The ultimate goal of this economic suppression was dependency—to ensure that both women and the Feminine Principle itself were permanently tethered to a system that controlled them.

The Masculinization of Human Civilization

With the Feminine Principle suppressed at every level, human civilization took on an increasingly Masculinized form—one defined by hierarchy, control, and mechanization. Stripped of its natural balance with the Feminine, the unhinged Masculine created a world obsessed with domination, efficiency, and conquest, where intuition, wisdom, and regenerative cycles were discarded in favor of rigid, extractive structures.

- **Governments became hierarchical and authoritarian** rather than cooperative and regenerative. The organic, community-driven leadership models of indigenous societies were replaced by rigid power structures where control, rather than harmony, dictated governance.

- **Economies prioritized endless growth and extraction** rather than sustainability and cyclical renewal. The natural rhythms of expansion and contraction were ignored in favor of perpetual economic expansion, creating massive inequality, environmental destruction, and systemic instability.

- **Education systems focused on logic, memorization, and obedience** rather than wisdom, creativity, and intuitive intelligence. Schools became mechanisms of indoctrination, training individuals to conform rather than think critically, suppressing innovation and emotional intelligence in the process.

- **The sciences rejected all that could not be measured or quantified**, dismissing the unseen, the intuitive, and the metaphysical as irrelevant. The wisdom traditions of ancient civilizations—rooted in direct experience, interconnectedness, and non-linear understanding—were discarded in favor of a strictly materialist worldview.

This extreme Masculinization of civilization did not create true progress—it created an imbalanced world that is now collapsing under the weight of its own rigidity. The obsession with control, expansion, and mechanization has led to a world devoid of harmony, operating in direct opposition to the intelligence of Life itself.

The next section will examine how the Feminist Movement, though born out of a rightful desire for justice, ultimately fought for access to an inherently broken system rather than challenging the paradigm itself—and why true feminine empowerment requires transcending, rather than integrating into, a system built on imbalance.

The Feminist Movement—Right Cause, Wrong Battle

Over the past century, the Feminist Movement has made significant strides in securing women's legal rights, education, and economic independence. Yet despite these legal victories, the deeper cultural imbalance between the Masculine and Feminine remains largely unresolved.

Why?

Because feminism, in its modern form, has been fighting for inclusion within a system architected around a hyper-Masculine paradigm—rather than transforming that paradigm altogether.

The very system that feminism sought entry into was—and remains—built on Masculine principles of control, competition, efficiency, and extraction. These are the values that govern modern economies, corporate structures, and political institutions. While these attributes have their rightful place, the imbalance arises because the Feminine's complementary values—intuition, nurture, regeneration, and cyclical intelligence—have never been fully integrated or honored within these systems.

The Feminist Movement focused on equality in participation, but not on redefining the game itself.

The result? Women have been granted access to the same careers, leadership positions, and societal roles as men—but they are often required to suppress their innate Feminine strengths to succeed. The modern corporate world does not reward intuition or emotional intelligence—it rewards linear thinking, relentless output, and aggressive ambition. Thus, the Feminine was not restored to its rightful place—it was merely allowed to compete on Masculine terms.

This is why modern feminism, as it currently exists, is not the solution.

True Feminine power does not come from becoming like men. It comes from reclaiming its own wisdom and strength and creating a new system where the Feminine is no longer marginalized, but honored as an equal force alongside the Masculine.

The next evolution of the Feminist movement must be transcendence.

This means moving beyond the fight for equality in an imbalanced system and instead establishing a harmonious co-evolutionary partnership between the Masculine and Feminine. This shift is not about competition—it is about restoring the Sacred Union that has been severed for millennia.

The Sovereign Feminine Archetype will rise—not by demanding a seat at the table of the old paradigm, but by co-creating an entirely new paradigm altogether.

The Feminine Rising—Change Is Coming

This is the world we live in today—a world still designed to suppress the Feminine and over-exalt the Masculine, leading to the widespread spiritual, ecological, and societal crises we now face.

But the Feminine cannot be erased forever. No matter how deeply it has been suppressed, it is written into the very fabric of existence itself.

The tide is turning.

The return of the Feminine is not just necessary—it is inevitable.

As the Masculine and Feminine begin to reconcile, we stand on the threshold of a new civilization—one that will either rise into harmony or collapse under the weight of its own imbalance.

The next section will examine how the suppression of the Feminine has shaped modern society, and why only by restoring this balance can humanity transcend its current crisis.

V. The Consequences of a World Without the Feminine

The suppression of the Feminine Principle has not only distorted the Masculine but has also led to a profound imbalance that permeates every aspect of human civilization. A world that dismisses the Feminine does not just become less compassionate—it becomes disconnected from the intelligence of Life itself.

This is the world we live in today.

Every major dysfunction we see—from environmental destruction to systemic oppression, from political corruption to the spiritual crisis of modernity—can be traced back to this fundamental schism. When wisdom is severed from action, when intuition is dismissed in favor of control, and when regeneration is sacrificed for endless extraction, the result is a civilization that devours itself.

The Erosion of Wisdom in Governance and Society

In the absence of the Feminine, governance ceases to be about service and wisdom—it becomes a mechanism for control, conquest, and enforcement. The decisions that shape civilization are made not with long-term, holistic understanding, but with short-term, linear thinking that prioritizes immediate power and dominance.

- Political systems prioritize control over coherence, treating governance as a game of strategy rather than a sacred responsibility to steward Life.

- Policies are dictated by economic interests rather than the well-being of people and the planet.

- Decisions are made without deep reflection, empathy, or foresight—resulting in conflict, oppression, and division rather than harmony.

This is the direct consequence of a world that has silenced the Feminine—the wisdom of interconnectedness, the ability to see the whole rather than just isolated parts, has been lost.

An Economy of Extraction Rather Than Regeneration

The modern economic system is built upon the hyper-Masculine model of endless expansion, conquest, and resource exploitation. It is not designed to nurture or sustain—it is designed to consume. The result is an economic system that:

- Views Nature not as a living intelligence, but as a commodity to be extracted, bought, and sold.

- Measures success in terms of GDP and market growth, ignoring the well-being of people and ecosystems.

- Treats workers as disposable resources, prioritizing efficiency over humanity.

- Creates artificial scarcity to maintain control rather than fostering true abundance.

Without the Feminine Principle—without the cyclical, regenerative wisdom that ensures sustainability—economies become machines of destruction rather than forces of prosperity.

A Mechanized, Soulless Education System

Education is meant to cultivate intelligence, creativity, and wisdom, yet in a world without the Feminine, it has become another system of mechanization. Instead of nurturing whole, sovereign individuals, it conditions people to conform, obey, and regurgitate information.

- Intuition, creativity, and emotional intelligence are dismissed as secondary to logic and memorization.

- Students are trained to become efficient workers, not free-thinking, self-actualized beings.

- The inner world—spiritual exploration, deep self-inquiry, and connection to purpose—is ignored in favor of external achievement.

An education system devoid of the Feminine produces individuals who may be intellectually capable but are spiritually and emotionally impoverished—leading to a civilization that is materially advanced but devoid of meaning.

A Healthcare System That Treats Symptoms, Not Causes

Modern medicine, in its obsession with mechanistic science, has abandoned the Feminine wisdom of holistic healing. The result is a healthcare system that:

- Treats disease as an isolated mechanical failure rather than as an imbalance in the whole being.

- Focuses on pharmaceutical intervention rather than preventative care and natural healing.

- Dismisses ancient healing modalities that have been practiced for millennia in favor of purely clinical approaches.

- Prioritizes profit over true well-being, creating a system that benefits from chronic illness rather than preventing it.

The loss of the Feminine in medicine has created a world where healing is no longer about restoration and wholeness—it is about control and symptom management, disconnected from the deeper intelligence of the body and Nature.

Technological Advancement Without Wisdom

Technology is neither good nor evil—it is simply a tool. But in a world where the Feminine has been suppressed, technological advancement is pursued without wisdom, ethics, or responsibility.

- Innovation is driven by profit and power, not by the well-being of humanity.

- Artificial intelligence, genetic modification, and bioengineering are pursued recklessly, without consideration of long-term consequences.

- The digital world has created unprecedented levels of disconnection—people are more "connected" than ever yet feel increasingly isolated and spiritually lost.

The Feminine would guide technology with wisdom, ensuring it is used in alignment with Life. In its absence, technology is accelerating humanity's disconnection from itself, from Nature, and from deeper Truth.

A Society Starved of Meaning

Perhaps the greatest consequence of suppressing the Feminine is the existential crisis gripping modern civilization. A world dominated by mechanization, control, and conquest leaves no room for the deeper dimensions of human existence—connection, wonder, intuition, and reverence for Life.

- People feel an inner void they cannot name, attempting to fill it with consumption, distraction, and external validation.

- Depression, anxiety, and spiritual emptiness are rampant—symptoms of a civilization that has lost touch with the very essence of what makes Life meaningful.

- Love has been commodified, relationships have become transactional, and human connection has been replaced by digital simulation.

A world without the Feminine is a world that has lost its Soul.

The next section will explore what this restoration looks like—not just in theory, but in practice. How do we reawaken the Feminine, individually and collectively? How do we build a world that honors both forces, creating a civilization that is whole, sustainable, and truly aligned with the intelligence of Life itself?

VI. The Restoration of the Feminine: Reharmonizing Civilization

The path forward is not about replacing the Masculine with the Feminine—it is about restoring their sacred harmony. The dysfunction of modern civilization is not due to the presence of the Masculine, but its detachment from the Feminine. A healed world does not diminish one force in favor of the other; it brings them into harmony, where action is guided by wisdom, expansion is tempered by regeneration, and power serves Life rather than subjugates it.

Rebalancing the Masculine and Feminine in Civilization

For humanity to transcend its Meta Crisis, every major system—governance, economics, education, healthcare, technology, agriculture—must be restructured to integrate both Masculine precision and Feminine wisdom.

Governance Rooted in Wisdom, Not Control

- Political systems must shift from mechanisms of force and enforcement to structures of stewardship and service.

- Leadership must be guided by wisdom and long-term vision rather than short-term gain and power consolidation.

- Decision-making must integrate logic with intuition, ensuring that policies honor Life rather than exploit it.

An Economy of Regeneration, Not Extraction

- The economic system must evolve beyond mechanistic capitalism, which values profit over people and the planet.

- True prosperity must be measured by sustainability, well-being, and collective flourishing—not just financial growth.

- Businesses must operate in service to Life, designing models that replenish rather than deplete.

A New Paradigm in Education

- Education must cultivate whole, sovereign beings, integrating emotional intelligence, creativity, and intuition alongside reason and knowledge.

- Learning must move beyond rigid structures of memorization and into dynamic, experiential understanding.

- The wisdom traditions of ancient cultures—holistic thinking, sacred geometry, and Natural law—must be reintroduced alongside modern sciences.

A Return to True Healthcare

- Healthcare must be reenvisioned to create true healing and holistic health, not a business that perpetuates chronic disease by treating symptoms with synthetic pharmaceutical interventions.

- All medicine, treatments, and interventions should be Nature-sourced, designed to restore the body's innate self-organizing intelligence (homeostasis).

- The wisdom of ancient cultures—Ayurvedic medicine, Chinese medicine, Indigenous herbal and plant medicines—must be reintroduced alongside modern homeopathic sciences.

Technology in Service to Life

- Innovation must be guided by ethical wisdom, ensuring that it serves humanity rather than enslaving it.

- Artificial intelligence, biotechnology, and space exploration must align with the principles of Life, not be driven by conquest and control.

- The digital world must enhance human connection and understanding, rather than replace real-world relationships and experiences.

Agriculture in Service to Health and Well-Being

- Food is the foundation of all health—physical, emotional, mental, and spiritual. The restoration of poisoned soils via regenerative agriculture plays an outsized and commonly overlooked role in transcending the Meta Crisis.

- Agricultural practices must be radically transformed to align with Natural law— this means outlawing chemical-based industrial farming and replacing it with regenerative and biodynamic farming that works in harmony with Nature.

- Livestock and farm animals should eat natural diets, graze or roam freely, and not be manipulated with synthetic growth chemicals. Their harvest should be conducted with reverence, as Indigenous cultures have always done. How we treat our animals directly affects human well-being.

The Return of Wisdom and Reverence

The restoration of the Feminine is the return of deep knowing, holistic intelligence, and reverence for Life. In practical terms, this means:

- Recognizing that intuition is not irrational—it is the highest form of intelligence, allowing us to perceive Truth beyond logic.

- Reintegrating cyclical wisdom—living in harmony with natural rhythms rather than forcing everything into linear, extractive systems.

- Elevating care, empathy, and collaboration as strengths rather than weaknesses.

- Healing the severance from Nature—restoring the Earth as a living intelligence, not a resource for exploitation.

- Reestablishing the role of Elders as wisdom keepers, ensuring that accumulated Life experience informs culture rather than being discarded.

- Reorienting toward family and community—not as a rigid, outdated structure, but as the foundation of emotional, spiritual, and social well-being.
  - The breakdown of the nuclear family has led to widespread disconnection, loneliness, and fragmentation, all symptoms of a world that has devalued the Feminine.
  - The restoration of intergenerational bonds, strong communities, and meaningful relationships is essential to healing humanity's Spiritual Crisis.
  - Family structures can take many forms, but at their core, they must be nurturing, supportive, and oriented toward the flourishing of Life rather than economic productivity alone.

The Consequences of Resistance

The world is already splitting into two timelines: those who embrace this harmony will flourish, while those who resist will continue down the path of entropy and collapse. A civilization that refuses to restore the Feminine will remain trapped in the cycles of war, resource depletion, and spiritual starvation. But a civilization that re-integrates the Feminine will usher in an era of unprecedented harmony, innovation, and human evolution.

The next section will explore how this restoration is not just a societal necessity but a deeply personal journey—one that requires every individual to reclaim and integrate their own inner Feminine.

VII. The Feminine in Every Individual – Reclaiming Wholeness

The restoration of the Feminine is not just a civilizational imperative—it is a deeply personal journey that each individual must undertake within themselves. The imbalance we see in the world is simply a macrocosmic reflection of the microcosm within each human being.

For too long, society has conditioned people to operate from a hyper-Masculine paradigm, favoring rationality over intuition, action over reflection, force over flow, and conquest over communion. The result is a world full of disconnected, fragmented individuals, struggling with burnout, emotional suppression, lack of purpose, and spiritual starvation.

To heal the world, we must first heal ourselves.

The Integration of the Masculine and Feminine Within

Every human being—regardless of gender—has both Masculine and Feminine energies within them. True self-mastery is the ability to integrate and balance these two forces:

- The Masculine is our drive, direction, structure, and execution—it is the force that allows us to manifest and create.

- The Feminine is our intuition, receptivity, wisdom, and emotional intelligence—it is the force that allows us to perceive, sense, and deeply understand.

A fully realized human being is one who has awakened both energies and allows them to work in coherence rather than in conflict.

The Consequences of Suppressing One's Inner Feminine

In a world that rewards hyper-Masculinity, many individuals have unknowingly repressed their inner Feminine, leading to:

- Emotional numbness—a disconnection from feeling, vulnerability, and authentic expression.

- Lack of meaning—an existence driven purely by external goals rather than inner fulfillment.

- Chronic stress and burnout—a constant state of doing, without the ability to rest and regenerate.

- Disconnection from intuition—an inability to trust one's own deep knowing and guidance.

- Fear of surrender—a belief that letting go is weakness rather than an act of wisdom.

- Broken relationships—struggles in intimacy due to an inability to receive, nurture, or express vulnerability.

This imbalance is not just seen in individual lives—it is what drives the global crises we now face.

Reclaiming the Inner Feminine

Restoring the Feminine within oneself is not about abandoning the Masculine—it is about creating inner harmony. This requires:

1. Developing Emotional Awareness

- Learning to feel deeply rather than suppress emotions.

- Recognizing that emotions are not weaknesses—they are a profound source of intelligence.

- Practicing self-inquiry and reflection to understand inner wounds, fears, and conditioned patterns.

2. Trusting Intuition

- Reconnecting with the inner knowing that does not rely on logic alone.

- Learning to make decisions based on coherence and felt wisdom, rather than just external validation.

- Spending time in silence and solitude to tune into inner guidance.

3. Embracing Flow and Surrender

- Releasing the need to control every outcome—understanding that Life unfolds in rhythms and cycles.

- Recognizing that not all progress is linear—sometimes rest, stillness, and reflection are just as powerful as action.

- Allowing oneself to receive, rather than always striving to achieve.

4. Reconnecting with Nature

- Spending time in natural environments to remember the intelligence of the Earth.

- Observing the cyclical nature of Life, rather than forcing everything into rigid structures.

- Honoring the body's natural rhythms, rather than ignoring them for productivity.

5. Cultivating Sacred Relationships

- Recognizing that true connection requires openness, vulnerability, and presence.

- Creating relationships based on deep communion, rather than competition or transactional exchanges.

- Honoring the Feminine in others—listening, nurturing, and allowing space for deep emotional Truth.

The Feminine and the Journey to Wholeness

When the Masculine and Feminine within an individual are harmonized:

- Purpose is no longer just external—it is deeply felt and lived.

- Action is guided by wisdom, not just blind ambition.

- Love is no longer transactional—it becomes sacred and deeply fulfilling.

- Life is experienced with depth, richness, and reverence, rather than just efficiency and achievement.

This inner balance is what allows individuals to transcend the Spiritual Crisis—because only a whole being can co-create a whole world.

The next section will explore how this restoration is not about men vs. women, but about humanity moving beyond polarization and into a new era of synthesis, integration, and higher-order intelligence.

VIII. The Higher Octave of Humanity: Transcending the Gender Wars

The path to restoring the balance between the Masculine and Feminine is not a battle of genders, nor is it a struggle for one to overpower the other. It is a reunion—a sacred reconciliation between these two forces, both within the individual and in human civilization at large.

The modern world, however, remains trapped in false battles—the so-called gender wars—where division, resentment, and ideological conflict have replaced genuine efforts toward unity and harmony. But these battles are distractions from the real issue:

The suppression of the Feminine has distorted both the Masculine and Feminine. To heal the world, they must be brought back into sacred partnership.

Beyond Feminism vs. Patriarchy: The True Solution

The Feminine has been repressed for millennia, and in response, the modern world has seen waves of feminist movements striving for equality. While these movements have led to undeniable progress, they have often fallen into the trap of seeking power within the same distorted paradigm that created the problem.

The true solution is not for the Feminine to compete with the Masculine in a broken system, but to restore an entirely new paradigm where both energies are equally valued, honored, and integrated.

- A civilization that thrives does not favor one energy over the other—it harmonizes them.

- The Masculine is not the enemy; it is simply lost without the Feminine to guide it.

- The Feminine does not need to dominate to reclaim its power—it simply needs to be restored to its rightful place as an equal force in creation.

This is not about external roles or power struggles—it is about aligning with the intelligence of Life itself.

Beyond Gender Debates: A Civilization Rooted in Meritocracy

The modern world still finds itself entangled in elementary debates over equal pay, gender roles, and opportunity—conversations that should have been transcended long ago. These discussions persist not because the answers are unclear, but because society remains trapped in old patterns of division, prejudice, and unconscious bias.

In a higher-order civilization, the following Truths become self-evident:

- All individuals should have equal access to opportunity based on their abilities, not their gender.

- Equal pay for equal work is not a debate—it is a given.

- Competence, skill, and contribution—not outdated gender roles—determine what one is capable of.

- A true meritocracy ensures that excellence, wisdom, and capability naturally rise to positions of influence, regardless of gender.

- This evolution is not limited to gender—it extends beyond all external identity markers. Sexual orientation, race, nationality, age, and religion become irrelevant personal identification markers as humanity awakens to a deeper Truth: our shared humanness is our unifying principle, not the constructs we have historically used to divide ourselves.

Rather than regulating fairness, a civilization rooted in higher intelligence naturally organizes itself around wisdom, integrity, and coherence.

The need for "equality debates" disappears when a civilization evolves beyond division, recognizing the Masculine and Feminine not as opposing forces, but as complementary energies that co-create reality.

Transcending the Gender Wars: A Unified Future

A civilization that is still debating gender roles is a civilization stuck in outdated constructs—one that has yet to evolve into a higher-order intelligence. The next evolutionary step for humanity is not political reform, nor is it another ideological movement—it is the transcendence of division itself.

This means:

- Recognizing that gender is not a battleground—it is a dynamic interplay of energies that must be brought into harmony.

- Moving beyond identity politics into the realm of true human sovereignty.

- Healing the wounds of the Feminine without turning against the Masculine.

- Creating systems where wisdom, intuition, and regeneration are valued as much as structure, strategy, and logic.

- Building a civilization where men and women—regardless of roles—stand as sovereign beings, contributing their unique gifts in a way that uplifts all.

A civilization that transcends these conflicts will not need "movements" to correct injustice—injustice itself will cease to be the foundation of society. The distortions of the past will not need to be continuously fought against, because they will no longer exist in the collective consciousness of an awakened humanity.

This is the true higher octave of humanity—the emergence of a civilization that operates in harmony with the intelligence of Life, rather than through artificial constructs of division, control, and opposition.

A Civilization No Longer Defined by Separation

The next phase of human evolution is not a battle for dominance between genders, but the restoration of sacred harmony between the Masculine and Feminine Principles—both within individuals and in civilization at large.

This is the higher octave of humanity—the emergence of a civilization that operates in harmony with the intelligence of Life, rather than through artificial constructs of division, control, and opposition.

However, restoring the Masculine and Feminine into harmony is only one piece of the larger transformation that humanity must undergo. The distortion of these fundamental forces has not only shaped human relationships and societal structures—it has also distorted our very understanding of law, order, and governance itself.

For thousands of years, humanity has believed that it can impose human-made laws over the immutable laws of Nature and the Cosmos. Just as the Masculine has sought to dominate the Feminine, civilization has sought to dominate Nature itself—believing it can legislate reality rather than align with it.

But no human law, no government decree, and no system of control can override the higher intelligence of the Universe. When humanity ignores or violates Natural law, suffering follows.

The next chapter will expose the grand illusion—that human civilization, in its arrogance, has attempted to replace the self-organizing wisdom of Life with its own artificial constructs. It will reveal how the root of all dysfunction stems from Mankind's failure to align with Natural law—and why any civilization that continues down this path is destined for collapse.

In every Crucible, there's a choice that must be made.

THE SACRILEGE OF THE FEMININE PRINCIPLE

EXECUTIVE SUMMARY

Why Should You Read This Chapter?

The suppression of the Feminine Principle is not just an issue of gender inequality—it is one of the deepest fractures in human civilization. It is a wound that has shaped history, distorted the Masculine, mechanized society, and severed humanity from its innate wisdom. The consequences of this disharmony are visible everywhere: in the desecration of Mother Earth, in extractive economies that prioritize conquest over regeneration, and in social systems that devalue intuition, emotion, and the unseen forces of Life. This chapter unveils how this imbalance has led to war, environmental destruction, and a civilization built on control rather than harmony.

This chapter is not about advocating for one force over the other—it is about revealing the sacred interplay between the Masculine and Feminine and why they must exist in harmony. It exposes the systematic erasure of the Feminine throughout history, the rise of a distorted Masculine that now dominates society, and the fundamental schism in Mankind's psychosis that results from this severance. But beyond diagnosis, it also points to the solution: the restoration of the Feminine as an equal force in civilization. Without this, humanity cannot transcend its dysfunction, cannot move beyond division, and cannot build a world that is truly aligned with the intelligence of Life itself.

Executive Summary: Key Takeaways

- **The Masculine and Feminine are the primordial creative forces of the Universe.** They are not biological constructs, but fundamental principles of existence. The Masculine represents structure, action, and direction, while the Feminine embodies wisdom, intuition, and regeneration. Both forces exist within every human being, and only through their balance can individuals—and civilization—achieve true harmony.

- **The desecration of Mother Earth is a direct reflection of the suppression of the Feminine Principle.** Nature, like the Feminine, has been treated as a resource to be conquered and exploited rather than honored and nurtured. The extraction-based economic model and the mechanization of Life itself mirror the way society has dismissed and devalued the Feminine's role in creation and wisdom.

- **The Masculine, when disconnected from the Feminine, becomes a force of domination rather than protection.** Instead of using its strength to uphold order and safeguard Life, the unbalanced Masculine seeks conquest, control, and endless expansion. This distortion has shaped human civilization into a system of mechanization, hierarchy, and oppression rather than one of wisdom, stewardship, and harmony.

- **The systematic suppression of the Feminine was not accidental—it was deliberately engineered.** Religious institutions erased goddesses and vilified women's spiritual power, economic structures commodified the Feminine as property, and social systems diminished emotional intelligence and intuition as "irrational." The Feminine was not silenced because it was weak—it was silenced because it was powerful.

- **The Feminine is the force of wisdom, coherence, and interconnected intelligence.** It perceives reality holistically rather than through fragmented analysis. By suppressing this energy, society has lost its ability to see the whole picture, leading to short-term, linear thinking that prioritizes immediate gains over long-term well-being. This severance is at the root of political dysfunction, environmental collapse, and social disconnection.

- **Governance, economics, education, healthcare, and technology have all been shaped by a hyper-Masculine paradigm.** Political systems enforce control rather than wisdom, economies value extraction over regeneration, education rewards memorization over intuition, healthcare treats symptoms instead of addressing root causes, and technology advances without ethical wisdom. Each of these dysfunctions stems from the absence of the Feminine's balancing force.

- **Modern feminism, while addressing key injustices, has often sought power within the same broken system rather than reimagining a new paradigm.** While legal equality is crucial, the true battle is not about gaining access to a hyper-Masculine world—it is about transcending it entirely. The real solution lies in restructuring society so that both the Masculine and Feminine energies are equally valued and integrated.

- **The so-called "gender wars" are a distraction from the real issue— humanity's severance from the sacred balance of these forces.** The fight between men and women is a symptom of a deeper wound. The Feminine has been wounded, and the Masculine has been distorted as a result. The solution is not division—it is reunification.

- **True meritocracy makes gender debates obsolete.** In a higher-order civilization, equal pay, equal opportunity, and equal rights are not controversial topics—they are self-evident Truths. Societies rooted in wisdom, integrity, and coherence naturally elevate the most competent individuals, regardless of gender or identity.

- **This transcendence is not just about gender—it extends to all artificial divisions.** In a world aligned with higher intelligence, race, nationality, age, religion, and sexual orientation become secondary to the recognition of our shared humanity. The notion of "identity politics" dissolves when society is no longer rooted in division but in unity and coherence.

- **A civilization that refuses to restore the Feminine will remain trapped in war, oppression, and self-destruction.** The over-dominance of the Masculine has led to mechanization, disconnection, and spiritual starvation. A world without the Feminine is a world that consumes itself.

- **The restoration of the Feminine is not about replacing the Masculine—it is about restoring harmony.** Action must be guided by wisdom, expansion must be tempered by regeneration, and power must be wielded in service to Life rather than for control. Societies that embrace this balance will flourish, while those that resist will continue their descent into entropy and collapse.

- **The next phase of human evolution is not a political movement—it is the transcendence of division itself.** It is the emergence of a civilization where the Masculine and Feminine are fully integrated—both within individuals and in the structures of society. This is the higher octave of humanity: the return to a world that is whole, coherent, and aligned with the intelligence of Life itself.

This chapter is a critical turning point in understanding why the world is in crisis—and, more importantly, how it can heal. Without restoring the sacred balance between the Masculine and Feminine, humanity will remain trapped in cycles of destruction. But by integrating these forces once again, civilization can rise to an entirely new level of consciousness, coherence, and creation.

THE ILLUSION OF HUMAN LAW OVER NATURAL LAW

I. What is Natural Law?

For millennia, Mankind has sought to impose order on civilization through human laws—legal codes, constitutions, and regulatory frameworks—believing these constructs to be the foundation of justice and social harmony. From Hammurabi's Code to modern constitutional democracies, these legal structures have shaped societal norms. Yet, no human-made law, regardless of its complexity, holds the same authority as the self-regulating intelligence that governs all of Life—Natural law.

Natural law is not a theoretical construct or a philosophical abstraction; it is not a human creation. Rather, it is the intrinsic order woven into the fabric of existence itself. It governs reality independently of human perception, ensuring coherence and sustainability across all dimensions of Life. As the fundamental order of existence—these principles that sustain the Cosmos, govern the cycles of Life, and dictate the cause-and-effect relationships that shape reality are immutable and omnipotent. It is the universal intelligence that ensures harmony and coherence, guiding everything from the movements of celestial bodies to the intricate symbiosis of ecosystems.

Mankind's great error has been its persistent attempt to override this inherent order—whether through centralized control of economic markets, the artificial reconfiguration of ecosystems, or the mechanization of human society. These efforts, while often well-intentioned, have disconnected humanity from the innate intelligence that sustains Life, leading to widespread disharmony and existential crises. This pervasive and enduring violation of Natural law lies at the very foundation of the Spiritual Crisis and Meta Crisis that now threaten civilization. When human-made laws attempt to replace or contradict Natural law; chaos, disorder, degeneration, and suffering inevitably follow.

Natural Law vs. Human Law

The key distinction between Natural law and Human law is fundamental: Natural law is discovered through observation and experience, while human law is an artificial construct born from social and political agendas. Natural law exists independently of belief systems, governing reality through immutable principles, whereas Human laws are often reactive, shifting in accordance with the interests of those who wield power:

- **Natural law is immutable; Human law is temporary.** The laws of gravity, the cycles of nature, and the principle of cause and effect do not change based on human opinion, political agendas, or cultural shifts. Human law, however, is constantly revised, repealed, and manipulated to serve the interests of those in power.

- **Natural law governs reality; human law attempts to govern perception.** Natural law governs the fundamental fabric of reality, operating independently of human acknowledgment. Human law, by contrast, is an attempt to govern our perception of reality—shaping collective behavior through legislation rather than genuine alignment with universal Truth.

- **Natural law ensures harmony; human law enforces compliance.** When societies align with Natural law, they thrive naturally. When they deviate, they create conflict, suffering, and decay, necessitating ever more coercion to sustain artificial structures.

History is littered with the remnants of civilizations that believed they could legislate reality. Empires have risen and fallen, not due to external threats alone, but because they structured their societies in contradiction to Natural law, ultimately collapsing under the weight of their own illusions.

The Core Principles of Natural Law

Natural law is not a set of commandments issued by an external authority—it is the inherent order that governs the unfolding of Life. Below are some of its foundational principles:

1. **Cause and Effect (The Law of Consequence)** - Every action has an equal and corresponding reaction. Whether in nature, society, or personal behavior, the consequences of one's actions are unavoidable. The modern world attempts to ignore this principle—polluting the planet, manipulating economies, and making decisions without accountability—but reality always restores balance.

2. **The Law of Interconnectedness** - All of Life is interconnected. Nothing exists in isolation. Every action ripples across the whole. When humanity sees itself as separate from Nature and each other, it creates fragmentation, which manifests as war, environmental destruction, and social decay.

3. **The Law of Free Will and Accountability** - Every individual possesses the power to create their reality through choice. However, with this power comes full accountability. Those who seek to evade responsibility—whether individuals,

governments, or corporations—ultimately suffer the consequences of their actions.

4. **The Law of Harmony and Balance** - Life sustains itself through equilibrium. When one force overpowers another—whether through environmental destruction, economic manipulation, or social oppression—imbalance leads to collapse. The modern world, driven by an over-dominant Masculine force, has created a system of endless expansion, conquest, and mechanization, severing itself from the natural rhythms of Life.

5. **The Law of Regeneration** - Natural systems are inherently regenerative. Life is cyclical, and sustainability depends on allowing natural renewal. However, modern civilization operates on a linear model of infinite growth, disregarding the necessity of rest, restoration, and renewal. The result is depletion—of the Earth's resources, of human well-being, and of civilization's long-term viability.

These principles are not imposed by any institution or ideology—they are the fabric of existence itself. Societies that honor these principles thrive, while those that attempt to override them inevitably decline.

The Consequences of Ignoring Natural Law

Human civilization is now facing the repercussions of its failure to align with Natural law. Every major crisis on the planet—economic instability, political corruption, environmental collapse, and social fragmentation—stems from this fundamental disconnection.

- Governments legislate control rather than cultivating wisdom and coherence.

- Economies are built on extraction rather than regeneration, leading to inevitable collapse.

- Technology, when severed from ethical wisdom, becomes an instrument of manipulation and coercion rather than liberation and true prosperity.

- The legal system incentivizes litigation and profiteering rather than genuine justice.

The fundamental illusion underlying Human law is the belief that it can dictate reality. Governments, institutions, and legal systems operate under the assumption that laws can reshape the natural order, yet no decree, policy, or regulation can override the cause-and-effect principles that govern existence itself. On the other hand, the abiding reality of Natural law is that it dictates human existence.

Mankind's Delusion: The Belief That It Can Rule Over Life

At the heart of the Meta Crisis is the belief that Mankind can impose its own order upon the Universe. This delusion has led to:

- The mechanization of Life, where humans function as economic units rather than sovereign beings.

- The destruction of ecosystems in the name of "progress" without acknowledging the intelligence of Nature.

- The proliferation of laws, regulations, and institutions that enforce compliance rather than foster wisdom and self-governance.

Yet no civilization that attempts to rule over Natural law has ever survived. History is littered with the ruins of empires that sought to control reality rather than align with it.

The Path Forward: Alignment, Not Legislation

The solution does not lie in an ever-expanding web of laws, policies, and regulations. While certain regulatory structures have, at times, aligned with Natural law—such as laws protecting clean water or ecosystems—these instances are more the exception, not the rule. The real path forward is a fundamental return to wisdom, coherence, and alignment with the governing intelligence of Life itself.

- Instead of trying to control the world, we must seek understanding it.

- Instead of enforcing artificial order, we must align with the harmony that already exists.

- Instead of dictating laws, we must cultivate wisdom and accountability.

Civilization does not need rulers—it needs alignment with Life itself. The world is not something to be mastered or conquered but something to be harmonized with—an intelligent, self-regulating living system that flourishes when aligned with Truth.

The next section will explore how Mankind's belief in human law has led to a system of force, coercion, and control, rather than one of wisdom, stewardship, and true justice. It will expose the false premise that government and legal systems are the ultimate arbiters of Truth, revealing how they have become tools of manipulation rather than facilitators of harmony.

II. The Arrogance of Human Law: How Man-Made Systems Became Tools of Control

Human civilization has long operated under the belief that laws, policies, and regulations are the foundation of order. Governments legislate, courts enforce, and societies are expected to comply. Yet, despite the endless creation of laws, humanity finds itself in deeper chaos—political corruption is rampant, legal systems are exploited for profit, and nations are in a perpetual state of conflict.

The fundamental error is this: Mankind believes it can legislate reality, rather than align with the immutable laws that govern existence. Instead of using law as a means to cultivate wisdom and accountability, human civilization has turned law into a weapon of coercion, oppression, and mechanized control.

The more disconnected a society becomes from Natural law, the more laws it creates to force compliance. Instead of fostering self-governance through wisdom, humanity has built vast bureaucratic systems that regulate every aspect of Life—criminalizing some actions while sanctioning others, regardless of whether they align with the intelligence of Life itself.

The Expansion of Human Law as a Sign of Civilizational Decay

A civilization in harmony with Natural law does not need endless rules, because its people live in alignment with Truth, responsibility, and integrity. However, when a society falls out of coherence, it attempts to control behavior through an ever-expanding legal code.

- Ancient tribal societies, rooted in natural wisdom, had minimal laws. They relied on common sense, community agreements, and personal accountability.

- The rise of empires and nation-states introduced complex legal systems, codifying laws to maintain order among growing populations.

- Modern societies now have millions of pages of legislation, yet corruption, injustice, and disorder are greater than ever.

Why? Because laws do not create wisdom. No legal system can force morality, nor can it replace an individual's ability to discern right from wrong. When a society becomes dependent on legislation rather than personal responsibility, it does not create order—it creates a culture of dependency, litigation, and exploitation.

The Legal System: A Mechanized Structure That Serves Power, Not Justice

Modern legal systems claim to uphold justice, yet they function primarily as instruments of control. The legal system does not exist to uphold Natural law—it exists to uphold the power of the ruling class.

- Justice is no longer about restoring harmony—it is about punishment and profit. Court systems hand out fines, prison sentences, and penalties not to create healing, but to maintain social control and feed an industrialized legal machine.

- Corporations manipulate legal loopholes to shield themselves from accountability. The wealthiest entities commit ecological destruction, financial fraud, and unethical business practices with impunity, while minor offenses from ordinary citizens are harshly penalized.

- Laws are written and rewritten to serve political and economic interests. Instead of reflecting universal Truth, human law is a shifting construct that changes based on the priorities of those in power.

Rather than acting as a guide for societal harmony, the modern legal system has become a labyrinth of technicalities, bureaucracy, and exploitation, ensuring that those who can afford the best legal representation wield the most power.

How Human Law Incentivizes Corruption

The distortion of human law is most evident in how it has become a tool for generating wealth rather than protecting justice. The modern legal system is not just flawed—it is profitable.

- Lawsuits have become an industry. In nations like the U.S., legal battles are waged not for justice, but for financial gain, with lawyers profiting from a system that rewards manipulation over morality.

- Prisons operate as businesses. Entire industries profit from mass incarceration, ensuring that justice is not about rehabilitation—but about maintaining a cycle of punishment.

- Regulations are designed to benefit the powerful. The legal code is riddled with tax loopholes, corporate protections, and legal shields for those who control wealth and influence.

The legal system, rather than protecting the people, has become a self-perpetuating machine that benefits those who understand how to exploit it. This is why laws do not apply equally—powerful elites commit egregious crimes and remain untouched, while the average person is punished for minor infractions.

The Overcriminalization of Society: Controlling the Citizenry Through Law

As societies grow more disconnected from Natural law, they attempt to legislate morality, behavior, and even thought itself. The result is overcriminalization—an excess of laws that dictate every aspect of human life.

- Citizens are burdened with endless regulations, permits, and taxes. Simple acts—like building a home, collecting rainwater, or growing food—are often illegal or heavily restricted.

- Nonviolent offenses are treated as crimes. From minor drug possession to small business infractions, people are punished for actions that violate no natural principle.

- Surveillance laws erode privacy. Governments justify mass surveillance in the name of security, yet the true intent is control.

A society that operates in harmony with Natural law does not require excessive legislation, because its citizens are aligned with Truth and accountability. When a society replaces wisdom with enforcement, it reveals its own spiritual immaturity.

The Delusion of "Righteous" Governance

One of the greatest illusions of modern civilization is the belief that government exists to serve the people. While this may have been the original intent in certain democratic systems, the reality is that governments primarily exist to preserve their own power.

- Most governments rule by coercion, not consent. Even so-called democracies rely on taxation, surveillance, and force to maintain control.

- Legal systems protect the state before they protect the individual. Governments create laws that criminalize dissent, restrict freedom, and reinforce systemic power structures.

- The concept of "justice" is often used to justify oppression. Tyranny is often disguised as public safety, ensuring that people comply with laws that strip them of sovereignty.

At its core, government should exist to serve the people—not to rule over them. The moment it becomes an entity that imposes control rather than facilitating wisdom, it has already violated Natural law.

The Path Back to True Justice: Natural Law Over Human Law

Humanity's crisis is not a political problem—it is a spiritual problem. The world does not need more laws—it needs alignment with higher-order intelligence. A just society does not emerge from the endless regulation of human behavior—it emerges when human beings reclaim their sovereignty and align their actions with Truth.

A society based on Natural Law would:

- Prioritize wisdom over regulation. Fewer laws would be needed because people would act with awareness, self-responsibility, and integrity.

- Focus on restoring balance rather than enforcing punishment. True justice seeks to heal and rehabilitate rather than simply penalize.

- Acknowledge that external governance is only necessary when internal governance is absent. A highly conscious civilization does not require coercion—it naturally organizes itself in harmony.

The challenge is clear: humanity must evolve beyond its reliance on laws as a mechanism for order and instead cultivate a society where individuals operate from a state of inner wisdom, integrity, and self-responsibility.

The next section will explore the true meaning of justice and why a legal system that is aligned with Natural law would look radically different from the corrupt, profit-driven system that exists today. It will reveal how justice should not be about punishment, but about restoring harmony—a principle that human law has long abandoned.

III. The Illusion of Government and Legal Systems

Governments present themselves as the ultimate authority over human civilization, dictating laws, regulating economies, and enforcing compliance through coercion. They claim to be the arbiters of order and justice, yet their existence is built on an illusion—the illusion that human law can override the immutable principles of Natural law.

But no government has ever created Life, sustained the Earth, or upheld the natural balance of the Cosmos. Governments do not govern reality; they attempt to manipulate it for the benefit of those in power. The idea that a governing body can dictate morality, justice, and the "rules of society" without aligning with the higher intelligence of Life is one of the greatest Falsehoods of modern civilization.

Governments Exist to Serve the People—Yet They Rule Instead

True governance is meant to be for the people, by the people—a system in service to the well-being of society, ensuring that collective decisions uphold harmony, fairness, and prosperity. However, most governments throughout history have operated under the opposite paradigm:

- They consolidate power rather than distribute it.

- They impose laws to control rather than to foster wisdom and responsibility.

- They serve the interests of the ruling elite rather than the collective good.

- They create dependency rather than encourage self-sovereignty.

What was originally meant to be an administrative structure designed to serve society has transformed into a system of domination, dictating nearly every aspect of Life. From taxation to regulation, from surveillance to censorship, modern governments have become engines of control rather than facilitators of freedom.

The Legal System: A Construct That Serves Power, Not Justice

Legal systems, much like governments, claim to uphold fairness, morality, and justice. In reality, they are built on arbitrary constructs designed to protect the interests of the ruling class while enforcing compliance on the masses.

Consider the following distortions in modern legal systems:

- Most laws are not based on universal Truths—they are written by those in power to protect their interests.

- Legal frameworks are complex by design, making justice inaccessible to those without wealth or influence.

- The court system is adversarial rather than reconciliatory, rewarding those who can manipulate the system rather than those who seek Truth.

- Justice is often determined not by moral clarity but by financial resources—who can afford the best lawyers, pay the highest fines, or manipulate legal loopholes.

At its core, the legal system is less about upholding justice and more about enforcing compliance within a system of control. It is not designed to restore harmony but to perpetuate the existing power structure.

The Fallacy of Legislating Morality

One of the great Falsehoods of human civilization is the belief that morality can be legislated into existence. Governments continually pass more laws in an attempt to create order, yet society remains filled with crime, corruption, and injustice. Why? Because morality cannot be dictated by written laws—it must emerge from the consciousness of individuals.

A truly just society requires minimal laws, because its citizens operate from a higher level of consciousness. When people live in alignment with Natural law, excessive regulation becomes unnecessary. Laws against theft, fraud, and violence would be irrelevant in a civilization where individuals act in coherence with Truth and integrity.

However, instead of fostering a society of sovereign, conscious individuals, governments seek to regulate society into compliance through endless rules, restrictions, and punishments. This approach is doomed to fail because it does not address the root issue—the consciousness of the people.

The U.S. Legal System: Justice as a Business

Perhaps no modern legal system exemplifies this dysfunction more than that of the United States. What was meant to be a justice system has become a profiteering industry, where:

- Lawsuits are weaponized as tools of financial gain rather than instruments of justice.

- The legal profession has evolved into a multi-billion-dollar industry fueled by endless litigation, loopholes, and technicalities.

- Exorbitant lawsuit settlements distort the purpose of the law, turning it into a game of financial exploitation.

- The prison system profits from incarceration, making rehabilitation secondary to profit motives.

Justice is not supposed to be a business. It is supposed to be a means of restoring harmony—ensuring that when wrongs are committed, balance is reestablished. Yet, under the current legal paradigm, punishment is the priority, and justice is measured in dollars and verdicts rather than in true reconciliation.

The Natural Law Alternative: Justice as Restoration

Under Natural law, justice is not about punishment—it is about the restoration of harmony. Instead of financial penalties, imprisonment, or retribution, true justice would be rooted in:

- Rehabilitation over incarceration—guiding individuals back into harmony rather than locking them away.

- Restitution over punishment—requiring those who harm others to make amends rather than simply serving time.

- Community-based resolution—where conflicts are resolved through dialogue, understanding, and mutual accountability rather than impersonal courts.

A society truly aligned with Natural law does not need complex legal codes, corporate-run prisons, or endless litigation. It functions from wisdom, responsibility, and coherence with Life itself—removing the need for artificial control structures.

The Transition to True Justice and Prosperity

The current legal and governmental frameworks are not sustainable—they are artifacts of a world operating from control rather than wisdom. As humanity awakens from its Spiritual Crisis and moves beyond its Meta Crisis, these systems will become increasingly obsolete. The question is not if they will collapse, but when—and what will replace them.

At the heart of this transition is the artificial economic system that fuels and sustains these structures of control. The modern economy is built on debt, scarcity, and infinite growth—all illusions that violate the regenerative cycles of Nature. Just as governance and legal systems must realign with Natural law, so too must our understanding of prosperity and wealth.

The next section will explore how the artificial economy, rooted in extraction and exploitation, has become one of the greatest distortions of Natural law—and why true prosperity can only emerge from alignment with the intelligence of Life itself.

IV. The Artificial Economy vs. Natural Prosperity

The modern economic system is not a natural phenomenon—it is an artificial construct engineered by human law, designed to concentrate power, control resources, and maintain dependence rather than create true abundance. It is a system that operates in direct violation of Natural law at every level, prioritizing profit over well-being, extraction over regeneration, and scarcity over abundance.

At its core, modern economics is based on a series of illusions—debt, infinite growth, and artificial scarcity—that contradict the fundamental regenerative cycles of Nature. This system is not failing because of poor policy, corruption, or mismanagement alone; it is failing because it is built on anti-Life principles that make collapse inevitable.

The Illusions That Drive the Modern Economy

The artificial economy is based on a framework that is fundamentally incompatible with the intelligence of Life. Some of its core distortions include:

- **The Illusion of Debt-Based Wealth**
  True wealth is derived from the natural world—food, water, energy, shelter, and human ingenuity. Yet, modern economics has disconnected prosperity from tangible, Life-sustaining resources and replaced it with debt. Money is created not from actual value, but from the expansion of debt. This means that the global economy requires perpetual borrowing to sustain itself, making it structurally unsustainable.

- **The Myth of Infinite Growth**
  Nature does not grow infinitely—everything in the natural world follows cyclical patterns of growth, rest, death, and renewal. Yet, the modern economy is built on the premise that expansion must be endless. Corporations, markets, and entire nations measure success by how much they grow, without acknowledging that unchecked growth in a closed system is the definition of cancer. True prosperity is not about infinite expansion—it is about sustainable regeneration.

- **Artificial Scarcity as a Control Mechanism**
  Despite living on a planet of abundance, the modern economic system manufactures scarcity to maintain control. Food, energy, medicine, and housing are all artificially restricted through patents, monopolies, and price manipulation to ensure dependency. In contrast, Natural law dictates that resources flow freely to where they are needed, sustaining all Life rather than enriching a select few.

- **The Monetization of Everything**
  The modern economy commodifies everything—Nature, human labor, even time itself. Rather than recognizing intrinsic value, it assigns artificial prices to things that should never be bought or sold, from fresh air and clean water to health and education. Under Natural law, true prosperity is not measured in financial wealth but in the abundance of well-being, harmony, and regenerative systems.

The Failure of the Current System: Why Collapse is Inevitable

The reason modern economies are failing is not a mystery—it is the natural consequence of violating the intelligence of Life. What is extractive will deplete, what is unsustainable will collapse, and what is out of harmony with Nature will be forced into course correction. The Meta Crisis humanity faces today—climate breakdown, financial instability, mass inequality—are not separate problems. They are symptoms of an economic system that is fundamentally anti-Life.

- **Endless extraction leads to resource depletion.**
  Forests are cut down faster than they can regrow, soils are stripped of nutrients, and oceans are overfished beyond their ability to replenish. This mirrors how the Feminine Principle has been suppressed in society—there is no focus on nurturing, restoration, or balance.

- **The financial system is a house of cards.**
  Debt expansion cannot continue indefinitely. The entire monetary system is based on confidence rather than actual value, making it one of the greatest illusions in human history. When that confidence collapses, so does the economy.

- **Economic inequality is a design feature, not a flaw.**
  The modern system was never intended to create widespread prosperity—it was built to consolidate power. This is why, despite unprecedented levels of technological advancement, poverty, hunger, and financial insecurity are still rampant worldwide.

- **The system incentivizes destruction rather than regeneration.**
  The most profitable industries today—war, pharmaceuticals, factory farming, and financial speculation—are all based on destruction rather than creation. Instead of rewarding what is in service to Life, the system funnels wealth into what is most extractive and degenerative.

Natural Prosperity: The Economic Model of the Future

A civilization aligned with Natural law does not function from scarcity, debt, or control—it thrives through coherence, reciprocity, and regeneration. The intelligence of Life dictates that what is regenerative will flourish, while what is extractive will perish. A truly prosperous economy must operate in harmony with Nature, rather than in defiance of it.

This means:

- **Shifting from extraction to regeneration**
  The future economy must be built on regenerative agriculture, renewable energy, and sustainable design—not on systems that strip the planet of its Life Force.

- **Decentralization and localization**
  Economic power must shift away from centralized institutions and global monopolies and return to local communities. When wealth is distributed at the local level, resilience increases, and societies thrive.

- **Value based on real resources and human well-being**
  Prosperity should be measured not by GDP or stock prices, but by food security, access to clean water, thriving ecosystems, and the overall health of the population.

- **Collaboration over competition**
  The highest intelligence is found in cooperation, not ruthless competition. Nature thrives through symbiotic relationships, not through domination.

- **Currency backed by real assets rather than debt**
  Money should reflect actual value—not be created out of thin air by central banks. A truly sound economy will be tied to energy, resources, and human ingenuity, rather than financial speculation.

The Cost of Defying Life's Intelligence

The collapse of the current economic system is not an isolated crisis—it is one of many symptoms of a civilization that has severed itself from the intelligence of Life. When economies are structured around artificial scarcity, debt-based control, and endless extraction, collapse is inevitable. But this is only one manifestation of a deeper problem: humanity's refusal to align with Natural law.

Every crisis we face—climate instability, financial collapse, political corruption, war, disease, and societal fragmentation—is not a separate issue to be solved in isolation.

They are all consequences of violating the fundamental laws that govern Life. The more humanity fights against these natural principles, the more suffering it creates for itself.

The next section will examine how every major breakdown in the modern world—economic, environmental, social, and political—is not random or accidental, but the inevitable result of a civilization that refuses to operate in accordance with Natural law.

.

V. The Consequences of Violating Natural Law

Modern civilization is unraveling—not because of unpredictable chaos, but because of systemic violations of Natural law. The breakdown of ecosystems, financial institutions, and social structures is not random—it is the inevitable result of a civilization built on principles that contradict the intelligence of Life itself.

Natural law is immutable. It cannot be overridden by legislation, technological advancements, or economic theories. When humanity insists on imposing artificial constructs that violate Life's inherent balance, the result is suffering, instability, and collapse. Every crisis humanity faces today—climate instability, financial collapse, political corruption, war, disease, and social fragmentation—is not an isolated problem to be fixed through policy or regulation, but a consequence of failing to live in harmony with Life's intelligence.

The Symptoms of a Civilization in Disharmony

1. Environmental Collapse

- o The mass extinction of species, deforestation, soil depletion, and ocean acidification are not simply the results of industrial activity—they are the consequences of an extractive, mechanized worldview that treats Nature as an object to be conquered rather than an intelligence to be honored.

- o The planet is not dying—it is recalibrating. When an ecosystem is pushed beyond its regenerative capacity, it will reset itself, often through mass die-offs, climate shifts, or resource depletion. The suffering this creates for humanity is self-inflicted—the Earth will recover, but civilization may not.

2. Economic Collapse

- o Modern economies are artificially engineered to contradict the regenerative cycles of Nature.

- The pursuit of infinite growth on a finite planet is not just unsustainable—it is delusional.

- Debt-based economies function as an inverted pyramid, requiring endless extraction and exponential consumption, making collapse an inevitability. The deeper issue is not "fixing" economic instability, but realizing that the system itself is built on anti-Life principles.

3. The Degeneration of Human Health

- A society that disregards Natural law will also disregard the biological and energetic intelligence of the human body.

- Industrialized food systems poison the population with chemical-laden, nutritionally dead products, severing people from the regenerative power of truly Life-giving nourishment.

- The modern medical system focuses on suppressing symptoms rather than healing root causes, creating an industry that profits from perpetual disease rather than restoring coherence.

- True health is not found in pharmaceuticals but in alignment with the intelligence of the body and the rhythms of Nature.

4. Political Corruption and Authoritarianism

- The more a civilization violates Natural law, the more force and coercion it requires to maintain order.

- Governments create endless laws, regulations, and surveillance measures—not to protect people, but to prop up a system that is inherently unsustainable.

- The rise of authoritarian control is not a sign of strength but of systemic fragility—a desperate attempt to enforce compliance with a reality that is breaking apart under its own contradictions.

5. Social Fragmentation and Spiritual Starvation

- A civilization that denies Natural law disconnects people from meaning, purpose, and belonging.

- Community, reverence, and interconnectivity are replaced by hyper-individualism, consumerism, and digital escapism.

- The epidemic of loneliness, anxiety, and depression is not a psychological crisis—it is a Spiritual Crisis, stemming from the loss of connection to the deeper intelligence of Life.

- No external solution can heal an internal disconnection—until humanity realigns with Natural law, no amount of therapy, self-help, or technological advancement will fill the void.

The Unavoidable Reckoning: Nature Always Wins

No civilization has ever escaped the consequences of violating Natural law. Whether through economic collapse, environmental reset, or societal breakdown, the natural order will always reassert itself. The question is not if humanity will face the repercussions—it is whether we will awaken and realign before those consequences become irreversible.

The next section will explore how civilization can realign with Natural law—not through force, control, or more regulation, but through surrendering to the higher intelligence of Life itself. True governance is not about imposing artificial order but about harmonizing with the self-organizing principles of the Universe. When humanity shifts from domination to stewardship, from mechanization to regeneration, and from control to coherence, civilization can finally break free from the cycles of collapse and step into its next evolutionary phase.

VI. Aligning Civilization with Natural Law

Humanity has spent millennia attempting to impose artificial order on the world—through laws, institutions, economic systems, and social structures—all in an effort to control Life rather than align with it. The result has been widespread suffering, environmental devastation, social unrest, and spiritual disconnection.

The solution is not more force, coercion, or control—it is surrendering to the higher intelligence of Life. True progress does not come from more laws, regulations, and policies, but from the realization that alignment with Natural law eliminates the need for excessive governance altogether.

A civilization that aligns with Natural law thrives effortlessly, without oppression, manipulation, or centralized enforcement. It is not a return to a primitive past, but a leap forward into a higher-order society—one that operates in coherence with the fundamental principles of Life itself.

The Shift from Control to Stewardship

For civilization to evolve beyond the cycles of collapse, it must shift its fundamental relationship with Life—from one of domination to one of stewardship.

- **Governments must transition from rule-makers and enforcers to facilitators of harmony.** A truly aligned society does not require excessive laws because its citizens act in accordance with higher intelligence.

- **Economies must evolve beyond artificial scarcity.** True prosperity is regenerative, not extractive—it is measured by well-being, sustainability, and abundance, not financial growth.

- **Education must prioritize wisdom over indoctrination.** Children should be raised to understand their sovereign nature and to think critically, rather than being conditioned into obedience and conformity.

- **Technology must serve humanity, not enslave it.** Innovation should enhance Life and deepen human potential, rather than mechanizing existence and severing people from their natural intelligence.

When civilization aligns with Natural law, systems function organically, fluidly, and efficiently—not through force or control, but through harmony with the intelligence of Life.

The Principles of a Civilization Aligned with Natural Law

For society to operate in accordance with Natural law, it must embody fundamental principles that mirror Life's intelligence:

1. **Self-Organization Over Centralized Control**

   o Natural systems do not require authoritarian rulers to function.

   o Governance must be decentralized, organic, and based on self-regulation rather than top-down enforcement.

2. **Regeneration Over Extraction**

   o Every system—economic, agricultural, technological—must contribute to Life rather than deplete it.

   o Resource use must be cyclical, not linear—what is taken must be replenished.

3. **Sovereignty Over Subjugation**

   o Individuals must reclaim their natural sovereignty rather than living as dependents of an external system.

   o A free society requires citizens who take full responsibility for their own lives, actions, and contributions to the whole.

4. **Coherence Over Competition**

   o Natural systems thrive through collaboration and synergy, not artificial competition.

   o A truly advanced society is cooperative, not adversarial—success is measured by collective well-being, not individual conquest.

5. **Inner Wisdom Over External Authority**

   o Society must prioritize inner knowing, intuition, and direct experience rather than relying solely on external experts, institutions, and dictated Truths.

   o A self-aware population does not need external governance—it is naturally aligned with Life.

The Misconception That Natural Law Means Chaos

One of the greatest misunderstandings is that a civilization without excessive laws and control would devolve into disorder. But this assumption is based on a flawed premise—that human beings are inherently chaotic and must be controlled to behave properly.

The Truth is the opposite:

- When people live in alignment with Natural law, they do not require coercion or enforcement.

- Chaos arises when artificial constructs attempt to override Life's inherent intelligence.

- A society rooted in Natural law does not need endless rules—it operates effortlessly because it mirrors the harmony of Nature itself.

The only reason modern civilization is drowning in laws, policies, and enforcement mechanisms is because it has strayed so far from coherence that excessive external control has become necessary to prevent complete collapse.

When society realigns with Natural law, the need for force dissolves—because Life itself is self-regulating.

The Path Forward: From Resistance to Alignment

The choice before humanity is simple:

- Continue fighting against Life, using force, control, and artificial constructs that will inevitably collapse.

- Or align with Life, surrendering to the intelligence that has sustained the Cosmos for eons.

A civilization that aligns with Natural law does not require oppression, manipulation, or coercion to function—it thrives in coherence, effortlessly sustaining its people, its systems, and its environment.

The next section will explore what this shift looks like at an individual level—because before humanity can realign civilization, each person must first realign themselves with the intelligence of Life.

VII. The Awakening of the Sovereign Being

At the foundation of human existence lies an inalienable Truth: every human being is born free and sovereign. This sovereignty is not granted by governments, institutions, or legal systems—it is endowed by the Creator and is intrinsic to the human experience. No external authority has the right to claim ownership over an individual's body, Mind, or Spirit.

Yet, throughout history, humanity has been conditioned to believe the opposite—to see freedom as something bestowed by rulers rather than something inherent. This illusion has led to widespread servitude, where people willingly surrender their sovereignty in exchange for security, convenience, and external validation.

The awakening of the sovereign being is not about rebellion—it is about remembering what has always been true. It is the realization that true power does not lie in governments, laws, or external structures, but within the individual themselves.

Sovereignty is a Birthright, Not a Privilege

- No government, institution, or ruler can take away that which was never theirs to give. Sovereignty is not a legal status—it is the fundamental state of every human being.

- Governments exist to serve the people, not to control them. True governance is a structure that facilitates harmony and protects sovereignty, not an entity that dictates, coerces, or subjugates.

- Freedom is not something to be granted—it is something to be claimed. A population that waits for permission to be free will always be enslaved.

Sovereignty is Not a One-Way Street: The Responsibility of the Citizen

The misunderstanding of sovereignty arises when people assume it means individual freedom without collective responsibility. But sovereignty does not mean isolation, selfishness, or lawlessness—it means existing in harmony with the whole, understanding that individual well-being is inseparable from the well-being of society.

- A sovereign being does not merely demand rights—they uphold responsibilities. True freedom requires accountability, self-mastery, and an active contribution to society.

- Government must serve the highest good of the collective, but the citizenry must also serve each other. A healthy civilization is one where service is reciprocated by service, where each person plays a role in the greater harmony of the whole.

- A society that upholds sovereignty is one where individuals recognize their role as stewards—not just of themselves, but of their communities, their environment, and future generations.

This is the great misalignment of modern civilization—people demand freedom while rejecting responsibility. They seek protection from government while simultaneously expecting government to solve all their problems.

A society that transcends its psychosis is one that balances sovereignty with service, where individuals take full ownership of their lives while also contributing to the well-being of the whole.

The Golden Rule: The Only Law a Sovereign Society Needs

In a civilization that has awakened beyond its Spiritual Crisis, governance does not need to be complex. Laws, regulations, and enforcement mechanisms become largely unnecessary when people operate from higher consciousness.

At the core of this wisdom is a single, universal principle:

"Do unto others as you wish to be done unto you."

This is not just a moral statement—it is the highest form of natural governance. When individuals live by this law, there is no need for excessive rules, policies, or control mechanisms, because every action is guided by mutual respect, integrity, and wisdom.

A civilization that has transcended its psychosis will no longer require:

- **Force-based governance**—because people will govern themselves through wisdom.

- **Punitive legal systems**—because justice will be based on restoration, not punishment.

- **Excessive laws and regulations**—because people will naturally act in accordance with coherence and Life-affirming intelligence.

This is the ultimate realization of sovereignty—a world where people are free not because they are granted permission, but because they have collectively risen into self-responsibility.

The Path Forward: The End of Force-Based Civilization

A sovereign civilization is one where people govern themselves not through external laws, but through internal wisdom. This is the true meaning of transcendence—not the abolition of governance, but the realization that the highest form of governance is self-mastery.

However, the transition to a world aligned with Natural law does not come without disruption. The systems built on force, exploitation, and artificial control are already crumbling under their own weight. What many perceive as instability and crisis is, in truth, the natural dissolution of structures that are no longer in alignment with Life.

The next section will explore the inevitable collapse of the old world and the emergence of a new civilization—one not dictated by rulers, governments, or economic elites, but one that arises organically as humanity returns to harmony with Natural law.

VIII. The End of the Old World and the Birth of the New

Humanity stands at a defining moment in history—a crossroads where it must choose between two radically different futures:

- Cling to the old world of control, coercion, and force—a world built on illusions, leading to further collapse and suffering.

- Or surrender to the intelligence of Life, realign with Natural law, and co-create a civilization that thrives in harmony with higher-order intelligence.

The current systems—governments, economies, legal frameworks—were all built upon the false premise that human authority can supersede Natural law. They have relied on force, manipulation, and artificial constructs to sustain themselves, but these foundations are crumbling. The collapse of outdated institutions is not a catastrophe—it is a necessary clearing of what no longer serves Life.

The Collapse of the Old World is Not the End—It is the Beginning

The downfall of the current system is not something to be feared. Just as a dying forest gives way to new Life, the decay of corrupted institutions is creating space for something new to emerge. This is not destruction—it is transformation.

The next evolution of civilization will not be dictated by governments, corporations, or centralized institutions. It will not come from policy, law, or ideological movements. It will emerge organically as humanity returns to harmony with Natural law.

The Internal Awakening Precedes the External Shift

Many believe that systemic change must come from political revolution, economic reform, or technological innovation. But true transformation does not begin with external structures—it begins within the individual.

- When people awaken to their own sovereignty, they will no longer give their consent to oppressive systems.

- When individuals realign their lives with Natural law, the artificial constructs of control will naturally dissolve.

- When humanity transcends its Spiritual Crisis, the external world will mirror this shift—because the world is always a reflection of human consciousness.

This is not a movement, not a revolution, not a policy change—it is an ascension in consciousness.

A Civilization That Thrives Effortlessly

A civilization that aligns with Natural law does not require force, regulation, or coercion to function. When humanity operates in coherence with the intelligence of Life, harmony arises effortlessly. This means:

- Governance is no longer about control—it becomes a form of stewardship and service.

- Economics is no longer about scarcity and extraction—it becomes a system of natural abundance.

- Technology is no longer used recklessly—it becomes a tool that serves humanity rather than enslaves it.

- Justice is no longer about punishment—it becomes a means of restoring harmony.

- Society is no longer fragmented by division—it becomes a living organism, thriving through unity and shared purpose.

The world that is coming is not a utopia—it is simply a civilization that operates in accordance with the higher intelligence of the Cosmos.

Transcending the Old World: The Next Phase of Humanity

Humanity stands at a crossroads: it can either recognize and realign with the immutable Truths of Natural law, or it can persist in the illusion that human-made systems of governance and legislation hold ultimate authority over Life itself. The more we attempt to impose artificial control over reality, the more suffering and disorder we create. The choice is not one of ideology or policy, but of coherence—will we surrender to the intelligence of Life, or continue down the path of forced compliance and inevitable collapse?

We can fight to preserve a dying system—one that is unsustainable, exploitative, and in direct violation of Life's principles. Or we can surrender to the intelligence of Nature, embrace its sovereign role as a co-creator, and allow the birth of an entirely new civilization.

This is not a prophecy. This is Natural law in action.

What is unsustainable must collapse.
What is coherent with Life will flourish.

And as this transformation unfolds, it is critical that humanity does not fall into the false solutions that have been presented as progress—solutions that are merely extensions of the same flawed thinking that created the crisis in the first place.

The next chapter will expose one of the greatest illusions of all—the Religion of Neoclassical Economics—revealing how an artificial economic system has perpetuated humanity's enslavement and how true prosperity can only emerge through alignment with Life's higher intelligence.

In every Crucible, there's a choice that must be made.

THE ILLUSION OF HUMAN LAW OVER NATURAL LAW

EXECUTIVE SUMMARY

Why Should You Read This Chapter?

Humanity has long operated under the illusion that man-made laws, governments, and economic systems are the ultimate authority in structuring civilization. But no government, legal system, or economic model has ever created Life, sustained the planet, or upheld the intricate balance of the Cosmos. These artificial constructs, built on control rather than wisdom, have severed humanity from the higher intelligence of Natural law–the immutable principles that govern all Life. This chapter exposes how human civilization, in its arrogance, has attempted to override these fundamental laws, leading to widespread dysfunction, corruption, and collapse.

The crises we face today–political corruption, economic instability, environmental destruction, and societal division–are not isolated issues. They are the inevitable consequences of violating Natural law. Civilization has become a machine of coercion and exploitation, enforcing compliance through legislation rather than wisdom, trying to regulate itself into harmony while ignoring the very fabric of Life's intelligence. This chapter reveals why governments, legal systems, and economic structures cannot create justice, prosperity, or peace unless they align with the higher-order principles of Nature. More importantly, it offers a pathway forward–one where sovereignty, prosperity, and social coherence arise not through control, but through alignment with Life's natural intelligence.

Executive Summary: Key Takeaways

- **Natural law is the supreme governing force of the Universe**–it dictates the cycles of Life, the principles of cause and effect, and the balance between expansion and regeneration. No human law, government, or ideology can override these immutable principles.

- **Mankind's psychosis is rooted in its belief that it can impose its own laws over the intelligence of Life.** Governments enforce control through legislation, but no system of authority has ever created or sustained Life–it merely attempts to manage it.

- **Human legal systems are artificial constructs** that do not reflect universal Truth. They are based on **control, punishment, and the consolidation of**

power, rather than the restoration of harmony and justice. Most laws serve the ruling class, not the well-being of the people.

- **The modern economy is an illusion that violates Natural law at every level.** Built on debt, scarcity, and infinite growth, it contradicts the regenerative cycles of Nature. True prosperity is not dictated by GDP or markets—it emerges when human systems align with Life's intelligence.

- **Humanity cannot regulate itself into harmony through endless laws.** The explosion of bureaucratic regulations, legal complexities, and governmental policies has not created peace or justice—it has created a system where control is enforced through coercion rather than wisdom.

- **The justice system has been hijacked into a business model.** The legal profession profits off of endless litigation, lawsuits have become a tool for financial gain rather than fairness, and the legal framework incentivizes exploitation rather than true resolution. Justice under Natural law is not about punishment—it is about restoring harmony.

- **Every crisis humanity faces—economic collapse, political corruption, environmental destruction—is a direct consequence of violating Natural law.** These are not random catastrophes but inevitable outcomes of a civilization that has severed itself from the intelligence of Life.

- **A society that aligns with Natural law does not need excessive laws, regulations, or authoritarian rule.** When people live in accordance with universal Truth, they act with integrity and mutual respect—negating the need for coercive control.

- **True sovereignty is the birthright of every human being, endowed by the Creator.** No government has the authority to take away what is intrinsic to human existence. However, sovereignty also comes with responsibility—citizens must contribute constructively to society rather than demand freedom without accountability.

- **The Golden Rule—"Do unto others as you wish to be done unto you"—is the only law truly required in a conscious society.** When individuals operate from a place of wisdom, mutual respect, and higher intelligence, excessive governance becomes unnecessary.

- **The collapse of outdated institutions and economic systems is not a catastrophe—it is a necessary clearing of what no longer serves Life.** The world is not ending; it is transforming. Those who resist this shift will experience suffering, while those who embrace it will thrive.

- **The next phase of civilization will not be dictated by governments or corporations—it will emerge organically as humanity realigns with Natural law.** This transition is not just an external restructuring—it is an inner awakening that begins at the level of individual consciousness.

- **Humanity stands at a crossroads: continue down the path of artificial control, or surrender to the intelligence of Life.** The old world is dying, and a new world is being born—one that thrives in **harmony, sovereignty, and alignment with the higher order of existence.**

IV – The Revelation: The Grand Hoaxes of Our Time

THE FICTITIOUS RELIGION OF NEOCLASSICAL ECONOMICS

I. The Mythology of Modern Economics: How It Became the Religion of Our Time

I did not come to this subject as an outsider. I was once fully immersed in the financial system, rising to the rank of senior executive (top 1%) within GE Capital, GE's financial and banking monolith, one of the world's largest financial institutions at the time. My academic pedigree—an Ivy League MBA—further entrenched me in the belief that modern economics was a legitimate science, governed by rational principles, empirical models, and self-evident Truths. It took me years of deconstruction to realize that what is taught in the halls of elite universities, practiced at the highest levels of finance, and enforced as gospel by policymakers is not science at all—it is a belief system. A fiction. A mythology masquerading as Truth.

Economics, as it is taught and practiced today, is not rooted in Natural law. It does not follow the intelligence of Life, nor does it align with the self-regulating, regenerative principles inherent in all living systems. Instead, it is built on abstractions, mathematical models detached from reality, and a mechanistic worldview that treats human beings, ecosystems, and societies as mere variables in an equation. It assumes that markets self-correct, that infinite growth is possible on a finite planet, and that money is the highest arbiter of value—all demonstrably false premises that have led to the economic, social, and environmental collapse we now face.

This chapter will dismantle the mythology of modern economics, exposing it as a fictitious religion designed to justify systemic wealth extraction, monopolization, and control. We will unravel the false dogma of neoclassical economics—the illusion of free markets, the myth of GDP growth as prosperity, the corruption of the Federal Reserve system, the unchecked expansion of derivatives, and the unsustainable nature of speculative finance. At its core, this is not just a critique of an academic discipline—it is an exposé of how a fabricated system of economic thought has been weaponized to concentrate power, subjugate populations, and sever humanity from its natural state of abundance.

Real wealth is not money. Real prosperity is not measured in GDP. And real economics—the kind that actually works—is not dictated by Wall Street, central banks, or policy think tanks, but by the immutable principles of Natural law.

The time has come to dismantle the illusion.

This section will deconstruct the false foundations of neoclassical economics, exposing its flawed assumptions, its destructive consequences, and its role in humanity's broader Meta Crisis. We will dismantle the notion that this system is the pinnacle of human progress and reveal it for what it truly is: a sophisticated illusion that is rapidly unraveling.

The Flawed Assumptions of Neoclassical Economics

At the core of neoclassical economics are fundamental misconceptions about human nature, markets, and prosperity. These assumptions are so deeply embedded in academic institutions, policymaking, and financial systems that they are rarely questioned—yet they are the very reason modern economies are unraveling.

1. The Myth of the Rational Economic Actor

- Neoclassical economics assumes that humans are rational, self-interested individuals who make decisions based purely on economic utility.

- In reality, human behavior is driven by emotion, intuition, reciprocity, and collective well-being—factors that cannot be captured by economic models.

- Behavioral economics has already debunked this myth, yet economic policies still operate under the false premise of homo economicus—the purely rational economic man.

2. The Delusion of Perpetual Growth

- The entire economic system is predicated on the presumption that perpetual growth is not just possible, but an inherent feature—despite operating within a world of finite resources with definitive limits to its regenerative capacity.

- True intelligence recognizes natural cycles of expansion and contraction—but modern economics demands perpetual GDP growth, regardless of its consequences.

- This obsession with endless growth fuels environmental destruction, financial instability, and social inequality—all in service of an illusion.

3. The Lie of Trickle-Down Economics

- Wealth does not "trickle down"—it concentrates at the top.

- Since the 1980s, corporate profits have soared while real wages have stagnated.

- The wealth gap is not an accident—it is the intentional outcome of a system designed to funnel resources upward, while placating the masses with debt and consumer distractions.

4. The Illusion of Market Efficiency

- Free markets do not always self-correct—they are highly susceptible to manipulation, speculation, and distortion.

- The financialization of the economy—where money is made from money rather than from creating real value—has turned markets into casino-like environments where speculation dictates outcomes rather than actual economic fundamentals.

- Far from ensuring efficiency, modern markets are characterized by speculative bubbles, recurring crashes, and systemic instability—as evidenced by the 2008 financial crisis and the ballooning derivatives market.

The Religion of the Market: Why Economics is Not Science

Despite its glaring flaws and contradictions, neoclassical economics is upheld as an unquestionable doctrine of Truth rather than a flawed ideological construct. It's an abstract theory of reality—not hard science— that is revered not because it is accurate, but because it serves the power structures that rely on its perpetuation.

- **It is faith-based, not evidence-based**—assumptions are treated as laws, despite mounting evidence to the contrary.

- **It is dogmatic, not adaptive**—even in the face of systemic failure, economists double down on the same flawed principles.

- **It is designed to benefit the elite**—policy decisions are crafted to maintain corporate dominance, financial speculation, and wealth consolidation, not to foster true prosperity.

This is not an economic system rooted in wisdom, intelligence, or harmony with Life— it is a control mechanism designed to keep humanity enslaved to debt, labor, and false scarcity. It is an artificial construct that must collapse, for it is fundamentally out of alignment with Natural law.

Next, we will dismantle the greatest deception of all—the myth of free markets, the unsound foundation upon which the entire modern economic system rests. While we are told that capitalism rewards competition, innovation, and efficiency, the reality is that markets are anything but free. They are carefully manipulated through monetary policy, central banking, corporate lobbying, and government intervention to ensure that wealth and power remain concentrated at the top. The promise of prosperity for all is an illusion—one that serves only those who control the levers of the system.

II. The Great Deception: Free Markets Are Not Free

The prevailing mythology of modern capitalism insists that free markets are self-regulating, efficient, and the best mechanism for wealth creation and prosperity. This is the core dogma of neoclassical economics, endlessly repeated in business schools, policy discussions, and media narratives. But this is a carefully constructed illusion—one designed to obscure the reality that modern markets are anything but free.

In Truth, markets do not operate on pure competition, nor do they naturally distribute wealth efficiently across society, let alone among nations. They are manipulated at every level—by central banks, government policies, corporate lobbying, and financial institutions that rig the game in favor of those who already control capital. The economy is not a free and open system—it is a closed loop that consolidates power in fewer and fewer hands.

This section will dismantle the myth of free markets, exposing how financial manipulation, stock buybacks, and policy distortions have turned the economy into a machine for wealth extraction, benefiting the elite while the masses are placated with debt, inflation, and stagnant wages.

The Hidden Hand of Market Manipulation

The notion that markets operate freely under pure supply and demand is a myth. The reality is that markets are constantly engineered in favor of those with the most power.

1. **Central Banks: The Ultimate Market Manipulators**

   o The Federal Reserve and other central banks do not allow free markets to operate naturally. They set interest rates, inject liquidity, and manipulate the flow of money to serve elite financial institutions.

   o Quantitative easing (QE)—the practice of printing money to prop up financial markets—has artificially inflated asset prices, disproportionately benefiting the wealthy who hold most of these assets.

   o The central banking system does not operate in the interest of the public; it is a private banking cartel designed to preserve the status quo of wealth consolidation.

2. **Government and Corporate Collusion**

   o Governments are not neutral arbiters of markets—they actively shape them to favor large corporations through tax incentives, subsidies, and favorable legislation.

   o Corporate lobbying ensures that laws and regulations are designed to benefit the largest players, creating barriers to entry that stifle true competition.

   o The revolving door between government and corporate executives ensures that the financial elite dictate economic policy, rather than serving the broader public interest.

3. **Monopoly Capitalism and the Death of True Competition**

   o Over the past several decades, markets have become increasingly monopolized. A handful of companies now dominate entire industries, from technology to banking to agriculture.

   o These monopolies control pricing, limit consumer choice, and use their power to suppress smaller competitors, further concentrating wealth at the top.

   o Anti-competitive practices, such as predatory pricing and strategic acquisitions, allow corporations to maintain dominance while pretending to operate in a "free market."

Stock Buybacks: A Legalized Ponzi Scheme

One of the most glaring examples of market manipulation is the widespread use of stock buybacks—a practice that was illegal until 1982 but is now a primary tool for corporate executives to enrich themselves at the expense of long-term economic stability.

- **What Are Stock Buybacks?** Rather than investing in innovation, employee wages and cost-of-living adjustments, or long-term value creation, corporations increasingly divert profits—and even borrowed money—into stock buybacks, a legalized form of market manipulation that artificially inflates share prices to enrich executives and shareholders.

- **Why This Benefits Executives**: CEOs and top executives are compensated primarily in stock options, meaning their personal wealth skyrockets when stock prices are manipulated upward.

- **Why This Hurts the Economy**: Instead of funding research, expansion, or fair wages, companies funnel trillions into buybacks, creating the illusion of prosperity while contributing to economic stagnation.

Stock buybacks are nothing more than legalized market manipulation—a way to extract value from the system rather than create it. This is the antithesis of a truly free market.

The Extractive Nature of the Financial System

The fundamental flaw of modern capitalism is that it is not regenerative—it does not reinvest its wealth into society to create lasting prosperity. Instead, it extracts value at every level, enriching a tiny percentage of the population while leaving the majority struggling to stay afloat.

- **Wage Stagnation & Inflation**: While stock prices soar, real wages have remained stagnant for decades. Meanwhile, inflation erodes purchasing power, ensuring that everyday people never truly get ahead.

- **Financialization Over Production**: The economy is no longer about making things of real value—it is about making money from money. Speculative finance dominates the modern economy, with hedge funds, derivatives, and high-frequency trading driving market activity rather than real economic productivity.

- **The Debt Trap**: To keep this illusion going, the masses are kept in a perpetual state of debt—whether through credit cards, student loans, or mortgages. Debt is not just a financial tool; it is a mechanism of control, ensuring that people remain trapped in a system that benefits the few at the expense of the many.

The so-called "free market" has become a predatory ecosystem where wealth flows upward, competition is suppressed, and financial engineering—not true economic productivity—determines market outcomes.

The Truth: Markets Serve Power, Not People

The grand deception of neoclassical economics is that free markets will solve all problems if left unregulated. But in reality, markets are engineered by those in power to serve their own interests.

- The stock market does not measure real economic prosperity—it measures how much wealth is being extracted from the working and middle class to fuel speculative gains for the elite.

- The modern economy is not about fair competition—it is about preserving dominance through financial manipulation and systemic inequality.

- The promise of trickle-down economics has failed—wealth does not trickle down; it inevitably and systematically hoards at the top.

The next section will expose how the Federal Reserve and central banking system perpetuate this economic illusion, creating artificial scarcity, fueling cycles of boom and bust, and maintaining control over the global financial system.

III. The Central Banking Cartel – The Engine of Perpetual Debt and Enslavement

At the heart of the modern economic system lies its most insidious illusion: money. The vast majority of people live their lives in servitude to it, governments wage wars over it, and entire civilizations rise and fall based on its perceived value. Yet, few ever stop to ask the most fundamental question—what is money, and who controls it?

Most assume that money is simply a neutral medium of exchange, a tool created to facilitate trade. But money is not just a tool—it is a mechanism of control. It is not scarce, nor is it tied to real-world value. It is conjured into existence by central banks at the push of a button, created out of thin air with no intrinsic backing.

To understand the illusion of money as well as modern economics, one must start with its beating heart: the central banking system. In the United States, at the core of this system is the Federal Reserve System, usually just referred to as the Federal Reserve—a de facto private banking cartel disguised as a public institution, wielding unchecked power over the money supply, interest rates, and the global financial order.

The average person assumes that the Federal Reserve is a government institution responsible for managing the economy for the public good. This is false. The Federal Reserve is neither federal nor does it hold real reserves. It is a privately controlled institution, deliberately structured to ensure that financial elites maintain dominion over the economy, the government, and by extension, the people.

The result is a monetary system based on perpetual debt, artificial scarcity, and cyclical crises. Every dollar in circulation is created as debt, ensuring that society remains trapped in an endless cycle of borrowing, inflation, and economic instability. This system is not a flaw—it is by design.

This section will expose how the Federal Reserve came to power, how central banking serves as an instrument of control, and why the global economy is now a ticking time bomb of debt that can never be repaid.

The Federal Reserve—A Private Cartel, Not a Public Institution

The greatest deception about central banking is the widespread belief that institutions like the Federal Reserve exist to serve the public good. This could not be further from the Truth. The Federal Reserve is not a government agency—it is a private banking cartel, designed not to ensure economic stability but to control the flow of money in ways that benefit the financial elite.

The story of the modern financial system begins not in Washington, but on a secluded island off the coast of Georgia.

Jekyll Island: The Birth of the Federal Reserve

In November 1910, a secretive meeting took place at Jekyll Island, a private retreat owned by a small group of the world's most powerful bankers. Among those in attendance were:

- Paul Warburg – German banker representing Rothschild interests.

- Senator Nelson Aldrich – Representative of Rockefeller interests.

- Henry Davison & Charles Norton – Senior partners at J.P. Morgan.

- Benjamin Strong – Future head of the New York Federal Reserve.

Together, these men devised a plan to create a central banking system that would allow them to privatize control over the U.S. money supply while giving the illusion that it was a government institution.

This plan was sold to the public as a way to prevent economic instability, yet its true purpose was to consolidate financial power into the hands of a select few. By 1913, their plan became law with the passage of the Federal Reserve Act, signed by President Woodrow Wilson.

Shortly after, Wilson realized the full extent of the power he had handed over:

"I am a most unhappy man. I have unwittingly ruined my country. A great industrial nation is controlled by its system of credit. Our system of credit is concentrated in the hands of a few men. The growth of the nation and all our activities are in the hands of a few men who necessarily, by very reason of their limitations, chill and check genuine economic development."
– President Woodrow Wilson

With the stroke of a pen, a handful of private banks gained control over the U.S. money supply, with the ability to create money out of nothing and lend it to the government at interest—enslaving the nation in perpetual debt.

When the Federal Reserve was established in 1913, it was sold to the American public as a safeguard against economic instability. In reality, it created a system where private bankers dictate monetary policy, setting interest rates, manipulating the money supply, and engineering economic cycles that enrich the few at the expense of the many.

The implications of this are staggering:

- The U.S. government does not issue its own currency—the Federal Reserve does. The government borrows money from the central bank and must pay it back with interest, perpetually indebting itself to private financial interests.

- Every dollar that enters circulation is created as debt—which means that, mathematically, there is always more debt in the system than actual money to pay it off. This ensures that society is permanently trapped in a cycle of borrowing.

- Central banks have the power to create or destroy wealth overnight simply by adjusting interest rates, expanding or contracting the money supply, or bailing out financial institutions at their discretion.

- Elected officials have no meaningful control over central banks—yet the decisions made by these unelected institutions determine the economic fate of entire nations.

In essence, central banking but especially the Federal Reserve due to its unique private ownership structure is a shadow government, operating above national sovereignty, answerable to no one, yet exerting absolute control over the financial lifeblood of civilization.

1971 - The Death of the Gold Standard and the Rise of Fiat Currency

For much of history, currencies were backed by gold—a natural form of monetary discipline that prevented reckless money printing.

However, in 1971, President Richard Nixon officially removed the U.S. dollar from the gold standard, severing its last tether to intrinsic value.

This moment was a watershed for the global economy:

- Before 1971, the U.S. dollar was backed by gold reserves, meaning every dollar in circulation represented real, finite wealth.

- After 1971, the U.S. dollar became a fiat currency—meaning its value was based solely on government decree and collective belief.

- This allowed for unlimited money printing, leading to massive inflation, rising debt levels, and a financial system increasingly detached from reality.

Today, the entire monetary system is built on air. The value of the U.S. dollar—and by extension, the global financial system—rests entirely on perception. Should confidence in the dollar erode, the entire structure could easily collapse within hours.

"Give me control of a nation's money supply, and I care not who makes its laws."
– Mayer Amschel Rothschild

This is not an economic system—it is a confidence game. A Ponzi scheme on a planetary scale. Let's explore next why debt is the reason why.

The FIAT Debt-Based Money System – The Ultimate Ponzi Scheme

The common belief is that when governments issue currency, they are simply creating money to facilitate trade and economic activity. In reality, money is not issued—it is loaned into existence, ensuring perpetual debt servitude. Here's why this is a mathematical death spiral: The Federal Reserve does not print money—it creates it out of nothing and loans it to the U.S. government at interest.

1. The money supply only expands when new loans are issued. When people, businesses, and governments borrow money from banks, new currency enters circulation even most of this is digital entry on the bank's ledgers.

2. But here's the catch—only the principal is created, not the interest. This means there is always more total debt (i.e. principal <u>and</u> interest) than actual money in existence.

3. This ensures that the debt can never be fully repaid. There is simply not enough money in the system to cover both principal and interest, forcing society to continuously borrow more just to keep the system from imploding.

This system functions as a self-replicating mechanism of control.

- If borrowing stops, the economy collapses.

- If debt repayment surpasses new borrowing, the economy collapses.

- If inflation runs too high, the economy collapses.

- If confidence in the currency falters, the economy collapses.

By design, the system is unsustainable—yet it is structured to extract maximum wealth and power before its inevitable implosion.

The Engineered Boom-and-Bust Cycle—How Central Banks Manipulate Economies

One of the most deceptive aspects of modern economics is the idea that recessions, depressions, and financial crises are natural occurrences—an unavoidable aspect of capitalism. In reality, these cycles are artificially engineered through central bank policy.

The pattern is predictable:

1. **Cheap Money Expansion** - Central banks lower interest rates and increase the money supply, encouraging borrowing, speculation, and asset inflation.

2. **Debt Accumulation** - As easy credit flows, businesses and individuals take on unsustainable levels of debt, inflating stock markets, real estate, and financial bubbles.

3. **Tightening and Collapse** - At a predetermined moment, central banks contract the money supply, raise interest rates, and pop the bubbles they created, triggering widespread bankruptcies, layoffs, and foreclosures.

4. **Wealth Transfer** - Assets that were once artificially inflated crash in value, allowing elite financial institutions to buy them for pennies on the dollar, further consolidating their wealth and power.

This cycle repeats itself over and over, each time transferring more wealth from the middle and lower classes to the financial elite while presenting the illusion that these economic crashes are natural and unavoidable.

Inflation—The Hidden Tax That Steals Wealth

One of the most deceptive tools of central banking is inflation—the gradual erosion of a currency's purchasing power over time. The public is led to believe that inflation is a natural phenomenon, but it is not. Inflation is engineered through monetary expansion and debt creation, and its primary function is to extract wealth from the working class.

Consider this:

- In 1913, when the Federal Reserve was created, one U.S. dollar had the purchasing power of what today would be worth over $30.

- The moment a dollar is "printed" into existence, it is already worth less because the total money supply has increased, diluting the value of all dollars in existence.

- Wages rarely keep pace with inflation—while the price of goods, services, and assets continues to rise, the real income of the average person stagnates or declines.

Inflation is not merely an economic policy—it is a silent wealth transfer, a hidden tax that disproportionately punishes those without appreciating assets, while enriching those who hold capital. Those who hold wealth in real estate, stocks, and commodities benefit from inflation, while those who live paycheck to paycheck lose purchasing power year after year. It is nothing more or less than a disingenuous system of covert wealth extraction.

The Debt Supernova - A System on the Brink of Collapse

The entire global economy is built on a system of perpetual debt. Governments, corporations, and individuals must continuously borrow to keep the system functioning, yet the amount of debt in circulation is mathematically impossible to ever repay.

- The U.S. national debt currently exceeds $34 trillion and continues to grow exponentially.

- The unfunded liabilities of Social Security and Medicare exceed $200 trillion.

- At the global level, total debt (including government, corporate, and consumer debt) now surpasses $300 trillion—an amount so large that it can never be repaid.

- While estimates vary widely, the global derivatives market notional value is estimated between $1 quadrillion and $2 quadrillion. Derivatives are not debt, but they are in Warren Buffett's words: "I view derivatives as time bombs, both for the parties that deal in them and the economic system."

- Debt ensures control—nations that fall too deep into debt become dependent on institutions like the International Monetary Fund (IMF) and the World Bank, which dictate economic policies that serve the interests of global finance, not sovereign nations.

The consequence? A world in which everyone—from individuals to entire nations—is enslaved to a system of artificial scarcity, forced to labor under conditions dictated by the very institutions that created the problem.

The Central Banking Illusion—Why This System Must Collapse

The modern financial system is not sustainable. It is an elaborate house of cards, built on manipulated interest rates, artificial money creation, and unsustainable debt. No system that violates Natural law—where harmony, reciprocity, and organic flow govern all living systems—can persist indefinitely.

- Nature does not operate on perpetual debt—it operates on cycles of renewal and regeneration.

- No natural system allows for the consolidation of resources into the hands of the few while depriving the many indefinitely.

- The artificial economy, built on credit, speculation, and monetary manipulation, will inevitably collapse under the weight of its own distortions.

The awakening to this illusion is growing. Alternative systems—decentralized finance, community-based economic models, and regenerative investment frameworks—are emerging as potential replacements.

The question is not whether this system will collapse, but when—and whether humanity will be prepared to replace it with something in alignment with Life itself.

This system will not last. It simply cannot last.

In the next section, we will examine the Wall Street casino—a system that thrives not by producing real value, but by leveraging financial speculation, insider manipulation, and derivative markets that have spiraled into a black hole of systemic risk.

IV. The Wall Street Casino: Financialization and Speculation Over Real Value

The financial sector was once a facilitator of real economic growth, designed to allocate capital toward productive enterprises—businesses that create jobs, develop infrastructure, and advance innovation. Today, that role has been almost entirely abandoned. The modern financial system does not generate wealth through production, but through speculation, leveraging money to create more money, often with little connection to tangible value.

Wall Street has transformed into a giant casino, where high-frequency trading, derivatives, and financial instruments exist for the sole purpose of maximizing short-term profits, regardless of long-term consequences. The economy is no longer about industry, innovation, or actual wealth creation—it is about financialization, where wealth is concentrated in the hands of a few who manipulate markets, exploit information asymmetry, and leverage systemic instability for personal gain.

This section will expose how the financial industry has decoupled from the real economy, how speculative markets have created a ticking time bomb of systemic risk, and how financial institutions have rigged the game to ensure that when they gamble and lose, it is the public that pays the price.

Derivatives: The Global Time Bomb

One of the most dangerous and least understood aspects of modern finance is the derivatives market—an unregulated, highly leveraged, and opaque part of the global financial sector. Estimates of the global derivatives market range widely, from $1 quadrillion to $2 quadrillion in notional value—an amount so large that even experts struggle to assess its systemic risk. While not all derivatives pose equal exposure, their interconnected leverage means that a single major failure could trigger cascading defaults, making toppling institutions worldwide a real and present danger.

Derivatives—often described as "financial weapons of mass destruction" by Warren Buffett—are contracts that derive their value from underlying assets like stocks, bonds, commodities, or interest rates. At their core, derivatives are bets on the future price movements of assets—yet the size of these bets often exceeds the value of the underlying asset itself, creating a financial illusion of wealth that far surpasses real economic value. Moreover, they are not simple hedging tools; they have become the primary mechanism for unchecked speculation, where financial institutions make massive bets on price movements with virtually no regulatory oversight.

The danger of derivatives lies in their interconnectedness—every derivative contract is dependent on counterparties being able to fulfill their obligations. This means that when one major player defaults, it can trigger a cascading collapse of financial institutions across the globe. Some warning signs have already emerged:

- **The "London Whale" Disaster (2012)** - A rogue trader at JPMorgan Chase made high-risk bets using credit default swaps (a form of derivative), leading to $6.2 billion in trading losses, shaking confidence in the stability of large financial institutions.

- **The Credit Suisse Collapse (2022)** - Once a pillar of European banking, Credit Suisse was forced into a government-mandated acquisition by UBS due to catastrophic losses, largely stemming from risky financial instruments and speculative trading gone wrong including losses in the billions due to the collapse of the hedge fund Archegos Capital. Archegos, a highly leveraged family office, collapsed in 2021 after a series of failed derivative trades, leading to over $10 billion in losses for major investment banks. This was a stark example of how hidden leverage and counterparty risk can unravel major financial institutions overnight.

- **A Hidden House of Cards** – Unlike traditional stock or bond markets, derivatives markets operate largely over-the-counter (OTC), meaning they are unregulated and opaque. Banks, hedge funds, and financial institutions engage in speculative derivatives trading with little accountability or disclosure.

The problem is exponential leverage—most derivatives are highly leveraged, meaning small fluctuations in market conditions can lead to outsized gains or catastrophic losses. The moment a major counterparty defaults, there's a significant risk to the system due to the domino effect that can readily come into play. This snowball effect where one major counterparty's default forces its counterparty in that trade-gone-bad to now default to other counterparties unrelated to the original trade can ripple through the system exponentially and spread globally in record time. Once this happens the illusion of stability will shatter, and the entire global financial system could unravel within days or possibly even hours.

The risk of financial contagion is not mere doom thinking. The magnitude of the derivatives market relative to the global economy and all money in circulation is so disproportional, there's simply not enough money in the system to bail out a systemic meltdown, especially when it spreads globally.

The Separation of Traditional Banking and Investment Banking: How Repealing Safeguards Led to Systemic Instability

For decades, there was a clear distinction between commercial banking (which handled deposits and loans for individuals and businesses) and investment banking (which engaged in riskier activities like securities trading, underwriting, and mergers & acquisitions). This separation acted as a safeguard—ensuring that speculative risk-taking did not endanger the savings and stability of ordinary depositors.

However, the repeal of Glass-Steagall (1933-1999) in the U.S. and similar deregulations worldwide blurred the line between banking and speculation, allowing financial institutions to gamble with customer deposits while leveraging their balance sheets to unprecedented levels.

The consequences of this deregulation were immediate:

- **Banks no longer had skin in the game.** Traditionally, investment banks were organized as partnerships, meaning that their partners had personal wealth at risk. But after deregulation, these institutions became publicly traded companies, shifting the risk onto deposit holders, shareholders, and, ultimately, the public.

- **"Too Big to Fail" institutions were born.** Merging investment banking with commercial banking created financial behemoths that were so interconnected that their collapse would have systemic consequences. This led to moral hazard—if banks knew they would be bailed out, they had every incentive to take reckless risks.

- **The 2008 financial crisis** was the direct result of banks engaging in highly speculative mortgage-backed securities trading, leveraging derivatives, and passing off toxic debt as safe investments. When the system collapsed, taxpayers footed the bill.

This consolidation of banking and speculation was not an accident—it was engineered by the financial elite to create a system where profits were privatized, but losses were socialized. When these speculative bets fail, the financial elite do not lose their wealth—taxpayers, pension funds, and ordinary workers absorb the damage, either through bailouts, inflation, or economic downturns. Nothing underscored this point more than that not a single senior bank executive in the '08 financial crisis was ever held accountable, in fact some received golden parachutes in the hundreds of millions of dollars.

How Wall Street Became a Predatory Machine

The financial industry no longer serves the economy—it extracts wealth from it. Instead of facilitating productive enterprise, Wall Street's dominant players—hedge funds, private equity firms, and speculative traders—have turned the market into a battlefield of exploitation, short-termism, and systemic instability.

Furthermore, it's important to note that Wall Street's predatory behavior does not exist in a vacuum—it is enabled by a revolving door between government and financial institutions. Politicians rely on campaign funding from major banks and investment firms, while former regulators often take lucrative jobs in the very industry they were supposed to oversee. This ensures that when crises emerge, the government does not hold Wall Street accountable—it bails it out, ensuring the cycle of financial corruption continues.

To be clear, there are legitimate banking operations that benefit the economy and society, but these tend to be plain vanilla banking operations and this is no longer where the big money is made. The big money is in what Wall Street calls financial ingenuity which is, in reality, an elaborate form of economic parasitism—one that siphons wealth from the real economy and funnels it to the 0.1% of the population that runs this highly sophisticated financial casino operation.

Conclusion: The Financial System Is Not Designed for Stability—It Is Designed for Exploitation

The modern financial system is not an engine of prosperity—it is a rigged game where those with access to capital, inside information, and regulatory influence control the outcomes. This is not free-market capitalism; this is financial oligarchy.

- Markets are manipulated, not self-correcting.

- Derivatives trading poses a catastrophic risk to global stability.

- The repeal of banking safeguards has led to reckless speculation.

- Hedge funds and private equity firms prioritize wealth extraction over productive enterprise.

- The system is designed to consolidate power at the top while socializing risk across society.

The financial system is not designed to create value—it is designed to concentrate wealth and power at the top. Those who run this casino are rewarded not just with obscene pay, but with disproportionate influence over governments, regulators, and policies that reinforce their dominance. And while workers are told to tighten their belts, corporate executives and Wall Street bankers continue awarding themselves record-breaking bonuses, even in years when their companies post losses or require taxpayer bailouts. Nowhere is this more evident than in the executive compensation racket, where the architects of this system enjoy astronomical rewards while workers struggle with stagnation, rising costs, and declining purchasing power.

In the next section, we will expose the deep corruption of corporate pay structures and how they fuel the growing chasm between the elite and the working class.

Section V: The Executive Compensation Racket

The justification for astronomical executive pay rests on a single premise: that CEOs and corporate leaders are uniquely skilled, irreplaceable visionaries who deserve disproportionate rewards for their contributions to a company's success. This argument is a myth. In reality, the modern system of executive compensation has been designed not as a meritocratic incentive, but as a self-reinforcing wealth extraction mechanism—a rigged game where corporate elites reward themselves through stock manipulation, rubber-stamped board approvals, and carefully crafted legal loopholes.

In 1965, the average CEO of a major U.S. company earned about 20 times the salary of their lowest-paid worker. Today, that ratio has exploded to over 400 times—a staggering increase that has little to do with merit and everything to do with systemic exploitation. This widening chasm is not the result of increased executive productivity or genius-level decision-making, but of structural distortions that have allowed a tiny fraction of corporate leadership to siphon wealth while suppressing wages, gutting job security, and externalizing financial risk onto employees and society at large.

This section will dismantle the mythology surrounding CEO compensation, exposing how the modern corporate pay system is built on stock buybacks, short-term incentives, financial engineering, and an incestuous network of corporate boards and compensation consultants—all designed to keep the wealth machine running for the few at the expense of the many.

The Myth of the Irreplaceable CEO

The first fallacy of the executive pay racket is the notion that today's CEOs are uniquely skilled individuals who command salaries proportional to their impact on corporate success. This argument collapses under scrutiny:

- No empirical evidence supports the claim that higher CEO pay leads to better company performance. In fact, a Harvard Business Review study found that higher-paid CEOs often underperform compared to their more modestly compensated peers.

- CEO turnover is high, yet companies continue to function. If top executives were truly irreplaceable, the departure of any single CEO would cause catastrophe—yet corporate history is filled with cases where a change in leadership has had little to no negative impact, and in many cases, actually improved performance.

- Most companies are not founder-led. The myth of the visionary leader is largely a tech-industry trope. In reality, the vast majority of S&P 500 companies are not run by founders, but by corporate bureaucrats who rotate between boardrooms, rarely having an outsized impact on the companies they run beyond what any other qualified CEO could have done.

- Unlike founders with large equity stakes, career CEOs are hired hands who have no real skin in the game. It's not their brainchild, not their company, not their money at stake, and so their risk is minimal to none yet they're get compensated as if none of the foregoing is the case—it's a massive distortion of their replaceability and the fact their risk profile matches that of any other employee.

This raises the question: if CEOs are not uniquely skilled value creators, then why are they paid so much? The answer lies not in merit, but in the systemic financialization of executive compensation.

Stock Buybacks: The Legalized Market Manipulation That Enriches Executives

One of the greatest scams in modern finance is the use of stock buybacks—a once-illegal practice that is now the primary driver of CEO wealth accumulation.

What Are Stock Buybacks?

A stock buyback occurs when a company uses corporate funds to purchase its own shares from the market, artificially inflating the stock price. Since most executive compensation is paid in stock options, this directly benefits corporate leadership while doing nothing to improve the actual health of the company.

Why is this a problem?

1. **Buybacks prioritize stock prices over productive investment.** Instead of funding R&D, employee raises, or infrastructure, companies spend billions repurchasing shares—artificially inflating market value without creating any real economic output.

2. **Executives cash out at the peak.** CEOs strategically time buybacks to maximize their personal stock option value—then dump their shares before the inflated bubble corrects.

3. **This used to be illegal.** Prior to 1982, stock buybacks were considered a form of market manipulation and were banned under U.S. securities law. But under the Reagan administration, the SEC lifted restrictions, effectively legalizing insider manipulation under the guise of "capital returns to shareholders."

The numbers speak for themselves:

- From 2010 to 2019, the 500 largest U.S. companies spent $6.3 trillion on stock buybacks—an amount that could have funded massive wage increases, innovation, or economic reinvestment.

- In 2021 alone, U.S. companies spent $882 billion on buybacks, breaking all previous records. Meanwhile, wages for American workers continued to stagnate.

- Studies show that over 50% of stock price gains in recent years have been driven by buybacks, rather than organic company growth.

Stock buybacks do not create real value—they redistribute wealth upward. While long-term shareholders benefit indirectly, the primary beneficiaries are the executive class, who strategically time buybacks to maximize their personal stock option gains. This is because the long-term shareholders could just as easily have been paid a dividend and they can always trade the stock if they feel the stock price is undervalued or overvalued, respectively.

The Incestuous Boardroom: How CEOs Set Their Own Pay

If CEO compensation seems absurdly high, it's because the system that determines executive pay is inherently corrupt.

- Corporate boards are filled with hand-picked allies. A CEO's salary is set by a board of directors—yet these same board members are often hand-selected by the very executives they are supposed to oversee.

- Board members have no incentive to limit executive pay. Many serve on multiple corporate boards, earning hundreds of thousands in fees for what amounts to a few meetings per year. The more they approve inflated pay packages for CEOs, the more likely they are to receive similar treatment in other boardrooms.

- Compensation consultants reinforce the illusion of merit. To justify astronomical salaries, boards hire compensation consultants who use misleading "peer benchmarking" techniques—arguing that CEOs must be paid top-tier wages to remain competitive. This creates a cycle where every company raises CEO pay simply because others are doing the same.

The result? An unchecked system where executives write their own paychecks under the illusion of independent oversight.

The Consequences of Runaway CEO Pay

The widening gap between CEO and the executive class pay and worker wages is not just an ethical issue—it is an economic destabilizer that fuels inequality, weakens purchasing power, and contributes to systemic instability.

- Wage Stagnation: While executive pay has skyrocketed, real wages for workers have barely increased in four decades. Productivity has risen 70% since 1980, yet worker compensation has barely budged.

- Short-Termism Over Long-Term Growth: CEOs focus on short-term stock price gains rather than long-term value creation—leading to underinvestment in innovation, employee training, and sustainable business practices.

- The Death of the Middle Class: When wealth is concentrated at the top, economic mobility collapses, leading to rising debt levels, social unrest, and declining standards of living.

In a rational system, CEO pay would be tied to actual long-term company performance—not manipulated stock prices, artificial financial engineering, or self-dealing board approvals.

The fundamental flaw of this system is not wealth itself, but the violation of harmony. Any system that hoards wealth at the top while hollowing out the middle is destined for eventual collapse.

"To be wealthy and honored in an unjust society is a disgrace."
– Confucius

Just to be clear, there's no problem for excellent CEOs and stellar executives to be very well-compensated for creating real value, but when their compensation skyrockets and the Middle and Lower Class are experiencing wage stagnation, you create disharmony within the company, communities, and society as it violates Natural law. It weakens the fabric of society, setting up an inevitable correction at some point as all things must eventually be restored to harmony under the immutable laws and principles of the intelligence of Life itself.

Conclusion: A System Built for Extraction, Not Creation

The executive compensation racket is not about rewarding talent—it is about wealth consolidation. It is a carefully engineered scheme that enables corporate elites to extract value without creating it, while the average worker struggles under stagnant wages, rising costs, and declining purchasing power.

The modern economy does not reward intelligence, ingenuity, or contribution—it rewards those who control the levers of financial manipulation.

Yet financialization is evolving. The same patterns of wealth extraction that define Wall Street have now found a new frontier—digital assets. A new wave of financial illusions has emerged—crypto, DeFi, NFTs. Sold as the future of financial freedom, decentralization, and democratization—yet beneath the surface, many of these so-called innovations resemble the same extractive schemes that have long defined financialized capitalism.

From cryptocurrencies and decentralized finance (DeFi) to NFTs and tokenized assets, the promise of a new financial paradigm has captured public imagination. Yet beneath the surface, much of this landscape functions as a digital Ponzi scheme—recycling old Wall Street tactics under a new banner, where early adopters extract wealth while latecomers are left holding the bag.

In the next section, we will dissect the world of crypto, NFTs, and digital assets—examining where they hold legitimate potential, where they serve as vehicles for unchecked speculation, and how they mirror the same boom-and-bust cycles that have long defined financialized capitalism.

VI. Crypto, NFTs, and the Digital Ponzi Scheme

Over the past decade, the world has witnessed the meteoric rise of cryptocurrencies, NFTs (non-fungible tokens), and decentralized finance (DeFi)—all marketed as revolutionary financial innovations that promise decentralization, financial sovereignty, and democratized wealth creation. Proponents claim that blockchain-based assets will replace the outdated banking system, empower individuals, and usher in a new era of economic freedom.

Yet beneath the surface, much of this emerging digital economy operates as a rebranded version of the same predatory financialization that has long plagued traditional markets. The fundamental patterns of Wall Street—speculation, artificial scarcity, wealth extraction, and boom-and-bust cycles—have been replicated within the crypto space, often with even fewer safeguards, transparency, or accountability.

While blockchain technology holds legitimate potential for innovation, the vast majority of cryptocurrency projects, NFT schemes, and DeFi applications function as Ponzi-like financial structures, where early adopters profit at the direct expense of later participants. The illusion of wealth is sustained through hype, speculation, and marketing narratives rather than the creation of real economic value.

This section will dissect the crypto economy, separating genuine technological promise from the rampant financial scams that dominate the industry. It will expose how the same forces of financialization—manipulation, speculation, and wealth concentration—have found a new playground under the guise of decentralization and digital freedom.

The Crypto Mirage: Decentralization or Financial Casino?

Cryptocurrency was originally envisioned as a decentralized alternative to fiat money—a peer-to-peer financial system immune from central bank manipulation and government control. Bitcoin, the first and most well-known cryptocurrency, was created in the aftermath of the 2008 financial crisis as a direct response to reckless monetary policies and banking failures.

However, while the ideology behind cryptocurrency is noble, its execution has largely fallen into the same traps as traditional finance. Rather than serving as a stable, decentralized store of value or medium of exchange, most cryptocurrencies today exist as vehicles for pure speculation, trading on hype rather than intrinsic utility.

The Reality of Crypto Markets

- **Volatility Over Stability** – The price of Bitcoin and other cryptocurrencies fluctuates wildly, often by double-digit percentages in a single day. This extreme instability makes crypto unsuitable as a reliable currency for everyday transactions.

- **Market Manipulation** – Unlike traditional financial markets (which, despite their flaws, have some oversight), crypto markets are rife with wash trading, pump-and-dump schemes, and insider manipulation—practices that would be illegal in regulated stock exchanges but are common in the crypto space.

- **Centralized "Decentralization"** – Despite being marketed as decentralized, most major crypto projects are controlled by a handful of individuals or development teams, often concentrated in venture capital-backed firms. A small group of insiders dictates supply, governance, and direction, contradicting the fundamental promise of decentralization.

- **Lack of Real-World Utility** – Despite years of development, very few cryptocurrencies serve any real-world purpose beyond speculation. Bitcoin remains inefficient for payments, Ethereum fees remain prohibitively high, and most altcoins exist purely for trading rather than practical applications.

- **Problematic Utility** – Due to its ability to facilitate transfers outside the conventional banking system, one area of utility been proven to be illicit payments related to drug smuggling, illegal weapons trade, human trafficking, and other nefarious uses.

Rather than replacing traditional finance, crypto has largely become an unregulated financial casino, where insiders use hype cycles to pump up prices before cashing out—leaving latecomers with worthless assets when the inevitable crash arrives.

NFTs: Digital Tulip Mania

NFTs (non-fungible tokens) were initially hailed as a groundbreaking innovation in digital ownership, allowing artists, musicians, and creators to monetize digital content in new ways. The idea was simple: blockchain-based ownership certificates would provide verifiable proof of ownership for digital assets, creating scarcity and value in the digital realm.

In practice, however, NFTs have become one of the most blatant speculative bubbles in financial history—reminiscent of the Dutch tulip mania of the 17th century, where the price of tulip bulbs reached astronomical levels before inevitably collapsing.

Why NFTs Are Financially Useless

- **They Are Not Truly Scarce** - While NFT marketplaces claim digital ownership is unique, the reality is that any digital image, video, or artwork can be copied infinitely. Unlike physical collectibles (paintings, rare coins, or historical artifacts), NFTs provide nothing beyond a blockchain entry saying "you own this token."

- **Massive Speculative Bubbles** - Many NFTs skyrocketed in value purely due to speculation. Celebrities, influencers, and financial insiders artificially pumped up prices—only for the market to collapse, leaving retail buyers with worthless tokens.

- **Rug Pulls & Wash Trading** - NFT marketplaces are filled with fraudulent projects where creators abandon their communities after making millions, or where prices are manipulated through fake transactions designed to create the illusion of demand.

- **The Illusion of Ownership** - Buying an NFT does not grant ownership of the underlying artwork or media. It merely gives the buyer a digital token pointing to a URL, which itself may become invalid if the hosting service shuts down.

By late 2022, the NFT market had already collapsed by over 90%, wiping out billions in speculative value. What was marketed as the future of digital ownership turned out to be little more than a short-lived gold rush, benefiting only the earliest adopters while leaving most investors with worthless digital tokens.

DeFi: The Shadow Banking System Without Regulation

Decentralized finance (DeFi) promised to revolutionize financial services by eliminating middlemen—allowing users to lend, borrow, trade, and earn interest without relying on banks or financial institutions. However, in practice, DeFi has simply recreated the same systemic risks as Wall Street, but in an even riskier, unregulated environment.

The Dark Side of DeFi

- **Ponzi-Like Lending Protocols** – Many DeFi lending platforms operate on circular lending, where users borrow funds, re-lend them, and use newly issued tokens as collateral—creating synthetic leverage bubbles reminiscent of subprime mortgage-backed securities before the 2008 crash.

- **"Yield Farming" & Unsustainable Returns** – DeFi platforms lured investors with promises of 100%+ annual returns, but these yields were often unsustainable—relying on new users to keep inflating token prices rather than generating real economic value.

- **Flash Loan Exploits & Hacks** – Without regulatory oversight, DeFi platforms have become hotbeds for hacks, exit scams, and rug pulls, where billions of dollars have been stolen due to vulnerabilities in smart contracts.

- **The Collapse of DeFi Giants** – High-profile failures such as Terra/Luna, Celsius, Three Arrows Capital (3AC), and Sam Bankman-Fried's FTX exposed the fragility of DeFi's interconnected lending ecosystem, triggering cascading liquidations and wiping out billions in investor funds.

Rather than offering true financial freedom, DeFi has so far largely become a high-risk house of cards, where unsophisticated investors are lured in by hype, only to be left holding the bag when liquidity evaporates.

Conclusion: Digital Alchemy, Same Old Scam

The world of crypto, NFTs, and DeFi promised a financial revolution—yet in practice, it has largely replicated the same extractive cycles of financial capitalism, but with even less transparency, regulation, or safeguards.

- Crypto has become a speculative casino, not a decentralized currency system.

- NFTs functioned as a pump-and-dump bubble, not a revolution in digital ownership.

- DeFi recreated Wall Street's financial engineering, but without any protections for retail investors.

This is not to say blockchain technology itself is without merit—there are real use cases in secure transactions, smart contracts, and transparent record-keeping. However, the vast majority of the crypto economy operates as a financial mirage, where artificial scarcity and speculative hype create fleeting wealth for insiders, while the majority of participants are left with devalued assets.

While crypto is often framed as an alternative to Wall Street's financialization, the reality is that it has merely become another playground for the same hedge funds, private equity firms, and institutional speculators who have long profited from market manipulation and wealth extraction. These financial behemoths are not just exploiting digital assets—they have spent decades perfecting the art of stripping real-world businesses for profit.

Nowhere is this more evident than in the shadow world of hedge funds and private equity, where financial predators acquire companies, load them with debt, extract as much value as possible, and discard the remnants—leaving workers, suppliers, and entire communities devastated. This is not capitalism—it is parasitism, fueled by financial engineering and the commodification of entire industries.

In the next section, we will expose the hedge fund and private equity scam, where firms extract wealth without creating it, manipulate markets for obscene personal gain, and sacrifice businesses on the altar of short-term profits—violating the very essence of the Feminine Principle in finance, which should be about nurturing and growing enterprises, not stripping them for parts.

VII. The Hedge Fund & Private Equity Ripoff

For decades, hedge funds and private equity firms have been portrayed as the elite class of finance—home to the sharpest minds, the best traders, and the most sophisticated investment strategies. In reality, these institutions have become the epicenter of financial parasitism, extracting wealth from businesses rather than building them.

Instead of driving innovation, creating jobs, or fostering long-term economic stability, hedge funds and private equity firms have engineered a shadow financial economy that rewards short-term gains at the expense of long-term sustainability. They acquire businesses, saddle them with debt, strip out assets, manipulate financial statements, and discard the wreckage—leaving workers, suppliers, and entire communities to deal with the consequences.

This is not capitalism in its true sense—it is financial looting disguised as investment. This section will expose how these firms operate, their devastating impact on businesses and workers, and how their practices violate the Feminine Principle in finance—the principle of nurturing, sustaining, and growing value rather than extracting and destroying it.

The Rise of Hedge Funds and Private Equity: A System Built for Exploitation

Hedge funds and private equity firms have positioned themselves as the masters of modern finance, promising superior returns through "alternative investments" that supposedly outperform traditional stock and bond markets. But beneath the marketing spin, their actual contribution to society is highly questionable.

- **Hedge funds do not create wealth; they extract and manipulate it.** Engaging in high-frequency trading, algorithmic manipulation, and speculative short-selling and other vulture strategies, they profit from market volatility rather than contributing anything of real economic value.

- **Private equity firms do not build companies; they extract from them.** Their primary model—the leveraged buyout (LBO)—saddles companies with unsustainable debt, slashes jobs, and liquidates assets to maximize short-term investor returns.

Together, hedge funds and private equity have hollowed out industries, pushed systemic risk into the global economy, and created an era of extreme financialization where real value takes a backseat to engineered profits.

Leveraged Buyouts: The Corporate Strip-Mining Model

At the core of private equity's business model is the leveraged buyout (LBO)—a predatory financial strategy that allows firms to acquire companies using borrowed money, extract as much short-term value as possible, and then leave the business to collapse under its own debt.

How a Leveraged Buyout Works:

1. **Private equity firms acquire a company using mostly borrowed money.** Instead of investing only their own capital, they use the target company's own assets as collateral to take out massive loans.

2. **The company, now owned by private equity, is immediately saddled with this debt.** What was once a healthy business is now burdened with obligations it never incurred on its own.

3. **Cost-cutting measures are imposed to maximize short-term profits.** This usually includes mass layoffs, pension fund cuts, outsourcing, asset sales, and slashing research & development budgets.

4. **The private equity firm extracts wealth through fees, dividends, and asset stripping.** Even if the company is bleeding cash, the private equity owners ensure they get paid first.

5. **Once the company is drained, it is either sold off at a premium or left to collapse under the weight of its debt.** Workers, suppliers, and communities are left to deal with the wreckage while private equity firms move on to the next target.

This is not true value-creation—it is corporate strip-mining. And it has left a devastating trail of destruction:

- **Toys "R" Us (2017):** Acquired through an LBO, the company was burdened with $5 billion in debt. Instead of reinvesting in the business, private equity owners extracted fees while cutting costs. Toys "R" Us eventually collapsed, leaving 33,000 employees jobless with no severance pay.

- **Sears (2004-2022):** Private equity owners loaded the retailer with debt, sold off its real estate assets for quick profits, and stripped the company to the bone. What was once an iconic American brand became a ghost of its former self before ultimately going bankrupt.

- **Hospitals & Healthcare (2000s-Present):** Private equity firms have increasingly targeted hospitals, cutting staffing, increasing patient costs, and prioritizing profits over care—leading to worse health outcomes for communities.

The common theme in all of these cases? Private equity extracts wealth without creating it, leaving financial devastation in its wake.

The Hedge Fund Model: Betting Against Society

Hedge funds, unlike private equity firms, do not acquire companies—they manipulate financial markets from the shadows. Their strategies are designed not to invest in companies, but to exploit weaknesses, inefficiencies, and volatility.

Hedge Fund Tactics:

- **Short-Selling Attacks** – Hedge funds bet against companies, often using media influence to create panic and drive stock prices down.

- **Algorithmic & High-Frequency Trading** – Instead of traditional investing, hedge funds use artificial intelligence and algorithmic trading to exploit microsecond price discrepancies, contributing nothing to actual economic growth.

- **Pump and Dump Schemes** – Some hedge funds manipulate stocks by hyping certain assets, cashing out at the peak, and leaving retail investors to take the losses.

- **Predatory Trading** - Through instruments like credit default swaps (CDS), hedge funds profit from economic crises by betting on corporate or national defaults—often exacerbating instability in the process.

- **Massive Leverage** - Many hedge funds borrow excessively to magnify returns, creating systemic risks that could collapse markets when trades go wrong.

In essence, hedge funds are not wealth creators—they are wealth extractors, siphoning billions through highly engineered financial games that provide no demonstrable tangible benefit to the real economy or society as a whole.

The 2/20 Compensation Model: Risk-Free Profits for the Financial Elite

One of the greatest scams in modern finance is the industry-standard hedge fund and private equity 2/20 compensation model—which ensures that fund managers get rich whether or not they actually generate returns.

How the 2/20 Model Works:

- **2% Management Fee**: Hedge funds and private equity firms charge investors (pension funds, endowments, etc.) an annual fee of 2% of total assets under management, no matter how well (or poorly) the fund performs.

- **20% Performance Fee**: In addition to the management fee, fund managers take 20% of any profits earned—ensuring they are rewarded handsomely for success, while bearing no risk for failure.

This model has created an asymmetrical system where financial elites profit regardless of market conditions:

- If the fund performs well, managers collect massive bonuses.

- If the fund collapses, investors lose their money, but fund managers still collect their management fees.

- If a fund is failing, managers can simply shut it down and start a new one, with no real accountability.

This structure has no downside risk for hedge fund and private equity executives—while ordinary investors, pension funds, and retirement accounts take the fall when speculative bets go bad.

Institutional Investors Keep the Scam Alive

Despite their destructive nature, hedge funds and private equity firms continue to thrive because institutional investors—pension funds, university endowments, and sovereign wealth funds—pour billions into them.

Why?

- **Illusion of exclusivity** – Many institutions believe hedge funds provide superior returns, despite multiple studies showing they underperform the broader market over the long run.

- **Short-term pressure** – Many fund managers are incentivized to chase short-term gains rather than long-term value creation.

- **Regulatory capture** – Hedge funds and private equity firms have successfully lobbied against regulation, ensuring their industry remains opaque and difficult to scrutinize.

In reality, these funds generate massive profits for insiders while exposing pensioners, retirees, and institutional investors to enormous risk.

The Feminine Principle Betrayed: The Desecration of Finance

At its core, finance should be about nurturing businesses, fostering growth, and ensuring economic sustainability. This is the Feminine Principle in finance—to care for, protect, and strengthen enterprises so they may thrive over generations.

Hedge funds and private equity firms violate this principle at every level:

- They **do not build, they dismantle**.

- They **do not nurture, they exploit**.

- They **do not create value, they extract it**.

This is financial capitalism at its most disharmonic, parasitic, and unsustainable. Any system that prioritizes extraction over creation is destined for collapse.

Conclusion: The Jackals at the Heart of the Financial System

Hedge funds and private equity firms represent the pinnacle of financial predation—they do not build businesses; they extract from them. Through leveraged buyouts, financial engineering, and speculative arbitrage, these firms treat businesses not as living, breathing entities that sustain communities, but as disposable assets to strip for short-term gain.

- Workers lose their jobs.

- Communities lose their economic backbone.

- Companies that took decades to build are gutted within months.

This is the sacrilege of the Feminine Principle in finance—the outright rejection of stewardship, nurturing, and long-term cultivation in favor of immediate liquidation and extraction. Under this system, money is the only metric that matters, and as long as an investment produces returns, no thought is given to its impact on people, society, or the planet.

But this begs a deeper question: what should investing look like in a world that values Life over mere financial gain?

Even Warren Buffett, the so-called "Oracle of Omaha" and the world's most celebrated investor, has built his fortune through a purely economic lens. Buffett is often praised as the ideal capitalist—rational, patient, and focused on long-term value. Yet his success, like all traditional investing, is measured by returns alone, without questioning whether those investments actually contribute to the well-being of humanity.

Take his beloved Coca-Cola investment—a company that has generated billions in profits, yet is one of the largest contributors to the global obesity and diabetes crisis. This is the paradox of modern investing: financial acumen and social responsibility are often at odds with one another.

In the next section, we will examine "The Warren Buffett Dilemma"—a case study in intelligent investing vs. ethical responsibility. In a post-psychosis world, financial success will no longer be measured by returns alone, but by the impact of capital on society, the environment, and collective well-being. The fundamental question is not "How much money does an investment generate?" but rather "What is the true cost of that profit?"

VIII. The Warren Buffett Dilemma: Intelligent Investing vs. Social Responsibility

Warren Buffett is often revered as the gold standard of investing—an oracle of financial wisdom who has built one of the most successful investment empires in history. Through his conglomerate, Berkshire Hathaway, Buffett has accumulated an empire spanning insurance, railroads, utilities, manufacturing, and consumer goods, consistently outperforming the market through disciplined value investing.

He is frequently portrayed as the benevolent capitalist, a man who preaches patience, long-term thinking, and ethical business practices. Unlike hedge fund managers or private equity predators, Buffett does not engage in reckless speculation, nor does he orchestrate leveraged buyouts that leave businesses gutted and communities in ruin.

And yet, Buffett exists as a paradox—the embodiment of financial genius within a system that fundamentally prioritizes profit over people. Despite his personal humility and ethical rhetoric, his investment strategy adheres to the same cold logic that drives financial capitalism: maximize returns, minimize risk, and extract value wherever possible, even at the expense of broader social consequences.

This section will examine the Warren Buffett Dilemma—the tension between intelligent investing and social responsibility, and whether it is truly possible to engage in ethical capitalism within an inherently exploitative financial system.

The Buffett Investment Model: A Masterclass in Value Investing

Buffett's success is rooted in the principle of value investing, a strategy pioneered by Benjamin Graham. Rather than chasing speculative trends or short-term market movements, Buffett's philosophy is to:

- **Buy undervalued companies with strong fundamentals.** He looks for businesses with competitive advantages (moats), strong cash flow, and reliable leadership.

- **Hold investments for the long term.** Unlike hedge funds that seek quick profits, Buffett's preferred holding period is "forever."

- **Prioritize financial discipline.** He avoids excessive debt, speculative bubbles, and market hysteria, focusing instead on fundamental business performance.

By following these principles, Buffett has amassed a net worth exceeding $120 billion, while Berkshire Hathaway has consistently generated superior returns for investors.

On the surface, this appears to be the epitome of responsible capitalism—investing in real businesses, not speculation, and allowing wealth to compound through organic growth. But a deeper examination raises uncomfortable questions:

- What are the social and ethical implications of Berkshire Hathaway's investments?

- Does investing in extractive industries make one complicit in their harm, even if done through a value-driven lens?

- Can capitalism ever be truly ethical, or is financial success inherently tied to systemic exploitation?

The Dark Side of Buffett's Investments

While Buffett has cultivated a reputation for financial wisdom and integrity, his portfolio tells a different story—one that reflects the same moral contradictions embedded in the broader financial system.

1. The Fossil Fuel Conundrum: Profiting from Environmental Destruction

Despite acknowledging the risks of climate change, Berkshire Hathaway remains heavily invested in fossil fuels. His conglomerate owns substantial stakes in companies like:

- **Chevron and Occidental Petroleum**, two of the largest oil producers in the world.

- **Berkshire Hathaway Energy**, which still relies on coal and natural gas despite gradual investments in renewables.

Buffett defends these investments as financially sound, arguing that the world will remain dependent on fossil fuels for decades. But this raises the ethical question: Should an investor with his influence prioritize financial returns over the long-term health of the planet?

Unlike hedge fund managers who actively resist climate regulation, Buffett remains neutral, taking a pragmatic approach that prioritizes profitability over proactive leadership. In doing so, he demonstrates the limits of ethical capitalism—if the highest returns come from extractive industries, even the most disciplined investors will continue to fund them.

2. Berkshire Hathaway's Labor Practices: A Benevolent Oligarch?

Buffett is often praised for allowing Berkshire Hathaway subsidiaries to operate independently, avoiding the heavy-handed management style of private equity firms. However, this decentralized model also means that:

- Many of his companies engage in anti-union practices to suppress wage growth and labor organizing.

- Manufacturing subsidiaries have been criticized for poor working conditions, particularly in railroads and energy infrastructure.

- Berkshire Hathaway companies, while profitable, do not lead the way in worker compensation or benefits.

Unlike activist investors who force layoffs to boost stock prices, Buffett does not actively strip companies of their assets. But at the same time, he does little to challenge the structural inequalities of capitalism, instead profiting from industries that rely on cost-cutting, wage suppression, and corporate consolidation.

In this sense, Buffett is not a financial predator—but neither is he a savior. He is a highly effective capitalist who operates within the system as it exists, without challenging its fundamental contradictions.

3. Tax Avoidance: Playing by the Rules of an Unfair System

Buffett has publicly advocated for higher taxes on the wealthy, famously criticizing the fact that he pays a lower tax rate than his secretary. And yet, Berkshire Hathaway itself engages in aggressive tax optimization strategies, utilizing loopholes that allow corporations to minimize tax burdens while accumulating massive profits.

This raises a central dilemma:

- Is Buffett's personal advocacy for higher taxes genuine, or merely rhetorical?

- Can ethical capitalism exist in a system where the most successful players use every legal loophole to avoid contributing their fair share?

Buffett's approach reflects a pragmatic complicity—he acknowledges the failures of the system while continuing to operate within it to maximize wealth accumulation.

The Limits of Ethical Capitalism

Warren Buffett represents the best-case scenario of capitalism—a disciplined, long-term investor who avoids speculation, prioritizes business fundamentals, and shuns the reckless financial engineering of Wall Street.

Yet his success still relies on a system that prioritizes shareholder value above all else. While he avoids the worst excesses of private equity and hedge funds, his investments still contribute to:

- **Environmental destruction** (fossil fuels).

- **Labor exploitation** (cost-cutting and anti-union practices).

- **Corporate consolidation** (monopolistic business strategies).

This presents a larger existential question: Can capitalism ever be truly ethical, or is financial success always tied to some level of systemic exploitation?

Buffett's model demonstrates that it is possible to be a disciplined capitalist without being an explicitly predatory one—but it still does not offer a path to true economic transformation. He does not strip-mine companies like private equity firms typically do, but neither does he challenge the structural incentives that prioritize profit over people.

His legacy is one of intelligent investing, not economic justice—and therein lies the dilemma.

Conclusion: The Warren Buffett Paradox

Warren Buffett serves as both an exemplar and a limitation of capitalism. He proves that financial success can be achieved without reckless speculation, yet his empire still operates within an economic system that prioritizes profit over people and planet.

While Buffett's approach is disciplined and measured, it does not challenge the fundamental flaws of modern finance. His success is not rooted in transformation but in mastery of the existing system. This raises a deeper question: Is it possible to align financial success with the flourishing of all Life, or does the current structure make this inherently unattainable?

As we move forward, the challenge is not just to refine capitalism but to evolve beyond it—to embrace an economic paradigm that prioritizes regeneration over extraction, circulation over hoarding, and the intelligence of Life over the logic of pure profit. The next section will explore the emergence of regenerative economics as a pathway toward this new vision.

IX. The Path to Regenerative Economics: Wealth in Service to Life

The current financial system is not merely broken—it is fundamentally misaligned with the intelligence of Life. Efforts to reform it within its existing structure will always fall short, as the system itself is designed to prioritize profit extraction over the well-being of people and the planet. True transformation does not come from regulation, redistribution, or policy tweaks; it emerges from an entirely new paradigm—one that views economics as an extension of Life's inherent intelligence rather than a mechanism for financial accumulation.

The Foundation of Regenerative Economics

Regenerative economics is not about replacing one ideology with another, nor is it about government intervention or wealth redistribution. It is about aligning economic activity with the intelligence of Life itself. This means creating financial and business systems that:

- Support Life-affirming enterprises rather than speculative gambling.

- Encourage wealth circulation rather than hoarding, mirroring Nature's ecosystems where nothing is wasted.

- Measure success by harmony, sustainability, and well-being rather than mere monetary growth.

John Fullerton's Regenerative Economics framework offers a guiding philosophy that rejects extractive capitalism in favor of economic principles that are symbiotic and self-renewing. The transition toward this new model is not something that can be centrally planned or imposed—it must emerge organically as humanity evolves in consciousness.

John Fullerton's Regenerative Economics Model

John Fullerton, a former Wall Street executive turned regenerative economist, has laid out a dynamic framework for economic transformation based on eight core principles. His work is not a rigid, top-down prescription but a set of guiding principles that foster the organic emergence of a regenerative economic system. These principles are:

1. **In Right Relationship** - Align economic activity with the health of the entire system, recognizing the interdependence of all Life.

2. **Views Wealth Holistically** - Redefine wealth beyond financial capital to include social, natural, and spiritual capital.

3. **Innovative, Adaptive, and Responsive** - Ensure economic structures evolve dynamically to meet the needs of a constantly changing world.

4. **Empowered Participation** - Foster inclusive economic systems where all individuals have agency and voice.

5. **Honors Community and Place** - Recognize that economies are rooted in specific cultural and ecological contexts, not abstract globalized systems.

6. **Edge Effect Abundance** - Encourage innovation at the intersections of different disciplines, industries, and cultures, just as biodiversity flourishes at ecological edges.

7. **Robust Circulatory Flow** - Ensure that money, resources, and energy continuously circulate rather than becoming concentrated and stagnant.

8. **Seeks Balance** – Recognize the need for equilibrium in economic systems, just as natural ecosystems regulate themselves.

Fullerton emphasizes that these principles do not provide a fixed formula but rather create the conditions necessary for a regenerative economy to emerge. Unlike conventional economic models that attempt to dictate outcomes through policy mandates, regenerative economics focuses on cultivating the right conditions for Life-affirming systems to develop organically.

Finance in Service to Life

The prevailing financial system rewards short-term gains at the expense of long-term vitality. A regenerative approach requires a fundamental shift:

- Capital must flow into businesses and initiatives that regenerate the Earth, nourish communities, and restore balance to the economic ecosystem.

- Investment must be decoupled from reckless speculation and redirected toward enterprises that contribute to social and environmental flourishing.

- Debt structures must be redesigned to empower rather than enslave, ensuring that financial leverage supports generative outcomes rather than extractive profits.

The Circulation of Wealth

In Nature, stagnation leads to decay, while circulation fosters vitality. The same principle applies to wealth. Hoarding capital in a way that concentrates power within a few hands leads to systemic imbalance. Instead, regenerative economics embraces:

- The dynamic movement of wealth through fair wages, shared ownership models, and reinvestment in Life-affirming projects.

- An economy where wealth functions like a river—flowing, nourishing, and sustaining all participants rather than accumulating in stagnant pools.

- Financial structures that incentivize collaboration over competition, ensuring that success is measured by collective well-being rather than individual accumulation.

The Emergence of a New Economic Paradigm

Regenerative economics is not something that can be mandated from above. It arises as a natural outgrowth of an awakened consciousness—one that recognizes the interconnectedness of all Life and rejects the mechanistic worldview that treats the economy as a machine to be optimized for maximum output.

As humanity continues its process of awakening, the old economic paradigm will gradually dissolve, not through force or revolution, but through obsolescence. The new paradigm will emerge as more individuals, businesses, and financial institutions align themselves with principles that serve Life rather than extract from it.

Conclusion: A Call to Participate

The path to regenerative economics is not a theoretical ideal—it is an invitation to participate in the creation of a world where wealth is a tool for all Life to flourish rather than a mechanism for control. The question is not whether this transition will happen, but whether we will actively choose to be architects of this new reality.

The next section will examine the broader implications of regenerative economics, exploring how business, finance, and governance can evolve in alignment with the intelligence of Life itself.

X. Conclusion: The Death of the Old and the Birth of the New

The unraveling of the current economic system is not a catastrophe—it is an essential clearing process. Just as a forest fire releases nutrients back into the soil for new growth, the collapse of artificial, extractive economies creates the space for an organic, Life-aligned economy to emerge.

The current financial system is unsustainable because it is built on a foundation of endless extraction, debt expansion, and short-term profit maximization. This model has reached its natural limit. Rather than resisting its decline, we must recognize it as an inevitable and necessary phase in the evolution of economic systems.

The Rebirth of an Economy in Service to Life

With the death of the old comes the birth of something new—an economy that regenerates rather than depletes, circulates rather than hoards, and honors rather than exploits. This is not an economy dictated by bureaucratic policies or government mandates, but one that arises naturally as individuals, businesses, and institutions align themselves with principles of regeneration.

The Future of Wealth: Stewardship Over Extraction

The future of wealth is not defined by accumulation but by stewardship. The regenerative economy is not about owning more, controlling more, or taking more. Instead, it is about participating in the great dance of Life—where prosperity arises from contributing to the whole rather than extracting from it.

This new economy will be governed by what can be called the **reverence economy**— an economic paradigm where success is measured by the well-being of ecosystems, communities, and future generations. In this paradigm:

- Wealth is a responsibility, not a privilege.

- Prosperity flows to those who nurture Life rather than exploit it.

- Economic activity aligns with the natural intelligence of ecosystems, ensuring perpetual renewal rather than depletion.

The Choice Ahead

The transition is already underway, and each of us has a role to play. The old world is unraveling. The new world is emerging. The question then is not whether this new economic paradigm will emerge—it is whether we will choose to embrace it with awareness and intentionality, or whether we will cling to the remnants of an outdated system until it crumbles beneath us.

A Transition to the Next Crisis: The Climate Change Fallacy

Yet, as the current economic system collapses, many will seek scapegoats and simplistic solutions. One of the most dominant narratives in this process is the climate change crisis, framed almost exclusively around CO_2 emissions. In the next chapter, we will challenge this reductionist approach, exposing why CO_2 is not the real crisis and exploring the deeper ecological and spiritual disconnection at the root of planetary degradation.

In every Crucible, there's a choice that must be made.

THE FICTITIOUS RELIGION OF NEOCLASSICAL ECONOMICS

EXECUTIVE SUMMARY

Why Should You Read This Chapter?

This chapter exposes the delusions of modern economics, illustrating how the financial system has become a distortion of real wealth. For decades, neoclassical economics has been treated as an unquestionable Truth—an almost religious doctrine that dictates how wealth should be created, how markets should function, and how progress should be measured. This chapter dismantles that fiction, exposing the deeply flawed assumptions that have shaped our financial and economic systems. From the myth of perpetual growth to the illusion of market efficiency, we reveal how these beliefs have led to systemic inequality, environmental degradation, and a financial order that prioritizes speculation over real value creation. If you have ever questioned why our economy seems to serve the few at the expense of the many, this chapter provides the clarity you need.

Beyond critique, this chapter closes out with a vision for what comes next. It introduces the concept of regenerative economics—not as an ideological alternative, but as a return to economic principles that align with the intelligence of Life itself. By understanding how wealth must shift from extraction to stewardship, you will see why the transition to a new economic paradigm is not a matter of policy but of consciousness. As the old world crumbles under its own weight, the question is not whether change will happen—it is whether you will be prepared to engage with it as a participant rather than a bystander.

Executive Summary: Key Takeaways

- **Neoclassical Economics as Dogma** - Economics is not a science but an ideological system that operates like a religion, enforcing unquestioned doctrines about growth, efficiency, and markets while dismissing alternative perspectives that honor the intelligence of Life.

- **The Illusion of Free Markets** - Free markets are a myth; they are systematically manipulated through central banking policies, corporate lobbying, and regulatory capture, ensuring that wealth concentrates at the top while the majority remain economic serfs.

- **The Federal Reserve and Monetary Deception** - The central banking system manufactures money out of thin air, indebting governments and individuals alike while using inflation to silently erode purchasing power and consolidate control.

- **Financialization Over Real Value** - The economy has become a casino, where speculative trading, derivatives, and leveraged debt create artificial bubbles, enriching a financial elite while detaching wealth from actual productivity and societal well-being.

- **The Corporate Greed Machine** - Executive compensation has skyrocketed from 20x to over 400x the lowest-paid worker, driven not by value creation but by financial engineering, stock manipulation, and a focus on short-term profit extraction.

- **The Crypto** Mirage - While blockchain technology has potential, much of the cryptocurrency space has devolved into a speculative playground for greed, leveraging hype and illusion to extract wealth from unsuspecting participants.

- **The Private Equity and Hedge Fund Scam** - These financial players strip companies of real value through leveraged buyouts, load them with debt, extract as much cash as possible, and then leave them to collapse, devastating workers and communities.

- **The Warren Buffett Paradox** - Even the most disciplined and ethical investors operate within a system that prioritizes returns above all else, demonstrating that financial success remains tied to systemic extraction rather than regenerative enterprise.

- **The Inherent Instability of the Current** System - An economic model built on infinite growth, consumption, and speculative finance is fundamentally unsustainable and has already begun to unravel, leading to inevitable collapse.

- **Regenerative Economics as the Alternative** - John Fullerton's framework provides an evolutionary path forward, prioritizing economic principles that mirror Nature's intelligence—where wealth circulates rather than accumulates, and economic success is measured by well-being, not mere financial returns.

- **The Death of the Old and the Birth of the New** - The collapse of artificial, extractive economies is not a failure but an essential clearing, creating space for a more harmonious, Life-affirming economic paradigm to take root.

- **Stewardship Over Extraction** - The future of wealth is not in hoarding or speculation but in the conscious stewardship of resources, enterprises, and ecosystems that sustain and regenerate Life.

•

THE CLIMATE CHANGE FALLACY: WHY CO_2 IS NOT THE REAL CRISIS

Advisory Note: This Manifesto is not a peer-reviewed research paper. While every effort has been made to ensure accuracy and verifiability of cited data, the purpose of this chapter is not to compile sources—it is to critically deconstruct the climate change narrative and expose its flawed assumptions and questionable, or at times even incongruous, conclusions. This entire Manifesto, including this chapter, is an invitation to think critically, investigate independently, and reclaim sovereignty over your own understanding of the issue.

To transcend our collective psychosis, we must reclaim control of the narratives shaping our world. This requires rejecting the passive consumption of prepackaged information and instead engaging in a proactive journey of fact finding and discernment. In the age of information abundance, we are both empowered and overwhelmed—Truth and Falsehood are interwoven, and it is our responsibility to sift through the noise, challenge assumptions, and seek knowledge beyond the boundaries of mainstream discourse. Complacency hands over control of our beliefs to external forces. True understanding demands curiosity, diligence, and the courage to question everything.

Section I - Introduction: The False Framing of the Climate Crisis

For decades, global discourse on environmental degradation has been dominated by a single narrative: carbon emissions as the root cause of planetary collapse. From international summits to corporate sustainability pledges, the reduction of CO_2 has been framed as the defining environmental challenge of our time. Governments have imposed carbon taxes, corporations have embraced net-zero pledges, and entire industries have been reorganized around the goal of reducing carbon footprints.

At first glance, this narrative appears logical—fossil fuel combustion releases CO_2, and CO_2 levels have risen alongside global temperatures. Yet correlation alone does not prove causation, and the deeper reality is far more complex. The CO_2 obsession is a deliberate oversimplification and misdirection—reducing a vast ecological crisis to a single, deceptive variable while ignoring the systematic destruction of Earth's living systems: *ecocide*.

While the political and corporate elite push policies designed to curb CO_2 emissions, they actively ignore the far more pressing and tangible causes of planetary collapse, including:

- **Toxic pollution of air, soil, and water** by heavy metals, pharmaceuticals, and synthetic chemicals.

- **Deforestation and habitat destruction** that disrupts global weather patterns and biodiversity.

- **Soil depletion and industrial farming** that have crippled Earth's natural ability to sequester carbon and sustain Life.

- **Mass overfishing and ocean acidification** that have driven marine ecosystems to the brink.

- **Decades of geoengineering and weather manipulation** that have altered global climate patterns but remain absent from climate models.

The reductionist CO_2 narrative ignores these ecological factors, reducing the infinitely complex global climate system to a single variable. This not only distorts public perception of the issue but has also led to policies that accelerate environmental destruction under the guise of "green" solutions.

The Illusion of Scientific Consensus

One of the most effective tools in promoting the CO_2 narrative has been the claim of scientific consensus—the assertion that 97% of climate scientists agree that man-made carbon emissions are driving catastrophic climate change. However, few take the time to question the underlying assumptions of this claim.

1. **Climate models are inherently unreliable** - Predictive climate models are based on assumptions about historical baselines, future emissions, and feedback loops. However, these models do not account for decades of geoengineering, land-use changes, or solar variability.

2. **No scientist can quantify the temperature reduction from CO_2 cuts** - Despite claims that CO_2 reduction is necessary, no climate scientist can quantify exactly how much temperatures will drop—or on what timeline—if emissions are reduced by a given amount. This exposes a fundamental weakness and glaring scientific gap in their conclusions.

3. **Climate science ignores long-term planetary cycles** - The Earth has undergone natural periods of warming and cooling for millions of years, influenced by factors such as solar radiation, ocean currents, and shifts in the

Earth's orbit. The idea that CO_2 is the sole driver of climate change is an oversimplification that ignores these far more powerful natural forces.

In reality, the climate system is infinitely complex, with global, regional, and local variables that interact in ways that modern science still does not fully understand. Factors that influence climate range from macro-level influences, such as variations in solar radiation, to micro-level disruptions, such as soil degradation and urban heat islands. Even at the regional level, local carbon and water cycles have intricate interdependencies that are still not fully understood. To reduce climate change to a single variable—CO_2—is not science; it is ideology.

The Role of CO_2 in Earth's Natural Systems

CO_2 is often portrayed as a pollutant, yet it is a natural and essential component of Life. The reality is that CO_2 levels have always fluctuated over geologic time scales, and the current focus on its rise from ~0.03% (c. 280ppm) from around 1900 (considered the pre-industrial level) to ~0.04% (c. 420ppm) today of the atmosphere ignores the far greater shifts that have occurred throughout Earth's history.

- **At ~0.02% CO_2 (180-200ppm), Earth would enter an ice age.** This highlights that CO_2 is essential for maintaining planetary warmth and sustaining ecosystems.

- **CO_2 is the foundation of plant life.** It is absorbed by trees, shrubs, and grasses through photosynthesis, converting it into oxygen and storing carbon in soil ecosystems.

- **The "excess" CO_2 in the atmosphere is not pollution—it is a resource.** If properly managed, this additional CO_2 could fuel a planetary-scale re-greening of deserts, forests, and grasslands.

- **The primary cause of desertification is not rising CO_2 levels, but deforestation and land mismanagement.** If human civilization shifted toward large-scale ecological restoration, Earth's capacity to regulate its own climate would be restored naturally, without the need for top-down global policies.

Conclusion: Setting the Stage for Deconstructing the Climate Narrative

Framing climate change as a CO_2 pollution problem is no accident—it is a calculated deception designed to divert attention from the wholesale environmental collapse already underway. By limiting the discussion to carbon emissions and framing CO_2 as pollution, the real forces driving planetary destruction—industrial pollution, deforestation, soil depletion, and ecological collapse—are largely left out of the conversation. Case in the point, the average person could not tell you what percentage of the atmosphere is made of CO_2, and they are typically dumbfounded to learn it's only ~0.04% as the climate change propaganda machine has caused them to believe we're drowning in CO_2. Meanwhile, the very corporations, governments, and global institutions pushing for net-zero policies continue to profit from environmental destruction while enforcing policies that have little impact on true ecological restoration.

The reductionist CO_2 narrative is not accidental—it has been engineered to serve economic and political interests. The next section will expose how the climate movement has been co-opted as a tool of control, consolidating power and wealth under the false pretense of environmental stewardship.

II. The Climate Change Narrative as Controlled Opposition

The exclusive focus on carbon emissions has created a carbon tunnel vision effect, leading policymakers, scientists, and activists to overlook the true drivers of planetary collapse. The Earth's climate system is governed by a complex interplay of factors, including:

- **Solar radiation and cosmic cycles** – Variations in solar activity have historically led to both warming and cooling periods, yet they are largely ignored in climate models. The Milankovich cycles – the eccentricity of the Earth's orbit, the tilt or obliquity of Earth's axis, and the Earth's wobble knows as the precession of the equinoxes – vary in predictable 100,000-year, 41,000-year, and 26,000-year cycles, respectively, and underline that changes in CO_2 concentrations have never have been the chief reason for warming and cooling in geological time.

- **Deforestation and land mismanagement** – The removal of forests is one of the greatest contributors to ecological collapse, disrupting both carbon and water cycles.

- **Toxic pollution and synthetic chemicals** – Heavy metals, endocrine disruptors, and persistent organic pollutants are poisoning ecosystems, yet they receive minimal attention.

The CO_2 fixation has blinded us to the true crises. Rather than addressing these crises, the climate movement focuses exclusively on CO_2, ensuring that the real culprits of environmental destruction remain untouched.

The Monetization of Fear: Turning Climate Panic into Profit

The climate crisis has been weaponized into a highly profitable financial industry, benefiting global elites while doing little to heal the planet. The mechanisms of this monetization include:

- **Carbon Credits & Offsets** – Under the guise of reducing emissions, corporations buy and sell carbon credits, creating a trillion-dollar market that allows polluters to continue business as usual.

- **ESG (Environmental, Social, and Governance) Scoring** – A mechanism that claims to reward sustainable investment but in reality funnels money into financialized "green" assets while ignoring actual ecological destruction.

- **Green Bonds** – Governments and corporations issue debt under the pretense of funding "climate-friendly" initiatives, yet much of this capital flows into industries with minimal environmental benefit.

The irony is that many of the world's largest polluters are profiting the most from the carbon economy—instead of stopping pollution, they turn it into a financial instrument, selling climate indulgences while continuing to extract and destroy at industrial scale.

Greenwashing the Crisis: How Corporations & Governments Exploit Climate Activism

Rather than implementing real environmental reforms, corporations and governments use greenwashing to maintain their profits while presenting a false image of sustainability. Tactics include:

- **Net-Zero Pledges Without Real Action** – Major companies pledge to be carbon neutral by 2050 while continuing destructive practices today.

- **Electric Vehicles as a False Solution** – EVs are touted as eco-friendly, yet their batteries require rare earth mining, child labor, and environmentally devastating lithium and cobalt extraction.

- **Biofuels & Palm Oil "Sustainability"** – Industries claim biofuels reduce carbon emissions while ignoring how deforestation for palm plantations devastates rainforests and biodiversity.

- **COP Conferences as a Boondoggle** – The Conference of the Parties (COP) climate summits are presented as critical global gatherings to address climate change, yet they have become largely performative. Often hosted by oil-rich nations, these conferences produce grand declarations and non-binding pledges while failing to implement meaningful environmental action. The 29 COP meetings held thus far have amounted to little more than diplomatic theater, placating activists while ensuring that economic interests remain protected. These events serve as a convenient platform for political and corporate elites to present an image of concern while perpetuating the very industries driving ecological destruction.

These deceptive practices mislead the public into believing progress is being made, when in reality, corporations simply rebrand environmental destruction as "sustainable development."

The Climate Emergency as a Psychological Control Mechanism

The climate crisis narrative has also been strategically used to justify expanding government control and centralization of power. Fear-based messaging conditions populations to accept restrictive policies, including:

- **Carbon Taxes & Personal Carbon Allowances** – Proposals that limit individual energy use, travel, and consumption under the guise of reducing emissions.

- **Climate Lockdowns** – Some policymakers and institutions have floated the idea of restricting movement and industry to "protect the planet," echoing pandemic-era lockdowns.

- **Censorship of Climate Skepticism** – Scientific debate on climate issues is increasingly suppressed, with dissenting voices being deplatformed and ridiculed.

By keeping the public in a constant state of alarm, governments and corporations expand their regulatory power while offering false solutions that concentrate wealth and control in the hands of the elite.

Conclusion: Setting the Stage for the True Crisis - Ecocide

The climate change movement has been hijacked to serve economic and political agendas. The real crisis is not CO_2–it is the destruction of Earth's natural systems. While the world obsesses over carbon footprints, the real catastrophe unfolds through deforestation, soil degradation, chemical pollution, and industrial-scale environmental destruction.

The next section will expose this crisis in full: Ecocide–the deliberate and systematic devastation of the planet's life-supporting ecosystems.

III. Ecocide: The True Crisis Destroying the Planet

The seven main pillars of ecocide represent the true causes of planetary collapse:

1. **Toxic Pollution** – The chemical poisoning of air, water, and soil.

2. **Chemical Warfare Against Nature** – Pesticides, herbicides, and GMOs destroying biodiversity.

3. **Soil Degradation & Desertification** – The collapse of Earth's carbon and water cycles.

4. **Deforestation & Water Cycle Disruption** – How cutting down forests alters planetary climate systems.

5. **Ocean Acidification & Overfishing** – How marine ecosystems are being annihilated.

6. **Geoengineering & Climate Manipulation** – Man-made interventions disrupting Earth's natural climate equilibrium.

7. **Cradle-to-Grave Industrial Manufacturing** – The planned obsolescence & waste economy that fuels environmental destruction.

Each of these crises will be examined in depth, exposing how human activity is driving Earth's life-supporting systems toward collapse.

1. Toxic Pollution: The Chemical Poisoning of Air, Water, and Soil

The industrial era has unleashed a torrent of toxic pollutants into the environment, poisoning Earth's life-supporting systems. These pollutants include:

- **Heavy metals** such as lead, mercury, and arsenic, which accumulate in water supplies and food chains, causing neurological and developmental disorders.

- **Endocrine-disrupting chemicals** found in plastics, pharmaceuticals, and agricultural runoff, which interfere with hormonal balance in both humans and wildlife.

- **Airborne toxins** from industrial emissions and synthetic chemicals that contribute to respiratory diseases and degrade atmospheric quality.

The consequences of this mass poisoning extend far beyond human health—entire ecosystems are collapsing under the weight of chemical overload, leading to biodiversity loss, habitat destruction, and the disruption of natural cycles essential for planetary balance.

2. Chemical Warfare Against Nature: Pesticides, Herbicides, and GMOs Destroying Biodiversity

The widespread use of pesticides, herbicides, and genetically modified organisms (GMOs) represents a systematic war against the natural world. Modern industrial agriculture, rather than working in harmony with ecosystems, has become an aggressive force that eradicates biodiversity and disrupts Earth's regenerative processes.

- **Pesticides & Herbicides:** Glyphosate (the active ingredient in Roundup) is now present in soil, waterways, and even human bloodstreams. These chemicals not only kill pests but also destroy microbial life critical to soil health and contribute to mass die-offs of pollinators such as bees and butterflies.

- **GMOs & Monocultures:** Engineered crops like Bt corn and Roundup Ready soybeans are designed to withstand heavy pesticide use. While they increase short-term yields, they deplete soil fertility, create superweeds resistant to herbicides, and eliminate genetic diversity crucial for long-term ecological resilience.

- **The Insect Apocalypse:** The industrial use of synthetic chemicals has led to a sharp decline in insect populations, with some studies suggesting a 75% reduction in biomass over the past 50 years. This disrupts food chains, leading to cascading ecosystem failures.

Rather than healing the land, modern industrial agriculture functions as an extractive system—one that poisons the soil, sterilizes landscapes, and renders ecosystems uninhabitable for Life.

3. Soil Degradation & Desertification: The Collapse of Earth's Carbon and Water Cycles

Soil is the foundation of Life on Earth, yet modern agricultural practices have severely degraded its ability to sustain ecosystems. Industrial farming, monocultures, and synthetic fertilizers have stripped the land of its natural fertility and ability to sequester carbon.

- **The Death of Soil Microbiology:** Healthy soil is a living system, teeming with microbial life that facilitates plant growth, nutrient cycling, and water retention. The widespread use of synthetic fertilizers and pesticides kills these microorganisms, leading to compacted, barren soil that can no longer support crops without artificial inputs.

- **Erosion and the Loss of Topsoil:** Industrial plowing and overgrazing accelerate soil erosion, causing the loss of topsoil at a rate far beyond natural replenishment. Scientists estimate that we have lost one-third of the world's arable land in the past 40 years, threatening global food security.

- **The Disruption of Carbon & Water Cycles:** Healthy soils store carbon and regulate the movement of water through ecosystems. When soil is depleted, it loses its ability to hold moisture, leading to increased desertification, drought, and more extreme weather patterns.

Rather than supporting Life, modern industrial farming extracts resources and depletes the very foundation of ecological stability. The solution is not more chemical inputs or genetically modified crops, but a return to regenerative agriculture—one that restores soil health, encourages biodiversity, and works in harmony with natural cycles.

4. Deforestation & Water Cycle Disruption: How Cutting Down Forests Alters Planetary Climate Systems

Forests are the lungs and circulatory system of the planet, playing a critical role in maintaining climate stability, biodiversity, and the regulation of the global water cycle. However, industrial logging, agricultural expansion, and urbanization have led to an unprecedented loss of forests, with catastrophic consequences.

- **The Role of Forests in Climate Regulation:** Forests act as carbon sinks, absorbing CO_2 while releasing oxygen. More importantly, they regulate moisture patterns and rainfall by capturing water in their canopies and releasing it through transpiration. When forests are removed, rainfall patterns shift, and entire ecosystems are thrown into imbalance.

- **The Disruption of the Water Cycle:** Deforestation leads to lower humidity, reduced rainfall, and prolonged droughts—a phenomenon known as desertification. The Amazon rainforest, often called the "lungs of the Earth," is already nearing a tipping point where deforestation could cause it to transition into a savanna, disrupting global weather patterns.

- **Increased Flooding and Soil Erosion:** Tree root systems anchor the soil and prevent erosion. When forests are clear-cut, topsoil is washed away by rain, rendering the land infertile and increasing the risk of catastrophic floods.

- **Biodiversity Collapse:** Over 80% of terrestrial species rely on forests for survival. Deforestation leads to mass extinction events, threatening food chains and ecosystem stability.

The Myth of Sustainable Logging & Palm Oil Plantations

Corporations often promote "sustainable" logging and replanting efforts, but these claims are largely greenwashing tactics. Secondary-growth forests and monoculture tree farms do not replace the biodiversity and ecological services of old-growth forests.

Similarly, the rise of palm oil plantations—marketed as a "renewable" alternative—has led to the destruction of millions of acres of rainforests in Indonesia, Malaysia, and the Amazon, killing orangutans, displacing Indigenous communities, and accelerating climate instability.

Reversing the Damage: Reforestation & Regenerative Land Management

The good news is that forests can regenerate when given the right conditions. Case studies from China's Loess Plateau, Costa Rica's rainforest restoration efforts, and permaculture-based land management have demonstrated that degraded landscapes can be revived.

A global shift towards reforestation, afforestation (planting forests where none existed), and regenerative land management could help stabilize the water cycle, restore biodiversity, and improve soil health. However, this requires a paradigm shift away from industrial agriculture and extractive land-use practices.

5. Ocean Acidification & Overfishing: How Marine Ecosystems Are Being Annihilated

The world's oceans, which cover over 70% of the planet's surface, are undergoing unprecedented destruction due to human activities. Two of the greatest threats facing marine ecosystems today are ocean acidification and overfishing, both of which have dire consequences for biodiversity, food security, and planetary stability.

- **Ocean Acidification: The Silent Killer of Marine Life**
  - The absorption of CO_2 by seawater leads to lower pH levels, disrupting the chemical balance of marine ecosystems.
  - Acidification weakens coral reefs, dissolves the shells of marine organisms, and threatens the entire food chain, from plankton to large predators.
  - Massive chemical-laden runoff from river tributaries have caused the chemicals we use on land to contaminate all our oceans.

- The Great Barrier Reef has experienced severe bleaching events, with over 50% of its coral cover lost in the past three decades.

- **Overfishing: The Industrial Plundering of the Seas**

  - Industrial-scale fishing has depleted fish populations at an unsustainable rate, with some species like bluefin tuna pushed to the brink of extinction.

  - Bottom trawling—where massive nets scrape the ocean floor—destroys marine habitats and releases carbon stored in seabed sediments.

  - The destruction of apex predators (such as sharks and whales) has thrown entire ecosystems off balance, leading to cascading effects throughout the marine food web.

The Illusion of Sustainable Fishing

- The global seafood industry markets "sustainable seafood" labels, but in reality, much of it is still tainted by illegal fishing, habitat destruction, and bycatch (the unintended capture of non-target species).

- Fish farms (aquaculture) are often presented as a solution, but they come with their own problems: pollution, genetic contamination of wild stocks, rampant "captivity" diseases not found in wild fish, and reliance on synthetic feed with chemical additives and wild-caught fish for feed.

Restoring the Oceans: The Need for Marine Protection & Regeneration

To reverse this crisis, bold action is needed:

- Establishing marine protected areas to allow fish populations and ecosystems to recover.

- Banning destructive fishing methods like bottom trawling and excessive bycatch practices.

- Promoting regenerative ocean farming, such as seaweed cultivation and shellfish reefs, to restore oceanic health and biodiversity.

The future of Life on Earth depends on healthy oceans. Without immediate intervention, the degradation of marine ecosystems will accelerate, leading to food insecurity, ecosystem collapse, and a further destabilized climate.

6. Geoengineering & Climate Manipulation: Man-Made Interventions Disrupting Earth's Natural Climate Equilibrium

While mainstream climate discourse focuses on anthropogenic CO_2 emissions, a far more immediate and concerning reality remains deliberately ignored—the extensive, decades-long manipulation of Earth's climate through geoengineering and weather modification programs. These interventions, carried out without public oversight, fundamentally disrupt natural climate cycles and could be exacerbating, rather than alleviating, climate instability. Furthermore, given many of these programs are shrouded in secrecy or classified, they severely undermine establishing a scientifically robust baseline of all forces—whether natural or manmade— at play in the already infinitely complex global weather system.

The Various Forms of Geoengineering and Weather Manipulation

1. **Stratospheric Aerosol Injection (SAI) - The Chemtrail Phenomenon**

   o Stratospheric Aerosol Injection (SAI) is the deliberate spraying of reflective particles, such as aluminum, barium, and sulfur dioxide, into the upper atmosphere to reduce solar radiation and cool the planet.

   o These aerosol particulates persist in the atmosphere, affecting weather patterns, blocking sunlight, and altering precipitation cycles.

   o While governments officially dismiss "chemtrails" as a conspiracy theory, numerous patents and military research documents confirm active experimentation in atmospheric aerosol spraying.

2. **Cloud Seeding - Artificial Weather Modification**

   o Cloud seeding involves the release of silver iodide, potassium chloride, or other chemicals into clouds to stimulate artificial precipitation.

   o Originally developed to mitigate droughts, this method has been widely used for military and economic purposes, including enhancing rainfall in certain regions while unintentionally depriving others.

   o China has the largest cloud seeding program in the world, actively modifying rainfall over vast regions, while countries like the UAE and the United States have engaged in similar programs with limited transparency.

3. **HAARP and Electromagnetic Weather Modification**

   o The High-Frequency Active Auroral Research Program (HAARP), based in Alaska, is a powerful ionospheric research installation capable of emitting high-frequency radio waves into the upper atmosphere.

   o This technology has been theorized to affect jet streams, disrupt natural storm formations, and potentially influence extreme weather events such as hurricanes and droughts.

   o Governments have long experimented with electromagnetic weather control, yet these activities remain classified or dismissed as pseudoscience despite mounting evidence.

4. **Carbon Capture and Solar Radiation Management (SRM)**

   o Geoengineering projects such as SRM aim to reduce solar heating by injecting sulfur particles into the stratosphere—a process that mimics the cooling effect of volcanic eruptions.

   o However, the unintended consequences include disrupting monsoon cycles, reducing agricultural yields, and increasing respiratory illnesses due to fine particulates in the atmosphere.

   o Many scientists warn that tampering with the delicate balance of Earth's climate system could have catastrophic, irreversible effects.

The Dangers and Consequences of Climate Engineering

- **Disrupting Natural Weather Cycles:** Weather modification alters precipitation patterns, leading to increased droughts in some regions while causing excessive flooding in others.

- **Unknown Long-Term Health Effects:** Aerosol spraying introduces toxic metals into the air, soil, and water supply, which accumulate in human and animal tissues.

- **Exacerbating Climate Extremes:** Instead of mitigating climate instability, geoengineering may be worsening hurricanes, heatwaves, and polar vortex anomalies by interfering with jet streams and atmospheric pressure systems.

- **Weaponization of Climate Control:** Weather manipulation has long been militarized, with historical projects such as Operation Popeye (Vietnam War) proving that governments weaponize environmental modification for strategic advantage.

The Lack of Public Transparency & The Suppression of Debate

Despite the overwhelming body of patents, declassified military documents, and academic research supporting the reality of geoengineering programs, mainstream climate science refuses to acknowledge these interventions.

- The official stance dismisses weather manipulation as "fringe science," despite evidence that government and private-sector experiments have been ongoing for decades.

- The public is not consulted, nor given any democratic input, on these large-scale interventions that affect global climate stability and human health.

- Scientists who question the risks of geoengineering face censorship, professional ostracization, or funding cuts, ensuring that only the official narrative–focused exclusively on CO_2–remains dominant.

Reclaiming Climate Integrity: Ending Unregulated Weather Modification

If humanity is to restore ecological balance, it must begin by demanding full transparency on geoengineering programs. The solution is not further artificial interventions but the cessation of weather manipulation, the restoration of natural climate rhythms, and the prioritization of ecosystem-based solutions.

7. Cradle-to-Grave Industrial Manufacturing & The Planned Obsolescence Economy

One of the most overlooked yet deeply embedded contributors to ecological collapse is the cradle-to-grave industrial manufacturing paradigm, which governs nearly every aspect of modern production and consumption. Under this model, products are designed with a limited lifespan, intentionally engineered to become obsolete, thereby fueling endless consumption cycles, waste accumulation, and environmental degradation.

The Planned Obsolescence Model: Waste by Design

- Many consumer goods, from electronics to automobiles, are deliberately designed with built-in failure points–whether through non-replaceable batteries, fragile components, or software updates that degrade functionality.

- The fast fashion industry churns out low-quality garments that wear out quickly, resulting in mountains of textile waste.

- Appliances and machinery, once built to last generations, are now designed for frequent replacement, benefiting manufacturers but straining global resources.

The Disposable Culture: Landfills Overflowing with Short-Lived Goods

- The majority of products today are designed with no end-of-life plan, meaning they inevitably end up in landfills or incinerators, leaching toxins into soil and waterways.

- Plastic packaging and single-use items dominate consumer markets, creating microplastic pollution that persists for centuries.

- Recycling is largely a myth—while marketed as a solution, most plastics and electronic waste are either downcycled or dumped in developing nations.

The Alternative: Cradle-to-Cradle Design & Regenerative Manufacturing

The solution lies in shifting from a cradle-to-grave model to a cradle-to-cradle paradigm, where products are designed for longevity, modular repair, and full material recovery at the end of their useful life.

- Modular design and right-to-repair legislation can extend product lifespans by allowing easy component replacement and refurbishment.

- Biodegradable and upcyclable materials can replace single-use plastics and toxic synthetic compounds.

- Circular economy models encourage companies to reclaim and repurpose materials, reducing environmental impact.

While this section provides an overview of planned obsolescence and industrial waste, a deeper exploration of how to transition toward regenerative manufacturing and economic models will be covered in Section VI of this chapter.

Conclusion: Recognizing Ecocide as the True Environmental Crisis

The destruction of Earth's natural ecosystems extends far beyond CO_2 emissions. The seven pillars of ecocide—ranging from soil degradation and deforestation to industrial waste and geoengineering—paint a far graver picture of environmental collapse than the mainstream climate narrative acknowledges. These are not distant or abstract threats; they are ongoing, measurable realities that directly impact the planet's ability to sustain Life. If humanity continues to ignore these deeper ecological crises, no amount of carbon reduction will prevent environmental disaster.

To move forward, we must recognize that climate stability is not solely determined by CO_2 levels but by the intricate, interwoven cycles of the biosphere. The next section will explore the true complexity of global climate, demonstrating why CO_2 is only one minor factor in an infinitely dynamic system that we are still only beginning to understand.

IV. The Complexity of Global Climate: CO_2 is Not the Primary Factor

The Earth's climate system is an infinitely complex, self-regulating network of interconnected forces that interact in ways we are still only beginning to understand. While mainstream discourse presents CO_2 as the primary driver of global climate changes, this is a gross oversimplification that ignores the vast array of natural and cosmic variables shaping our planetary environment.

CO_2: A Minor Gas in a Vast Atmospheric System

- CO_2 comprises only ~0.04% of the atmosphere—an incredibly small fraction when compared to water vapor, which is the dominant greenhouse gas and has far greater influence on temperature regulation.

- The assumption that CO_2 alone dictates global climate ignores the far greater impact of solar activity, oceanic currents, volcanic activity, and natural carbon sinks.

- Historically, the Earth has experienced both warmer and colder periods with significantly lower and higher CO_2 levels, demonstrating that CO_2 is not the primary climate driver.

The Sun, Milankovitch Cycles, and Cosmic Influences on Climate

- Solar activity cycles, including the 11-year sunspot cycle, play a significant role in global temperatures. Periods of high solar activity correlate with warming, while solar minimums are associated with cooling events such as the Little Ice Age (1300-1850 AD).

- Milankovitch Cycles describe how variations in Earth's orbit, axial tilt, and planetary wobble affect climate over thousands of years, driving glacial and interglacial periods independent of CO_2 fluctuations.

- Galactic Cosmic Rays (GCRs), modulated by solar activity, influence cloud formation and precipitation patterns, further impacting global climate dynamics.

How Earth's Natural Carbon Cycle Actually Works

- CO_2 is constantly cycled between the atmosphere, ocean, soil, and plant life in a dynamic equilibrium.

- Oceans absorb and release massive amounts of CO_2, acting as a primary regulator of atmospheric carbon levels.

- Forests, wetlands, and soil systems naturally sequester CO_2, reinforcing the point that healthy ecosystems—not arbitrary carbon reduction policies—are the key to climate stability.

- Volcanic eruptions and natural methane releases contribute significant greenhouse gases, dwarfing anthropogenic contributions in many instances.

The Role of Water Vapor and Ocean Currents in Climate Regulation

- Water vapor is the most dominant greenhouse gas due to its abundance, yet it is rarely mentioned in mainstream climate discourse. Unlike CO_2, which has a long atmospheric lifespan, water vapor varies dynamically and has an immediate effect on temperature through cloud formation and precipitation.

- The Thermohaline Circulation (Global Ocean Conveyor Belt) drives major climate shifts by redistributing heat across the planet. Disruptions to these currents—such as those caused by freshwater influx from melting ice sheets—have historically led to abrupt climate changes.

- El Niño and La Niña events, driven by ocean temperature variations in the Pacific, cause significant shifts in global weather patterns, proving that climate fluctuations are complex and multi-causal.

CO_2 as Plant Food: The Untold Benefits of a Greener Planet

- Plants rely on CO_2 for photosynthesis, meaning that increased atmospheric CO_2 accelerates plant growth and enhances agricultural yields.

- Some studies suggest that higher CO_2 concentrations could help restore degraded ecosystems, enabling reforestation and greening of previously barren landscapes.

- Instead of demonizing CO_2, humanity should focus on restoring forests, regenerating soils, and optimizing land use to allow the planet's natural carbon cycle to function properly.

The Need for a Holistic Climate Science Approach

- Climate science should incorporate a full-spectrum understanding of natural variables rather than focusing exclusively on CO_2.

- Policies that prioritize CO_2 reduction while ignoring deforestation, soil depletion, pollution, and geoengineering will fail to address the root causes of environmental decline.

- A shift toward systems-based ecological thinking is essential for real climate solutions that work with nature rather than against it.

A true understanding of Earth's climate must go beyond the carbon tunnel vision that dominates today's discourse. While CO_2 without any doubt plays a role in planetary regulation, it is not the primary factor driving climate change. Natural cycles, oceanic patterns, solar fluctuations, and terrestrial ecosystems are far more significant in shaping the Earth's climate and that's saying nothing about the joker card in all of this—the large-scale global weather manipulation which we know has been going on for many decades but otherwise this factor is opaque and unquantifiable by scientists due to its clandestine nature. Rather than engaging in policies that attempt to control carbon output through taxation and restriction, the real focus should be on restoring natural systems, protecting biodiversity, and revitalizing Earth's regenerative processes.

The next section will explore how industrial agriculture—one of the most destructive forces on the planet—is the true disruptor of Earth's natural climate systems.

V. The Industrial Agriculture Crisis: Destroying Earth's Natural Cycles

Industrial agriculture is arguably the greatest disruptor of Earth's natural climate cycles, yet it remains largely absent from mainstream climate discourse. Instead, fossil fuels are scapegoated while the devastating impact of industrial farming on soil, water, and atmospheric health is ignored. The reality is that modern farming practices, driven by monoculture, synthetic inputs, and corporate profit motives, have decimated the planet's carbon and water cycles, contributing to desertification, biodiversity collapse, and the depletion of essential ecosystems.

Industrial Agriculture: The True Climate Disruptor

- Monoculture farming strips soil of its organic matter, leaving it unable to retain water and carbon, leading to desertification and weakened plant resilience.

- Chemical fertilizers, pesticides, and herbicides kill essential soil microbes, preventing natural carbon sequestration and disrupting underground ecosystems vital for plant health.

- Industrialized livestock operations generate toxic waste lagoons, pollute waterways, and contribute to antibiotic resistance, yet they are framed as climate villains solely due to methane emissions—ignoring their broader environmental destruction.

- Feedlot cattle are raised on unnatural diets of GMO soy, corn, and grains, requiring vast amounts of arable land to grow feed rather than allowing them to graze naturally. This inefficiency highlights the irrationality of modern livestock production.

The Collapse of the Soil-Carbon Cycle

- Healthy soil is the largest terrestrial carbon sink, naturally absorbing and storing CO_2 through microbial processes.

- Industrial plowing and chemical exposure destroy soil structure, reducing its capacity to hold moisture and carbon, making it more prone to erosion and degradation.

- The result is increasing desertification, which further exacerbates extreme weather conditions and climate instability.

Chemical Warfare Against the Land: The True Environmental Toxin

- Synthetic fertilizers and pesticides destroy beneficial soil bacteria and fungi, preventing natural nutrient cycling.

- Herbicides like glyphosate (Roundup) kill off essential microbiomes, weakening plant defenses and leaching into water systems.

- Runoff from industrial farms contributes to ocean dead zones, where excess nitrogen and phosphorus create algae blooms that suffocate marine ecosystems.

The Inhumane & Unsustainable Model of Factory Farming

A higher-order intelligence would recognize that the health and well-being of animals directly impact the quality of food consumed by humans. Yet, industrial agriculture treats animals as production units rather than living creatures, creating a system that is both inhumane and nutritionally deficient.

- Cattle, poultry, and pigs are crammed into confined spaces, deprived of natural movement and diets, and pumped with antibiotics to prevent disease outbreaks caused by overcrowding.

- Meat from factory-farmed animals is nutritionally inferior to that of pasture-raised animals, with lower omega-3 content and higher inflammatory omega-6 fats.

- The psychosis of industrial farming is that it mass-produces diseased animals for human consumption, ultimately feeding sickness back into the human population.

Regenerative Agriculture: A Real Climate Solution

Rather than taxing carbon and implementing ineffective market-driven "green" policies, a true climate solution lies in regenerative agriculture—a holistic, nature-based approach that restores ecosystems while rebalancing the carbon and water cycles.

- Diversified crop rotations rebuild soil health, preventing desertification and strengthening plant resilience.

- Cover cropping and no-till farming restore microbial activity and carbon storage within the soil.

- Holistic grazing methods mimic natural herd movements, replenishing grasslands, increasing biodiversity, and naturally sequestering carbon without synthetic interventions.

- Decentralized, small-scale farming models reduce dependency on corporate agribusiness, creating regional food sovereignty while enhancing environmental health.

- Regenerative livestock systems integrate animals into natural landscapes, allowing them to graze freely while restoring soil health and strengthening ecological resilience.

If the goal is truly to restore planetary balance, the emphasis must shift away from fossil fuel reductionism and toward healing the land, replenishing soil systems, and reintegrating agriculture with natural cycles. Without addressing the devastation caused by industrial farming, any climate policy is destined to fail.

The obsession with CO_2 emissions has diverted attention away from industrial agriculture's role in dismantling the planet's life-support systems. While global leaders push carbon taxes and emissions reductions, they ignore the rampant soil degradation, water cycle disruption, and destruction of natural ecosystems caused by corporate agribusiness. The same institutions that champion "climate action" have done little to challenge the real environmental offenders—instead, they have created new markets for profit while avoiding fundamental change.

This pattern of false solutions extends beyond agriculture and into the broader energy sector. The next section will expose the great deflection—how Big Oil is painted as the villain while electric vehicles (EVs) are framed as the solution, despite their own environmental catastrophe and corporate-driven deception.

VI. The Great Deflection: Big Oil and EVs

The dominant climate narrative has positioned Big Oil as the primary villain while presenting electric vehicles (EVs) as the solution to planetary salvation. This false binary ignores a deeper Truth: while fossil fuels have an undeniable environmental impact, EVs are not the clean alternative they are made out to be. In reality, the entire transition to electrification is a corporate strategy, not an ecological one—one that sustains centralized energy monopolies while suppressing truly sustainable energy alternatives.

Big Oil: The Necessary Scapegoat

- While demonized as the main driver of climate change, modern civilization still depends on oil for energy, transportation, plastics, agriculture, and industrial production.

- The claim that we can simply "end oil" tomorrow is naive; a realistic transition requires viable, scalable alternatives, not reactionary policies.

- Many anti-oil protests and climate movements are indirectly funded by interests pushing green energy markets, ensuring oil remains the villain while distracting from deeper systemic exploitation.

The Greenwashing of EVs: The Hidden Environmental Cost

- EVs are marketed as "zero-emission," yet their production, energy sourcing, and disposal tell a different story.

- Lithium, cobalt, and rare-earth metal mining for EV batteries devastates landscapes, poisons water supplies, and exploits child labor in developing nations.

- The power grids that charge EVs still rely on fossil fuels, meaning that much of their energy comes from coal and natural gas.

- Battery disposal remains an unresolved crisis—toxic waste from spent EV batteries will pose an increasing environmental hazard in the coming decades.

The Suppression of Hydrogen and Alternative Energy Solutions

- Hydrogen fuel cells offer a far cleaner, scalable alternative to both fossil fuels and lithium-ion batteries, yet development remains artificially suppressed.

- Unlike battery-powered EVs, hydrogen-powered vehicles produce only water vapor as a byproduct, making them genuinely emission-free.

- The existing retail gas infrastructure could be easily converted to distribute hydrogen, eliminating the need for massive new charging infrastructure.

- The energy monopolies resist hydrogen because it eliminates their scarcity-based profit model—hydrogen is the most abundant molecule in the Universe.

The Unspoken Reality: Technological Suppression

- The history of energy innovation is filled with technologies that could have transformed energy consumption but were mysteriously shelved or discredited. Makes you wonder what was so vital that the FBI removed Nikolas Tesla's "free energy" research papers from his safe when he died in 1943?

- Stanley Meyer's water-powered car, which allegedly extracted hydrogen efficiently from water, disappeared after his sudden and suspicious death.

- Other decentralized energy solutions have faced legal, financial, and political roadblocks that keep energy systems centralized under corporate control.

The False Choice: Trading One Monopoly for Another

- The forced transition to EVs is not about saving the planet—it's about shifting control from one energy monopoly (fossil fuels) to another (battery and grid-based electrification).

- Oil companies and battery manufacturers are not at odds—they are often the same financial players profiting from both industries.

- Governments are using subsidies, mandates, and legislation to ensure the public funds the transition, while corporations continue extracting wealth and resources with no accountability for the long-term environmental damage.

A Truly Sustainable Future Requires Energy Sovereignty

- The real conversation should be about energy sovereignty—empowering decentralized, clean energy systems that remove dependency on any singular corporate-controlled model.

- Expanding localized renewable solutions, investing in hydrogen, permaculture-based biofuels, and other non-extractive energy sources, and breaking free from artificial scarcity models are the real keys to planetary restoration.

- Without addressing the energy monopoly structure, the transition from fossil fuels to EVs will merely replace one extractive system with another, leaving the core issues of environmental destruction unresolved.

The energy debate is not about "saving the planet"—it is about who controls the energy future. While the public is sold a simplistic battle of Big Oil vs. Green Energy, the Truth is that the same elite forces are engineering the transition in a way that consolidates their power, suppresses true alternatives, and ensures continued corporate dominance.

The next section will address another critical, yet overlooked, piece of the environmental puzzle—the waste economy, planned obsolescence, and how our current industrial paradigm is designed to generate infinite waste rather than sustainability.

VII. The Cradle-to-Cradle Economy: Breaking Free from Planned Obsolescence

The industrial economy is designed for waste. From disposable plastics to short-lifespan consumer goods, modern production is built on an extractive 'cradle-to-grave' model—where products are manufactured, used briefly, and discarded into landfills or incinerators. This approach fuels endless consumption while devastating ecosystems and depleting finite resources. A true environmental revolution requires abandoning this paradigm in favor of a regenerative 'cradle-to-cradle' system, where waste is eliminated, and all materials are continuously reused or upcycled.

Planned Obsolescence: The Engine of Waste

- Modern products—everything from cars, electronics, clothing, furniture, to household appliances—are deliberately designed with short lifespans, forcing continuous replacement and maximizing corporate profits.

- Software-driven obsolescence ensures that even functional devices become outdated as companies disable updates, restrict repairs, or design products that cannot be easily fixed.

- The fast fashion industry churns out low-quality clothing designed to deteriorate quickly, driving massive textile waste and pollution. Behind the glamour and marketing facade of fashion hides a global textile industry that's the second most polluting industry in the world, after oil and gas. It's responsible for a significant amount of greenhouse gas emissions, water pollution, and microplastic pollution. Fashion accounts for approximately 10% of global carbon emissions and 20% of global wastewater. Basically, Zara is not much different from ExxonMobil, except nobody is protesting "no more fashion."

- Historical examples show a stark contrast: Household appliances from the mid-20th century were designed to last for decades, yet today, they fail within a few years by design. The shift from durability to disposability reflects a deliberate strategy to increase consumption rather than efficiency.

The Environmental Cost of Disposable Culture

- Plastics and electronic waste clog landfills and oceans, leaching toxic chemicals into water supplies and harming wildlife.

- Microplastics are now found in human blood, organs, and even placental tissue, indicating how deeply embedded plastic pollution has become in the global ecosystem.

- The throwaway economy depletes critical resources such as rare-earth metals, which are mined under hazardous conditions with severe environmental damage.

The Cradle-to-Cradle Revolution: Rethinking Production

- To become truly regenerative—going beyond sustainability—means designing products for longevity, repairability, continuous reuse, and with their eventual recycling or upcycling already designed in.

- Modular electronics and appliances—where worn-out components can be replaced instead of discarding the entire device—offer a blueprint for the future.

- Some companies are already proving this model works: Patagonia, for example, has pioneered a repair service that extends the life of its outdoor gear. Rather than discarding damaged items, customers can send them in for repair, using leftover materials from production that are stored and catalogued specifically for this purpose. This is a practical example of a business model that prioritizes durability over disposability.

- Circular economies create closed-loop systems where all materials are reclaimed, eliminating the concept of waste—nothing is ever wasted in Nature, everything is repurposed in service to Life.

Near-Sourcing: Rethinking Global Supply Chains

- A cradle-to-cradle economy must include near-sourcing—producing goods closer to where they are consumed to reduce the environmental costs of long-distance shipping and distribution.

- The reliance on globalized, outsourced manufacturing has led to massive emissions from transportation, often negating the benefits of so-called "green" products.

- Localized production models reduce energy consumption, increase product traceability, and promote community-based economies that support regional sustainability.

Rethinking Packaging and Material Selection

- Product design must phase out synthetic, non-biodegradable plastics in favor of biodegradable or compostable alternatives.

- Hemp, bamboo, and mushroom-based packaging offer sustainable, regenerative options that decompose naturally without polluting the environment.

- The integration of biodegradable plastics and plant-based alternatives must be prioritized to replace petroleum-based materials that persist in landfills for centuries.

From Extraction to Regeneration: A New Industrial Paradigm

- The transition from an extractive, linear economy to a regenerative, circular model would fundamentally reshape global supply chains.

- Policies that incentivize repairability, durability, and material recovery are essential to reversing the waste crisis.

- The ultimate shift requires moving beyond profit-driven production toward a system that aligns with the intelligence of nature—where waste ceases to exist.

- The shift to a regenerative 'Cradle-to-Cradle' economy is not primarily a technological challenge—it is a shift in consciousness, requiring us to transcend short-termism in how we design economies, manufacture goods, and engage with consumerism itself.

The final three sections will examine the broader implications of how industrial civilization must evolve beyond its current destructive paradigms and embrace a truly regenerative model—one that is not based on scarcity, waste, and depletion, but on harmony, renewal, and intelligent design.

However, many so-called 'green technologies'—from electric vehicles to wind and solar power—are being promoted as solutions while hiding their own extractive, environmentally destructive processes. The next section will expose the fallacy of green technology as a solution and reveal how lithium mining, rare-earth extraction, and carbon offset schemes are nothing more than another iteration of industrial exploitation disguised as sustainability.

VIII. The Fallacy of Green Technology as a Solution

The modern environmental movement promotes green technology as the ultimate solution to the climate crisis. Governments, corporations, and activists alike champion electric vehicles, wind turbines, and solar panels as the future of sustainability. But what is rarely discussed is the immense environmental cost of these so-called "green" solutions. In reality, these technologies often replicate the same extractive, polluting, and exploitative models they claim to replace.

The EV Small Print Nobody Reads: Lithium Mining & Battery Waste

- Electric vehicles (EVs) are marketed as "zero-emission," yet the environmental devastation caused by lithium, cobalt, and nickel mining is rarely acknowledged.

- Lithium mining requires massive amounts of water, leading to desertification and water shortages in regions like Chile, Bolivia, and Argentina.

- Cobalt extraction, a critical component in EV batteries, relies on child labor and inhumane working conditions, particularly in the Democratic Republic of Congo.

- Battery disposal remains an unsolved crisis—lithium-ion batteries degrade over time, and recycling technologies are still inefficient, creating new layers of toxic waste and heavy energy consumption during recycling.

- The global rush for battery materials is fueling neo-colonial resource exploitation, where developing nations bear the brunt of environmental destruction while wealthier nations consume the "clean" products.

The Solar & Wind Mirage: Hidden Costs of Renewable Energy

- Solar panels and wind turbines rely on rare-earth metals and intensive mining operations, often in ecologically fragile regions.

- Solar panel production generates toxic byproducts, including cadmium and lead, which contaminate groundwater and soil.

- Wind turbines require enormous amounts of steel, concrete, and fiberglass, leading to high emissions during production and massive waste disposal issues when they reach the end of their lifespan.

- Despite being hailed as "clean," both solar and wind farms have significant land-use impacts, often disrupting ecosystems, wildlife habitats, and agricultural land.

- The intermittency problem—wind and solar require backup from fossil fuels or massive battery storage, creating an indirect dependence on the very energy sources they aim to replace.

The Myth of Net Zero: Carbon Offsets as a Corporate Loophole

- The concept of net zero emissions allows corporations to continue polluting while purchasing carbon credits, effectively outsourcing their environmental destruction.

- Carbon offset programs often rely on questionable tree-planting initiatives that do little to sequester long-term carbon or address root causes of pollution.

- Many offset programs are fraudulent, with companies double-counting credits or funding projects that would have occurred anyway.

- The net zero narrative provides a convenient smokescreen for industries to avoid true systemic change while maintaining their bottom lines.

The Bigger Picture: Greenwashing the Climate Crisis

- The transition to green technology does not solve the deeper issue of ecological destruction—it merely shifts the burden elsewhere.

- By focusing on energy "solutions" while ignoring soil depletion, deforestation, pollution, and industrial waste, the mainstream climate agenda remains reductionist and ineffective.

- While solar and wind energy have a definitive use case and place in transitioning away from dirty energy sources like coal and gas, they are not the panacea, and their environmental drawbacks must be addressed through technological advances and use of eco-friendlier materials.

- The real path to planetary healing requires moving beyond extractive economies altogether and embracing regenerative solutions rooted in alignment with nature.

The next section will explore what a truly regenerative energy and economic system would look like—one that moves beyond both fossil fuels and extractive "green" technologies toward a Life-affirming paradigm built on the intelligence of Nature.

IX. Realigning Civilization with Natural Law: The Only True Path to Restoration

The solution to the planetary crisis does not lie in global governance, carbon markets, or technological interventions. True regeneration requires realigning civilization with the intelligence of Life itself—working with, rather than against, Natural law.

Humanity has spent centuries attempting to dominate and control nature, seeing itself as separate from the intricate systems that sustain Life. This mindset has led to widespread ecological destruction, systemic imbalance, and a complete disconnect from the wisdom that has governed natural ecosystems for millennia. If we are to restore balance, we must first acknowledge that nature already possesses all the intelligence required for renewal—our role is to support, not interfere.

The Return to Nature's Wisdom

History has shown that top-down solutions imposed by centralized institutions rarely lead to genuine ecological restoration. Governments, the UN, and corporate-backed climate initiatives prioritize economic and political interests over environmental well-being. In contrast, true sustainability emerges from localized, decentralized solutions that empower communities to steward their own natural resources in alignment with local ecosystems.

Indigenous cultures have long understood this principle. Their agricultural practices, rotational grazing, and polyculture farming techniques have allowed them to live in harmony with the land for thousands of years, without the ecological devastation seen in modern industrial civilization. By reintegrating these time-tested approaches, we can begin to reverse the damage inflicted by exploitative economies.

Localized economies also play a critical role in ecological restoration. When food, energy, and essential goods are produced regionally rather than being transported across the globe, the environmental strain caused by logistics and industrial-scale farming is significantly reduced. Strengthening community-based economies creates resilience, self-sufficiency, and a direct connection between people and their environment.

Restoring Earth's Regenerative Capacity

Nature's capacity to heal itself is nothing short of extraordinary. Forests can regrow, soil can be rebuilt, and oceans can recover—but only if human interference is minimized and the right conditions for regeneration are created.

One of the most immediate changes that must be made is the end of industrial monoculture farming. The practice of growing single crops over vast areas has devastated soil health, disrupted carbon and water cycles, and destroyed biodiversity. Transitioning toward regenerative agriculture and agroforestry can rapidly restore soil fertility, water retention, and natural carbon sequestration.

Similarly, allowing damaged ecosystems to rewild themselves can lead to rapid biodiversity recovery. Entire landscapes can be restored within decades if human activity ceases and regenerative forces are allowed to take over. This is seen in cases where deforested land, when left untouched, naturally reverts to thriving ecosystems over time.

In the oceans, overfishing bans and marine sanctuaries have demonstrated that aquatic life rebounds remarkably fast when left undisturbed. Rather than continuing to expand industrial fishing operations, policies that protect vital marine habitats and limit human extraction can allow nature to restore balance on its own terms.

The Ultimate Truth: Natural Law Cannot Be Violated Without Consequence

The greatest mistake of modern civilization has been its belief that nature can be manipulated, controlled, or "fixed" through technological intervention. Every major environmental crisis today is a direct result of violating Natural law. From industrial-scale deforestation to chemical-laden farming, from overfishing to geoengineering, every attempt to "improve" upon nature has led to cascading ecological disasters.

Regeneration is not about finding a technological "fix" for climate change or devising complex schemes for carbon trading—it is about working with Nature in creating the conditions that allow her to heal, restore, and regenerate. Until human civilization understands this fundamental Truth, no policy, market mechanism, or invention will create real sustainability.

The future must be built not on false scarcity, extractive systems, and artificial economic models, but on the principles of abundance, renewal, and deep ecological integration. Only by relinquishing the illusion of control and aligning with the intelligence of Life can we begin to restore planetary harmony.

The final section will explore how this paradigm shift can be practically implemented—not through policies or market mechanisms, but through a fundamental change in how we live, produce, and interact with the natural world.

X. Conclusion: The Illusion of Control vs. The Path to True Regeneration

The mainstream climate change narrative is a carefully constructed deception—one that reduces the immense complexity of ecological destruction to a single, convenient villain: CO_2.

By fixating on carbon emissions, the real crisis—the systematic dismantling of Earth's life-support systems—is obscured from public discourse. The result? Policies that enrich financial elites and entrenched commercial interests while leaving the root causes of environmental collapse unaddressed.

CO_2 is not the enemy. Life itself is being destroyed. Forests, oceans, and soils—the true regulators of planetary health—are being degraded at an unprecedented rate. Yet, instead of directing attention to restoring these ecosystems, the global agenda revolves around carbon credits, greenwashed technologies, and coercive policies that do nothing to halt ecocide.

The solution is not in technological interventions, centralized mandates, or corporate-driven sustainability programs. It lies in a fundamental return to reverence, stewardship, and alignment with Natural law. Regeneration is not something to be engineered—it is the natural state of Life when left undisturbed. Our role is not to control nature, but to create the conditions in which nature can heal itself.

Humanity stands at a crossroads: We can either cling to the illusion of control—placing faith in false solutions that perpetuate exploitation—or awaken to the Truth that genuine restoration begins with humility: recognizing that Nature, not man, holds the key to harmony and renewal.

The next chapter will reveal who benefits from these manufactured crises, and why keeping humanity distracted by false narratives serves a larger and much more sinister agenda—maximum profits at any cost, even human health.

In every Crucible, there's a choice that must be made.

THE CLIMATE CHANGE FALLACY: WHY CO$_2$ IS NOT THE REAL CRISIS

EXECUTIVE SUMMARY

Why Should You Read This Chapter?

For decades, the climate change debate has been dominated by a singular focus on CO$_2$, portraying it as the existential threat to humanity. This reductionist narrative has served as a distraction, keeping attention away from the far more pressing issue: ecocide—the systematic destruction of Earth's life-support systems. The climate movement has been weaponized, not to protect the planet, but to advance financialized schemes, regulatory control, and corporate greenwashing that do little to halt environmental destruction.

This chapter methodically deconstructs the climate change narrative, exposing how the obsession with carbon emissions is a false framing that benefits elites while leaving the real crisis unaddressed. It explores the true drivers of planetary collapse, from industrial agriculture to soil depletion, pollution, and deforestation, while dismantling the myths surrounding green technology, carbon markets, and corporate sustainability initiatives. Finally, it lays out the only real solution—realigning civilization with Natural law by restoring Earth's regenerative capacity instead of trying to engineer false solutions.

Executive Summary: Key Takeaways

- The False Framing of the Climate Crisis – The climate change debate has been oversimplified into a singular focus on CO$_2$, while the real drivers of planetary collapse—deforestation, soil depletion, pollution, and industrial waste—are ignored. The carbon narrative is a misdirection that serves financial and political agendas rather than true environmental restoration.

- The Climate Change Narrative as Controlled Opposition – The climate movement has been co-opted by corporations, financial elites, and global institutions to push greenwashed solutions that serve profits over the planet. Carbon credits, ESG scoring, and net-zero policies allow the worst polluters to buy their way out of accountability while continuing to exploit nature.

- Ecocide: The True Crisis Destroying the Planet – The real environmental crisis is the destruction of Earth's carbon and water cycles, biodiversity, and soil fertility. The chapter outlines seven key pillars of ecocide, including toxic pollution, deforestation, ocean depletion, and geoengineering.

- The Complexity of Global Climate: CO_2 is Not the Primary Factor – The Earth's climate is governed by a complex interplay of solar cycles, ocean currents, water vapor, and natural carbon cycles. The overemphasis on CO_2 ignores these far more influential climate drivers while failing to account for long-term planetary cycles we still do not fully understand.

- The Industrial Agriculture Crisis: Destroying Earth's Natural Cycles – Industrial farming is the largest disruptor of the planet's climate systems, not fossil fuels. Monoculture farming, chemical fertilizers, and pesticides destroy soil's ability to store carbon and water, making ecosystems more fragile and prone to collapse.

- The Great Deflection: Big Oil and EVs – While oil companies are vilified as the sole enemy of the climate, the real agenda is the forced transition to electric vehicles (EVs), which rely on lithium, cobalt, and rare earth mining that devastate the environment. At the same time, truly sustainable alternatives like hydrogen and decentralized energy solutions are suppressed.

- The Cradle-to-Cradle Economy: Breaking Free from Planned Obsolescence – The throwaway economy has been engineered to maximize corporate profits while accelerating planetary destruction. A cradle-to-cradle approach—focusing on longevity, repairability, and regenerative materials—is the only viable path forward.

- The Fallacy of Green Technology as a Solution – Solar panels, wind turbines, and electric vehicles require resource extraction on a massive scale, often as destructive as fossil fuels. The "net-zero" movement is a corporate loophole that allows pollution to continue under the guise of sustainability.

- Realigning Civilization with Natural Law – The only real solution is not in technology but in restoring Earth's natural regenerative cycles. Nature does not need intervention—it needs humanity to step aside and stop interfering. Decentralized, local solutions—not top-down global mandates—are the key to long-term planetary healing.

- The Illusion of Control vs. The Path to True Regeneration – Humanity has been conditioned to believe that climate change can be "managed" through taxes, policies, and technological fixes. But the real problem is a civilization that is completely disconnected from the intelligence of nature. Until we recognize that Nature—not man—holds the key to planetary balance, no policy or invention will lead to true sustainability.

HEALTHCARE, BIG PHARMA, AND BIG FOOD: THE CHRONIC ILLNESS & MALNUTRITION CARTEL

I. Introduction: The Business of Sickness, Not Health

Modern healthcare is not structured to prioritize healing but rather to sustain a profitable, repeat-business model that thrives on chronic illness and pharmaceutical dependency. Rather than focusing on preventing disease and fostering long-term well-being, the system is designed to manage symptoms, ensuring a steady stream of repeat patients and pharmaceutical consumers. The incentive structures of healthcare institutions, pharmaceutical companies, and insurance providers prioritize financial gains over true wellness.

At its core, Western medicine operates within a reductionist framework—treating the human body as a collection of isolated parts rather than as a holistic, interconnected system. For example, a patient with high blood pressure is typically prescribed medication to lower it, rather than being guided to address potential root causes like stress, poor diet, or hormonal imbalances. This approach leads to a heavy reliance on prescription drugs, invasive procedures, and temporary fixes, rather than addressing the root causes of disease. The result is a society plagued by chronic illness, where dependency on medication is normalized rather than questioned.

The interconnected web of Big Pharma, processed food conglomerates, and industrial agriculture has created a self-perpetuating cycle where nutrient-deficient foods contribute to chronic disease, leading to increased pharmaceutical consumption, while regulatory agencies and corporate interests work to sustain this profitable model. Highly processed foods loaded with refined sugars, seed oils, and synthetic additives fuel metabolic disorders, while toxic agricultural chemicals like glyphosate contribute to systemic inflammation. Pharmaceuticals then mask these symptoms rather than addressing the underlying dietary and environmental imbalances. It is a perfectly engineered cycle of sickness, sustained by policies, corporate interests, and regulatory agencies that serve industry profits rather than human health.

To break free from this paradigm, individuals must reclaim sovereignty over their own well-being by prioritizing whole-food nutrition, adopting preventative health practices, reducing dependency on pharmaceuticals, and seeking out holistic healing modalities. True health is not found in a doctor's office or a prescription bottle—it begins with restoring the body's natural resilience through proper nutrition, regenerative agriculture, and holistic healing practices. Only by rejecting the industrialized medical model and embracing whole-food nutrition, regenerative agriculture, and holistic healing modalities can individuals escape the perpetual cycle of disease management and reclaim true vitality.

II. The Sick Care Model: A System Designed for Dependency

The modern healthcare system is structured not to promote health, but to manage illness in a way that ensures lifelong dependency. A 2017 study published in the Journal of the American Medical Association found that only 3% of healthcare expenditures in the U.S. are allocated toward preventive health measures, underscoring the system's focus on treatment rather than prevention. Rather than seeking to prevent disease and enhance well-being, it operates as a reactive system that focuses on managing symptoms rather than addressing root causes. This approach ensures a continuous stream of patients who require long-term pharmaceutical and medical interventions, creating a profitable cycle of chronic illness.

At the core of this model is a fundamental shift that has taken place over the past century: the corporatization of healthcare. What was once a field dedicated to patient care has been transformed into an industry driven by financial interests, insurance policies, and medical bureaucracy.

- **Healthcare is a trillion-dollar industry**—not because it cures disease, but because it maintains chronic illness. Modern medicine is designed to keep patients in a state of managed sickness, where they require ongoing treatments, medications, and procedures.

- **The elimination of natural remedies**—Traditional healing methods such as homeopathy, herbal medicine, acupuncture, and holistic wellness practices have been systematically marginalized and discredited, not because they are ineffective, but because they do not generate continuous revenue for the medical industry.

- **The suppression of preventative medicine**—Rather than promoting lifestyle changes, proper nutrition, and early intervention, the system teaches doctors to diagnose and prescribe. This ensures that patients remain dependent on medical interventions rather than empowered to prevent disease themselves.

- **The role of medical schools and Big Pharma**—Medical education is largely funded by pharmaceutical companies, ensuring that doctors are trained within a framework that prioritizes pharmaceutical and surgical interventions over holistic healing. This has now creates a several generations of healthcare providers who view medicine through the lens of pharmaceutical dependency rather than prevention and root-cause healing.

- **The corporatization of hospitals and medical practices**—Private equity firms and massive healthcare conglomerates have taken over hospitals, private practices, and specialty clinics, shifting the focus from patient well-being to profit generation. Doctors who once had the autonomy to care for their patients holistically are now constrained by insurance reimbursement policies, corporate cost-cutting, and productivity quotas that force them to see more patients in less time while adhering to rigid, standardized treatment protocols.

- **Insurance companies dictate medicine**—Rather than doctors determining the best course of treatment, Insurance companies dictate medical treatment by determining which procedures, tests, and medications will be reimbursed, often prioritizing cost-effectiveness over patient outcomes. Preauthorization requirements delay or deny necessary treatments, forcing doctors to prescribe medications or interventions that align with insurance policies rather than those best suited for individual patients. Many holistic or alternative therapies, despite proven efficacy, are excluded entirely because they do not generate high-profit margins for the medical-industrial complex.

As a result, modern medicine has moved further away from its true purpose—healing—and has become an industry designed for financial gain. Breaking free from this paradigm requires reclaiming personal health sovereignty and rejecting the dependency model that has been imposed on society. The only path to true well-being is through prevention, holistic healing, and restoring the body's natural balance through regenerative lifestyle choices.

III. Big Pharma: Engineering Lifelong Customers

The pharmaceutical industry is not in the business of curing disease; it is in the business of managing symptoms and creating lifelong customers. For example, rather than funding research into reversing Type 2 diabetes through diet and lifestyle, pharmaceutical companies develop medications that patients must take indefinitely to regulate their blood sugar. Statins prescribed for high cholesterol rarely address the dietary and metabolic causes of the condition, leaving patients on medication indefinitely. Similarly, antidepressants such as SSRIs alter brain chemistry without addressing underlying factors like gut health, trauma, or nutritional deficiencies— leading to long-term dependency rather than true mental health restoration. The more people depend on medications, the more profitable the industry becomes. This is the foundation of the Big Pharma profit model—turning chronic illness into a permanent revenue stream rather than seeking to eliminate it.

- **The profit model of disease** – Chronic conditions like diabetes, heart disease, and autoimmune disorders are rarely cured but instead controlled through expensive prescription drugs. Pharmaceutical companies prioritize treatments that require lifelong adherence rather than those that lead to full recovery.

- **The psychiatric drug racket** – The rise of over-diagnosed and overmedicated mental health disorders has led to a booming psychiatric drug market. Conditions such as ADHD, depression, and anxiety are often misdiagnosed or exaggerated, leading to mass medication that numbs rather than heals. Many of these drugs, such as SSRIs and benzodiazepines, come with severe withdrawal symptoms, further trapping individuals in dependency.

- **The vaccine-industrial complex** – Vaccines have become a primary revenue driver for pharmaceutical companies due to government mandates and legal immunity from liability.

  - **The pediatric vaccine gold rush** – Vaccines now represent the primary profit engine for pediatricians, who receive bonus incentives from insurance providers for high patient compliance with vaccine schedules.

  - **The exponential rise in childhood vaccines** – In the 1960s, children received just 6 vaccine doses. Today, the CDC schedule recommends 72 doses by age 18, despite a lack of long-term studies assessing cumulative effects.

  - **The 1986 National Childhood Vaccine Injury Act** – This act removed pharmaceutical companies' liability for vaccine injuries, creating a massive financial incentive to rapidly develop and deploy new vaccines without adequate safety trials.

- **The COVID-19 Vaccine Debacle** – The COVID-19 vaccines represent one of the most glaring examples of rushed pharmaceutical development and regulatory failure.

  - **Operation Warp Speed and the illusion of rigorous testing** – Traditional vaccine development takes 10-15 years, yet COVID vaccines were produced, tested, and approved in under a year.

  - **Sealed trial data and suppressed transparency** – Pfizer and Moderna attempted to seal trial data for 75 years, raising serious concerns about safety and efficacy but even more so transparency as this undermined independent peer review which is an essential element of true science.

- The shifting narrative on efficacy – Initially marketed as nearly 100% effective, later studies showed the vaccines neither prevented infection nor transmission, yet mandates and coercive policies persisted.

- The rise of vaccine injuries and lack of accountability – Reports of myocarditis, blood clotting disorders, and autoimmune issues have emerged, yet pharmaceutical companies remain shielded from liability.

- Many questions of culpability remain unanswered – According to the VAERS database statistics, the COVID vaccines have more deaths and permanent injuries attributed within a mere three years than all other vaccines combined since the VAERS database started in the early 1960s.

- **The opioid crisis as a case study** – Big Pharma knowingly fueled the opioid epidemic, leading to millions of addictions and deaths. Companies like Purdue Pharma aggressively marketed OxyContin as a "low-risk" painkiller, despite internal knowledge of its highly addictive nature. The opioid crisis demonstrates how profit motives supersede public health concerns in the pharmaceutical industry.

- **The FDA as a captured agency** – Rather than acting as a neutral regulatory body, the Food and Drug Administration (FDA) functions as an extension of Big Pharma.

  - The majority of the FDA's drug approval budget comes from fees paid by pharmaceutical companies.

  - Regulatory agencies have a revolving door with industry executives, ensuring pharmaceutical interests dictate public health policies.

  - Many drugs that later prove dangerous—such as Vioxx—were fast-tracked for approval despite evidence of severe side effects.

Big Pharma thrives on dependency and creating long-term predictable profit streams, with regulatory agencies often complicit in this model. The FDA, for example, receives nearly 45% of its drug approval budget from pharmaceutical industry fees, raising concerns about regulatory capture and conflicts of interest. Chronic illness is extraordinarily profitable; healing is simply not. True health sovereignty requires moving beyond the chemical dependency model imposed by Big Pharma and embracing holistic, regenerative, and preventative approaches to well-being.

IV. The Processed Food and Agricultural Cartel: Manufacturing Sickness

The modern food system is designed for mass production, maximum shelf life, and corporate profit—not human health. The processed food industry, industrial agriculture, and government-backed nutritional guidelines have created a population that is simultaneously overfed and undernourished, leading to an epidemic of obesity, diabetes, cardiovascular disease, autoimmune disorders, and other chronic illnesses.

- **The toxic standard American diet (SAD)** – The standard Western diet is built on highly processed foods, refined sugars, and industrial seed oils, which are linked to inflammation, insulin resistance, and metabolic dysfunction. These foods are cheap to produce, highly addictive, and create a perpetual cycle of cravings and disease.

- **The fast food epidemic** – Fast food has become a cornerstone of many Americans' diets, filled with preservatives, additives, and low-quality ingredients designed for long shelf life rather than nutrition. Morgan Spurlock's famous documentary *Super Size Me* demonstrated how consuming fast food exclusively for a month led to severe declines in liver function, mood swings, fatigue, depression, and weight gain—all symptoms of processed food toxicity.

- **The connection between food and disease** – Chronic conditions such as diabetes, heart disease, cancer, and neurodegenerative disorders are not random occurrences; they are a direct result of decades of malnutrition and exposure to toxic food products. Industrial food processing removes vital nutrients, while artificial additives, preservatives, and synthetic ingredients accumulate in the body, disrupting metabolic function and gut health.

- **The weaponization of nutritional science** – Decades of corporate-funded studies and government dietary recommendations have misled the public about what constitutes a healthy diet. The demonization of saturated fats, the promotion of high-carbohydrate and low-fat diets, and the glorification of synthetic, processed foods have left generations malnourished and sick.

  - **The food pyramid myth** – Originally designed based on agribusiness lobbying rather than science, the traditional food pyramid promoted excessive consumption of grains, processed carbohydrates, and vegetable oils, while downplaying the importance of healthy animal fats and proteins.

  - **The demonization of saturated fats** – Corporate-backed studies falsely linked cholesterol and saturated fats to heart disease, paving the way for industrially processed seed oils and trans fats, which have since been proven far more harmful.

- **Big Ag's role in soil depletion and nutrient loss** - Modern agriculture prioritizes yield and profitability over soil health, leading to widespread depletion of essential minerals, destruction of microbial ecosystems, and loss of soil carbon. This means that even fresh produce today contains a fraction of the nutrients it did just decades ago.

  - **Monoculture farming destroys ecosystems** - Industrial farming strips the soil of biodiversity, requiring more synthetic fertilizers and chemical interventions to sustain production.

  - **Chemical fertilizers and pesticides kill soil health** - Synthetic nitrogen fertilizers, herbicides, and pesticides disrupt the natural microbiome of the soil, reducing its ability to retain nutrients and sequester carbon.

  - **Overwhelming correlation soil and human microbiome** - There's now overwhelming scientific evidence that the health of our soils is directly correlated with human health—when we poison our soils and disrupt its microbiome, we're in effect poisoning ourselves and disrupting our own microbiome.

The food system is not broken—it is functioning exactly as it was intended: to create dependency on industrially produced, nutrient-deficient food that fuels chronic disease, which in turn feeds the pharmaceutical and healthcare industries. For example, the widespread use of high-fructose corn syrup and trans fats in processed foods has been directly linked to obesity, diabetes, and cardiovascular disease, conditions that drive pharmaceutical sales and medical interventions. The only path to true wellness is to reject industrialized food and return to regenerative, whole-food nutrition.

V. The Synthetic Health Illusion: From GMO Foods to Lab-Grown Meat

The biotech industry has expanded into the food system under the guise of sustainability and food security. But instead of promoting natural, regenerative agriculture, these corporations push synthetic, genetically modified, and lab-grown alternatives designed to monopolize food production and increase consumer dependency on industrial food sources.

- **The rise of genetically modified foods (GMOs)** - GMOs have been marketed as the solution to world hunger, yet they have resulted in higher pesticide use, destruction of crop biodiversity, and increasing corporate control over seed patents. Farmers are forced into contracts with companies like Monsanto (now Bayer), which patent their genetically modified seeds, restricting farmers from saving and replanting their own crops.

- GMOs have been directly linked to the depletion of nutrient density and the notion they create "empty calory" food sources which contribute to the obesity and chronic illness epidemic.

- New medical research into the human microbiome and its role in our health is now even postulating the synthetic genetic code of GMOs cannot be "read" by the trillions of microbes that function as the functional intelligence of our intestinal system in filtering out the beneficial nutrients that are to be passed through our single-cell gut wall and the harmful nutrients or poisons that should be excreted.

- **The fallacy of plant-based processed foods** – The explosion of highly processed vegan and plant-based "meat" products has been framed as a move toward sustainability. However, these foods are made from ultra-processed soy, seed oils, and chemical additives, leading to the same health issues as other industrially manufactured food products.

  - Many plant-based alternatives are owned by the same multinational food corporations responsible for decades of health crises.

  - Lab-created protein substitutes often contain synthetic ingredients and genetically engineered compounds that have unknown long-term effects on human health.

- **Lab-grown meat: A manufactured solution to a manufactured problem** – The push for lab-grown meat is driven by billion-dollar investments from corporations and billionaires who seek to control the global protein supply.

  - These synthetic meats require immortalized cell lines, a process that involves cancerous cells, fetal bovine serum, and genetic manipulation– raising major concerns about safety, long-term health effects, and ethical considerations.

  - Lab-grown meat is energy-intensive, requiring vast amounts of resources to produce, making it neither environmentally sustainable nor scalable as a true alternative to regenerative farming.

- **The World Economic Forum's food control agenda** – The same globalist organizations that promote synthetic foods are also working to eliminate traditional farming practices.

- Government-backed campaigns against natural animal agriculture, raw dairy, and small regenerative farms are increasing, with stricter regulations that favor corporate-controlled food production.

- The goal is to create a fully centralized, controlled food supply where consumers have no choice but to eat engineered, mass-produced food substitutes.

- **The attack on natural, whole foods** – Regenerative farmers, small organic producers, and raw dairy advocates are increasingly targeted by government agencies and global regulatory bodies.

  - Despite being consumed for thousands of years, raw milk is demonized, while synthetic, factory-processed dairy replacements are promoted.

  - The push for insect protein – As synthetic meat is marketed as the future of protein, mealworms, crickets, and insect-based food sources are being introduced as a "sustainable" alternative, further shifting food control toward industrialized sources.

  - Many different kinds of bacteria that are known to make people sick have been found in insects including E. coli and Campylobacter. In addition to these bacteria, viruses, parasites, heavy metals, and fungi are also possible forms of biological contamination.

The future of food is being engineered for dependency, not health. If humanity is to restore true health sovereignty, it must reject synthetic food monopolies and return to decentralized, regenerative, and locally sourced nutrition. Without a restoration of our physical health and well-being, there is little hope to escape our psychosis as much of the psychosis has an underpinning in the disruption of our endocrine system which regulates our hormones, which in turn are directly correlated with our clarity of Mind, emotional stability, and mental health.

VI. Restoring True Health Sovereignty

The current healthcare and food systems have been engineered to create dependency, chronic illness, and pharmaceutical reliance. To break free from this medical-industrial complex, humanity must reclaim sovereignty over health, nutrition, and healing. This requires a return to natural medicine, regenerative agriculture, and holistic well-being rather than outsourcing personal health to corporate entities that profit from sickness.

- **Healing is not a business model** – The modern healthcare system operates on profit-driven treatment, not prevention. True health will never come from a system where wellness is not profitable. The fundamental shift must come from empowering individuals with the knowledge and resources to maintain health without pharmaceutical intervention.

- **The return of regenerative food systems** – Industrial agriculture has created nutrient-depleted, chemically altered food that weakens human health. The future of true health lies in regenerative agriculture, which restores soil health, produces nutrient-dense food, and eliminates toxic pesticides and synthetic fertilizers.

  - **Decentralized food networks** – Local farms, community-supported agriculture (CSA), and small-scale regenerative farming must replace the corporate-controlled, genetically modified, and industrially processed food supply.

  - **Nutrient-dense foods as medicine** – Health must return to the kitchen, not the pharmacy—prioritizing organic, pasture-raised, and whole foods rather than lab-created, synthetic substitutes.

- **Decentralizing healthcare and restoring holistic healing** – The reductionist, pharmaceutical-driven model of medicine has disempowered individuals from understanding and managing their own health.

  - **Holistic medicine and alternative healing** – Traditional systems such as Ayurveda, Traditional Chinese Medicine (TCM), naturopathy, and herbalism have been suppressed in favor of synthetic drugs. These ancient systems treat the root causes rather than just masking symptoms.

  - **Reclaiming personal health sovereignty** – Rather than relying on government agencies and corporate interests to dictate health choices, individuals must take ownership over their well-being through informed decision-making, critical thinking, and proactive wellness practices.

  - **Transforming the Western medical school curriculum** – There must be a radical shift from the orientation of treating symptoms of illness to the creation and restoration of health and well-being. Fundamentally, all healthcare should be oriented towards preventing illness in the first place, restoring true health holistically, and a preference of homeopathic medicine and treatment options over synthetic pharmaceutical interventions.

- **The role of the Feminine Principle in medicine** - The modern healthcare system embodies a mechanistic, reductionist, and interventionist approach that prioritizes synthetic treatments over the body's natural regenerative capacity.

  - **True healing is a holistic process** - Ancient healing traditions recognized the connection between body, Mind, and Spirit. Modern medicine must reintegrate compassion, intuition, and holistic wellness, aligning with the Feminine Principle of nurturing and regeneration rather than mechanical symptom suppression.

  - **From dominance to cooperation with nature** - Instead of forcing the body into compliance with drugs, surgery, and artificial interventions, medicine must evolve to work with the body's innate intelligence and self-healing mechanisms.

- **True health is self-governance** - The path forward requires individuals reclaiming their well-being rather than outsourcing it to the medical-industrial complex.

  - **Informed consent and bodily autonomy** - Every individual has the right to understand and choose what they put into their body, whether food, pharmaceuticals, or medical interventions.

  - **Breaking the dependency cycle** - Moving away from chronic reliance on medications, processed foods, and centralized healthcare systems is the only way to restore true health freedom and resilience.

Humanity is at a crossroads: continue down the path of synthetic health, dependency, and disease, or reclaim the wisdom of natural healing, regenerative food, and self-governed health sovereignty. The existing medical-industrial complex cannot be reformed—it must be transcended by those willing to take responsibility for their own well-being and the creation of a whole new reimagined holistic healthcare system.

VII. Conclusion: The Future of Health Lies Outside the System

The modern healthcare and food systems are not designed for human well-being—they are structured for control, dependency, and profit. For decades, the corporate-driven medical-industrial complex has framed health as something to be outsourced to pharmaceutical companies, government agencies, and industrial food conglomerates. This paradigm has led to an epidemic of chronic illness, malnutrition, and reliance on synthetic interventions rather than genuine healing.

But a great awakening is taking place. More people than ever before are beginning to see the failures of mainstream healthcare and industrial food production. They are realizing that true health does not come from a pill, a vaccine, or a highly processed, lab-engineered meal—it comes from nature, sovereignty, and self-responsibility.

- **The rise of holistic healing** - Alternative health practices once dismissed as "pseudoscience" are now gaining widespread recognition. Traditional medicine, herbalism, naturopathy, and regenerative nutrition are being restored as viable paths to wellness.

- **Rejecting corporate control over health** - As trust in pharmaceutical companies, the FDA, and industrial agriculture declines, individuals are taking proactive steps to reclaim their well-being by adopting whole-food nutrition, natural medicine, and regenerative lifestyles.

- **Health sovereignty as a revolutionary act** - In a system built on dependency, the greatest act of defiance is to break free and restore self-sufficiency. True health cannot be dictated by corporate interests or government mandates—it must be cultivated through conscious choices, education, and alignment with nature's intelligence.

The intersection of physical, emotional, mental, and spiritual health is undeniable. Chronic illness is not just a physical condition—it is also a manifestation of a disconnected Mind, a deregulated emotional body, and a suppressed Spirit. True healing must address all aspects of human well-being, not just treat symptoms with synthetic chemicals.

As we close this chapter, the question becomes: Who benefits from keeping humanity sick, weak, and dependent? The next chapter explores how the same corporate forces that control healthcare and food also shape governments, economies, and societies— engineering human behavior for their own benefit. The failure of modern healthcare is not an isolated problem; it is part of a much larger web of political and social engineering designed to maintain control through dependency. Breaking free requires a radical shift in mindset—one that rejects blind faith in corporate-controlled medicine and embraces personal responsibility for health. This means supporting regenerative agriculture, prioritizing whole-food nutrition, seeking alternative healing modalities, and demanding transparency and accountability from medical institutions. The choice is clear: remain a passive participant in a system designed for control, or reclaim health sovereignty through informed, conscious action.

In every Crucible, there's a choice that must be made.

HEALTHCARE, BIG PHARMA, AND BIG FOOD: THE CHRONIC ILLNESS & MALNUTRITION CARTEL

EXECUTIVE SUMMARY

Why Should You Read This Chapter?

The modern healthcare system is not designed to make people well—it is structured to keep them sick, dependent, and profitable for the pharmaceutical, agricultural, and medical industries. From the rise of chronic illness to the infiltration of processed, nutrient-deficient foods, this chapter exposes how the business of medicine and food is engineered to sustain disease, not health.

You will learn how Big Pharma profits from managing symptoms rather than curing diseases, why the industrial food system has been designed to create malnourished yet overfed populations, and how modern medicine has become a corporate-driven model of intervention rather than prevention. Most importantly, this chapter will illuminate how true health sovereignty is possible—not through government policies or pharmaceutical interventions, but by reclaiming autonomy over food, medicine, and well-being.

If you have ever questioned why society is growing sicker despite advancements in medicine, or why billions of dollars are spent on "healthcare" while chronic illness skyrockets, this chapter will provide the missing pieces of the puzzle. The key to true health and freedom is not found within the system—it lies in stepping outside of it and returning to the intelligence of Nature.

Executive Summary: Key Takeaways

- **The modern healthcare system is structured as a business, not a healing system.** It prioritizes profit over wellness, ensuring that chronic illness remains a permanent revenue stream.

- **Big Pharma profits from managing symptoms rather than curing diseases.** Pharmaceutical companies design medications that require lifelong use, keeping people trapped in a cycle of dependency.

- **The vaccine industry operates as a protected profit machine.** Since the 1986 National Childhood Vaccine Injury Act removed liability from manufacturers, the number of recommended childhood vaccines has skyrocketed from 6 in the 1960s to 72 today.

- **The COVID-19 vaccine rollout exemplified regulatory failure and corporate profiteering.** Rushed approvals, hidden trial data, and shifting narratives on efficacy and safety raised unprecedented concerns about public health decision-making.

- **The processed food industry is engineered to create sickness.** Industrialized food is devoid of nutrients and filled with harmful additives, leading to obesity, diabetes, cardiovascular disease, and autoimmune disorders.

- **The connection between food and health has been deliberately obscured.** Government-backed nutritional guidelines, corporate-funded studies, and processed food marketing have misled the public into consuming diets that fuel chronic disease.

- **The agricultural system has been hijacked by corporate interests.** Industrial farming depletes soil health, destroys biodiversity, and contaminates food with synthetic fertilizers, pesticides, and GMOs.

- **GMOs have fundamentally altered food quality.** They not only increase dependence on corporate-controlled seed patents but also degrade the nutrient density of food, leading to the rise of "empty calorie" consumption.

- **Lab-grown meat and synthetic food are the next frontiers of food control.** Backed by billionaires and corporations, these products are designed to monopolize food production, not to promote human health.

- **The Feminine Principle must be restored to medicine and food.** True healing requires nurturing, regeneration, and working with nature rather than dominating and exploiting it.

- **Health sovereignty is the only path forward.** Breaking free from pharmaceutical and industrial food dependency requires a return to natural medicine, regenerative agriculture, and conscious self-care.

- **The intersection of physical, mental, and spiritual health is undeniable.** True wellness is multidimensional and cannot be reduced to pharmaceuticals or medical interventions alone.

- **The next chapter will expose how the same corporate interests controlling health also engineer political and social structures.** The web of political and social engineering extends far beyond healthcare, influencing every aspect of modern society.

·

THE FAILURE AND INSIDIOUS NATURE OF POLITICAL & SOCIAL ENGINEERING

I. Introduction: The Illusion of Governance in a Controlled System

Governance, as it exists today, is not what it appears to be—instead, it is a carefully curated illusion. The notion that elected officials truly represent the will of the people is a mirage perpetuated to maintain social order while shielding the reality of centralized control. Governments no longer serve the people—they serve the financial and corporate entities that dictate global policy behind closed doors. The ideological battle between political parties is a well-orchestrated performance, carefully scripted to pacify the masses while preserving the illusion of democracy.

The Illusion of Democracy: Elections as Theater

Modern electoral systems function within tightly and covertly controlled boundaries, ensuring that regardless of the outcome, real power remains in the hands of the ruling class. While citizens are encouraged to vote, the candidates and policies available to them are carefully selected by powerful lobbying groups, corporate donors, and media conglomerates that shape public opinion.

- **Two-Party Monopoly:** In many so-called democratic nations, such as the United States, the political landscape is dominated by two primary parties that ultimately serve the same economic interests. Both sides engage in performative opposition, but when it comes to issues such as foreign policy, corporate bailouts, and mass surveillance, they act in lockstep.

- **Corporate and Financial Influence:** The political system is bankrolled by billionaire donors, multinational corporations, and global financial institutions—not out of altruism, but as a strategic investment. Their return comes in the form of favorable legislation, regulatory loopholes, and economic policies that prioritize their interests over the public good.

- **Mainstream Media as a Propaganda Arm:** Corporate media does not challenge corruption—it upholds it. Instead of investigative scrutiny, it perpetuates the system's legitimacy by amplifying trivial debates, sensationalizing scandals, and presenting political theater as governance.

The Real Divide: The Governed vs. The Controllers

While the masses are conditioned to believe in the left vs. right political divide, the actual power dynamic is between the ruling elite and the governed population. The governing class—comprising ultra-wealthy donors, politicians, bureaucrats, corporate executives, media moguls, and technocratic decision-makers—exerts control over public perception, economic conditions, and legislative frameworks to serve their own interests. The general population is kept in a state of division, ensuring that they remain too distracted to challenge the real power structures.

- **Political Puppetry:** Leaders are often handpicked long before elections, groomed by think tanks and globalist organizations such as the World Economic Forum, the Council on Foreign Relations, and the Bilderberg Group.

- **Controlled Dissent:** Even opposition movements are frequently co-opted to provide an illusion of resistance while maintaining the integrity of the system.

- **Endless Distractions:** Manufactured social issues, outrage cycles, and crises are strategically introduced to keep the public emotionally invested in the political spectacle rather than recognizing the overarching deception.

The modern political system is not designed for self-governance—it is structured to maintain dependency. Centralized institutions create the illusion of choice while ensuring that all major political outcomes align with the interests of those in power. Laws, policies, and economic measures are dictated by a web of unelected technocrats, corporate boards, and international financial institutions.

- **Regulatory Capture:** The very agencies tasked with oversight—such as the FDA, SEC, and EPA—are frequently staffed by former executives from the industries they claim to regulate, ensuring policies serve corporate interests rather than the public good.

- **The Watershed Supreme Court Ruling: Citizens United** - The 2010 Supreme Court decision in *Citizens United v. Federal Election Commission* effectively removed all barriers to corporate and wealthy donor influence over the political system by eliminating limits on independent political expenditures. By equating corporate financial contributions to free speech, this ruling legalized unlimited political spending through Super PACs and dark money networks—effectively auctioning elections to the highest bidder. As a result, elections became for sale where the highest bidders could drown out the voices of ordinary citizens, further entrenching the interests of powerful elites while masquerading as democratic participation.

- **International Governance:** Organizations such as the International Monetary Fund (IMF) and the World Bank dictate economic policies that override national sovereignty under the guise of financial stability.

- **The Surveillance State:** The expanding power of intelligence agencies, data collection firms, and digital tracking technologies ensures that governments maintain near-total visibility over their populations, solidifying their control over dissent and social movements.

Conclusion: Awakening to the Reality of Control

The first step toward reclaiming true sovereignty is recognizing that the governance structures in place are not designed to serve the people but to preserve and expand the power of a global ruling elite. By shifting the focus away from the carefully manufactured political theater and toward the mechanisms of real control, individuals can begin to understand the true nature of the system. Only through this awareness can we begin dismantling these structures and start cultivating transparent, representative, citizen-centric systems of governance based on distributed powers that prioritize sovereignty over subjugation and human autonomy over centralized authority.

Recognizing the system for what it truly is represents a profound loss of innocence. Many cling to the romanticized belief that governments exist to serve the people, unaware that these ideals function more as rhetoric than reality. Abraham Lincoln's famous words from the Gettysburg Address in 1863, stating that government is "of the people, by the people, for the people," have been so deeply ingrained in the collective psyche that most assume they are enshrined in the U.S. Constitution. Yet, these words are nowhere to be found in the Constitution; they exist only in Lincoln's address. This revelation underscores how powerful narratives shape perception and how deeply ingrained myths about governance must be reevaluated. Recognizing this Truth is not an exercise in cynicism but rather an essential step toward breaking free from illusions and reclaiming genuine self-governance.

II. The Manufactured Political Divide: Keeping the Masses Distracted

In modern society, political division is not an organic byproduct of differing ideologies but a deliberately manufactured construct designed to keep populations distracted and in conflict with one another. The illusion of choice in democratic systems serves to maintain control while fostering an environment of perpetual discord. This carefully orchestrated division ensures that the masses remain preoccupied with superficial battles rather than addressing the fundamental power structures that govern them.

Left vs. Right: A False Dichotomy

One of the most effective tools of social engineering is the artificial division between left and right political ideologies. This construct forces individuals into ideological camps, making them believe they must choose a side while failing to see that both sides ultimately serve the same ruling interests.

- **Two Parties, One Agenda:** In nations such as the United States, the Democratic and Republican parties present themselves as ideological opposites. However, both are funded by the same corporate interests, influenced by the same think tanks, and committed to the same overarching globalist policies. While they may differ on social issues, their economic and foreign policies often align to preserve the existing power structure.

- **Theatrical Opposition:** Politicians engage in highly publicized battles over hot-button issues such as immigration, gun control, and social justice while quietly collaborating behind closed doors on matters that truly impact the balance of power, such as military expansion, surveillance, and economic deregulation.

- **Controlled Opposition:** Even grassroots movements and third-party candidates that appear to challenge the status quo are often absorbed, diluted, or neutralized before they can pose a genuine threat to the system.

How Social Issues Are Weaponized

Beyond maintaining a two-party illusion, the ruling elite actively weaponize social issues to keep the public emotionally invested in political theater rather than questioning systemic corruption.

- **Emotional Manipulation:** Topics such as race, gender, abortion, and LGBTQ+ rights are frequently used to divide people along ideological lines. While these issues are important, their true purpose within political discourse is often to inflame division and rally voters rather than to achieve genuine solutions.

- **Media Amplification:** Corporate media outlets selectively highlight specific narratives that deepen political divides, reinforcing echo chambers where individuals only consume information that aligns with their existing beliefs.

- **Crisis Manufacturing:** Events such as riots, protests, and mass shootings are often exploited—if not outright engineered—to stoke societal tensions, creating the illusion of widespread civil unrest that necessitates greater government control.

Identity Politics and the Divide-and-Conquer Strategy

Identity politics has become a primary tool for fragmenting society. By encouraging people to define themselves primarily by race, gender, sexuality, or other immutable characteristics, the ruling elite successfully prevent unity among the masses.

- **Fragmentation of Society:** When individuals prioritize group identity over shared interests, they become more susceptible to external manipulation and less likely to unite against the true sources of oppression.

- **False Narratives of Oppression:** While real injustices exist, many are exaggerated or selectively highlighted to drive a wedge between groups, making solidarity nearly impossible.

- **The Hijacking of Social Movements:** Genuine grassroots movements, from civil rights to labor unions, are often co-opted and redirected to serve the interests of elites rather than those of the people.

The Perpetual Political Circus: Outrage Cycles and Controlled Narratives

The political landscape is intentionally structured to keep the public in a constant state of reactionary outrage. This cycle prevents deep, critical thinking and ensures that people remain emotionally engaged with the system, believing that they can enact meaningful change through the next election cycle.

- **Scandal-Driven Politics:** Each election season brings a new wave of scandals, investigations, and controversies designed to distract the public from long-standing systemic issues.

- **Short-Term Focus:** Politicians and the media direct public attention toward fleeting, high-emotion issues rather than addressing long-term structural problems such as wealth inequality, corporate monopolization, and perpetual warfare.

- **Manufactured Heroes and Villains:** Political figures are presented as either saviors or existential threats, ensuring that voters remain emotionally invested in supporting or opposing them rather than questioning the legitimacy of the system itself.

Social Media as the Amplifier of Division

Social media platforms play a crucial role in reinforcing and accelerating political division. Algorithms prioritize sensationalist and polarizing content, ensuring that users remain addicted to political outrage.

- **Echo Chambers and Radicalization:** Individuals are funneled into ideological bubbles where they only engage with like-minded individuals, deepening polarization and making productive discourse nearly impossible.

- **Censorship and Narrative Control:** Tech giants actively suppress dissenting viewpoints that challenge mainstream political narratives while promoting state-approved messaging.

- **The Weaponization of Misinformation:** Both mainstream and alternative media sources exploit the digital landscape to spread half-Truths, disinformation, and emotionally charged content that fuels division and paranoia.

Conclusion: Breaking Free from the Political Illusion

Understanding that the political divide is a manufactured construct is the first step toward transcending its control. The ruling elite have no interest in solving society's greatest problems because their power is dependent on keeping the masses divided and distracted.

- **Reclaiming Independent Thought:** Individuals must detach from partisan identities and evaluate political narratives with skepticism.

- **Focusing on Shared Interests:** Issues such as economic freedom, corporate corruption, and personal sovereignty transcend party lines and should be prioritized over ideological battles.

- **Recognizing the True Power Structure:** Instead of engaging in the false dichotomy of left vs. right, people must acknowledge the broader framework of control and work towards decentralizing power.

By breaking free from the illusion of political division, individuals can reclaim sovereignty over their own beliefs, decisions, and actions. Only then can meaningful change begin to take shape outside the carefully controlled structures of political theater.

III. The Deep State and the Hidden Hand of Control

Throughout modern history, governments have projected an image of public accountability, democratic integrity, and institutional transparency. However, beneath the surface exists a shadowy network of unelected power brokers—an entity often referred to as the Deep State. This network comprises intelligence agencies, military contractors, multinational corporations, think tanks, globalist organizations, and high-level bureaucrats who collectively steer policy beyond the reach of electoral oversight. The Deep State functions as the true mechanism of governance, ensuring continuity of power regardless of who holds public office.

The Revolving Door Between Government, Corporations, and Think Tanks

One of the defining characteristics of the Deep State is the seamless movement of individuals between the highest levels of government, multinational corporations, and influential think tanks. This system ensures that the same interests remain in control, regardless of which party or political figure is in office.

- **Corporate-Government Symbiosis:** High-ranking officials frequently move between roles in government agencies, financial institutions, and multinational corporations. Former defense secretaries take positions on the boards of weapons manufacturers, ex-Wall Street executives dictate economic policy, and pharmaceutical lobbyists transition into regulatory agencies meant to oversee the very industry they once represented.

- **Think Tanks as Policy Architects:** Organizations such as the Council on Foreign Relations (CFR), the Trilateral Commission, and the World Economic Forum (WEF) play an outsized role in shaping global policies. These entities bring together politicians, CEOs, military generals, and media elites to ensure policy alignment across nations, often without public scrutiny or accountability.

- **The Undemocratic Nature of Bureaucracies:** Government agencies, particularly those related to national security and finance, operate with little oversight. Institutions such as the Federal Reserve, the CIA, the FBI, and the NSA wield immense power without being directly answerable to voters. Their continuity ensures that fundamental policies remain unchanged, no matter who is elected to office.

How Intelligence Agencies Manipulate Policy, Public Perception, and Global Events

The intelligence apparatus serves as a key instrument of the Deep State, influencing both domestic and international affairs while shielding its actions under the guise of national security.

- **Surveillance and Data Collection:** Intelligence agencies such as the NSA, CIA, and MI6 conduct mass surveillance on both domestic and foreign populations, harvesting vast amounts of data to monitor dissent and predict social movements.

- **Regime Change and Foreign Interventions:** The Deep State has a long history of orchestrating coups, backing opposition movements, and manipulating elections to install leaders that serve Western geopolitical and economic interests. Examples include CIA-backed coups in Iran (1953), Chile (1973), and Ukraine (2014).

- **Media Manipulation and Psychological Operations:** Agencies such as the CIA have infiltrated media organizations through programs like Operation Mockingbird, ensuring that mainstream narratives align with governmental and corporate interests. Disinformation campaigns, controlled opposition, and smear tactics are routinely employed to discredit dissenting voices.

The Role of Globalist Organizations in Shaping Policy Beyond National Governments

Many of the most consequential policies implemented by national governments do not originate from elected representatives but from unelected global institutions that exert influence over sovereign nations.

- **The World Economic Forum (WEF):** This organization, composed of corporate and political elites, promotes global policies on economics, digital identity, and social governance. Under the banner of the "Great Reset," the WEF has advocated for drastic shifts in economic structures, wealth redistribution, and increased reliance on artificial intelligence and automation.

- **The International Monetary Fund (IMF) and World Bank:** These financial institutions impose economic conditions on indebted nations, often forcing austerity measures, privatization of national resources, and economic policies that serve the interests of multinational corporations rather than the populations they affect.

- **The United Nations and WHO:** While often presented as humanitarian organizations, these institutions have been used to set international policies that override national sovereignty, from pandemic responses to climate regulations that consolidate power within centralized governing bodies.

Silencing Dissent: How Whistleblowers and Journalists Are Suppressed

Those who expose the corruption and inner workings of the Deep State often face severe repercussions, as the system has developed numerous mechanisms to silence dissent and control information.

- **Whistleblower Persecution:** Figures such as Edward Snowden, Julian Assange, and Chelsea Manning revealed how intelligence agencies spy on citizens and manipulate global events. Instead of being protected under whistleblower laws, they were branded as criminals and forced into exile or imprisonment.

- **Corporate Media Censorship:** Media conglomerates, often beholden to the same corporate and governmental interests they report on, routinely bury stories that challenge the narrative of the Deep State. Alternative voices are marginalized, de-platformed, or smeared as conspiracy theorists.

- **Big Tech's Role in Information Control:** Social media giants collaborate with intelligence agencies to suppress dissenting views, using algorithmic suppression, content moderation, and outright bans to stifle opposition and maintain a tightly controlled narrative.

The Deep State's Influence on Global Conflicts, Financial Crashes, and Social Movements

A core function of the Deep State is engineering crises that consolidate power, justify policy shifts, and maintain the structures of global control.

- **Perpetual War as a Business Model:** The military-industrial complex relies on endless wars to sustain profitability. Conflicts are often prolonged or manufactured under the guise of national security, ensuring continued weapons sales, military contracts, and government funding.

- **Financial Manipulation and Economic Control:** The Deep State plays a direct role in orchestrating financial crashes that facilitate wealth consolidation. The 2008 financial crisis, for example, resulted in massive bailouts for banks while average citizens suffered from job losses, foreclosures, and austerity measures.

- **Social Engineering Through Crisis Exploitation:** Whether through pandemics, climate emergencies, or civil unrest, the Deep State utilizes crises to introduce new laws, surveillance measures, and economic shifts that further entrench their power.

- **Patriot Act** - In the aftermath of the 9/11 attacks, the Patriot Act was rushed through Congress with little debate, dramatically expanding the surveillance powers of the U.S. government. Under the guise of national security, this legislation stripped away key privacy protections, allowing intelligence agencies unprecedented authority to monitor phone calls, emails, financial transactions, and personal records without a warrant. The act also weakened due process by enabling indefinite detention of suspects and secret court proceedings through the Foreign Intelligence Surveillance Court (FISA). Far from being a temporary measure, the Patriot Act set the precedent for a vast surveillance apparatus that continues to erode civil liberties, normalizing government overreach and the mass collection of data on ordinary citizens.

Conclusion: Recognizing and Resisting the Hidden Power Structure

The Deep State is not a myth but a deeply entrenched system that operates beyond the boundaries of electoral politics. While it may not be possible to dismantle it overnight, the first step is widespread awareness and acknowledgment of its existence.

- **Decentralization as the Path Forward:** Moving away from centralized governance and fostering local, self-sufficient communities can minimize the influence of the Deep State.

- **Independent Media and Critical Thinking:** Supporting alternative news sources, whistleblowers, and open discourse is essential to counteract the controlled narratives of mainstream media.

- **Personal Sovereignty and Resilience:** Ultimately, resisting the Deep State requires individuals to become less dependent on government-controlled systems, fostering economic and intellectual independence.

By understanding the true mechanisms of power and rejecting the illusion of democratic control, people can take meaningful steps toward reclaiming autonomy and charting a course toward genuine self-governance.

IV. Endless Wars and Geopolitical Conflict: The Military-Industrial Complex at Work

War is not an unfortunate consequence of geopolitical tensions—it is a deliberate and profitable enterprise that sustains an entire economic and political ecosystem. The military-industrial complex thrives on perpetual conflict, ensuring that war remains a constant fixture in global affairs. The financial and political elites who benefit from war have little incentive to pursue peace when conflict drives profits, expands influence, and justifies ever-growing government power.

How Perpetual War is a Feature, Not a Flaw, of the System

Contrary to the conventional view that wars are fought solely for national security or ideological differences, many conflicts are strategically prolonged or deliberately ignited to serve entrenched interests. The economic and political machinery behind warfare ensures that peace remains elusive.

- **The War Economy:** Defense spending constitutes a significant portion of national budgets, particularly in the United States. Billions of taxpayer dollars flow into defense contracts, fueling a self-sustaining war economy.

- **The Illusion of Peacemaking:** Even diplomatic efforts often serve as mechanisms to justify further militarization. Negotiations are used to set the stage for future conflicts rather than to achieve lasting resolutions.

- **Political Expediency:** Leaders frequently use war as a political tool to distract from domestic crises, unify a divided electorate under a common enemy, or justify authoritarian measures under the guise of national security.

The Military-Industrial Complex: Profiting from Endless War

The term "military-industrial complex" was first popularized by President Dwight D. Eisenhower in his 1961 farewell address, warning of an entrenched system where defense contractors, lobbyists, and politicians form a symbiotic relationship that prioritizes war over peace.

- **Defense Contractors and Arms Manufacturers:** Companies such as Lockheed Martin, Boeing, and Raytheon rake in billions from government contracts, ensuring a constant demand for weapons, aircraft, and military technology.

- **Private Military Firms and Mercenaries:** The rise of private military companies (PMCs) like Blackwater (now Academi) and Wagner Group has privatized warfare, allowing governments to engage in conflicts with minimal public scrutiny.

- **Revolving Door Politics:** High-ranking military officials and government leaders frequently transition into lucrative positions within defense corporations, ensuring continuous advocacy for militarization.

False Flags and Manufactured Enemies: The Justification for Military Expansion

Governments have historically used false flag operations—events staged or manipulated to frame an enemy—as a means to justify war.

- **Historical Precedents:** The Gulf of Tonkin incident (1964) was used to escalate the Vietnam War, despite later revelations that the attack may have been misrepresented or fabricated.

- **Weapons of Mass Destruction (WMD) Narrative:** The 2003 Iraq War was largely justified by claims that Saddam Hussein possessed WMDs, a claim that was later proven false but successfully rallied public support for invasion.

- **The War on Terror:** Following 9/11, sweeping military campaigns were launched across the Middle East, creating prolonged instability and lucrative opportunities for defense industries.

The Role of the U.S. in Global Interventions: Spreading "Democracy" or Expanding Dominance?

The United States, under the pretext of promoting democracy and human rights, has engaged in numerous interventions that serve broader economic and geopolitical interests.

- **Regime Change Operations:** The CIA and other U.S. agencies have played a role in toppling governments unfavorable to Western corporate and financial interests, such as Iran (1953), Chile (1973), and Libya (2011).

- **Geopolitical Control:** Military bases span across the globe, ensuring U.S. dominance in strategic regions and safeguarding resource access, trade routes, and economic leverage.

- **Selective Humanitarianism:** While interventions are framed as efforts to stop human rights abuses, military action is often absent when no strategic interests are at stake (e.g., conflicts in Central Africa and Myanmar).

How War Distracts Populations While Enriching the Ruling Class

War serves not only as a tool for financial profit but also as a mechanism of societal control.

- **Fear-Based Compliance:** Governments exploit war to introduce policies that limit civil liberties, expand surveillance, and justify state overreach.

- **Media Manipulation:** Corporate media outlets amplify pro-war narratives while suppressing anti-war dissent, ensuring public support remains strong.

- **Economic Wealth Transfer:** While the average citizen bears the costs of war through taxes and inflation, the financial elite continue to profit from government contracts, resource plundering, and economic restructuring in war-torn regions.

Conclusion: Ending the Cycle of Manufactured Wars

To break free from the cycle of endless war, a radical shift in public consciousness is required. The military-industrial complex operates under the assumption that the public will remain passive and uninformed about its true motives.

- **Challenging the War Narrative:** Recognizing the patterns of manufactured conflict and questioning mainstream media narratives can weaken the justification for interventionist policies.

- **Ending Corporate Influence in Government:** Reducing the power of defense lobbyists and enforcing strict regulations on the military-industrial complex can limit the incentives for war.

- **Investing in Peace-Building Alternatives:** Shifting resources from militarization to diplomacy, economic cooperation, and conflict prevention would create a more stable and prosperous world.

By exposing the mechanisms behind perpetual war and refusing to participate in its narrative, individuals and societies can begin dismantling the war economy and reclaiming their agency over geopolitical affairs.

V. The Weaponization of Crises: Engineering Consent for Control

Crises—whether real, exaggerated, or manufactured—have long served as a powerful tool for governments and elites to expand control over populations. By leveraging fear, uncertainty, and chaos, authorities justify sweeping changes to laws, policies, and societal norms that would otherwise be met with resistance. Throughout history, crises have been used as a means to increase surveillance, curtail civil liberties, centralize power, and push forward agendas that benefit a select few while diminishing the freedoms of the many.

The "Problem-Reaction-Solution" Cycle: How Governments Manufacture Consent

One of the most effective strategies used by ruling elites is the "Problem-Reaction-Solution" model, which operates as follows:

- **Problem:** A crisis emerges, whether organically, through negligence, or as a result of deliberate orchestration.

- **Reaction:** The public, driven by fear and uncertainty, demands swift action and solutions from the government.

- **Solution:** Authorities implement sweeping measures—often pre-planned—that expand state power, restrict freedoms, and consolidate control.

By framing their responses as necessary for security, stability, or the greater good, governments are able to normalize policies that would have been unthinkable under ordinary circumstances.

The Role of Fear in Shaping Public Compliance

Fear is the most effective psychological tool for mass control. When individuals perceive a direct threat to their safety—whether from terrorism, disease, economic collapse, or climate catastrophe—they are far more likely to accept draconian measures in exchange for a false sense of security.

- **Terrorism as a Justification for Surveillance:** After 9/11, governments worldwide introduced extensive surveillance programs, most notably through the Patriot Act, which permitted warrantless wiretaps, indefinite detention, and the bulk collection of personal data.

- **Public Health Crises and Biosecurity Measures:** The COVID-19 pandemic saw the normalization of lockdowns, digital tracking, vaccine mandates, and restrictions on movement—policies that once seemed inconceivable but were rapidly accepted under the pretext of public health.

- **Financial Crises and Economic Restructuring:** Recessions and stock market crashes have historically been used to justify massive bailouts for corporations and banks, while the working class absorbs the financial burden through austerity measures and increased taxation.

Emergency Powers as Permanent Governance

A recurring pattern in crisis response is the implementation of "temporary" emergency powers that, rather than being rescinded once the crisis subsides, become a permanent feature of governance.

- **The War on Terror:** Initially framed as a response to 9/11, the global war on terror evolved into an indefinite justification for mass surveillance, preemptive wars, and extraordinary rendition programs.

- **The Expansion of Police Powers:** Crises such as riots, mass shootings, and civil unrest have been used to militarize police forces, increase government surveillance, and introduce broad counterterrorism measures that often target dissenters rather than actual threats.

- **Digital IDs and Social Credit Systems:** Under the guise of security and efficiency, governments push for centralized digital identities and tracking systems that make individual freedoms contingent on compliance with state directives.

The Climate Change Agenda: Environmentalism or Power Consolidation?

While environmental concerns are real, the narrative around climate change has been increasingly leveraged as a tool for control.

- **Carbon Taxes and Economic Control:** The push for carbon taxes and emissions restrictions is often framed as a necessary step for the planet, yet it disproportionately impacts small businesses and individuals while allowing corporations to continue polluting through carbon offset schemes.

- **The "Great Reset" and Green Policies:** Global institutions such as the World Economic Forum have openly advocated for radical economic transformations under the banner of sustainability, promoting ideas such as "you will own nothing and be happy."

- **Climate Lockdowns and Mobility Restrictions:** Proposals for climate-related restrictions on transportation, energy consumption, and food production are already being discussed as potential emergency measures to combat global warming.

Digital IDs, Central Bank Digital Currencies (CBDCs), and the Future of Control

The increasing digitization of identity, finance, and commerce presents new avenues for control under the pretext of security and economic stability.

- **The End of Cash:** Governments are pushing for the elimination of physical currency in favor of digital currencies controlled by central banks. This shift would grant authorities complete oversight over individual transactions and the ability to restrict spending on non-compliant individuals.

- **Programmable Money:** Unlike traditional currency, CBDCs can be programmed with expiration dates, spending restrictions, and behavioral incentives—allowing governments to dictate how and when people use their own money.

- **Integration with Social Credit Systems:** In countries like China, digital payment systems are already linked to social credit scores, determining an individual's ability to travel, purchase goods, or access services based on their compliance with government mandates.

Conclusion: Recognizing and Resisting the Weaponization of Crises

Understanding the pattern of crisis exploitation is the first step in resisting its effects. Every crisis presents an opportunity for power consolidation, but awareness of these tactics allows individuals to critically evaluate proposed solutions before surrendering their freedoms.

- **Demanding Accountability:** Governments must be held accountable for the policies they enact under emergency conditions, with clear sunset clauses to prevent indefinite overreach.

- **Decentralization as a Safeguard:** The more localized and self-sufficient communities become, the less dependent they are on centralized systems that exploit crises for control.

- **Maintaining Critical Thinking:** Instead of reacting emotionally to crises, individuals should analyze the long-term consequences of proposed solutions and consider who truly benefits from them.

- **Level of Consciousness:** While technologies such as Central Bank Digital Currencies (CBDCs) and digital tracking systems are not inherently malevolent, their implementation is heavily influenced by the collective level of consciousness of society. At lower levels of awareness—where fear, control, and manipulation dominate—these tools are often misused to centralize power and suppress individual freedoms. However, in a society guided by higher-order intelligence, ethical governance, and spiritual maturity, these innovations could be harnessed for the greater good, enhancing transparency, efficiency, and equitable resource distribution. The key distinction lies not in the technology itself but in the consciousness of those wielding it.

By recognizing these patterns and refusing to be manipulated by fear, individuals can begin to reclaim their sovereignty and resist the creeping encroachment of authoritarian governance.

VI. The Social Engineering of Humanity: Control Through Culture

The most effective form of control is not brute force—it is the ability to shape perception, belief systems, and social norms. When engineered correctly, people do not need to be forced into compliance; they willingly accept and even defend the narratives that govern their lives. Through media, entertainment, education, and cultural shifts, the ruling elite have orchestrated a slow but deliberate transformation of human society to make populations more passive, obedient, and dependent on centralized authority.

How Media, Entertainment, and Education Mold Public Perception and Behavior

Modern media, entertainment, and education systems are not designed to inform, enlighten, or empower individuals. Instead, they serve as mechanisms for conditioning mass behavior and reinforcing controlled narratives.

- **News as a Propaganda Tool:** Corporate-controlled media dictates the scope of public discourse. What is reported, how it is framed, and what is omitted altogether serves the interests of those in power.

- **Hollywood and Predictive Programming:** Movies and TV shows introduce and normalize ideas long before they are implemented in reality. Science fiction dystopias, once seen as warnings, now function as blueprints for governance.

- **The Education System as Indoctrination:** Schools no longer teach independent thought but enforce ideological compliance. Critical thinking, logic, and deep inquiry are replaced with rote memorization of state-approved narratives.

The Destruction of Traditional Values and the Rise of State-Engineered Morality

For a population to be fully controlled, its moral compass must be dictated by external forces rather than innate human principles.

- **The Attack on Faith and Spirituality:** Organized religion and personal spirituality have historically provided moral grounding and resistance to tyranny. The erosion of these institutions creates moral relativism, where values can be dictated by the state.

- **The Redefinition of Ethics:** Right and wrong are no longer based on universal moral principles but are dictated by shifting cultural trends designed to suit the needs of the ruling elite.

- **The Breakdown of Intergenerational Wisdom:** Older generations, once revered for their knowledge and Life experience, are dismissed as outdated, creating a society disconnected from its historical roots.

The Deliberate Weakening of Critical Thinking—Education as Indoctrination, Not Empowerment

An informed and intellectually empowered population poses a threat to centralized control. The modern education system ensures this never happens.

- **The Rise of Emotional Thinking Over Rational Analysis:** People are trained to react emotionally rather than think critically. This makes them more susceptible to manipulation and social engineering.

- **The Marginalization of Classical Education:** Studies in philosophy, logic, and rhetoric have been replaced with curricula that prioritize ideological conformity over intellectual rigor.

- **The Cult of Experts:** People are conditioned to trust authority figures, media personalities, and self-appointed "experts" without questioning their motives or biases.

The War on Masculinity, Femininity, and the Nuclear Family

Strong families, defined roles, and natural gender dynamics provide stability and resilience. The ruling elite seeks to dissolve these structures, making individuals more reliant on the state.

- **The Demonization of Masculinity:** Strength, leadership, and assertiveness—historically male virtues—are now framed as toxic traits to weaken natural male leadership and protection instincts.

- **The Rewriting of Femininity:** Nurturing, motherhood, and family-building have been replaced with hyper-independence and state dependency, eroding women's traditional societal roles.

- **The Dissolution of the Family Unit:** A strong nuclear family serves as a buffer against state overreach. By normalizing fragmented families, single parenthood, and detachment from ancestral lineage, populations become easier to manipulate and control.

Social Credit Systems, Cancel Culture, and Corporate Censorship—How Dissent is Punished and Compliance Rewarded

The emergence of digital surveillance, social credit scores, and online censorship serves as the enforcement arm of cultural control.

- **The Expansion of Surveillance:** Social media activity, personal opinions, and associations are now monitored, cataloged, and used to determine access to financial services, travel, and employment.

- **Cancel Culture as a Modern Inquisition:** Those who deviate from the state-approved narrative are systematically vilified, ostracized, and deplatformed, creating an environment of self-censorship.

- **Corporate Censorship as a Proxy for Government Control:** Technology companies increasingly enforce policies that align with state interests, eliminating opposition under the guise of "combating misinformation."

How Wars, Violence, Gore, and the Bizarre Are Woven Into Hollywood, TV, Video Games, and Music to Normalize These Elements Through Subliminal Programming

One of the most insidious aspects of cultural programming is the deliberate desensitization of humanity to violence, depravity, and chaos.

- **Hyper-Violence in Entertainment:** Movies, video games, and music increasingly glorify violence, war, and brutality, conditioning younger generations to accept these as normal parts of Life.

- **The Fetishization of the Bizarre:** Absurdity, grotesqueness, and moral degeneracy are celebrated in media, creating a nihilistic culture where nothing is sacred and everything is permissible.

- **Subliminal Programming and Predictive Conditioning:** Many entertainment products include subtle symbols, messaging, and repeated themes designed to shape subconscious beliefs and perceptions.

Conclusion: Reclaiming Cultural Sovereignty

To break free from cultural social engineering, individuals must become conscious of the mechanisms at play and take active steps to reclaim their own moral and intellectual sovereignty.

- **Rebuilding Independent Thought:** Seeking Truth beyond mainstream narratives and prioritizing logic over emotional manipulation restores mental autonomy.

- **Restoring Strong Families and Communities:** A return to intergenerational wisdom, strong family units, and natural gender roles fosters societal resilience.

- **Creating Alternative Cultural Institutions:** Independent media, alternative education, and grassroots artistic expression must replace corporate-controlled programming.

The path forward is not passive resistance—it is active creation. By consciously rejecting engineered cultural narratives and embracing Truth, beauty, and virtue, humanity can reclaim its sovereignty and shape a future free from manipulation and control.

VII. The Future of Politics: Breaking Free from the Control Grid

The traditional political paradigm—one based on centralized authority, hierarchical governance, and mass compliance—is rapidly losing legitimacy. The cracks in the system are visible, and more people than ever are awakening to the realization that true freedom cannot be granted from above; it must be reclaimed from within. The future of politics is not about reforming the existing power structures, but about transcending them entirely and building a new system rooted in self-governance, decentralization, and sovereignty.

Centralized Systems Will Never Be Reformed from Within—The Solution is Decentralization

The illusion of political reform has been a primary tool used to pacify the masses. Whether through elections, activism, or legislative changes, the system ensures that no real challenge to its control is ever allowed to materialize.

- **The Cycle of False Hope:** Every few years, citizens are given the illusion of choice in elections, yet policies that serve elite interests remain unchanged.

- **Entrenched Bureaucratic Power:** Politicians come and go, but unelected technocrats, globalist institutions, and corporate cartels maintain continuity in governance.

- **Regulatory Capture:** Every major industry—finance, healthcare, energy, and media—is controlled by a small elite, ensuring that governments serve corporate interests rather than the people.

- **Why Decentralization is the Only Option:** Instead of seeking permission from the system to change, individuals and communities must take proactive steps to create alternatives beyond centralized control.

Self-Governance and Localism: The Future of Political Organization

Rather than top-down governance, the future belongs to self-sustaining, autonomous communities that operate independently of centralized states. These communities will redefine how political structures function, prioritizing cooperation over coercion.

- **Localized Decision-Making:** Small-scale governance ensures accountability and prevents the corruption that plagues large bureaucracies.

- **Resource Independence:** Food, energy, and economic sovereignty allow communities to function without reliance on global supply chains controlled by corporate interests.

- **Technological Sovereignty:** The use of decentralized technologies such as blockchain, encrypted communication, and peer-to-peer systems ensures privacy and freedom from surveillance.

The Power of Opt-Out Strategies: Parallel Economies, Decentralized Networks, and Sovereign Living

To break free from the control grid, individuals must actively disengage from the centralized systems that enslave them. This means creating parallel structures that operate outside government oversight.

- **Opting Out of the Fiat Economy:** Central bank digital currencies (CBDCs) and government-controlled monetary policies aim to track and restrict financial autonomy. Cryptocurrencies, barter systems, and local trade networks offer alternatives.

- **Independent Media and Information Channels:** Corporate media will always serve as a mouthpiece for the establishment. Alternative platforms, decentralized social media, and direct peer-to-peer communication bypass censorship.

- **Education Beyond Indoctrination:** Rather than state-controlled schooling that conditions obedience, real education must focus on critical thinking, self-sufficiency, and skill-building for an independent Life.

- **Sovereign Health and Wellness:** The pharmaceutical industry profits from dependency. A future outside the control grid requires a return to natural healing, regenerative medicine, and holistic wellness practices.

How True Change Happens at the Level of Consciousness, Not Policy

Politics is downstream from consciousness. The reason centralized control persists is that people continue to outsource their sovereignty and believe in the necessity of rulers. The true revolution is not in laws, policies, or governance—it is in awakening to the reality that no external authority has the right to rule over another.

- **The Psychological Chains of Statism:** People are conditioned from birth to believe that authority is legitimate, necessary, and moral. Breaking this programming is the first step toward true freedom.

- **Raising Consciousness Through Self-Mastery:** When individuals reclaim responsibility for their own lives, they no longer require government intervention to dictate their decisions.

- **Rejecting the Fear-Based Paradigm:** The state operates on fear—of chaos, scarcity, and disorder. A higher level of consciousness recognizes that order emerges naturally from self-governance and cooperation, not coercion.

The Path Forward: Not Choosing Better Rulers, But Rejecting the Need for Rulers Altogether

A free society does not require masters or overseers. The very notion of political leadership is outdated and serves only to consolidate power into the hands of the few at the expense of the many. Instead of looking for better politicians or new ideologies, humanity must recognize that external governance is a relic of a past consciousness that no longer serves. While it will take some time for humanity to evolve into these new paradigms, as a higher-order intelligence civilization this is where humanity will be headed:

- **Beyond Representative Government:** The idea that a handful of elites can represent the interests of millions is inherently flawed. More direct and active participation in community governance, rather than primary reliance on electoral politics, will be the way forward.

- **Beyond the Nation-State:** Artificial borders, imposed identities, and state-issued rights are all constructs that limit true human potential. The future belongs to self-organizing networks, not governments.

- **Beyond the Illusion of External Control:** No ruler, party, or movement can bring true freedom—it can only be claimed on an individual level, then expanded outward through voluntary cooperation.

Conclusion: The Future is Decentralized, Sovereign, and Beyond Politics

The collapse of the old political order is inevitable. Centralized systems are unsustainable, and their increasing dysfunction is a sign of their impending failure. The only question is whether people will passively suffer under their decline or take proactive steps to build the new paradigm.

- **Withdraw from the System:** Stop participating in its illusions of reform, control, and dependency.

- **Build Parallel Structures:** Invest in decentralized economies, local governance, and independent knowledge networks.

- **Embrace Sovereignty:** The future belongs to those who refuse to be governed and instead choose self-mastery, voluntary cooperation, and autonomy.

The revolution is not coming—it is already here, for those who have eyes to see it. The control grid only exists as long as people believe in it. The moment enough individuals choose sovereignty over submission, the system will crumble under its own weight.

VIII. Conclusion: The Awakening to Sovereignty

The transformation of humanity's political and social order is not an act of destruction, but an act of creation. It is not a rebellion fueled by anger, but a reimagining guided by wisdom. While the old structures crumble under the weight of their own incoherence, the emerging reality is one aligned with the laws and principles of Nature—one in which governance serves Life rather than controlling it.

This transition will not be without turbulence. The phase shift from a centralized, mechanistic world to a decentralized, life-honoring system will bring choppy waters. Those who have relied on external authority will experience disorientation, and the ruling class will resist their obsolescence. Yet, this is not a collapse into chaos, but an evolution into higher order. Just as forests rejuvenate after wildfires, the destruction of outdated institutions paves the way for new growth—one that is more resilient, more aligned, and more coherent with the deeper intelligence of Life itself.

This is Not the Abolishment of Governance—It is Its Evolution

The awakening to sovereignty does not mean the radical abolition of all governance, nor does it entail anarchy in the conventional sense. Governance is not inherently evil—it is only its corrupted, unnatural forms that enslave rather than serve. The future does not demand the absence of governance, but its reimagining.

- **Governance Aligned with Natural Law:** Instead of arbitrary man-made regulations that serve power and profit, governance will reflect the intrinsic harmony of Nature—upholding principles that foster thriving, harmony, and self-responsibility.

- **Leadership as Stewardship, Not Control:** Leaders will no longer be rulers—they will be guides, facilitators, and protectors of the natural order, ensuring that human structures serve Life rather than suffocate it.

- **The Death of Bureaucracy, the Birth of True Self-Organization:** Hierarchical bureaucracies will be replaced by decentralized, self-organizing systems where decisions are made at the most local level possible, honoring the intelligence and autonomy of individuals and communities.

The Benevolent Revolution: Navigating the Transition with Wisdom

Unlike the revolutions of the past, which were marked by bloodshed and the replacement of one form of tyranny with another, this revolution is different—it is a revolution of consciousness. The shift we are undergoing is not a violent overthrow but a gradual and organic restructuring, guided by the higher intelligence of Life itself.

- **From Resistance to Creation:** The old world cannot be fought into submission—it must simply be left behind. Rather than spending energy resisting corrupt systems, we must focus on building the new in their place.

- **From Dependence to Sovereignty:** The transition will require individuals to take responsibility for their own lives—economically, spiritually, and intellectually—rather than outsourcing their well-being to external institutions.

- **From Fear to Trust in the Process:** The turbulence of transition is inevitable, but those who see beyond the immediate instability will recognize the emergence of something greater—a system rooted in Life, not in control.

The Future Belongs to Those Who Embrace the New Paradigm

The old paradigm was built on coercion, scarcity, and the illusion of separation. The new paradigm is emerging through sovereignty, abundance, and the recognition of Life's interconnected intelligence. Those who cling to the old world will find themselves increasingly disoriented, while those who align with the new will be part of something extraordinary—the rebirth of governance in harmony with Life itself.

- **Those Who Seek Control Will Be Left Behind:** The structures of domination and coercion will be rendered obsolete as people choose voluntary cooperation over enforced compliance.

- **Those Who Build the New Will Lead:** Leadership in this new world will not be granted through titles or elections, but through wisdom, embodiment, and service to Truth and the greatest good of all.

- **Those Who Reclaim Sovereignty Will Thrive:** The individuals and communities that embrace self-responsibility and self-governance will become the blueprint for what comes next.

The Final Truth: The Only Real Revolution is a Revolution of Consciousness

No policy, government, or external force can "fix" the system we live under—it is the collective level of human consciousness that creates our reality. Political systems are merely an outer reflection of the inner state of those who inhabit them. As long as people believe in the necessity of control, coercion, and hierarchy, such systems will manifest. But as more individuals awaken to their true sovereignty, new structures will emerge naturally—ones that are rooted in coherence rather than force.

This is the true awakening—not a rebellion against the old, but an alignment with what has always been true: That Life is sovereign, intelligence is self-organizing, and true governance is not a system of control, but a system of service to the greater whole.

As we cross the threshold into this new reality, the question is not whether the system will change—it is inevitable. The only question is whether we will navigate the transition with fear and resistance, or with wisdom and trust in the intelligence of Life itself.

With this, we conclude Part IV of the Manifesto, a deep examination of the pervasive dysfunctions across our economic, medical, political, and social institutions. We have unveiled how power has been consolidated into the hands of the few, how human sovereignty has been systematically eroded, and how the prevailing governance structures stand in stark opposition to the inherent intelligence of Life. We have also dismantled the false narrative that climate change is merely a CO_2 issue, exposing the deeper reality of ecocide—the wholesale destruction of natural living systems. This understanding is critical, but it is only the beginning.

Now, as we move into Part V: *The Path Forward—The Restoration of Intelligence & Cosmic Order*, the focus shifts from deconstructing the system's failures to actively envisioning and giving concrete form to the blueprint of what must come next. If Part IV illuminated what must be left behind, Part V will chart the course for what must take its place. This is not about ideological debates or theoretical discussions—it is about the practical, tangible steps required to reclaim intelligence, restore harmony with Natural law, and construct a civilization that thrives in alignment with the Grand Architecture of Creation.

The path forward is unmistakable: we must move beyond the obsolete structures of the past and into a higher-order reality—one that honors Truth, Wisdom, and the sacred intelligence woven into the fabric of existence.

In many ways, we have now thoroughly deconstructed the Polycrisis and its countless manifestations. While understanding these crises is essential, what is far more important is recognizing their true origin—Mankind's psychosis. The Polycrisis is not the root problem; it is merely the symptom. At its core, what we face is a Meta Crisis—a Spiritual Crisis that has shaped the world as we see it today.

The real work, then, is not to endlessly analyze the dysfunction, but to transcend it. To rise above the illusion, to reclaim intelligence, and to restore coherence with the natural order of Life.

That is what comes next.

In every Crucible, there's a choice that must be made.

THE FAILURE AND INSIDIOUS NATURE OF POLITICAL & SOCIAL ENGINEERING

EXECUTIVE SUMMARY

Why Should You Read This Chapter?

For decades, we have been conditioned to believe that governance is a system designed for the betterment of society. Yet, a closer examination reveals that modern political structures function primarily to consolidate power, manufacture consent, and control the masses. The institutions that claim to serve the public interest are, in reality, instruments of coercion and social engineering. Governments do not operate in isolation—they are deeply entangled with corporate conglomerates, intelligence agencies, and globalist organizations that manipulate narratives and enforce division to maintain control.

This chapter exposes the hidden mechanics of political and social engineering, revealing how power structures operate behind the façade of democracy. It explains why partisan politics is nothing more than a distraction, designed to keep the masses divided while those in control continue their agenda unchallenged. Furthermore, it dissects how perpetual war, economic crises, and cultural programming serve as tools of mass manipulation. Understanding these mechanisms is essential—not to incite fear or resistance, but to empower individuals to see beyond the illusion and reclaim their sovereignty. True change does not come from electing better leaders or reforming corrupt institutions; it comes from transcending the system altogether and realigning with the intelligence of Life itself.

Executive Summary: Key Takeaways

- **Governance as a System of Control:** Governments no longer serve the people; they serve corporate, financial, and military-industrial interests, maintaining a façade of democracy while ensuring continuity of the ruling class.

- **The Manufactured Political Divide:** The left vs. right dichotomy is an illusion meant to keep people emotionally reactive and distracted, preventing them from uniting against their true oppressors.

- **Deep State Influence:** Unelected bureaucracies, intelligence agencies, and globalist organizations manipulate policy, public perception, and global conflicts behind the scenes.

- **Perpetual War as an Economic Model:** The military-industrial complex thrives on engineered conflicts, using false flags and manufactured enemies to justify endless war, enriching the ruling elite while distracting the populace.

- **The Weaponization of Crises:** Governments exploit terrorism, pandemics, and economic crashes to expand control, implement emergency powers, and justify mass surveillance.

- **Social Engineering Through Culture:** Education, media, entertainment, and technology are used to weaken critical thinking, erode traditional values, and normalize control mechanisms such as censorship, cancel culture, and social credit systems.

- **Breaking Free from the Control Grid:** Centralized political systems will never be reformed from within. The path forward is decentralization, self-governance, and a return to Natural law.

- **The Benevolent Revolution:** The transition will not be a radical, anarchic rejection of governance but a reimagining of leadership as stewardship—aligned with Life's intelligence rather than coercion and exploitation.

V – The Path Forward: The Restoration of Intelligence & Cosmic Order

TRANSCENDING THE PSYCHOSIS: THE ONLY WAY OUT

Section I - Introduction: The Ultimate Realization

The Fundamental Premise: A Spiritual Crisis of Consciousness

Every major crisis unfolding on this planet today—geopolitical conflict, economic instability, environmental degradation, societal polarization, or institutional corruption—are not isolated events. These are not random malfunctions of an otherwise sound system; they are the symptoms of an existential Spiritual Crisis. We are in a race to raise human consciousness—everything else is just details.

To many, consciousness may seem abstract or mystical, but it is neither—it is simply our level of awareness and perception of reality. It is the operating system of humanity—determining our level of thinking, how we perceive and experience Life, what we value, how we organize society, and ultimately, what kind of world we create.

The external world is a mirror of our collective consciousness. Just as an individual's Life is shaped by their beliefs and perceptions, the world reflects humanity's predominant state of awareness. In our fractal-based Universe—meaning everything is a fractal across a wide range of scales—our shared outer world is simply the macrocosm of the microcosm that is Mankind's inner world.

A world in harmony and coherence can only emerge from a species in harmony and coherence. Likewise, a world in chaos, division, and dysfunction is nothing more than an outward projection of a species in chaos, division, and dysfunction.

This is the realization we must come to terms with: The external world is not something separate from us—it is us.

Why External Solutions Have Failed—and Will Always Fail

The natural impulse when faced with crisis is to solve it externally—to create new policies, new laws, new technologies, new movements, new leaders. This has been the approach of humanity for centuries. And yet, every revolution, every government intervention, every reform has failed to produce lasting change.

Why?

Because all these efforts attempt to address symptoms rather than the root cause. They attempt to reorganize the structure of the system without addressing the consciousness that built the system in the first place.

Consider this:

- Why does corruption persist despite endless reforms and anti-corruption laws?

- Why do wars continue despite global institutions created to prevent them?

- Why does environmental destruction accelerate despite international climate agreements?

- Why does economic inequality widen despite new policies aimed at redistribution?

The answer is simple: No policy can override the level of consciousness that created the problem in the first place.

If the underlying level of consciousness remains the same, then no matter how many times we rearrange the external system, it will always regress back to dysfunction. A corrupt system does not sustain itself because of its design; it sustains itself because the level of consciousness that built it still exists.

Fixing external problems without transforming consciousness is like rearranging furniture in a burning house.

This is the critical distinction that separates true transformation from illusionary change.

The System is a Mirror—Not an Enemy

Many view the system we live under as an external enemy—a force imposed upon us by corrupt elites, politicians, or institutions. This perspective, while understandable, is incomplete.

The system is not an imposition of random external forces—it is a mirror of our collective internal state. The governments, corporations, financial institutions, and social structures that exist today did not emerge from nothing; they are a manifestation of humanity's collective level of consciousness.

- **When we exist in fear, we seek security over freedom**—and thus create a world of control and surveillance.

- **When we operate from scarcity and greed**—we build economies based on hoarding and exploitation.

- **When we embrace division**—we create governments and ideologies that keep us polarized.

- **When we disconnect from nature and wisdom**—we create a world of degeneration and artificiality.

In other words, the system does not create our consciousness—our consciousness creates the system.

Until we recognize this Truth, we will stay locked in an endless cycle of blame and resistance—chasing illusions instead of addressing the real cause.

The Only Path Forward: Transcendence

If the system is a mirror of our collective consciousness, then fighting the system is like fighting our own reflection. The more we resist it, the more we engage with it, the more energy we give it. What we resist, persists. By engaging with the system through opposition, we remain in reaction to it—ensuring its continued relevance. True transformation does not come from tearing down the old; it comes from making the old obsolete by embodying something higher.

The solution is not resistance but transcendence—a leap in consciousness so profound that the old system collapses, not by force, but by irrelevance.

- A corrupt political system does not collapse when it is overthrown; it collapses when people rise in awareness and no longer consent to its rule.

- A broken economic system does not collapse through regulation; it collapses when people stop participating in its illusions of debt and scarcity.

- A dysfunctional food system does not change through policy; it changes when people elevate their food choices, creating demand for integrity-based alternatives that render the old paradigm unviable.

- A society of division and fear does not heal through activism; it heals when people stop identifying with false labels and step into unity.

This is the power of transcendence. The system does not need to be defeated—it needs to be rendered obsolete.

Understanding that external solutions have failed and that the system itself is merely a projection of collective consciousness leads us to the next realization: fighting it is like wrestling with a shadow—it only strengthens the illusion of its power. Many believe that exposing corruption or dismantling oppressive structures will create change. Yet history proves otherwise—resistance alone does not liberate; it reinforces the very system it seeks to overcome. In Section II, we will explore why resistance fails, how it keeps us trapped in the same dysfunctional paradigm, and why true transformation requires a different approach altogether.

Section II – Why Resistance Fails

The Illusion of Fighting the System

One of the greatest misconceptions in the pursuit of change is the belief that resisting, exposing, or dismantling a corrupt system will lead to its downfall. While this perspective appears logical on the surface, history has repeatedly shown that resistance alone does not create transformation—it ensures entanglement.

Revolutions have been fought, governments have been overthrown, and economic systems have been restructured, yet the fundamental dysfunction of human civilization remains. Why? Because each of these efforts has focused on changing external structures rather than elevating the consciousness that creates them.

The idea that we must "fight the system" assumes that the system is an external force imposing itself upon us. However, as we established in Section I, the system is not separate from us—it is a direct manifestation of humanity's collective consciousness. Fighting it is like attacking a shadow while ignoring the object casting it. The more we engage with the shadow, the more we keep it alive.

The Pattern of Revolutions – Why the Cycle Repeats

History is a revolving door of revolutions. Societies rise up against oppressive regimes, overthrow their leaders, implement new systems, and yet, within a few generations, they find themselves back in the same dysfunction—only with new faces and slightly altered structures.

- The **French Revolution** overthrew monarchy, only to fall into dictatorship under Napoleon.

- The **Russian Revolution** replaced the Tsar with Communist rule, leading to massive state oppression.

- The **Arab Spring** sought democracy, yet many nations that participated ended up under different forms of authoritarian control.

Each of these movements sought to destroy the old but failed to elevate human consciousness beyond the patterns that created the old system in the first place.

Until humanity transcends the level of consciousness that produces corruption, greed, control, and division, no amount of external change will produce lasting transformation.

Why What We Resist, Persists

Engaging in resistance locks us into the frequency of what we oppose. This is not just a philosophical idea—it is a fundamental law of reality. The more we fight something, the more we remain in a state of reaction to it, ensuring its continued relevance in our lives.

- **Resisting authoritarianism strengthens its justification**—leaders use the opposition to justify even tighter control.

- **Resisting economic oppression fuels the system**—activism often operates within the same financial structures it seeks to dismantle.

- **Resisting war fuels conflict**—history shows that wars fought to end oppression often lead to new forms of subjugation.

This is why resistance fails: it operates at the same level of consciousness as the system it seeks to change. True transformation requires an entirely different approach.

Transcendence as the Only Real Solution

If resistance perpetuates the problem, then what is the alternative? The answer is transcendence—stepping completely out of the paradigm that keeps the dysfunctional system alive.

- Instead of **resisting** corrupt governance, we embody **sovereignty** and create new decentralized models of leadership.

- Instead of **fighting** against economic enslavement, we exit the dependency cycle and reclaim self-sufficiency.

- Instead of **warring** against manipulation, we rise in discernment and no longer fall prey to deception.

Transcendence is not about fixing the old—it is about rendering it obsolete by shifting into a higher mode of being. This is why history's greatest paradigm shifts did not come from wars or protests, but from breakthroughs in consciousness and ways of living.

The Unseen Trap - How Resistance Keeps You in the Game

The most sophisticated mechanism of control is the illusion that fighting back is the solution. The system depends on our engagement—whether through compliance or opposition—to sustain itself. It does not care whether you are for it or against it—it only cares that you remain locked in the paradigm it has created.

- **Political systems thrive on division.** When we fight against one ideology, we strengthen the polarity that keeps the system intact.

- **Financial systems thrive on dependency.** When we engage in financial activism, we often reinforce the legitimacy of centralized economies.

- **Media thrives on outrage.** The more we react, the more attention and energy we feed into the cycle.

Breaking free requires no longer playing the game at all. The moment enough people disengage from the framework of fear, dependency, and reaction, the false system collapses—not by force, but by irrelevance.

Moving Beyond Resistance to True Change

This leads us to the inevitable conclusion: Real change is not achieved by fighting the system—it is achieved by embodying a new way of being that makes the system obsolete.

In Section III, we will explore what this shift actually looks like in practice—how individuals and communities can rise above the game entirely and begin constructing a world that does not require opposition to exist.

Section III - Why Transcendence Works

Transcendence as the Only Real Solution

A dysfunctional system does not collapse because it is attacked or destroyed; it collapses because it becomes irrelevant. Fighting a decaying structure only prolongs its existence by keeping it relevant. The only true way to move beyond dysfunction is to create something superior—something that naturally outcompetes the old system, rendering it obsolete.

This is the essence of transcendence: not opposing the old, but rising beyond it.

The False System Harvests Energy

The system we live under does not sustain itself through genuine power, but through our unconscious participation. It thrives by feeding on fear, division, and compliance.

- **The system is not inherently powerful**—it only survives because we continue to invest our energy into it.

- **Fear and division serve as fuel**—the more people remain in conflict, the more they sustain the structures they claim to oppose.

- **The illusion of authority persists as long as people believe in it**—the moment enough people withdraw belief in its legitimacy, it crumbles.

Historical Examples of Natural Collapse

History has repeatedly shown that dysfunctional systems do not collapse due to external attack but because they become untenable from within. The greater the disharmony within a system, the closer it moves toward inevitable dissolution.

- **The Soviet Union** did not fall due to military defeat; it imploded under its own inefficiencies and contradictions.

- **Ancient empires**—such as Rome and Byzantium—did not collapse due to external threats alone but because of internal corruption, stagnation, and loss of coherence.

- **Modern empires**—The once almighty General Electric Company went from one of the largest and most revered companies in the world to being dismantled, sold off in parts, and now only lives on in a few remaining legacy businesses. All of this happened in the span of less than 15 years, showing how even corporate giants are not immune to internal inefficiencies and loss of adaptability.

- **Technological and societal evolution** naturally renders outdated systems obsolete.
  - The horse and buggy were not banned; they simply faded as automobiles provided a superior alternative.
  - Centralized media lost control over narratives not because of regulation, but because decentralized digital platforms emerged.

The Inevitable Shift

When people stop participating in dysfunctional systems—when they remove their energy and shift toward higher-order alternatives—the old world collapses by default. This is not an act of war or opposition; it is the natural process of evolution.

In Section IV, we will explore how this process can be accelerated and what practical steps individuals can take to consciously shift toward a more coherent, Life-affirming reality.

Section IV – The System Crumbles When Enough People Withdraw Their Energy

The Power of Collective Disengagement

No system—no matter how powerful—can survive without the participation of those it seeks to control. The moment enough individuals withdraw their energy, the very foundations of that system begin to erode. History has shown time and again that when people cease to comply, the structure collapses—not through force, but through irrelevance.

This section outlines the key areas where disengagement leads to systemic dissolution and the emergence of new, Life-affirming paradigms.

Fear-Based Narratives and the Collapse of Propaganda

The primary tool of control has always been fear. Governments, media conglomerates, and corporate entities rely on fear to manufacture consent and shape public behavior.

- When enough people stop participating in fear-based narratives, propaganda loses its hold.

- Fear works only if people believe it. Once the illusion is exposed, mass manipulation becomes ineffective.

- Truth does not need enforcement; it stands on its own. Falsehood, on the other hand, requires constant reinforcement through repetition, censorship, and coercion to maintain its illusion of legitimacy. When enough people stop internalizing deception, the entire apparatus of control collapses under its own weight.

Rejecting Financial Slavery and the Decline of the Debt-Based Economy

The modern economic system is built on debt and dependency, ensuring that the majority remain subservient to financial institutions.

- When enough people exit the cycle of debt and dependency, the debt-based economy loses its grip and begins to unravel.

- This does not require a revolution—it requires individuals choosing financial sovereignty through alternative economic models.

- Decentralized finance, community exchange systems, and self-sufficiency render centralized control structures obsolete.

Reclaiming Sovereignty and the Dissolution of Centralized Control

Centralized systems of governance depend on obedience, regulation, and top-down authority. The moment individuals recognize their innate sovereignty, these control structures begin to disintegrate.

- When enough people reclaim their sovereignty, centralized control erodes naturally.

- True governance arises from self-responsibility, not imposed authority.

- Localized, community-driven leadership becomes the natural alternative to distant bureaucracies.

The Medical-Industrial Complex and the Shift to True Well-Being

Pharmaceutical companies and institutionalized healthcare thrive on a population that remains sick, dependent, and uninformed about true health.

- When enough people choose health over pharmaceuticals, the medical-industrial complex loses its grip.

- Natural healing, holistic medicine, and preventative care become the default.

- Wellness becomes a sovereign choice rather than a commercialized dependency.

Transforming the Food System Through Conscious Choices

The global food industry is structured around profit-driven mass production, often at the cost of health, sustainability, and nutrition.

- When enough people uplevel their food choices, the entire food system transforms.

- Organic, regenerative farming replaces processed, chemically-laden agriculture.

- Profit-oriented corporations inevitably respond to demand—when people stop consuming toxic foods, better alternatives become dominant.

Breaking Free from Manufactured Division

The system thrives on keeping people trapped in false external identities—political, racial, national, ideological—because division ensures control.

- When enough people stop identifying with false external labels, the manufactured division collapses.

- The more people step beyond labels and into their sovereignty, the entire mechanism of control breaks.

- True unity is not forced—it emerges naturally when people see beyond imposed narratives.

- The illusion of separation is the bedrock of control; when individuals see beyond these artificial divisions, the entire structure of manipulation loses its foundation.

The Ultimate Dissolution of the False World

All of these shifts point toward one fundamental Truth:

- When enough people commit to the inner work to elevate their consciousness, the false world dissolves by default.

- It does not need to be overthrown—it simply becomes irrelevant.

- A new paradigm does not need to be enforced; it emerges organically when the old paradigm is no longer sustained. This is not an abstract ideal—it is an observable, cyclical pattern in history, biology, and social evolution. What is incoherent and disharmonious cannot sustain itself indefinitely. No empire, ideology, or control structure has ever withstood the natural forces of entropy and evolution. The shift is not a matter of 'if' but 'when'—and the timeline of transcending this collective Spiritual Crisis will be determined by how quickly individuals will embody these principles.

Now that we've established how corrupted systems collapse, the next step is to explore how to consciously create the world that follows—one that does not rely on control, coercion, or fear to function. In Section V, we will outline the inner revolution that must take place in each of us in order for the regenerative, Life-affirming systems to emerge that naturally replace the dysfunctional structures of the past.

Section V – The Path to Transcendence: The Inner Revolution

It Begins with the Individual

The transformation of the world does not begin with governments, institutions, or mass movements. It begins with the individual. Every external change in human civilization has always been preceded by an internal shift in human consciousness. It is the awakening of individuals, not collective mandates, that drives evolution.

- Societies evolve when individuals rise beyond fear and limitation.

- Systems change when individuals withdraw their energy and participation from those that do not serve them.

- A new world does not emerge from the top down—it is built from within, one sovereign being at a time.

If we look at history, the great shifts in human civilization—whether in philosophy, governance, or science—began not with mass uprisings, but with a few individuals seeing beyond the constraints of their time and choosing to embody a higher possibility.

This is the true path to transcendence.

The False World Will Not Be Overthrown—It Will Be Left Behind

The old paradigm is built on fear, control, and separation. Many believe that to create a better world, we must first defeat the current system. But this is an illusion. What is built on fear cannot be dismantled through opposition—it dissolves only when it is no longer needed.

- You do not defeat the system; you outgrow it.

- You do not fix the old world; you first envision a higher possibility, then design its foundations, create its blueprint, and finally build it into form—until the old world becomes irrelevant and fades away.

History is filled with failed attempts to overthrow corrupt systems, only for new ones—equally dysfunctional—to rise in their place. Why? Because the consciousness that created the problem was never transcended.

The way forward is not to fight against the existing structures but to move beyond them entirely by embodying a new way of being.

Practical Aspects of Transcendence

Transcendence is not a theoretical concept; it is a lived experience. It requires conscious effort, discipline, and an unwavering commitment to inner transformation. Here are the essential aspects:

Step Out of Fear

Fear is the foundation of the current paradigm. Every system of control—whether political, financial, or social—relies on keeping people in a state of fear.

- **Fear fuels the system**—the more we react from fear, the more we sustain it.

- **Sovereignty dissolves fear**—when we step into self-mastery, the illusions lose their grip.

- **Inner stillness is the antidote**—clarity and peace make manipulation impossible.

Transcendence begins when individuals stop making decisions out of fear and instead align with courage, wisdom, and inner knowing.

Reclaim Your Energy

Where you place your attention, you place your power. The system thrives on distraction, emotional reactivity, and endless engagement with external dramas. Reclaiming your energy means consciously choosing where to direct your focus.

- **Stop feeding the illusions**—withdraw from narratives that perpetuate division, victimhood, and fear.

- **Master your attention**—cultivate presence rather than being consumed by external chaos.
- **Engage only with what expands you**—invest energy in creation, Truth, and self-evolution.

When enough individuals do this, the external world shifts automatically, without force or opposition.

Live in Alignment with Natural and Cosmic Law

The false world is built on artificial constructs—man-made laws, institutions, and ideologies disconnected from Truth. The new world—the one that is already emerging—is governed by Natural and Cosmic law.

- **Natural Law**: The fundamental principles that govern Life—reciprocity, coherence, integrity, and the inherent intelligence of nature.
- **Cosmic Law**: The deeper universal order that guides the unfolding of reality—higher intelligence, consciousness, and the interconnectedness of all things.

Living in alignment with these laws means:

- Reclaiming sovereignty by engaging in true critical thinking—seeing beyond partisanship, escaping echo chambers, and recognizing Truth beyond ideological filters.
- Devotion to self-mastery and taking responsibility and accountability for healing our own triggers, wounds, and traumas.
- Acting from Truth rather than compliance.
- Choosing coherence over conflict.
- Embracing that Nature thrives on diversity, not uniformity. We are all unique by intelligent design, so we must stop seeing it as a design flaw.
- Trusting Life's intelligence rather than artificial control mechanisms.

When enough people embody these principles, the old world does not need to be dismantled—it simply ceases to function.

The Threshold of Evolution

We stand at a threshold—the choice between remaining entangled in a collapsing paradigm or stepping fully into a higher octave of consciousness. The path forward is not through external battles, but through internal revelation. Not by memorization, but by remembrance. Not through logic alone, but by direct intuitive knowing. This is the path of spiritual initiation.

As individuals reclaim sovereignty, step out of fear, and align with universal Truth, a new world will emerge organically and spontaneously—not through force, but through the natural order of evolution.

The revolution is not external. It is inner. And it has already begun.

Now that we have established that true transcendence begins within, we must recognize that the old world is already in freefall. The question is no longer whether change is coming—it is already here; the unraveling has long been in motion.

What remains is the choice: will we cling to the crumbling structures of fear, control, and dependency, or will we step into sovereignty, coherence, and higher intelligence? In the next section, we will explore this crucible moment—the time to choose between two diverging realities unfolding in parallel.

Section VI – The Crucible Moment: The Time to Choose

The Collapse is Inevitable—The Transition is Up to Us

The old world is already falling apart. The systems and structures that once appeared stable are now visibly disintegrating under the weight of their own incoherence. This collapse is not theoretical or distant—it is happening now, in real-time, across every domain: political, economic, environmental, and societal.

But collapse alone does not ensure transcendence. Throughout history, civilizations have collapsed, only to be replaced by new versions of the same dysfunction. The critical factor is how humanity chooses to transition—whether through fear and control, or through sovereignty and higher intelligence.

This is the crucible moment. The time to choose.

Two Diverging Paths Exist Simultaneously

The collapse and the transcendence are not separate events occurring at different times. They are happening simultaneously—two realities unfolding in parallel. The world is bifurcating, and each individual is faced with a fundamental choice: which path will they align with?

Path One: Collapse into Fear and Control

- More centralization, more surveillance, more coercion.

- Increased dependence on artificial systems—governments, corporations, pharmaceuticals, technology.

- Amplified division—tribalism, ideological warfare, and externalized blame.

- An existence dictated by fear, reaction, and submission to external authority.

Path Two: Transcend into Sovereignty and Coherence

- Embracing personal responsibility and self-governance.

- Reconnecting with nature, intuition, and higher intelligence.

- Creating decentralized, Life-affirming systems outside of institutional control.

- Stepping beyond fear, division, and external dependency into a reality of Truth, coherence, and unity.

This bifurcation is not a future event—it is happening **now**. The choices made today determine the trajectory of each individual and, collectively, the trajectory of humanity.

The Illusion of a Neutral Ground

For those who believe they can remain neutral, undecided, or simply "wait and see," there is a hard Truth to face: there is no neutral ground in a collapsing paradigm.

- To not choose is, by default, to remain embedded in the old system, subject to its limitations and control.

- Avoiding the choice does not stop the bifurcation—it simply ensures that the choice is made for you.

- The external world will continue shifting regardless; the question is whether one will actively shape the new reality or passively remain in the collapse of the old.

The Time to Choose is Now

This is not a call to arms; it is a call to alignment. No external savior will lead humanity out of this moment—only those who step into their own power, discernment, and Truth will make the transition successfully.

Every action, every belief, every investment of time, energy, and attention is a vote for one reality or the other. The false world continues only because people continue participating in it. The new world emerges only when enough individuals consciously build it into being.

The time to choose is not in the future.

The time is now.

Having established the necessity of choice in this crucible moment, we now arrive at the final realization: there is no external solution to humanity's predicament. No policy, reform, or revolution will create the world we long for—only a fundamental leap in consciousness can.

In the next section, we explore the deeper Truth behind all transformation: the false world does not need to be destroyed; it simply dissolves when something higher emerges. This is the final choice—are you ready to let go of the old and step fully into the new?

Section VII – The Final Realization

The Only Way Out is Through Transcendence

Humanity's predicament cannot be solved through external means. No political solution, financial reform, or social movement will bring about the transformation we seek. The old world is not failing because of a lack of better policies, governance, or economic models—it is failing because it is built on a foundation of incoherence, division, and fear. No external restructuring can remedy a system that is the byproduct of a dysfunctional level of consciousness.

The only way out is through transcendence—a complete elevation in how we perceive and engage with reality. This is not an abstract concept; it is the fundamental Truth underlying all great shifts in history. When consciousness expands, the world naturally reorganizes itself to reflect that higher state.

- The problem is not the system—it is the consciousness that created it.

- The solution is not a new ideology—it is a new way of being.

- The only true revolution is an inner one.

Reality Evolves, It Is Not Fought Over

For centuries, humanity has operated under the belief that change comes through conflict—overthrowing governments, dismantling institutions, and waging ideological wars. But history reveals a deeper Truth: reality does not evolve through destruction—it evolves through emergence.

- The false world does not collapse because it is destroyed—it collapses because something higher takes its place.

- This is a fundamental law of Evolution—when a higher-order system emerges, the lower-order system dissolves by default.

- We do not need to dictate what comes next—it will emerge naturally, guided by Life's intelligence, but only if we collectively create the conditions for it to arise.

When humanity rises into a higher state of coherence, the structures of the past become irrelevant. They no longer need to be fought; they simply cease to function. We are not here to fix a broken system—we are here to create what comes after.

This is the Final Choice

Everything has led to this moment. The choice is simple but profound: Are you ready to let go of the false world and embody the new?

- The world of fear, control, and division is available to those who choose it.

- The world of sovereignty, coherence, and Truth is available to those who step into it.

- Both realities will continue to unfold, but only one leads to true freedom.

There is no more waiting. There is no more external battle to fight. The path forward is clear: transcend or remain entangled in the collapse.

This is the final realization—the culmination of everything that has been explored in this chapter.

The only question that remains is: What will you choose?

You can fight the old, or you can transcend it and birth the new—those are the only two choices.

Wealth Harmony—A New Socio-Economic Principle

As we transcend the limitations of the old world, we must reexamine our understanding of wealth. The dysfunction of modern economies—and society as a whole—is not rooted in inequality alone, but in a deeper disharmony.

In the next chapter, we explore a new principle: Wealth Harmony—where true prosperity is measured not just in financial terms, but in health, justice, safety, happiness, and opportunity for all. The future of wealth is not about forced redistribution or artificial balance—it is about restoring harmony with the principles of Life itself.

In every Crucible, there's a choice that must be made.

TRANSCENDING THE PSYCHOSIS: THE ONLY WAY OUT

EXECUTIVE SUMMARY

Why Should You Read This Chapter?

The world is at a breaking point, and the collapse of the old paradigm is already underway. But destruction alone does not bring transformation. This chapter reveals the only true path forward: transcendence. No external movement, political shift, or economic restructuring will save us—only a fundamental shift in consciousness can. Here, you will discover:

- Why external solutions fail to create lasting change.

- How reality evolves through emergence, not opposition.

- The final choice humanity faces: cling to the collapsing world of fear and control, or step into sovereignty and coherence.

This chapter is not about theory—it is about the decision that will shape your Life and the world to come. The time to choose is now.

.

Executive Summary: Key Takeaways

- **The collapse of the old world is already happening**—but destruction alone does not lead to transformation. The political, economic, and social structures that once seemed unshakable are crumbling under their own weight. However, collapse does not automatically result in something better. Without a shift in consciousness, the same dysfunctional patterns will re-emerge under a different form. True transformation is not about tearing down the old, but about what we choose to create in its place.

- **No external solution will save us**—political, economic, and social reforms fail when the underlying consciousness remains unchanged. Throughout history, revolutions and systemic overhauls have only replaced one form of control with another. The dysfunction is not in governance, money, or policy—it is in the consciousness that gives rise to them. The only real solution is an internal shift in perception, responsibility, and awareness.

- **Reality does not evolve through conflict—it evolves through emergence—** the old dissolves when something higher takes its place. Attempting to fight against corruption, control, and manipulation only reinforces their existence. Instead of engaging in opposition, the focus must be on embodying and creating what comes next. When enough people step into higher intelligence, the outdated structures simply fade away due to irrelevance.

- **The only true revolution is an inner one—**transcendence is the only viable path forward. Every external revolution in history has ultimately failed to bring lasting peace or harmony. This is because the root cause—humanity's fragmented consciousness—was never addressed. The only real revolution is the one that happens within, as individuals awaken to a higher state of coherence and alignment with Life.

- **The false world cannot be fought or reformed—**it will collapse naturally when humanity shifts to a higher state of coherence. Dysfunctional systems persist because people still feed them with their energy and belief. The moment enough individuals disengage, these structures begin to dissolve. Instead of waging war against corruption, we must embody a reality where corruption has no place, thus making the old paradigm obsolete.

- **Two realities are unfolding in parallel—**one of deeper control, fear, and division; the other of sovereignty, Truth, and harmony. As the collapse unfolds, individuals are choosing—whether consciously or unconsciously—between two diverging paths. Some will tighten their grip on external authority and fear-based narratives, while others will step into personal sovereignty and coherence. Both realities will exist simultaneously, but only one leads to true liberation.

- **There is no neutral ground—**to not choose is to remain in the collapsing paradigm by default. Many believe they can remain on the sidelines, waiting to see how events unfold. But reality does not work that way. The bifurcation is already occurring, and inaction is itself a choice. Those who do not actively align with a higher reality will find themselves swept along with the old system's descent.

- **Transcendence is not a passive process—**it requires conscious participation, alignment, and the creation of new systems. Stepping beyond the collapsing paradigm does not mean sitting back and waiting for a new world to appear. It requires deliberate action—releasing fear, reclaiming sovereignty, and engaging in the creation of new, Life-affirming structures. Transcendence is an active embodiment of a new reality, not merely an intellectual understanding of it.

- **The final choice is here: fight the old or transcend it and birth the new.** Every individual must decide whether they will remain entangled in the dysfunction of the old world or step into something greater. This is not a choice to be made in the distant future—it is happening now, moment by moment, through every action, thought, and belief. The only question that remains is: What will you choose?

WEALTH HARMONY:
REDEFINING PROSPERITY FOR A NEW ERA

I. Introduction: The Crisis of a Narrow Definition of Wealth

For centuries, society has equated wealth with financial accumulation, propelling civilization into ever-increasing unhinged material gluttony and insatiable consumption—deeply hollowing out the meaning of Life with true fulfillment as mere collateral damage. This narrow belief that wealth is synonymous with money and financial accumulation has led to deep imbalances—economic growth pursued at the cost of human and planetary well-being. Despite unprecedented material wealth, society faces record levels of chronic illness, depression, anxiety, loneliness, and existential emptiness—revealing the cruel paradox of modern prosperity.

The consequences of this reductionist view are severe:

- Financial success is often achieved at the expense of health, relationships, meaning, and well-being.

- Nations celebrate rising GDP—an abstract economic metric—while mental illness, chronic disease, opioid addictions, poverty and homelessness, and social unrest grow unchecked. By all objective measures, this reveals a deeper, underlying crisis: Mankind's psychosis.

- The global economy prioritizes profits while ignoring justice, fairness, sustainability, and human health, dignity, and inner fulfillment.

This is not merely an economic crisis—it is a crisis of meaning and well-being, the very hallmarks of a deeper Spiritual Crisis. The true path forward requires a radical expansion of what we define as wealth.

A New Paradigm: Wealth as a Holistic State of Abundance

True wealth transcends financial metrics; it is a dynamic, multidimensional state of prosperity that includes:

- **Health & Vitality:** A strong body and Mind.

- **Emotional & Social Connection:** Love, compassion, and a sense of belonging.

- **Meaning & Purpose:** A deep connection to Life's greater purpose.

- **Time & Freedom:** The ability to live Life on one's terms.

- **Justice & Opportunity:** Human dignity, fairness and access for all.

- **Harmony with Nature:** A regenerative relationship with the Earth.

The old paradigm prioritizes financial accumulation at the expense of all else. The new paradigm recognizes that true wealth is not about hoarding resources but about cultivating a holistically abundant Life of fulfillment, meaning, health, opportunity, freedom, safety, dignity, and regenerative financial prosperity (note: circulating financial resources vs hoarding them)—in other words, a soulful Life instead of a soulless existence.

Wealth Harmony: A Dynamic and Fluid Force

Wealth Harmony is not a static equation to be precisely balanced—it is a dynamic, living principle that evolves with the rhythms of Life, personal growth, and natural cycles. Just as nature moves through phases of growth, decay, and renewal, so too must our understanding of wealth remain adaptable.

At times, certain aspects of wealth will require greater attention, while others recede into the background. The key is not perfection, but coherence. When we experience disharmony—whether in health, relationships, or purpose—Life is signaling that it is time to recalibrate and bring all aspects of wealth back into a harmonic orchestra.

This process will look different for every individual. Each of us has a unique rhythm, and the orchestration of wealth will vary based on our personal journey. However, while the balance shifts, we cannot ignore any of these pillars—neglecting one inevitably leads to disharmony across all. Wealth Harmony is about cultivating an awareness of this ever-changing dynamic, learning to flow with Life rather than against it.

This chapter will explore how humanity can break free from an extractive, imbalanced economic model to one that fosters true prosperity—where wealth is measured not just in money, but in the abundance of all aspects that make Life truly worth living.

II. Expanding the Definition of Wealth: The Nine Pillars of True Prosperity

Wealth, in its truest form, is not confined to material riches. While financial resources play a role in security and opportunity, they are merely one facet of a much greater tapestry of abundance. A truly prosperous Life is multidimensional, enriched by factors beyond money—our well-being, relationships, sense of purpose, and connection to the world around us.

The nine pillars of wealth introduced in this chapter should not be mistaken for a definitive or exhaustive list of what constitutes a meaningful Life. Rather, they serve as a framework to help us understand the breadth and depth of multidimensional abundance—showing us a clear pathway into creating a Life of true wealth. Just as an ecosystem thrives when its elements function in harmony, true human prosperity is achieved when these core aspects of Life exist in dynamic coherence. This framework helps us see that wealth is not about equal distribution across all areas at all times, but about maintaining a fluid, responsive orchestration that adapts to the rhythms of Life.

There is no universal formula for how these aspects should be prioritized—each individual's experience of abundance will vary depending on Life's seasons, personal growth, and external circumstances. Yet, while the expression of wealth is unique for each person, neglecting any one of these pillars creates disharmony, ultimately pulling Life out of alignment. Recognizing this interconnectedness allows us to navigate our journey with greater clarity and intention, ensuring that prosperity is both sustainable and deeply fulfilling.

The following are the nine pillars of true prosperity:

1. **Financial Wealth (Financial Security & Material Resources)**

   o Money is a tool, not the destination. It enables security but cannot substitute for health, relationships, or purpose.

   o True prosperity ensures financial stability without compromising well-being.

2. **Physical Wealth (Health, Vitality & Longevity)**

   o A wealthy person who is sick is still impoverished.

   o A truly prosperous society prioritizes clean food, holistic healthcare, and regenerative living.

3. **Emotional Wealth (Love, Connection & Compassion)**

   o Meaningful relationships are a cornerstone of wealth—without love, family, and human connection, financial riches are empty.

   o Societies obsessed with material wealth often suffer from chronic loneliness and emotional detachment.

4. Mental Wealth (Knowledge, Wisdom & Creativity)

- o A civilization's true wealth is in its intellectual and creative capital.

- o Education should cultivate critical thinking and wisdom, not just economic productivity.

5. Spiritual Wealth (Meaning, Purpose & Inner Peace)

- o True wealth includes a connection to something greater than oneself, be it spirituality, philosophy, or deep self-awareness.

- o Without purpose, even the richest people experience existential emptiness.

6. Social Wealth (Community, Trust & Shared Prosperity)

- o Societies built on cooperation, trust, and fairness flourish, while those that prioritize competition and exploitation collapse.

- o Justice, freedom, and opportunity for all are non-negotiable elements of wealth harmony.

7. Environmental Wealth (Harmony with Nature & Regenerative Stewardship)

- o The Earth is the foundation of all wealth—destroying nature is the ultimate form of self-impoverishment.

- o True prosperity is regenerative, not extractive.

8. Time Wealth (Freedom, Leisure & Presence)

- o The wealthiest people are those who control their time—modern society glorifies overwork, yet time is the most finite resource.

- o True wealth is the freedom to spend time on what truly matters.

9. Creative Wealth (Creative Expression)

- o Life itself is a creative act, to be fully alive and live a full and fulfilling Life we must engage with Life through creating.

- o True wealth is creating the Life we love living.

The Interconnected Nature of Wealth Harmony

These nine pillars are not isolated—they are deeply interconnected, forming a holistic framework for a truly abundant Life. When one pillar is neglected, the others inevitably suffer, leading to a Life that feels incomplete or out of alignment.

For example, financial success means little if it comes at the cost of physical health and emotional fulfillment. Likewise, a strong sense of purpose and inner peace can sustain a person through financial difficulties, but persistent economic insecurity will ultimately erode well-being. The goal is not to rigidly balance these aspects at all times but to recognize when they fall into disharmony and take steps to restore coherence.

Understanding wealth in this expanded way invites us to rethink our relationship with work, success, and societal structures. It forces us to ask: Are we truly wealthy, or are we simply accumulating money at the cost of everything else?

In the next section, we will explore how the current economic system has created a deep disharmony among these pillars—leaving humanity fragmented, exhausted, and unfulfilled.

III. The Disharmony of Our Current Economic System

The modern economic system has led to a profound fragmentation of wealth, prioritizing financial accumulation at the expense of other essential forms of prosperity. In its current form, this system is neither sustainable nor aligned with human well-being—it is extractive, exploitative, and deeply disconnected from the natural rhythms of Life.

Instead of fostering true abundance, our global economy has:

- **Monetized every aspect of Life**, reducing relationships, health, and even time itself into commodities.

- **Created structural inequities**, where a select few accumulate vast wealth while billions struggle to meet their basic needs.

- **Encouraged unsustainable consumerism**, leading people to seek fulfillment through material goods rather than meaningful experiences.

- **Exploited natural resources**, treating the Earth as an infinite source of extraction rather than a living system to be nurtured.

The Worship of Money as the Sole Metric of Value

In today's world, money reigns as the ultimate measure of success, dictating what we value, respect, prioritize and pursue—often at the cost of human and planetary well-being. In this system, the only things that matter are those that can be readily converted into cash at the Altar of Money. Wisdom, integrity, art, and even love itself have been relegated to secondary importance because they cannot be readily monetized. This false hierarchy has created a reality where:

- People are willing to sacrifice health, relationships, and purpose for financial success, only to realize too late that these were their true sources of wealth.

- Entire industries exist not to create real value but to manipulate perception and extract profit, leading to a world where financial gain trumps ethical considerations.

- The false scarcity mindset prevails, convincing humanity that there is never "enough," driving perpetual accumulation at the expense of well-being.

The Reduction of Life to Transactions

As wealth has been equated solely with money, human existence has been reduced to an endless series of transactions:

- Relationships are now commodified—dating apps, networking events, and even friendships become strategic exchanges rather than genuine connections.

- Healthcare is not a fundamental right but a for-profit industry, where cures are secondary to maintaining a steady stream of lifelong customers.

- Time, the most finite resource of all, has been financialized, forcing individuals to sell their hours in pursuit of an illusionary security that never arrives.

The Market as the Ultimate Authority

We live in an era where market forces dictate morality, culture, and even identity:

- Governments and policies are shaped by corporate interests, not by what is best for human flourishing.

- Economic indicators like GDP are treated as the ultimate measures of progress, even when they signal environmental destruction and human suffering.

- The financial system rewards short-term profit maximization, ensuring that decisions are driven by immediate returns rather than long-term wisdom.

The Consequences of Living in a Wealth-Disharmonic Society

This distortion of wealth has led to profound consequences:

- A rise in mental health crises—anxiety, burnout, and existential despair are symptoms of a world that values productivity over well-being.

- A deepening spiritual starvation—people increasingly seek fulfillment through consumption, distraction, and addiction, yet find themselves more disconnected than ever.

- A culture of exploitation rather than regeneration—when wealth is extracted at the expense of human dignity and planetary health, society begins to unravel.

The Need for a Paradigm Shift

The current economic model is built on disharmony, disconnection, and short-term gain at the expense of lasting prosperity. It is neither sustainable nor compatible with human fulfillment. The time has come to move beyond this outdated paradigm and establish a system that values holistic wealth, coherence, and regenerative abundance.

In the next section, we will explore how we can transition toward a new paradigm—one that restores harmony among all aspects of wealth, allowing individuals and societies to thrive in a way that is regenerative, fulfilling, and aligned with Life itself.

IV. The Principle of Wealth Harmony

The transition from a fragmented and extractive economic model to one of true prosperity requires a fundamental shift in how we understand wealth. Wealth Harmony is not about simply redistributing financial assets or tweaking existing structures—it is about redefining the core principles that govern human prosperity.

At its essence, Wealth Harmony recognizes that true wealth is achieved when all aspects of prosperity exist in coherence, rather than competition. This means creating harmony between financial, emotional, spiritual, and environmental wealth, ensuring that individuals and societies do not have to sacrifice one form of wealth to achieve another.

This principle does not reject financial wealth but rather places it in proper relationship with other aspects of well-being. Money is a tool, not an end in itself—when it is aligned with purpose, meaning, and regeneration, it becomes a force for holistic prosperity rather than an instrument of control or extraction. When money serves humanity, it enables prosperity; when humanity serves money, it creates suffering.

Syntropy vs. Entropy: The True Nature of Wealth

o grasp Wealth Harmony, we must recognize that the Universe thrives on syntropy—the continuous renewal of Life—rather than mere entropy and decay. On the surface, all physical matter appears to be subject to entropy—aging, decaying, and ultimately perishing into chaos. Yet, when examined more deeply, nothing ever truly dies; it transforms, offering itself in service to the continuation of Life itself. The cycle of birth, decay, and renewal reveals a higher-order intelligence at work, ensuring that nothing is ever truly lost—it is simply rearranged into a new form of expression.

For example, a supernova explosion appears, at first glance, to be an act of destruction—obliterating a star. Yet, this explosion scatters stardust across the Universe, forming the very building blocks of new Life, new planets, and new galaxies. In this way, what seems to be an end is actually a catalyst for regeneration. This is the true nature of Wealth Harmony—it is not about stagnation or rigid balance, but about continuous transformation and renewal. True wealth, like Life itself, is syntropic, ever-expanding and evolving in service to something greater.

Core Tenets of Wealth Harmony

- **Flow Over Accumulation** - True wealth is not hoarded but circulates dynamically, enriching both individuals and the collective.

- **Value Creation Over Extraction** - Financial success must stem from authentic value creation, not through exploitation or manipulation.

- **Beauty Over Profits** - Beauty—whether in architecture, art, nature, or relationships—is a direct manifestation of coherence. When we prioritize beauty, we align with the deeper intelligence that governs all of Life. Profits, when properly aligned, emerge naturally from this state of flow.

- **Regenerative Finance** - Economic systems must be designed to support Life, communities, and ecosystems rather than degrade them.

- **A New Purpose for Wealth** - Wealth exists to enhance the human experience, fostering creativity, freedom, and collective well-being, rather than serving as a metric of power or dominance.

- **Harmony and Alignment** – Wealth should be distributed in a way that supports both individual self-actualization and collective flourishing, ensuring that no one form of wealth is pursued at the sacrifice of another.

A New Vision for Prosperity

A thriving society is one in which people are not forced to trade their health for income, time for productivity, or purpose for profit. The old paradigm of wealth, built on control, scarcity, and competition, is no longer viable. In its place, a new socio-economic principle must emerge—one that acknowledges the interconnectedness of all dimensions of wealth and fosters an environment where financial stability, well-being, and purpose coexist in harmony.

Wealth Harmony is not a utopian ideal but an attainable reality when we shift our economic and cultural structures to reflect higher intelligence, creativity, human well-being, and sustainability. It requires a fundamental realignment of priorities—one that ensures that financial wealth does not eclipse the other vital elements that make Life truly rich.

As we move forward, consider: In what ways is your own wealth in harmony or disharmony? What shifts in perspective or action would bring greater coherence to your Life?

In the next section, we will explore practical pathways to integrate Wealth Harmony into our economic systems, businesses, and personal lives, enabling a more just, abundant, and fulfilling world for all.

V. The Path Forward: Designing a Future of Wealth Harmony

The realization of Wealth Harmony requires more than theoretical understanding—it demands tangible, systemic shifts in how we structure our economies, businesses, and personal lives. Moving from an extractive, scarcity-based system to one that fosters coherence, regeneration, and true abundance means rethinking the foundational pillars that govern our society.

Redefining Success: Shifting from GDP to Well-Being Metrics

- Current economic models prioritize growth at all costs, using GDP as the primary measure of progress. Yet, rising GDP often correlates with increased environmental destruction, mental health crises, and social inequities.

- We must adopt **new metrics** that measure holistic well-being, such as:

  - **Genuine Wealth Index (GWI)** – Tracks financial stability, health, education, and Life satisfaction.

  - **Regenerative Prosperity Index (RPI)** – Measures economic activities that enhance, rather than degrade, ecosystems and human well-being.

  - **Time Sovereignty Index (TSI)** – Evaluates how much freedom individuals have over their time, rather than simply measuring productivity.

Business as a Force for Holistic Prosperity

- Companies must move beyond profit-maximization models and embrace Wealth Harmony principles in their operations.

- Business leaders should shift from extraction-based economics to models of value creation and regeneration, ensuring that:

  - Employee well-being is prioritized over sheer efficiency.

  - Supply chains operate ethically and in alignment with sustainability.

  - Organizational success is measured not only by revenue but also by positive impact on society and nature.

Reframing the Employer-Employee Relationship: A Symbiotic Partnership

For true Wealth Harmony to exist in business, the outdated paradigm of employees as mere resources to be managed, optimized, or extracted from must be discarded. A company is not a machine where labor is a cog; it is a living system that thrives only when all parts work in mutual support.

At a higher-order level of intelligence, both the business and the employee recognize their interdependence—they exist in a symbiotic relationship where both must contribute and both must thrive.

- The employer is in service to the employee, ensuring the conditions for creativity, well-being, and prosperity to flourish. When employees thrive, they bring their highest levels of energy, innovation, and dedication to their work.

- The employee, in turn, is in service to the company, recognizing that without contributing to the organization's success, the business cannot generate the wealth necessary to support and uplift its people.

- This mirrors the same principle seen at the societal level, where citizens and communities must actively contribute to collective well-being, just as a thriving society must provide opportunity, support, and dignity to its members.

The future of business lies in moving away from a hierarchical, control-driven model to one of shared stewardship, where leadership is measured not by how well employees are controlled but by how well they are empowered to bring their best selves to their work.

A Regenerative Economic Model

- The financial system must evolve from an accumulation-based structure to one that flows, circulates, and nourishes Life.

- Strategies for creating a regenerative economy include:

  - **Circular Economic Systems** – Transitioning away from wasteful, linear production models toward regenerative cycles that reuse and repurpose resources.

  - **Decentralized Wealth Distribution** – Empowering local economies through community-driven financial models, reducing dependence on centralized financial institutions.

  - **Conscious Capital Deployment** – Redirecting investment capital towards ventures that align with Wealth Harmony rather than speculative markets detached from real-world value.

Personal Wealth Alignment: Living in Harmony with Life's Rhythms

- Individuals can integrate Wealth Harmony into their lives by:

  - Shifting their definition of success from external accumulation to inner fulfillment.

  - Prioritizing time wealth—fostering autonomy over one's schedule rather than being enslaved by overwork.

  - Cultivating regenerative relationships—valuing love, trust, and collaboration over competitive gain.

Society as a Reflection of Who We Are

For society to become a safe, kind, tolerant, and peaceful place, each of us must embody those very qualities in our daily interactions. Society is not an external entity operating separately from us—it is a mirror reflecting who we are collectively. If we desire a world of kindness, we must first be kind to others. If we seek a just and peaceful society, we must ourselves act with fairness and peacefulness in all our dealings. The world does not arbitrarily bestow prosperity, harmony, or goodwill—it reflects back the energy and behaviors we contribute.

Being polite, courteous, and respectful is not a sign of weakness; rather, it is a sign of higher-order intelligence. These qualities generate positive reciprocity, drawing better experiences into our lives. Conversely, bitterness, anger, and condescension inevitably invite back the very same negativity we put forth into the world. The fundamental Truth is this: the world is not happening to us—it is responding to us. By embodying the values we wish to see in the world, we become active participants in the manifestation of a society built on Wealth Harmony rather than dysfunction.

We stand at a crossroads—one path continues the relentless worship of money, leading to systemic collapse and spiritual depletion. The other path embraces a multidimensional vision of wealth, one where prosperity is not measured by numbers alone but by the depth of our relationships, the vitality of our environment, and the well-being of our communities. The choice is ours, and the time to choose is now.

Conclusion: The Future Is Created Now

Wealth Harmony is not just an economic or social theory—it is a new way of living and organizing society. It is the recognition that true wealth extends beyond financial capital to include well-being, purpose, justice, safety, freedom, happiness, and the opportunity for all to flourish. This shift requires a fundamental transformation in how we perceive value, success, and prosperity.

If we continue to worship money at the expense of all else, civilization will collapse under the weight of its own incoherence. When financial accumulation becomes the sole metric of wealth, it erodes the very foundation upon which Life is meant to thrive. We have already seen the consequences—rising inequality, environmental degradation, spiritual depletion, and a pervasive sense of emptiness despite material abundance. A world that prioritizes profit over people, power over purpose, and consumption over connection cannot sustain itself.

Yet, there is another path—one that embraces a multidimensional view of wealth and creates a society where prosperity is not confined to a select few but is experienced by all. This is not about rejecting money or material success but about placing them in proper relationship with the full spectrum of human and planetary well-being. Wealth, in its truest form, is regenerative. It does not accumulate in stagnant reservoirs but flows, nourishes, and uplifts all aspects of Life.

The real question is not "How much money have we accumulated?" but "Are we truly wealthy in every aspect of Life—our health, relationships, purpose, and legacy?" Are we cultivating the kind of wealth that endures—the wealth of meaningful relationships, vibrant health, creative expression, inner peace, and a thriving world for future generations?

The future is not something that happens to us—it is something we create. The age of scarcity, competition, and extraction is coming to an end. The age of Wealth Harmony is beginning. The question is—will we rise to meet it?

VI. Conclusion: The Future of Wealth Harmony

We are now at a defining moment in history—where the way we perceive and create wealth will determine the trajectory of civilization. The outdated model, where wealth is hoarded by the few and measured solely in monetary terms, has led us into crisis after crisis, fostering inequality, environmental collapse, and societal discord. If we remain on this path, the consequences will be catastrophic.

However, the collapse of the old paradigm presents an extraordinary opportunity—to rebuild our economic and social structures on the foundation of Wealth Harmony. This is not just an expression of higher-order intelligence; it is a Life-or-Death practical choice that humanity must collectively make. According to the Global Footprint Network, a non-profit sustainability science lab, already more than 80 percent of the world's population lives in countries that are running ecological deficits, using more resources than what their ecosystems can regenerate. If the rest of the world aspires to the Western lifestyle of consumption, the entire living system of the planet will readily collapse.

Hence, Wealth Harmony is not a theoretical ideal—it is the only practical solution that aligns with both the survival of civilization and the well-being of individuals. We must wean ourselves off the illusion that materialism will fulfill us, when the data clearly shows that it does not. Instead, excessive consumption has created profound negative consequences, from chronic illness and mental health epidemics to the opioid crisis and widespread ecological destruction.

A Spiritual Crisis cannot be transcended through materialism or other hollow markers of success such as fame, status, or prestige. The hunger of the Soul is not satisfied by accumulation, but by experiencing true wealth—the kind that money cannot buy: love, purpose, deep connection, and inner peace. Wealth Harmony is not just about economics; it is about restoring what has been lost in our relentless pursuit of external validation.

If we embrace a multidimensional view of wealth, one that recognizes financial prosperity as just one pillar among many, we can create a world where abundance is not a privilege of the few, but a shared experience for all. The reality is that true wealth is not about accumulation—it is about flow, connection, and regeneration.

This shift requires a radical realignment of our priorities. Instead of asking how much we can extract, we must ask how much we can contribute. Instead of measuring our worth by net worth, we must measure it by the depth of our impact, the richness of our relationships, and the coherence of our existence.

The window to make this shift is closing rapidly. If we do not consciously transition to a Life-sustaining model of wealth, the collapse of the old system will not be a choice—it will be an inevitability.

The task ahead is not to reform broken systems but to transcend them altogether—to birth an entirely new way of being, one that aligns with the intelligence of Life itself. The question is no longer whether we have enough money, but whether we have cultivated true wealth—the kind that nourishes the human Spirit, restores the natural world, and honors the sacred interconnectedness of all things.

A future of Wealth Harmony is not something we wait for—it is something we create, now, through every choice we make. The choice we have before us is clear: cling to a crumbling system built on illusion and extraction, or step boldly into an era of coherence, regeneration, and shared prosperity—where true wealth uplifts humanity and restores our planet.

Next Up: The Grand Odyssey of Evolution

But why is all of this happening? Why would a Cosmic Order allow such suffering? The answer lies in evolution—a process in which God experiences every aspect of itself through this grand dream, and we, as its fractals, are an essential part of this unfolding journey. Humanity must come to know the dark so that it can transcend it and, in doing so, realize its Divine origins. As we move forward, we will explore the deeper meaning of this evolutionary process and how it shapes the destiny of both individuals and civilization itself.

In every Crucible, there's a choice that must be made.

WEALTH HARMONY:
REDEFINING PROSPERITY FOR A NEW ERA

EXECUTIVE SUMMARY

Why Should You Read This Chapter?

Wealth has long been measured solely in financial terms, yet true prosperity encompasses much more. This chapter challenges conventional economics and introduces Wealth Harmony—a multidimensional approach integrating financial, emotional, spiritual, and ecological well-being.

If we continue prioritizing money over meaning and consumption over sustainability, civilization will collapse under its own weight. The Western world on average already consumes resources at roughly five times the planet's regenerative capacity. If this model spreads, ecological disaster is inevitable.

Transitioning to Wealth Harmony is not just a noble idea—it is a practical necessity. True wealth is not mere accumulation but the quality of our lives, our relationships, and our alignment with Life itself.

By reading this chapter, you will gain insight into:

- How our economic system fuels crisis and disharmony
- Why wealth must include health, purpose, connection, and sustainability
- How Wealth Harmony offers a path to prosperity without ecological collapse
- The role of spiritual fulfillment in redefining true abundance

The question before us is clear: Will we cling to a system unraveling before our eyes, or will we embrace higher intelligence and co-create a future of true wealth and regeneration?

Executive Summary: Key Takeaways

- **Wealth Harmony redefines prosperity** beyond financial accumulation by integrating health, purpose, connection, and sustainability. True prosperity cannot be measured solely by the numbers in a bank account but by the well-being of individuals, communities, and the planet. A world that prioritizes only financial wealth while neglecting other dimensions of Life is destined for fragmentation and crisis.

- **The Western world consumes resources at five times Earth's regenerative capacity**, a model that, if scaled globally, will lead to ecological collapse. Our planet's natural systems cannot sustain the level of extraction and waste we currently impose upon it. Without a shift toward regenerative and Life-affirming economic models, humanity will deplete the very foundation that makes prosperity possible.

- **Material wealth alone does not equate to fulfillment**—rising chronic illness, mental health crises, and social fragmentation prove this. Despite unprecedented material abundance, millions suffer from stress, anxiety, and a lack of purpose. True wealth must encompass well-being, inner peace, and meaningful relationships rather than being reduced to material accumulation.

- **The current economic system fosters disharmony** by prioritizing short-term financial gain over long-term well-being. Companies, governments, and individuals are trapped in a cycle of maximizing profit without considering the broader consequences. This extractive model leads to burnout, inequality, and environmental degradation, all of which erode the very fabric of human flourishing.

- **True wealth flows rather than accumulates**—it must be regenerative, nourishing both individuals and the planet. Like a healthy ecosystem, a thriving economy should circulate resources in a way that benefits all participants rather than hoarding them in stagnant reservoirs of power and privilege. Wealth Harmony recognizes that abundance is not about taking more but about ensuring that prosperity moves and enriches all aspects of Life.

- **A new economic paradigm must emerge** that values contribution, coherence, and interconnectedness over extraction and control. Instead of seeking relentless economic growth at any cost, we must build systems that regenerate communities, restore ecosystems, and support human well-being. Wealth must be measured by its ability to sustain and enhance Life, not by how much can be accumulated.

- **Time, relationships, and spiritual fulfillment are core components of true wealth** and must be prioritized alongside financial stability. A society obsessed with endless work, consumerism, and productivity often sacrifices what matters most—meaningful human connection, time to reflect, and the inner peace that comes from living in alignment with one's values.

- **Businesses must move from exploitation to value creation**, fostering environments where employees and communities thrive. A truly prosperous enterprise is not one that maximizes shareholder profits at any cost but one that nurtures its workforce, supports local communities, and operates in harmony with nature. The future of business must be regenerative, not extractive.

- **Society reflects who we are collectively**—if we want a just and harmonious world, we must embody those qualities ourselves. A culture of greed, competition, and selfishness creates a world of division and instability, whereas a culture based on generosity, cooperation, and integrity fosters true prosperity. The transformation of our systems begins with the transformation of our consciousness.

- **The transition to Wealth Harmony is not optional—it is a necessity** if humanity is to survive and flourish in the long term. The old paradigm of materialism, hyper-consumption, and disconnection is collapsing under its own weight. We stand at the threshold of a new way of being, one where wealth serves Life rather than destroys it.

- **The question is no longer "How much money do we have?" but rather "Are we truly wealthy in every aspect of Life?"** Financial success alone does not determine a fulfilling Life. True wealth is measured in the richness of our relationships, the vitality of our health, the integrity of our actions, and the sustainability of our world. The time has come to redefine prosperity on terms that honor Life, rather than diminish it.

THE GRAND ODYSSEY OF EVOLUTION

Section I: The Eternal Unfolding of the Cosmos

An Odyssey Without End

To truly grasp evolution, we must expand our vision beyond the conventional constraints of time. Evolution is not a mere linear ascent or confined to biological adaptation—it is an unfolding symphony of the highest order intelligence expressed through form, spanning eons beyond human comprehension. And yet, despite its vastness, we are not mere spectators to this grand unfolding; we are participants, woven into the very fabric of existence itself.

The term *Odyssey* signifies more than a journey; it is a purposeful adventure marked by trials, revelations, and transformation. The Cosmos itself is on a *Grand Odyssey*; an infinite unfolding that stretches across time, space, galaxies, Universes, and whatever might be beyond. While modern science seeks to map the contours of this vast terrain through equations and observations, the ancient wisdom traditions understood something even deeper: evolution is not merely a process, it is a mystery—an infinite act of creation in which consciousness seeks to know itself.

A Universe Without Expiry

Observational evidence suggests the Universe has no definitive expiration. It expands and contracts, births stars and swallows them in black holes, cycles through destruction and renewal with a rhythm that suggests something far greater than randomness. To the ancient Vedic seers, this was the *Lila*, the divine play of existence, an eternal cosmic dance with no beginning and no end. The Taoists called it the *Tao*, the formless way that moves through all things. The Egyptians saw it as the breath of Atum, an unceasing act of creation and dissolution.

The mechanistic worldview of reductionist science attempted to strip evolution of its inherent mystery, reducing it to random mutations and selection pressures. But even in the heart of modern physics, we now glimpse what the ancients long understood: the Cosmos is not a lifeless machine, but an intricate, self-organizing intelligence. The vast web of galaxies, the mathematical harmony in nature's design, and Life's emergence from apparent chaos all point to an underlying higher order intelligence engaged in a Cosmic symphony of eternal creative unfolding.

The Golden Ratio and the Blueprint of Life

If there is a universal signature of this intelligence, it is found in the *Golden Ratio* (Phi, 1.618...). Unlike the Fibonacci sequence, which only approximates this ratio, the Golden Ratio is an irregular, infinite pattern woven into the fabric of Nature itself. It manifests in the spirals of galaxies, the proportions of the human body, the structure of DNA, the arrangement of sunflower seeds, and the symmetry of seashells. It is a mathematical constant that suggests not randomness, but coherence—an intrinsic intelligence shaping the material world.

This ratio is not just an aesthetic marvel; it is evidence that evolution is not arbitrary—it follows an unseen order, a deeper intelligence that we are only beginning to grasp. To recognize this is to realize that humanity itself is not an accident. We, too, are expressions of this intelligence, designed to unfold in ways that harmonize with the larger symphony of existence.

The Ancient Understanding of Evolution

Long before Darwin, long before genetic theory, the ancients understood evolution— not in the limited sense of biological adaptation, but as the evolution of consciousness through form. The Vedic tradition spoke of vast cycles known as *Yugas*, where human consciousness expands and contracts in rhythm with cosmic forces. The Greeks had their Ages of Man, where civilizations rose and fell according to the spiritual state of humanity. The Hopi and other indigenous cultures spoke of multiple worlds—each a phase of transformation leading to greater understanding.

Unlike the modern scientific narrative, which frames evolution as a series of random occurrences leading to ever-increasing complexity, these traditions discerned a deeper pattern, purpose, and progression. Evolution was not seen as the mere survival of the fittest, but as a sacred journey—an Odyssey—of intelligence awakening to itself.

Humanity at the Threshold

As we stand at this moment in history, we are not at the pinnacle of evolution, as we often like to believe. We are at an inflection point—a *Crucible*. The choices we make, the consciousness we cultivate, and the way we perceive our role in this unfolding story will determine whether we stagnate or ascend. Every civilization before us has faced this moment—a reckoning where the collective must choose between self-destruction or stepping into a higher octave of intelligence. The difference now is that our civilization is planetary, and there is nowhere left to retreat. The next phase of human evolution is not about further dominion over matter but about attuning to the intelligence that governs Life itself.

The Grand Odyssey of Evolution does not unfold outside of us where we are the passive witness; it unfolds through us and we are its active participant. We are both its creation and its co-creators. The question is no longer whether evolution is unfolding—the question is whether we will embrace our role within it or resist and endure the inevitable cataclysm of rejecting the forces that govern us.

Section II: Humanity's Place in the Grand Evolutionary Arc

The Four Evolutionary Stages of Human Consciousness

Throughout history, human consciousness has evolved through distinct phases, each marked by a shift in how we perceive ourselves, nature, and our place in the Cosmos. These stages are not merely social or technological advancements; they represent transformations in our fundamental awareness and interaction with reality. The journey of human evolution is not yet complete—we stand at a threshold between our current paradigm and the emergence of a new way of being.

1. **Primitive Instinct (Survival-Oriented Consciousness)**

   o Early humans lived in direct harmony with nature but operated primarily on instinct.

   o Tribal existence was based on survival, fear of the unknown, and a deep reliance on primal emotions.

   o Spirituality was animistic—rooted in an intuitive sense of nature's forces and ancestral wisdom.

2. **Structured Mind (The Birth of Civilization, Religion, and Rationalism)**

   o The rise of agriculture and settled societies led to hierarchical structures, organized religions, and the codification of knowledge.

   o Logic and rational thought emerged, giving rise to philosophy, science, and formal education.

   o Humanity shifted from animism to structured belief systems, often centering around divine authority figures.

3. **Awakening to Interconnection (Holism, Systems Thinking, and Consciousness Studies)**

    o With the advent of quantum physics, psychology, and systems theory, a new understanding of interconnectivity began to emerge.

    o Ancient wisdom resurfaced, aligning with modern discoveries about consciousness and the non-material aspects of existence.

    o This stage recognizes that intelligence is not confined to human cognition but is embedded in all aspects of Life and the Cosmos.

4. **Homo Luminous (Future Human Evolution—Integration of Matter and Spirit)**

    o The next stage of evolution is not technological but consciousness-based.

    o Humanity will move beyond rigid materialism into a state of integrated awareness—where the physical and the spiritual are no longer seen as separate.

    o This stage represents a harmonic alignment with the intelligence of Life itself, leading to new ways of being, relating, and creating.

Patterns of Rise and Collapse in Civilizations

History reveals a cyclical pattern in the rise and fall of civilizations. While each era believes itself to be unique, the underlying causes of societal decline remain eerily consistent: disconnection from higher wisdom, moral decay, unsustainable systems, and an overemphasis on external power. Past civilizations have faced a crucial choice—adapt and transcend or collapse under the weight of their own incoherence.

- **The Sumerians, Mayans, Romans, and Byzantines** all experienced this pattern of ascent, stagnation, and decline.

- Each reached a point where material progress outpaced spiritual and ethical wisdom, leading to internal fragmentation.

- **The difference today is that our civilization is planetary**—our choices affect the entire species and biosphere.

- **Myth and archetype have always pointed the way**—the Phoenix rising from the ashes, Prometheus bringing fire to mankind, the Hero's Journey—all stories of death, transformation, and rebirth.

The Inflection Point: Humanity's Current Spiritual Crisis of Low Levels of Consciousness

We are at a precipice unlike any before. The challenges we face—environmental destruction, political instability, social fragmentation—are symptoms, not causes. The root issue is a spiritual crisis of low levels of consciousness: our inability to perceive ourselves as an intrinsic part of the grand evolutionary arc.

- **The Illusion of Separation**: Humanity has long operated under the illusion that we are separate from nature, each other, and even our own deeper selves.

- **The Crisis of Meaning**: Modern Life is characterized by existential disconnection—an inability to find purpose beyond material accumulation and societal validation.

- **The Reckoning of Choice**: Unlike past civilizations, we now possess the knowledge, tools, and awareness to consciously shift the trajectory of evolution.

The question is: Will we step into the next phase of evolution, or will we resist and repeat the cycles of collapse?

Evolution as Conscious Participation

The evolution of humanity is not an external process—it is an internal transformation. As we awaken to the intelligence of Life, we move beyond the outdated paradigm of control and manipulation into one of harmony and co-creation.

- Our evolution is no longer about physical survival, but about the expansion of awareness.

- We are not separate from the evolutionary arc—we are its conscious agents.

- Each of us plays a role in determining the future of our species.

To embrace this moment is to recognize that we are no longer passive participants in evolution. We are the threshold generation, the ones who must choose whether humanity rises into its next octave of consciousness and its higher-order intelligence or remains shackled to outdated paradigms of fear and fragmentation.

What does Homo Luminous look like in action?

- A being who operates from love and wisdom, rather than fear and division.

- Someone who sees intelligence as not merely intellectual, but as an alignment with the flow of Life.

- An individual who embodies unity consciousness, moving beyond competition and separation into cooperation and creation.

The Grand Invitation

The Grand Odyssey of Evolution is not something that happens to us—it happens through us. This moment in history is not random—it is a call to those who are ready to step forward and embody the new way of being. The future is not preordained—we are its architects.

The invitation is clear: Step into the next phase of conscious evolution, or remain bound to a world that no longer serves the intelligence of Life.

Section III: The Cosmic Cycles of Birth, Death, and Rebirth

Earth as a Living System Undergoing Its Own Evolution

For centuries, humanity has viewed Earth as an inert backdrop to human affairs—a collection of resources to be extracted, tamed, and controlled. But this mechanistic perspective is increasingly proving to be a dangerous illusion. The Gaia Hypothesis, first proposed by scientist James Lovelock, offers a radically different understanding: Earth is not an object, but a living, self-regulating system. It is a vast intelligence unto itself, dynamically adapting and evolving just as all living organisms do. Indigenous traditions have long understood this Truth, referring to Earth as a great mother, a conscious being in her own right, rather than merely a collection of inorganic matter.

If we accept that Earth is alive, then we must also accept that it is undergoing its own evolutionary process, independent of yet intertwined with humanity's fate. Just as human beings go through cycles of death and rebirth, so too does the planet. Natural disasters, climate shifts, and mass extinctions are not random catastrophes—they are part of Earth's cyclical rhythm, its way of shedding outdated structures and regenerating new Life.

Throughout geological history, the Earth has experienced dramatic transformations—ice ages, great floods, and massive extinction events—all of which have paved the way for new evolutionary leaps. Life is not destroyed by these cycles; rather, it is purified, refined, and reorganized into more sophisticated, adaptable forms. Today, we are witnessing another great planetary transition, one that will determine whether humanity aligns with the next stage of evolution or resists it to its own peril.

Humanity's Role: Parasites or Stewards?

Humanity stands at a crossroads. For too long, we have acted as parasites, consuming the planet's resources without regard for long-term consequences. We have poisoned the waters, desecrated the soil, and disrupted the delicate ecological balance upon which all Life depends. We have convinced ourselves that nature is something to be dominated, rather than something to be in sacred relationship with. The result has been an escalating crisis—rising temperatures, collapsing ecosystems, and the mass extinction of species. If we continue down this path, we may soon find ourselves expelled from the planetary body, much like an infection the immune system can no longer tolerate.

But there is another choice. We can step into our rightful role as stewards—not rulers, not exploiters, but conscious participants in the grand evolutionary dance of Life. Many indigenous traditions have long understood this responsibility. They did not see themselves as separate from nature, but as co-creators within it, tasked with maintaining harmony and ensuring the continuity of Life for future generations. They understood that true intelligence is not about control, but about alignment—working in concert with the natural rhythms of the planet rather than imposing our own artificial order upon it.

This is the great invitation before us. Will we continue to act as parasites, accelerating the planet's destruction and sealing our own fate? Or will we evolve into conscious stewards, attuned to the wisdom of the living Earth, and actively participating in its renewal?

The Role of Crisis in Evolution

Crisis, catastrophe, and calamity are Divine gifts wrapped in sandpaper—they are the mechanisms through which the Universe propels evolution forward. Growth does not emerge from comfort; it arises from challenge. Just as muscles tear before they strengthen, just as fire clears the forest floor to make space for new growth, suffering is the necessary catalyst for transformation. Without discomfort, there would be no impulse to evolve, no reason to transcend outdated paradigms.

Every major evolutionary leap—biological, societal, and spiritual—has been preceded by a moment of reckoning, an existential test that forces individuals and civilizations to rise to new levels of intelligence. The Black Plague gave way to the Renaissance. The collapse of empires birthed new ways of governance. The crises of today are not the signs of doom but the initiatory fires of something greater.

This cycle of suffering, transformation, and rebirth is embedded in mythology across cultures. The Descent of Inanna in Sumerian tradition, the Resurrection of Osiris in

Egyptian mythology, and the death and rebirth of Dionysus in Greek lore all reflect the Truth that hardship is the crucible of renewal. These myths were not simply tales of the past—they were archetypal blueprints for the journey that all individuals and societies must undergo.

The Crucible Climax—The Final Resistance Before Transformation

Every transformation, whether personal or collective, reaches a Crucible Climax—a moment of immense pressure where the old paradigm fights to hold on even as the new one emerges. This is the final resistance before breakthrough, the point at which fear, doubt, and inertia surge to keep things as they are. In mythology, this is the Threshold Guardian, the great obstacle that must be overcome before the hero can claim their higher destiny. Today, humanity is facing its own Crucible Climax, and the resistance to change is palpable. Systems of power, entrenched belief structures, and fear-based conditioning are all fighting to maintain control—but they cannot stop the inevitable.

The question is: Will we break through, or will we collapse under the weight of our own resistance?

A Vision Beyond Crisis—What Lies Ahead?

If we are to embrace crisis as a catalyst, we must also envision what lies beyond it. The Black Plague gave birth to the Renaissance, an era of profound art, philosophy, and human potential. What kind of world can emerge from the challenges we face today?

A world awakened to the wisdom of nature, where humanity no longer operates in opposition to the living systems of the Earth but in co-creation with them. A civilization that understands intelligence is not merely technological but rooted in alignment with Life itself. A society where spiritual maturity replaces material obsession, and governance is based on wisdom rather than control.

This is not a utopian fantasy but a reality that is already stirring within those who see beyond the ashes of the old world. The turbulence of crisis is not an end, but the birth pangs of something greater. The only question is: will we embrace the transformation, or will we resist it, prolonging the pain of rebirth?

If we embrace this perspective, we cease resisting the inevitable turbulence of transformation. Instead, we move with it, seeing crisis as the means by which we break free from stagnation. This is the moment to evolve—not despite the storm, but because of it.

Section IV: The Next Evolutionary Leap—The Emergence of Homo Luminous

The Birth of a New Human Archetype

For millennia, Homo sapiens has defined itself through its dominance over nature, its ability to manipulate the environment, and its relentless pursuit of survival and expansion. But as we reach the limits of this paradigm, it is becoming clear that the next evolutionary leap is not technological—it is one of consciousness. Humanity is at a juncture where it must transcend the fear-based survival programming that has governed its past and step into an entirely new archetype: Homo luminous—the illuminated human.

Moving from Homo Sapiens to Homo Luminous

Homo luminous is not a new biological species but a profound transformation of human consciousness. It is a shift from separation to unity, from control to co-creation, from intellect to wisdom. This is the evolutionary leap from materialism to spiritual integration, where humanity no longer identifies solely with the physical body and ego, but as conscious beings interconnected with the fabric of existence itself.

Many wisdom traditions have long predicted this emergence. The Vedic concept of Satya Yuga describes a future era of divine consciousness, where humans live in harmony with Truth and Natural law. The Mayan prophecies of the 2012 baktun cycle did not foretell an apocalyptic end but the dawn of a new era—one where human beings awaken to their higher nature. Similarly, the Christian mystic tradition speaks of a "New Earth," a realm where enlightened humanity transcends the limitations of fear and fragmentation. These ancient prophecies all point to the same Truth: the emergence of a new archetype of human, one that aligns with the intelligence of the Cosmos rather than fights against it.

Systems That Thrive on Control Will Fight to Maintain the Status Quo

As the light of Homo luminous begins to rise, the shadows of the old paradigm fight to hold on. Systems built on hierarchy, fear, and control will not dissolve without resistance. The entrenched powers—whether political, economic, or ideological—will attempt to reinforce their structures through surveillance, coercion, and division. Their survival depends on humanity remaining in a state of dependence, blind to its own sovereignty and power.

This resistance is not new. Every great shift in consciousness has been met with fierce opposition. The mystics, sages, and revolutionaries who spoke Truth throughout history were persecuted, not because they were wrong, but because they threatened the illusion of control. Socrates, Yeshua, Hypatia, and countless others were silenced, yet their wisdom endured, planting the seeds of future awakenings. From the persecution of Galileo for challenging dogma to modern-day whistleblowers revealing systemic deception, these cycles repeat. And yet, Truth always outlives suppression.

Expect Turmoil, Backlash, and Chaos as the Old Paradigm Resists Its Own Demise

Just as a dying star erupts in one final, violent burst before collapsing into something new, so too will the old world convulse in its final throes. Economic systems will falter, institutions will lose legitimacy, and cultural divisions will widen. These are not signs of failure but of transformation.

Crisis is not merely destruction—it is a forcing function. It strips away what is incoherent, leaving only what is essential. Humanity is not given the luxury of choosing whether to evolve; rather, it is being compelled to evolve by the sheer unsustainability of the old paradigm. When something is misaligned with the intelligence of Life itself, it must either adapt or dissolve.

Chaos is not the end—it is the birth canal of the new. Those who understand this will not be swept away by fear, but will stand firm, knowing that destruction is the precursor to rebirth. It is during these moments of uncertainty that Homo luminous must anchor itself in Truth, love, and wisdom, acting as a beacon for those caught in the storm.

What Does an Awakened Humanity Look Like?

An awakened humanity is one that no longer operates from the paradigm of scarcity, competition, and control but from abundance, cooperation, and wisdom. Homo luminous does not see itself as separate from nature or from others but as part of an indivisible whole. This fundamental shift in awareness would manifest as:

- **Co-Creation Over Control:** No longer seeking to dominate nature, Homo luminous works in conscious partnership with the intelligence of the Earth, using technologies and systems that regenerate rather than deplete.

- **Inner Sovereignty Over External Authority:** Rather than relying on external institutions to dictate morality and Truth, an awakened humanity would operate from direct knowing, discerning Truth through deep inner alignment.

- **Heart-Centered Intelligence Over Cold Rationalism:** The union of intellect with love, where decision-making is guided by wisdom rather than mechanistic efficiency.

- **Embodied Spirituality Over Dogma:** Instead of seeking salvation in hierarchical religious systems, Homo luminous recognizes that divinity is not external—it is the very fabric of their being.

This shift will not happen overnight, nor will it occur through top-down institutional change. It is an individual awakening that reaches a critical mass, rippling through the morphogenetic field, until it becomes the new dominant paradigm.

The Role of Love, Wisdom, and Truth as Guiding Evolutionary Forces

At the core of this transformation are three immutable forces: **Love, Wisdom, and Truth.** These are not abstract concepts; they are the **structural forces of higher consciousness** that govern all of evolution.

- **Love is the unifying force**—it is what dissolves the illusion of separation and realigns humanity with the greater whole. In its highest form, love is not emotion, but the recognition of oneness.

- **Wisdom is the refinement of intelligence**—it is what allows humanity to align with the higher order of Life rather than working against it. Wisdom is intelligence tempered by experience, humility, and spiritual insight.

- **Truth is the luminous thread that connects all reality**—it is the Divine architecture of existence. As humanity awakens, Truth is no longer something debated or imposed; it becomes something self-evident.

These three forces are the signposts of Homo luminous. To embody them is to move beyond survival consciousness and step into the role of conscious co-creators with the Cosmos.

This is the path of the illuminated human, the great evolutionary leap that has been written in the stars, encoded in the myths of our ancestors, and whispered by sages across time. The question is no longer whether this transformation is happening—it is. The only question is: who among us will choose to embrace it?

Signs That the Shift Is Already Happening—The Global Spiritual Awakening and the Resurgence of Ancient Wisdom

Everywhere we look, there are signs that humanity is undergoing a profound awakening. A growing number of individuals are breaking free from outdated paradigms, questioning the structures that once seemed immutable, and seeking deeper meaning beyond material success. This awakening is not a fringe movement—it is a planetary shift, one that is drawing wisdom from the deep well of ancient teachings and integrating them with modern understanding.

The resurgence of interest in indigenous knowledge, Eastern mysticism, and esoteric traditions reflects a hunger for Truth that transcends dogma. The Hermetic principles, the teachings of the Tao, the wisdom of the Vedas, and the spiritual practices of the Andean and Native American traditions are being rediscovered—not as relics of the past, but as blueprints for navigating the present and future. What was once hidden in secret schools is now emerging into collective consciousness, forming the foundation for a new way of being.

Science Converging with Mysticism—Quantum Physics, Non-Locality, and the Nature of Reality

For centuries, science and spirituality seemed to be at odds, each claiming dominion over different aspects of reality. But as scientific inquiry pushes further into the mysteries of existence, it is beginning to validate what mystics have long known: reality is not solid, fixed, or mechanical, but fluid, interconnected, and governed by unseen forces.

Quantum physics has revealed that at the subatomic level, particles exist in a state of potentiality, influenced by observation itself. The principle of non-locality suggests that everything in the Universe is interconnected in ways that defy classical understanding. This aligns perfectly with the ancient concept of Indra's Net, a Vedic metaphor describing the Universe as an infinite web of interconnected jewels, each reflecting the whole.

The convergence of modern physics with mystical traditions is not accidental—it is part of the great unveiling, a moment where humanity is beginning to see beyond the illusion of separation. As these insights permeate collective consciousness, they lay the groundwork for a civilization that operates from the principles of unity rather than fragmentation.

The Resistance of the Old World—Systems That Thrive on Control Will Fight to Maintain the Status Quo

As the light of Homo luminous begins to rise, the shadows of the old paradigm fight to hold on. Systems built on hierarchy, fear, and control will not dissolve without resistance. The entrenched powers—whether political, economic, or ideological—will attempt to reinforce their structures through surveillance, coercion, and division. Their survival depends on humanity remaining in a state of dependence, blind to its own sovereignty and power.

This resistance is not new. Every great shift in consciousness has been met with fierce opposition. The mystics, sages, and revolutionaries who spoke Truth throughout history were persecuted, not because they were wrong, but because they threatened the illusion of control. Socrates, Yeshua, Hypatia, and countless others were silenced, yet their wisdom endured, planting the seeds of future awakenings.

Expect Turmoil, Backlash, and Chaos as the Old Paradigm Resists Its Own Demise

Just as a dying star erupts in one final, violent burst before collapsing into something new, so too will the old world convulse in its final throes. Economic systems will falter, institutions will lose legitimacy, and cultural divisions will widen. These are not signs of failure but of transformation.

Chaos is not the end—it is the birth canal of the new. Those who understand this will not be swept away by fear, but will stand firm, knowing that destruction is the precursor to rebirth. It is during these moments of uncertainty that Homo luminous must anchor itself in Truth, love, and wisdom, acting as a beacon for those caught in the storm.

We Must Navigate This Transition Without Fear

Fear is the fuel of the old paradigm, and it will be wielded as a weapon to keep humanity tethered to the past. But those who step into the light of Homo luminous must reject fear, seeing through the illusion of control and embracing the infinite potential that lies ahead.

The choice before us is simple: succumb to fear and regress, or rise into the next octave of human evolution. The time has come to choose.

And this choice is not theoretical—it must be embodied. The shift to Homo luminous is not something that will be handed to humanity; it is something that must be lived, breathed, and enacted daily. The structures of the old world will not simply vanish; they must be transcended through conscious action, radical alignment with Truth, and unwavering commitment to wisdom.

The time of passive spectatorship is over. Every individual is now faced with the question: Will I be a passive observer of this transition, or will I embody the principles of Homo luminous and become a force for the new world?

Section V: Conclusion—Embracing the Grand Odyssey

The Future Is Not Preordained—We Are Co-Creators

The story of human evolution is not written in stone. It is an unfolding narrative, shaped by the choices we make—individually and collectively. Evolution is not something happening *to us*; it is something happening *through us.* We are not passive observers of this transition but active co-creators of the next phase of human consciousness.

The power of choice has never been more critical. Do we resist the call of higher intelligence and remain bound to the old paradigm, or do we step boldly into the unknown, trusting that an entirely new way of being is possible? The future is not something imposed upon us by fate—it is an emergent reality shaped by the thoughts we think, the actions we take, and the values we embody.

Each of us carries the potential for awakening. Each of us has the power to accelerate this transition—not by waiting for external systems to change, but by becoming the change itself. The transformation to Homo luminous does not require permission from institutions or validation from the outside world. It begins within, in the silent, unwavering decision to live in alignment with the intelligence of Life itself.

Living the New Paradigm Now

Many look toward an idealized future—a golden age of enlightenment, peace, and unity—without realizing that this shift is not a distant utopia; it is an emergent reality already unfolding. The consciousness of Homo luminous is not something that will manifest overnight, nor will it be granted by external forces. It is a lived experience, one that must be embodied in every thought, action, and relationship.

How Can We Embody the Consciousness of Homo Luminous Today?

The transition to an evolved humanity does not begin with grand movements or systemic overhauls—it begins in the micro-moments of everyday Life. It is the quality of our awareness, the depth of our integrity, and the coherence of our actions that determines whether we align with the new paradigm or remain shackled to the old.

Here are practical ways to align with evolutionary intelligence in daily Life:

- **Operate from Love, Not Fear:** Make decisions that reflect unity, compassion, and wisdom, rather than reactionary fear and control.

- **Engage in Deep Inquiry:** Question narratives that perpetuate separation and division. Seek universal Truth beyond societal programming.

- **Honor the Intelligence of Nature:** Align your actions with Life-affirming principles, respecting the Earth as a living, conscious being.

- **Cultivate Inner Sovereignty:** Reclaim the power of your own discernment rather than outsourcing Truth to external authorities.

- **Embody Co-Creation:** Live as if the new world is already here. Speak, act, and build as though the paradigm of Homo luminous is fully realized.

The more individuals embody these principles, the more the morphogenetic field shifts toward coherence. This is not philosophy; it is physics. The dominant energetic blueprint of humanity is being rewritten, one awakened Soul at a time. And once the critical threshold—the tipping point— is reached, the shift will become unstoppable.

The Grand Odyssey of Evolution is not ending—it is expanding. We are standing at the precipice of the greatest leap in human consciousness ever recorded.

The question is no longer whether evolution is happening—the question is whether we will participate in it consciously. Will we resist and stagnate, or will we step boldly into the unknown, surrendering to the intelligence that has been guiding this Universe from the beginning?

The time for speculation is over. The time for embodiment is now.

You and I are the call. The choice is now.

The Final Call—Mankind's Phoenix Rising

Every great transformation in nature, myth, and human history reaches a climactic moment—a crucible of intense pressure that forces either collapse or rebirth. We are now entering that Crucible Climax, where the full weight of our individual and collective Spiritual Crisis collides with the urgency of planetary awakening.

Part VI is the final call, where the path of Homo luminous is no longer an abstract concept but the decisive factor that determines whether humanity rises like the Phoenix or succumbs to planetary cataclysm. There is no middle ground.

In Chapter 19—Humanity's Crucible: Planetary Cataclysm or the Phoenix, we will confront the stark reality that we stand on the precipice of either total collapse or a radical transformation. The forces of destruction and renewal are converging, and we must understand how to navigate this critical juncture with clarity, strength, and wisdom.

Then, in Chapter 20—The Christos Revolution: The Unraveling of the Universe Within, we will explore the deeper spiritual revelation at the heart of this transition. The Christos is not a religious figure but a state of Divine consciousness—one that has been seeded in humanity for millennia, awaiting activation. This is the final initiation, the unraveling of the Universe within, where the individual and collective awakening become one.

The Grand Odyssey of Evolution has led us here, to the threshold of a new world. But thresholds demand a choice. Do we step through and claim our higher nature, or do we turn away and retreat into the familiar darkness?

Part VI is the answer to that question. It is the final revelation, the last initiation, and the greatest challenge we have ever faced.

The Phoenix is calling. Will we rise?

In every Crucible, there's a choice that must be made.

THE GRAND ODYSSEY OF EVOLUTION

EXECUTIVE SUMMARY

Why Should You Read This Chapter?

This chapter challenges the conventional understanding of evolution, shifting the narrative from mere biological adaptation to a grand odyssey of consciousness expanding through form. Humanity is not at the peak of its development, but at a pivotal juncture—one where it must choose between stagnation and transcendence. This choice is not simply about technological advancement or economic stability, but about the very fabric of our awareness and the way we engage with existence itself.

As civilizations before us have reached moments of great crisis, they have either collapsed under the weight of their unconsciousness or transcended into a higher order of wisdom. We are now facing a similar moment, but on a planetary scale. This chapter invites you to step beyond the illusion of separateness, competition, and control, and into a deeper understanding of what it means to be truly human. It explores how our crises—whether environmental, social, or existential—are not external problems but manifestations of a deeper Spiritual Crisis that can only be resolved through an inner transformation.

If you seek a deeper understanding of why the world appears to be unraveling, and why these seemingly chaotic times are, in fact, an evolutionary Crucible, then this chapter is essential. It will show you why the emergence of Homo luminous is not just a speculative idea but an inevitable shift that is already unfolding—and how you, as an individual, can play an integral role in this transformation.

Executive Summary: Key Takeaways

- **Evolution is not purely biological but a grand odyssey of consciousness expanding through form.** While Darwinian evolution explains survival mechanics, it does not address the deeper intelligence that guides Life toward greater complexity, coherence, and harmony. The true nature of evolution is not random—it is the unfolding of an inherent intelligence embedded in the fabric of reality. Humanity is not an endpoint of evolution but an ongoing experiment in consciousness, now facing a choice to align with higher intelligence or remain trapped in self-destructive patterns.

- **Humanity is at an inflection point where it must choose between stagnation and transcendence.** Every great civilization before us has faced a moment of reckoning—some have collapsed due to their inability to evolve, while others have risen by aligning with higher wisdom. We now face a planetary reckoning, where technological advancement without spiritual evolution will only lead to further fragmentation. The path forward is not about external progress alone, but about inner transformation, without which no true progress can be sustained.

- **Our crisis is not environmental, technological, or political at its core—it is a crisis of consciousness, a Spiritual Crisis that determines all external realities.** The dysfunctions we see in the world today—climate change, social unrest, economic instability—are not isolated crises, but symptoms of humanity's disconnection from higher intelligence. Without restoring inner alignment with Truth, wisdom, and love, no external solutions will be truly effective. The way forward is not just through policy or innovation, but through an inner revolution in how we perceive and engage with Life itself.

- **The emergence of Homo luminous is the next evolutionary leap—a shift in consciousness from fear and control to unity and co-creation.** Just as Homo sapiens emerged from prior species through a leap in cognitive awareness, humanity now stands on the edge of another profound transition. Homo luminous is not a new physical species but a new way of being—one that transcends scarcity, fear, and separation, embracing wisdom, coherence, and interconnectedness. The emergence of this archetype is already underway, but its full realization depends on whether enough individuals embody it in their daily lives.

- **This transformation is not something happening to us; it is something happening through us. We are the co-creators of our collective destiny.** Evolution does not impose itself upon us—we participate in it, either consciously or unconsciously. The shift toward Homo luminous is not an event that will arrive externally, but a state of being that must be cultivated within. Every individual who awakens to this Truth accelerates the transformation of the collective, bringing the new paradigm closer to full realization.

- **The resistance of the old paradigm—hierarchical systems based on fear and control—will intensify as the new paradigm emerges.** Every major shift in human history has been met with resistance. The systems built upon control, exploitation, and fragmentation will not surrender willingly. Instead, they will fight to maintain their grip through fear-mongering, coercion, and division. Understanding this resistance is key, as it allows us to navigate the transition without succumbing to fear or despair.

- **Living the new paradigm now is the key to accelerating the transition—by embodying love, wisdom, Truth, and inner sovereignty in daily Life.** The shift into Homo luminous is not something that will happen in the distant future—it is happening now, through every choice we make. The more we align with higher intelligence, act from love rather than fear, and reclaim our inner sovereignty, the more rapidly the new paradigm crystallizes. This is not an abstract concept; it is an active practice of being.

- **We are now entering the Crucible Climax, where humanity faces the ultimate choice: collapse into chaos or rise into a new era of higher intelligence and divine embodiment.** Every transformative process involves pressure. We are in that crucible now—the moment where everything is being tested, refined, and ultimately restructured. This is not a time for passivity, but for conscious participation. The choice before us is clear: will we rise into coherence, or will we dissolve in the entropy of our own unconsciousness?

VI – The Final Call: Mankind's Phoenix Rising

HUMANITY'S CRUCIBLE: PLANETARY CATACLYSM OR THE PHOENIX

I. Introduction: The Crossroads of Humanity

Humanity stands at the precipice of its greatest reckoning—a Crucible where our collective fate will be forged in the fires of choice. This is not just a crisis of systems, politics, or economies; it is an existential initiation—a test that has been foretold in myth, scripture, and prophecy across cultures and eras.

Throughout history, all civilizations have faced their Crucibles. The Egyptians spoke of the Bennu, the divine bird that rises from the ashes, a precursor to the Phoenix of Greek mythology. The Hindus described the cycles of creation and destruction through the Yugas, with the Kali Yuga marking an era of darkness before renewal. The Hopi warned of a time when humanity would be forced to choose between a spiritual path and self-destruction. The Alchemy of the ancients was not just about transforming metals—it was the science of transmuting the Soul, of burning away the dross to reveal pure gold.

What these traditions describe is not a random catastrophe, but a sacred pattern, a recurring event in the Grand Architecture of all Creation. Each time humanity reaches the precipice of its own undoing, it is met with a choice: to remain in spiritual ignorance and perish, or to rise in wisdom and be reborn.

Today, we face the Meta Crisis—the root from which all Earthly crises have emerged. The Polycrisis—failing institutions, ecological devastation, perpetual war, and economic instability—are merely the outward manifest symptoms of a deeper unmanifest cause. The real crisis is spiritual. Humanity has become disconnected from Truth, from its intrinsic Sattva—the state of purity, coherence, and harmony with Life itself. This is the real battleground. And as all wisdom traditions have taught, without inner alignment, external solutions are futile.

This is the fire we stand before. The Phoenix does not rise by resisting the fire—it surrenders to it and is reborn *because* of it. The question is no longer whether the fire will come, but how we will meet it: as the conscious architects of renewal or the unconscious victims of entropy?

II. The Two Paths: Collapse or Rebirth

The civilizations before us have crumbled under the weight of their own incoherence. Rome, Byzantium, the Indus Valley, the Maya—each rose to prominence, only to succumb to the same internal entropy that now grips modern humanity. The difference? Never before has collapse been a planetary event. Never before has the fate of all Life hung in the balance of a singular species' choices.

Humanity's trajectory is reaching a climax, and the choice before us is stark: we either submit to the forces of entropy and face collapse, or we embrace the fire of transformation and emerge reborn.

Path One: Planetary Cataclysm

If we remain on our current path of incoherence—ecological devastation, spiritual alienation, synthetic control mechanisms, and economic servitude—the result is inevitable:

- **Ecological Breakdown:** The unchecked destruction of the biosphere accelerates, leading to mass extinctions, desertification, rising sea levels, and irreversible climate shifts. Nature, which has always been self-regulating, will remove what does not align with its rhythms. Humanity is not exempt from this law.

- **Spiritual Collapse:** As materialism deepens its grip, people become further disconnected from meaning, purpose, and the higher intelligence that governs Life. Nihilism, depression, and escapism (through addiction, entertainment, and technology) consume the masses, leading to widespread psychological and emotional instability.

- **Mass Displacement and War:** Resource scarcity—food, water, arable land—will trigger the largest human migrations ever recorded. Nations will fracture, and wars will erupt over dwindling supplies, furthering the cycle of destruction.

- **Technocratic Control and Loss of Autonomy:** In response to the chaos, centralized powers will seize greater control under the guise of "safety." Surveillance, digital currencies tied to behavioral compliance, and a loss of personal freedoms will redefine human existence.

- **The Descent into Totalitarianism:** As desperation grows, societies will gravitate toward authoritarian leaders who promise security in exchange for sovereignty. This cycle has played out throughout history, but never before on a global scale.

This is the natural outcome of unchecked spiritual decay. When mankind forgets its divine nature, it descends into a beastly existence where fear, survivalism, and control dictate reality.

Path Two: The Phoenix Rising

The alternative is the path of conscious transformation—not a passive hoping for things to change, but an active participation in the alchemy of renewal. This requires stepping into the fire willingly, undergoing the necessary purification, and co-creating a new paradigm in harmony with Life's intelligence.

The rise of the Phoenix is not an easy path, but it is the only path that leads to true regeneration. It demands:

- **A Return to Spiritual Intelligence:** Recognizing that we are not separate from the Cosmos but deeply woven into its fabric. Aligning our actions with higher order intelligence rather than mechanistic, reductionist thinking.

- **Rebuilding from a Foundation of Sattva:** Sattva, the state of purity, harmony, and coherence, must become the new standard for our individual and collective decisions. This means moving beyond fear-based, reactive choices into decisions that are in service to Life.

- **Dismantling the False Systems:** The institutions that perpetuate disharmony— whether financial, educational, medical, or political—must be dissolved and replaced with structures that are regenerative and aligned with Truth.

- **A Revolution in Human Consciousness:** This is not merely about policy changes or technological advancements; it is about a complete shift in how we relate to reality itself. A civilization of awakened individuals does not need to be forced into order—it will self-organize into coherence and harmony with the intelligence of Life itself.

The Crucible is Already Here

The window of opportunity is closing. The choice is no longer theoretical; it is being made every day by individuals, leaders, and nations.

The Phoenix does not rise in comfort. It rises through fire.

The question is: Will we choose to be burned by unconscious destruction, or will we step into the fire of transformation and emerge reborn?

III. The Reality of Collapse: What Cataclysm Looks Like

Throughout history, civilizations have collapsed under the weight of their own corruption, hubris, and misalignment with the natural order. The fall of Rome, the disintegration of Byzantium, and the decline of Weimar Germany all followed eerily similar patterns—social fragmentation, economic instability, overreach of centralized power, and a deep moral and spiritual decay. The difference today is that collapse is no longer isolated to one empire or region—it is planetary.

Phase 1: The Early Symptoms (Denial & Disruption)

- **Economic Volatility:** Inflation surges, markets become unstable, and supply chains buckle under pressure. Governments implement short-term fixes, which only exacerbate systemic failures. Hyperinflation and recession cycles become common.

- **Political Distrust:** Corruption is exposed at unprecedented levels. Public confidence in institutions erodes. Governments become more authoritarian in their responses to dissent, using fear to maintain control.

- **Psychological & Spiritual Breakdown:** Anxiety, stress, and fear rise as uncertainty dominates. Many seek escape in addiction, material distractions, or digital realities, while others fall into despair and nihilism.

- **Technocratic Crackdowns:** Governments increase surveillance, impose digital compliance measures (such as social credit systems), and control financial transactions under the pretense of "stability."

- **Growing Social Unrest:** As frustration mounts, civil disobedience, mass protests, and violent riots escalate. Communities fracture along ideological lines, creating heightened polarization.

Phase 2: The Tipping Point (Survival Mode)

- **Resource Wars Begin:** Food and water scarcity become dire. Conflicts over resources erupt, first between smaller factions and later between entire nations. Energy crises deepen as fossil fuel reserves diminish and alternative systems remain underdeveloped.

- **Mass Migrations Escalate:** Entire populations are forced to flee regions affected by famine, war, and environmental collapse. Borders close, refugee camps overflow, and human trafficking networks expand.

- **The Breakdown of Law & Order:** Governments struggle to maintain order. Some nations descend into civil war, while others impose martial law. Private security forces and warlords rise as traditional enforcement structures fail.

- **Global Governance Attempts to Tighten Control:** Elite groups push for a centralized global governance model, using digital IDs, biometric tracking, and AI policing to "restore order." Compliance becomes mandatory for access to food, work, and mobility.

- **Spiritual & Existential Crisis Deepens:** People either awaken to a deeper Truth or fully submit to despair. Some rediscover the wisdom of ancient spiritual traditions, while others turn to cult-like ideologies and extremist movements.

Phase 3: The Descent into Chaos (Total System Failure)

- **Complete Economic Collapse:** Fiat currencies hyperinflate, losing all value. Banking systems fail, leading to a transition to barter economies. Only those with tangible resources (land, food, water, skills) survive with autonomy.

- **Technocratic Governance Reaches a Breaking Point:** The centralized control system either consolidates total power—turning society into a digital feudal state—or collapses under its own inefficiencies, leading to lawless anarchy.

- **Spiritual Reckoning:** Humanity faces a stark divide—those who have transcended the illusion of control and reconnected with the intelligence of Life thrive in new, localized communities, while those who cling to the old paradigm are consumed by fear and chaos.

Reframing Collapse as a Spiritual Test

History teaches us that collapse is not simply an economic or political failure—it is the natural consequence of a civilization that has lost its way. The external breakdown is merely the reflection of internal fragmentation.

- Collapse does not destroy Truth—it only burns away the Falsehoods and illusions that could never stand.

- It is not merely an end, but an initiation—a purification by fire.

- Those who cling to the old systems will suffer the most; those who align with universal Truth and coherence will navigate the transition.

The real question is not whether collapse can be avoided. It cannot. The real question is: Will you face it as a victim of entropy or as an architect of renewal?

The next section will explore the fire of transformation—the necessary purification that leads to the Phoenix's rise.

IV. The Necessary Fire: A Purification, Not a Punishment

Throughout history, fire has been both a destroyer and a purifier. In the Vedic traditions, fire is central to the concept of Agni, the divine force that consumes impurities and transforms offerings into blessings. In alchemy, fire is the great catalyst, burning away the dross to reveal the philosopher's stone. In Christian mysticism, the "baptism by fire" signifies a profound spiritual awakening. And in the Phoenix myth, fire is the essential force of rebirth.

Fire does not destroy for destruction's sake—it purifies, clears away the false, the stagnant, and the corrupt to make way for something new, vibrant, and aligned with higher intelligence.

Humanity now stands in the flames of its own making. Whether we experience this as a cataclysmic inferno or a transformative initiation depends entirely on how we engage with it.

The Nature of This Purification

What is being burned away is not Life itself, but the incoherent structures that oppose it. This is a necessary dissolution—not a punishment, but a consequence of misalignment.

What must be sacrificed to the fire:

- **Corrupt Institutions:** Political, economic, and social systems built on manipulation, greed, and control.

- **Materialist Dogma:** The belief that only the physical is real, that existence is mechanistic, and that meaning is an illusion.

- **Spiritual Bypassing:** The false notion that awakening means escaping reality rather than engaging with it.

- **The Victim Mindset:** The refusal to take responsibility for one's consciousness and actions, externalizing blame onto the system, elites, or fate.

- **Technocratic Illusions:** The belief that technology alone can solve the crisis, without addressing the spiritual and ethical distortions that created it.

Everything that lacks coherence with Truth will burn—because it must. The fire is neither personal or discriminates. It is not punishment—it is purification by operation of immutable Cosmic law.

The Role of Sattva in the Purification

In the Vedic tradition, Sattva represents purity, harmony, clarity, and alignment with Life's intelligence. It is the quality of consciousness that sees reality as it is, unclouded by fear or illusion.

To navigate the fire, we must embrace Sattva—not as an abstract ideal, but as a way of being.

- **Truth over Comfort:** Choosing to see what is real, even when it is difficult.

- **Simplicity over Excess:** Releasing attachment to the superficial distractions that keep us asleep.

- **Harmony over Struggle:** Aligning with the natural flow of Life instead of fighting against it.

- **Inner Sovereignty over Dependence:** Reclaiming our ability to think, feel, and act from our own center.

The fire is already burning—and the more we resist it, the more painful it becomes. But those who embrace purification willingly will emerge lighter, clearer, and ready to build the world that comes next.

Rebirth Through the Flames

The Phoenix does not rise because it fears death; it rises because it surrenders to it.

This is not just an abstract lesson—it is the reality of our time. What is false will burn. What is true will remain.

The question is: Will you allow yourself to be transformed, or will you be consumed?

The next section will explore how we move forward—how to step beyond collapse into the conscious creation of a new paradigm.

V. Transcending the Illusion of Apocalypse

Collapse is not the end—it is a transition to the next phase of evolution. Throughout history, humanity has perceived great collapses as apocalyptic finalities, yet each time, a new paradigm emerges from the ashes of the old. The fall of Rome paved the way for the Renaissance. The Black Plague gave rise to radical shifts in human consciousness and governance. What seems like destruction is often the fertile ground for something greater to be born.

The ego fears death because it cannot see beyond itself; in Truth, this is a shedding of illusion. Much of what humanity clings to today is ephemeral—constructed identities, material excess, power structures built on false premises. The deeper reality is that all that is unaligned with Truth must dissolve, making space for something more coherent, more authentic, and more in tune with the intelligence of Life itself.

Just as the Phoenix does not resist the fire but surrenders to it, we are called to embrace the necessary transformation that is upon us. Resisting only deepens suffering. The fear of collapse is, at its core, the fear of loss—the loss of familiarity, the loss of control, the loss of old identities. Yet, just as day follows night, rebirth follows dissolution. Those who recognize this transition for what it is—a gateway rather than an end—will find themselves leading the way into a new world.

This is the Crucible where only Truth survives. The illusions of control, of permanence, of separation from Life are melting away. What remains is that which is unshakable— the eternal, the intrinsic, the foundational principles that have guided enlightened civilizations throughout history. To transcend the illusion of apocalypse, we must release attachment to the false and step into the unknown with trust.

The question is not *whether* transformation will happen—it is already underway. The only question that remains is: Will we surrender to the fire and rise anew, or will we cling to what is crumbling and be consumed by it?

VI. The Phoenix Code: Humanity's Path to Resurrection

The Phoenix is one of the most enduring symbols of transformation across ancient traditions. The Greeks saw it as a mystical bird that self-immolated and emerged reborn from its own ashes, embodying the cycle of death and renewal. In Egyptian mythology, the Bennu bird was a divine being linked to the sun god Ra, signifying the Soul's resurrection. In Hindu and Buddhist thought, the Phoenix aligns with the cycles of karma and reincarnation, reinforcing that destruction is never the end, only a doorway to another phase of existence. Even in Christian mysticism, resurrection is central—the metaphor of being "born again" through trials, shedding the old self to emerge as something greater.

The Phoenix Code is not just mythology—it is a fundamental law of transformation. Civilizations rise and fall, individuals go through dark nights of the Soul, and ecosystems cycle through death and rebirth. This process is encoded into the very fabric of existence, and now, humanity itself is facing its own Phoenix moment. The question is not whether we will undergo this transformation—it is already happening. The question is: Will we embrace it consciously, or will we resist and suffer the flames?

The path forward requires intentional action. How do we consciously embrace the path of rebirth?

1. **Sacrifice the Old:** Let go of the dying world and its false promises. The systems built on deception, control, and unsustainability must dissolve to make room for something new. This is not about destruction for its own sake, but about creating space for higher-order coherence. Just as a forest fire clears dead wood to allow new growth, we must release what no longer serves Life.

2. **Step Into the Fire:** Transformation requires actively engaging with the process of purification. This is the alchemical fire—burning away illusions, attachments, and fears that hold us back from true evolution. Those who resist will suffer, while those who surrender to the process will emerge purified, refined, and capable of co-creating a new reality.

3. **Reclaim Sovereignty:** Humanity must take responsibility for its own awakening—no external savior is coming. The greatest deception of the modern world is the belief that solutions lie in external authorities, technologies, or institutions. True sovereignty begins within—when individuals reclaim their inner power, their divine intelligence, and their capacity to shape reality.

4. **Align With Life's Intelligence:** The new world must emerge from alignment with Natural law and the grand architecture of Life itself. The mechanistic worldview that treats existence as a dead machine has failed. The only sustainable path forward is one of coherence, interconnection, and reverence for the intelligence embedded in all things. This is not a return to primitivism but an ascension into a higher-order civilization that thrives in harmony with the Cosmos.

The Phoenix does not lament what has burned—it rises anew, transformed, and unburdened. Just as individuals must pass through their own Crucible to achieve enlightenment, humanity as a whole must pass through its trial by fire.

To embrace the Phoenix Code is to step into this transformation willingly—to recognize that the end of one world is merely the beginning of another. Those who cling to the ashes of the past will find themselves trapped in suffering, while those who rise will become the architects of a new era.

This is the path of humanity if we choose it.

VII. The Final Choice

We have reached the defining moment—the crucible where humanity decides its future. Everything discussed up to this point has led to one ultimate question: Will we remain bound to the collapsing remnants of an old paradigm, or will we step forward into the unknown and co-create a new world?

This is not a theoretical question. It is a choice each individual must make now, because the transition is already unfolding. The structures of the past are crumbling, revealing their inherent unsustainability. The Falsehoods and illusions that held them together are dissipating, leaving only raw Truth in their place. There is no refuge in neutrality, no escaping forces grander than us. The old world is collapsing—will you rise with the Phoenix or perish in its ashes?

The Fork in the Road: Collapse or Co-Creation

1. **Clinging to the Old:** Fear-driven Minds will seek to restore the past, desperately holding onto power structures, material excess, and hierarchical control systems. But this is like trying to rebuild a house that has already burned down—the foundation is gone.

2. **Embracing the New:** Those who awaken to the deeper reality will walk forward—not in blind optimism, but with the clarity that this moment is an initiation into something radically new. They will build regenerative systems, align with natural intelligence, and lay the groundwork for a civilization that operates in coherence with Life.

The Role of Conscious Individuals

It is a fallacy to believe that humanity must collectively choose the same path for transformation to occur. The Truth is, transformation begins with individuals who lead the way. Throughout history, profound shifts have always been initiated by those who saw beyond the collapse and had the courage to act in accordance with higher Truth.

- **You are not powerless in this process.** Your choices, actions, and consciousness contribute to the formation of what comes next.
- **Small groups of awakened individuals**—not vast majorities—will establish the templates for the new paradigm.
- **The morphogenetic field of consciousness** is shaped by those who hold the highest frequency of Truth, coherence, and alignment with Life.

The Time of Decision Is Now

There is no waiting for a "better time" to awaken. There is no savior coming to rescue humanity from itself. The moment of reckoning is already upon us, and we are being called to make a choice:

- **Fear or Truth**
- **Submission or Sovereignty**
- **Entropy or Creation**
- **Extinction or Evolution**

The Phoenix has already taken flight—will you rise with it, or will you remain in the ashes?

A Glimpse into What Comes Next

The Copernican Revolution forced mankind to realize it was not the center of the Cosmos. It shattered illusions and reoriented humanity's understanding of its place within the grand design. Now, a new revolution is upon us—one that does not change our place in space, but our very perception of self.

The Christos Revolution is upon us—a revelation that will shatter the illusion of separation, awakening mankind to its true sovereignty, intelligence, and Divine essence. This is not merely a shift in thought; it is the unraveling of a false reality that has conditioned humanity for millennia.

This is the call: Transcend our psychosis. Restore harmony. Reclaim Truth. The next chapter will illuminate the final step in this journey—the revolution within.

In every Crucible, there's a choice that must be made.

HUMANITY'S CRUCIBLE:
PLANETARY CATACLYSM OR THE PHOENIX

EXECUTIVE SUMMARY

Why Should You Read This Chapter?

Humanity is standing at its defining moment—a Crucible of transformation where we must decide whether to embrace rebirth or succumb to collapse. The Polycrisis we see today—geopolitical instability, economic turmoil, environmental degradation, and societal fragmentation—is not the real crisis. These are merely symptoms of the Meta Crisis, a deeper spiritual disconnection that has left mankind lost, fragmented, and in disharmony with Life itself. This is not just a moment of collapse—it is an initiation.

This chapter examines the two diverging paths ahead:

- **Planetary Cataclysm**—a descent into entropy where humanity clings to outdated paradigms, leading to war, economic collapse, mass migrations, authoritarian control, and a complete loss of autonomy.

- **The Phoenix Rising**—humanity's conscious rebirth, where we willingly sacrifice Falsehoods, embrace purification, and co-create a reality rooted in Truth, sovereignty, and alignment with Life's intelligence.

The fear of collapse often stems from a misunderstanding of its true purpose. This chapter reframes collapse not as an end, but as a gateway—a necessary fire that burns away illusions, clears out corruption, and creates space for something new. It invites the reader to transcend fear, embrace transformation, and take an active role in shaping the emerging world.

If you want to understand why our world is unraveling, what this transition truly means, and how to navigate it with clarity and purpose, this chapter provides the necessary insights to move beyond fear and into conscious creation.

Executive Summary: Key Takeaways

- **Collapse is a spiritual initiation, not just a material breakdown.** The fall of civilizations has always mirrored the disintegration of collective consciousness. What we are experiencing now is a planetary initiation, forcing us to either evolve or perish.

- **The Polycrisis is the symptom, not the root cause.** Ecological devastation, economic instability, and geopolitical turmoil are manifestations of a deeper disease—the fragmentation of human consciousness and our disconnection from Life's intelligence. Until this root cause is addressed, no external solution will be sufficient.

- **Fear of collapse stems from attachment to illusion.** The greatest suffering comes not from change itself, but from our **resistance to it. When we recognize that the old systems were never sustainable to begin with,** we can let go and step into transformation rather than clinging to what is already crumbling.

- **The Phoenix Code is a universal pattern of transformation.** Mythology and history reveal that all great transitions follow a cycle of destruction, purification, and rebirth. From alchemy to spiritual traditions, the Phoenix archetype teaches us that fire is not the enemy—it is the path to renewal.

- **The world is not ending; it is unraveling to reveal Truth.** Just as the Copernican Revolution shattered humanity's false perception of the Cosmos, this moment is dissolving the illusion of separation and control. This unraveling is necessary for the restoration of harmony.

- **Regeneration is not a passive process—it requires conscious engagement.** Those who simply wait for external events to dictate their future will be swept away by entropy. Those who actively engage with transformation will be the architects of the new paradigm.

- **A small number of awakened individuals can shift the entire trajectory.** History has shown that meaningful change has never required the majority—only a critical mass of individuals aligned with higher Truth. Consciousness moves in quantum leaps, not linear progression.

- **The final choice is upon us.** Humanity stands at a fork in the road—one path leads to chaos, the other to coherence. The question is not whether we will undergo transformation; it is whether we will embrace it consciously or be forced into it through suffering.

- **The Christos Revolution will be the great awakening of our time.** Just as past revolutions forced humanity to expand its understanding of reality, the Christos Revolution will reveal the greatest Truth of all—that we have been trapped in illusion, disconnected from our divine intelligence. The call is clear: transcend the psychosis, restore harmony, and reclaim Truth.

THE CHRISTOS REVOLUTION: THE UNRAVELING OF THE UNIVERSE WITHIN

Section I: Introduction to Christos

The Christos Revolution is the apex of spiritual sovereignty—an awakening to our Divine essence and the remembrance that we are, and always have been, conscious co-creators of reality. It is not a religious movement, nor does it require submission to any external authority. Instead, it is a revolution of inner realization, liberation, and divine embodiment.

For too long, humanity has been conditioned to look outside itself for salvation—through institutions, doctrines, and intermediaries who claim to hold the keys to the Divine. The Christos Revolution shatters this illusion. It is not about kneeling before a throne but rising into our own Divine inheritance. Spiritual initiation has always been about reclaiming one's sovereignty, yet over time, religious systems have distorted this universal Truth, demanding submission to external figures who present themselves as gatekeepers of enlightenment.

The Christos—also referred to as Christ Consciousness—is not exclusive to Christianity but rather a universal principle embedded in all great wisdom traditions. It is the same spiritual principle known as Buddha Nature in Buddhism, Atman in Hinduism, and Higher Self-awareness in many other traditions. Names change, but the essence remains the same—the direct experience of Divine awareness beyond the limitations of the ego.

The term Christos comes from the Greek word for "anointed," referring to the Divine Spark within each being. It signifies the awakening to one's inherent Divinity—the realization that the sacred flame of the Divine is not something external but something already embedded within the Soul.

Hence, Christos is not an ordinary state of consciousness—it is an exalted state, a pinnacle of spiritual evolution. To step fully into Christ Consciousness is not something we achieve overnight, nor even in a single lifetime. It is the highest spiritual aspiration, requiring deep devotion, purification, and lifetimes of unfolding. Yet, nothing is more important than embarking upon this path. The Christos is not a goal to be reached but a journey to be walked with reverence, discipline, and love. Every step forward refines our awareness, aligns us with higher Truth, and draws us ever closer to the luminous brilliance of Divine embodiment.

The Christos Revolution is not a ritual but a fire test—an alchemical Crucible where all illusions of false identity are incinerated, revealing only the untarnished gold of our Divine Truth. This is not about believing in something outside of ourselves but about *becoming* what we were always meant to be.

At the heart of this Revolution lies *autopoiesis*—the divine self-poetry of our Becoming. We are not just participants in Life; we are its poets, its sculptors, and its masterpieces all at once. Every choice, every thought, every act of creation is a line of poetry written onto the living canvas of the Universe. To awaken the Christos within is to recognize that our Life itself—who we are Being—is a work of Divine art, shaped by our conscious will and intention.

The Christos Revolution is already unfolding—not in the future, but right now. It is manifesting in every individual who chooses to step into their own power, embody their Divine nature, and express the highest Truth of their Being. The question is not whether it will happen. The only question is: will we answer its call?

Why Should You Read This Chapter? This chapter is the transcendent purpose of *The Crucible Manifesto*. It is both a revelation and an invitation—a call to recognize that your liberation, your sovereignty, and your highest creative expression are already within you. The Christos Revolution is not something distant, nor something external— it is already alive within you. Will you step into the fire and become what you were always meant to be?

Section II: The Path of Initiation

To embark upon the Christos Revolution is to walk the Path of Initiation—a sacred journey of transformation that has been encoded in spiritual traditions throughout the ages. This is not an intellectual pursuit nor a passive belief system; it is a radical transformation that demands everything of the seeker—body, Mind, and Soul. True initiation is not merely about knowing but about *becoming*.

Initiation vs. Indoctrination: The Liberation of the Soul

For centuries, religious institutions have replaced initiation with indoctrination, transforming the process of ascending into spiritual sovereignty into one of descending into external dependence. Indoctrination demands submission to an external doctrine, often mediated by clergy, institutions, or sacred texts. It establishes a hierarchy of knowledge where spiritual Truths are filtered through intermediaries who claim authority over divine wisdom. By contrast, true initiation does not seek to constrain or control—it seeks to liberate.

The Christos Revolution is a return to authentic spiritual initiation, one that requires no external validation or approval. It is the unveiling of one's own divine knowing, a direct communion with higher intelligence. The Christos is not something to be *believed in*—it is something to be *embodied*. The only authority in this process is the inner compass of Truth that lies within each Soul.

The Threefold Fire of Initiation

Throughout history, esoteric traditions have spoken of the three great fires that all initiates must pass through. These are:

1. **The Fire of Purification** - The burning away of egoic illusions, false identities, and attachments that tether one to lower states of consciousness.

2. **The Fire of Transformation** - The deep inner work of restructuring one's reality, shedding conditioned patterns, and forging a new foundation based on divine wisdom and universal Truths.

3. **The Fire of Embodiment** - The final stage where all separation dissolves, and Life itself becomes the stage for the unfettered expression of Divine artistry. Here, one no longer seeks enlightenment—they are it.

Each fire tests the seeker. Many resist the first fire, unwilling to release the comfortable illusions of the false self. Others linger in the second fire, struggling with the magnitude of internal transformation. Few reach the third fire, where all that is false has been transmuted, and Life itself becomes a radiant expression of Divine essence.

The Role of Suffering and the Dark Night of the Soul

Initiation is not a comfortable process. It is often accompanied by suffering, trials, and the collapse of everything one once believed to be true. This is the Dark Night of the Soul, a Crucible of despair where all external meaning falls away, leaving the seeker naked before the unknown. But within this darkness, a light begins to emerge—the light of the Christos within. The deeper the descent, the greater the revelation.

This is not punishment but an act of supreme grace—an unmaking of the false so that the indestructible Truth may stand revealed. Those who endure the Dark Night with courage and surrender emerge reborn, their consciousness no longer confined to the limitations of the material world but infused with the living wisdom of higher reality.

The Journey of a Lifetime (or Many Lifetimes)

To walk the Path of Initiation is to commit to a lifelong, and often multi-lifetime, journey of refinement. There is no shortcut, no fast track, no external savior who can do the work on our behalf. The Christos Revolution is not an event—it is a state of becoming. And every step forward, every moment of revelation, every conscious act of Truth and love brings us closer to embodying that which we seek.

The true initiate understands that there is nothing more important than this journey—that every other worldly concern pales in comparison to the liberation of the Soul. When one steps onto this path, there is no turning back, for to taste the nectar of divine Truth is to forever hunger for its fullness. The Christos within us calls not for blind faith, but for devotion, courage, and unwavering commitment to Truth.

Will You Walk This Path?

What lies ahead on this path? The trials, the revelations, the Crucible that transforms the seeker into the Christos embodied. In the next section we'll delve into the path that's the journey to Christ Consciousness and demystify some of the facets of spiritual initiation.

Section III: The Journey to Christ Consciousness

The journey to Christ Consciousness is the greatest spiritual pilgrimage—a return to the original, undistorted state of Being. This path is not about attaining something external but about remembering and reclaiming what has always been within us. It is a process of deep unlearning, shedding false identities, and stepping into the full radiance of our Divine essence.

The Christos as a Living Force

Christ Consciousness is not an abstract ideal but an exalted state of Being—a direct reunion with the living higher order intelligence that creates and animates all things. It is not something we attain, but something we remember and restore within ourselves. It is the primordial creative force behind all existence, the underlying structure of Divine creation. To awaken to our Christ Consciousness within is to become a conduit for Divine will, embodying wisdom, love, and creative power in perfect harmony.

This is not a metaphor—it is an actual shift in vibrational state, awareness, intelligence, and our entire state of Being. The more one aligns with Christ Consciousness, the more Life itself becomes an expression of Divine artistry.

The Obstacles to Christ Consciousness

The greatest barrier to Christ Consciousness is the false self, or the egoic identity. Conditioned beliefs, trauma, and collective programming obscure the Christos within, keeping us tethered to fear, scarcity, and separation.

Key obstacles include:

- **Ego Attachment** – The illusion of self-importance and separation from the Divine.

- **Mental Constructs** – Conditioned beliefs that distort Truth and limit perception.

- **Emotional Wounds** – Unprocessed trauma and unresolved pain that block divine flow.

- **External Distractions** – The relentless pull of societal expectations, materialism, and artificial identities.

Dissolving these barriers reclaims our sovereignty, allowing us to gradually rise into higher octaves of consciousness.. This is the inner revolution that births the Christos fully realized.

Initiatory Stages of Christ Consciousness

There are **three fundamental stages** on the path:

1. **Awakening to the Christos Within** – The initial realization that the Divine is not separate but inherent within.

2. **The Purification Process** – Deep inner clearing, releasing distorted perceptions, attachments, and conditioning.

3. **Embodiment & Expression** – Living in full alignment with Divine Truth, becoming a beacon of Christ Consciousness in the world.

Each stage requires courage, humility, and a willingness to surrender to Divine intelligence. It is not a straight path but a spiral—returning again and again to deeper layers of realization.

The Christos and Autopoiesis: Becoming a Spiritual Poet

As we step deeper into Christ Consciousness, we engage in *autopoiesis*—the sacred art of the self-poetry of our existence. We are not merely awakening to Truth—we are sculpting it through the art of our Being. Every thought, action, and expression is an extension of the intelligence of Life, a brushstroke upon the grand canvas of existence.

To fully embody Christ Consciousness is to become the living art of Creation itself—not in an abstract sense, but as an actualized, breathing reality. It is to become the poet, the sculptor, and the Divine masterpiece simultaneously.

For the spiritual Poet, Life itself is the ultimate canvas—never finished, only refined, as da Vinci so wisely observed: *"Art is never finished, only abandoned."*

The Invitation to Rise

The journey to Christ Consciousness is open to all, but it requires radical authenticity, unwavering devotion, and the courage to walk the unknown path. Most often, we don't choose to awaken—the Universe chooses for us. Once the Truth serum has been dropped, we have the choice of when we're willing to go on the Path of Initiation, but the Path itself is no longer an option.

Many approach this path but hesitate at its threshold, retreating when the fires of transformation burn too brightly. Few press forward, yet those who do come to know a reality more beautiful, vast, and alive than they ever imagined. This is not a path for the many—but it is a path for the willing.

Section IV: Dissolving the Illusion of Separation

The greatest deception of the false self is the illusion of separation—the belief that we are isolated fragments adrift in an indifferent Universe. This illusion fuels the mechanics of fear, scarcity, division, and control, ensuring that we remain disconnected from the Truth of our divine nature.

In the Vedic traditions, this veil of illusion is called Maya—the grand deception that convinces us that reality is only what we perceive with our five senses. Maya is the play of form, the constantly shifting and impermanent nature of the material world, which keeps us bound to cycles of ignorance and suffering. The deeper reality, however, is hidden beneath this veil—a reality where all things are interconnected, where nothing is separate from Source, and where duality itself is an illusion.

Similarly, in Gnosticism, the veil is personified as the Archons, forces that keep humanity blind to its Divine origins. The Gnostics understood that the material world, as perceived by the unenlightened, is a construct designed to trap Souls in ignorance. Only through direct knowledge—gnosis—does one pierce the veil and reclaim awareness of their Divine nature. This same understanding can be found across esoteric traditions: the recognition that separation is not real, but a mental construct imposed by the conditioned Mind.

The **false self thrives** on:

- **Fear** - The belief in vulnerability, isolation, and the threat of annihilation.

- **Scarcity** - The illusion that love, time, resources, or worth are finite.

- **Division** - The perpetual categorization of self and others, fueling polarization, separation, and conflict.

- **Control** - The impulse to dominate external reality rather than master our inner world.

By contrast, the **Christos within exists in a state of:**

- **Love** - The recognition that all of existence is held in the embrace of Divine intelligence and unconditional Love.

- **Abundance** - The understanding that the Source is infinite, and we are direct emanations of it.

- **Unity** - The knowing that separation is an illusion and that all things are interconnected.

- **Sovereignty** - The realization that our true power arises from inner alignment, not external dominance.

Shattering the Mechanistic Worldview

For centuries, humanity has been conditioned to perceive the Universe as a lifeless, mechanistic system—a soulless machine operating on cold, impersonal laws. This materialistic worldview has severed our recognition of the intelligence of Life itself, leaving us stranded in a paradigm of disconnection.

But science, spirituality, and metaphysics are now converging to reveal a far deeper reality:

- The Universe is not a random, dead system but a living, intelligent, interconnected field of energy and consciousness.

- Quantum physics, sacred geometry, and esoteric wisdom all point to the same Truth: everything is vibrational, everything is interwoven, and intelligence permeates all things.

- Mystics, sages, and visionaries have always known what science is just beginning to confirm: the Universe is alive, conscious, and self-organizing.

When we awaken to this, the illusion of separation dissolves. We no longer see ourselves as isolated entities but as integral expressions of a vast, interconnected Whole. This inner shift in awareness is the Christos Revolution.

Recognizing the Veil of the Egoic Mind

The egoic Mind is the architect of separation. It constructs a veil—a perceptual filter that distorts reality, keeping us trapped in limitation. It whispers that we are alone, powerless, and finite, feeding the false identity that clings to fear and control.

But the Christos within sees through this veil. It recognizes that there was never separation, only the illusion of it. The invitation of the Christos Revolution is to step beyond the confines of the egoic Mind and into higher awareness—to see the unity behind all apparent dualities, the intelligence behind all seeming randomness, and the love that underlies all things.

To pierce the veil is to reclaim our true sight. It is to remember that the Divine spark has never left us—we have only been looking through a fog of conditioned perception. The deeper we go within, the more clearly we see that we were never separate, never alone, and never disconnected from the whole of Creation.

This is the dissolution of the illusion.

This is the return to Truth.

The question is: Are we ready to see?

Section V: The Role of Suffering & The Dark Night of the Soul

All revolutions begin with crisis—the Christos Revolution is no different. The process of spiritual awakening often emerges from the depths of suffering, when the old structures of identity, belief, and reality begin to crumble. This collapse, while painful, is not a punishment but an invitation—an initiation into a higher state of being.

The Dark Night of the Soul as an Initiation

Despite its name, the Dark Night of the Soul is rarely a singular event, nor is it limited to just one "night." It can last for days, weeks, months, or even years, depending on the depth of transformation required. It is one of the most profound spiritual initiations, a rite of passage that many seekers undergo multiple times in their journey of awakening. As we continue seeking higher consciousness and greater expansion, we will likely encounter many Dark Nights—each one serving as a deeper purification of the self.

This experience is not meant to break us, though it often feels that way. It is a necessary destruction of the false self, the ego-constructed identity that clings to illusion and separation. The Dark Night strips away all that is not real, exposing the Soul to the raw essence of Truth. The death of the old self becomes the fertile ground upon which the new, awakened self may rise.

Yet, as we progress on the spiritual path, we gain greater mastery over these Dark Nights. We develop tools, awareness, and inner strength that allow us to navigate them with more grace. Rather than being consumed by suffering, we learn to surrender to it as part of the sacred alchemy of transformation. The Dark Night, then, is no longer perceived as something to be feared but as an integral part of spiritual evolution.

Suffering as a Catalyst for Awakening

Though suffering is often viewed as something to be avoided, in the grand design of spiritual evolution, it serves a sacred purpose. Suffering is an alchemical force, a Crucible that refines and purifies which translates into rising in level of consciousness. It is through pain, loss, and hardship that we are often forced to look beyond the illusions of the material world and seek the eternal Truths that lie beyond form.

To those who resist it, suffering feels like an unbearable weight. To those who embrace it with awareness, suffering becomes the very fire that transfigures our ignorance into awareness, and our awareness into lived wisdom. Every challenge, heartbreak, and moment of despair carries within it the seed of higher awakening.

The Christos Revolution calls for a new way of seeing suffering—not as a curse, but as a doorway to rebirth. When we stop resisting our trials and instead lean into them, we begin to see that every dark night carries the promise of dawn. The light we seek is already within us; suffering merely burns away the veils that prevent us from seeing it.

This is the path of transformation.

This is the passage through fire.

This is the Soul's rebirth.

Section VI: The Collective Christos Revolution

The awakening to Christ Consciousness may begin as an individual journey, but it does not remain isolated—it expands beyond the self, reverberating through the collective field. Higher levels of consciousness resonate at higher frequencies and vibrations, and as individuals ascend, their creative force and electro-magnetic imprint on the morphogenetic field expands exponentially, influencing the morphogenetic field of the collective at ever-increasing levels. As the field rises in frequency and vibration, all of humanity is lifted in a way akin to a rising tide lifting all boats.

The 100th Monkey Effect: How Consciousness Shifts Collectively

Both scientific inquiry and esoteric wisdom point to a profound Truth: consciousness operates within a morphogenetic field, where individual awakenings accumulate until a critical mass is reached—a threshold that shifts the collective as a whole. This phenomenon, often called the 100th Monkey Effect, illustrates how a shift in individual consciousness, when adopted by a sufficient number of people, suddenly spreads across the collective. It is as if a threshold is crossed, and what was once difficult to attain becomes natural for all.

Throughout history, we have seen this pattern emerge in social, scientific, and spiritual revolutions. The Christos Revolution follows this same trajectory: at first, it is an isolated movement of pioneers, but as more individuals awaken, the frequency of divine awareness saturates the field, accelerating the transformation of humanity as a whole.

Dismantling the Old Paradigm Through Transcendence, Not Resistance

The Christos Revolution does not engage in opposition—it renders opposition unnecessary. Rather than battling the existing power structures, it moves beyond them, dissolving their hold through the sheer force of awakened consciousness. Resistance only strengthens the system it seeks to overthrow. The old world order—rooted in control, manipulation, and scarcity—collapses not because it is forcibly dismantled, but because it no longer finds resonance in an awakened humanity.

Power structures are sustained by fear and dependency. When enough awaken, a critical mass of energy gets withdrawn from these false systems, and like a house without a foundation, the illusion collapses. This is why true revolution is not an act of violence, but an evolutionary leap. It is an ascension of consciousness that renders the old ways irrelevant.

A Peaceful, Evolutionary Leap Beyond the Old World

Unlike past revolutions, which were marked by bloodshed and conflict, the Christos Revolution is not a battle—it is a shift. It is a turning away from the broken mechanisms of the past and an embrace of a new way of Being.

- It does not seek to overthrow governments; it seeks to make them unnecessary.

- It does not attack institutions; it dissolves the need for them.

- It does not fight the old; it simply builds the new, until the old is left behind like a discarded shell.

This is not an external war, but an inner transformation that reshapes the world by reshaping the individual. When enough individuals embody Christ Consciousness, the world itself must change, for the outer world is only a reflection of the inner.

The Universality of Spiritual Awakening

True spirituality does not demand allegiance to any particular doctrine, text, or esoteric wisdom teaching. It does not matter whether one is inspired by the Vedic traditions, Gnosticism, Taoism, Buddhism, or any other path of initiation—what matters is the authentic pursuit of higher Truth. As the ancient axiom states: "There are many roads, but they all lead to Rome." Each Soul resonates with different spiritual languages, yet all sincere seekers ultimately converge upon the same Divine realization—the awakening to unity, love, and Christ Consciousness.

The Call to Collective Awakening

The Christos Revolution is already underway. It is happening in individuals, in communities, and across the energetic field of humanity. The question is not if it will reach its tipping point, but when.

Every person who steps into their Divine nature accelerates this shift. Every act of love, Truth, and wisdom moves the collective closer to its awakening. The invitation is clear:

The tide of awakening is rising. It is no longer a question of if this revolution will reach its tipping point, but who among us will rise to meet it. Who will step forward as a beacon of Divine embodiment? Who will become the bridge to a higher humanity? Will we be the generation that steps beyond limitation? Will we be the ones who embody Christos not just as individuals—but as the very fabric of a new humanity?

Section VII: Embodying the Christos

The Christos Revolution is not merely a realization—it is a way of Being. To awaken to Christ Consciousness is one thing, but to embody it is another. Embodiment is the highest expression of spiritual mastery; it is the active, living manifestation of Divine Intelligence in thought, word, and deed.

What It Means to Embody Christ Consciousness

To truly embody Christos is to integrate it into every aspect of Life. It is not an abstract philosophy, nor a belief system confined to scripture or meditation—it is a lived reality. Those who walk this path express Christ Consciousness through:

- **Acting with Love, Integrity, and Sovereignty** - Every action is aligned with Truth and guided by the intelligence of Life itself.

- **Seeing the Divine Spark in All Beings** - Recognizing that every Soul, regardless of its stage of evolution, is an emanation of the One.

- **Living in Harmony with Natural Law** - Understanding that Divine Will is not arbitrary but encoded in the fabric of existence, guiding all things toward coherence and evolution.

Embodiment is not perfection—it is presence. It is the ability to stay rooted in Divine awareness, even in the face of chaos. The world may remain in disharmony, but the embodied Christos moves through it with clarity, grace, and unwavering Truth.

Personal Responsibility as a Spiritual Act

Many seek external solutions for the dysfunctions of the world, yet few recognize the inner transformation required to truly create change. Embodying Christos is an act of radical responsibility, for our inner state shapes the outer world.

- **Consciousness is Co-Creative** - We are not passive observers of reality; we are active participants in its unfolding. Every thought, intention, and action contributes to the collective field.

- **Sovereignty is Essential** - True awakening is the recognition that authority does not lie outside of us—it emanates from the Divine spark within.

- **The External is a Reflection of the Internal** - The distortions we see in the world are manifestations of deep unconsciousness. When we reclaim our own Divine alignment, we restore harmony within—and by extension, to the world around us.

The Christos Revolution does not happen through force; it happens through each individual taking full responsibility for their spiritual embodiment. It is not about waiting for salvation but becoming the salvation we seek.

Shifting from Passive Belief to Active Embodiment

The world is filled with those who believe, but few who embody. Many intellectually grasp spiritual principles, yet continue to live in opposition to them. The Christos path demands more—it requires full integration, where knowledge is no longer something held in the Mind but something lived through every breath.

The shift from belief to embodiment is not just a stage of spiritual evolution—it is the essence of spirituality itself. In the end, all theory, all knowledge, and all teachings are meaningless if they are not lived. Embodiment is the only true measure of awakening. It is the difference between reading or talking about love and becoming love, between knowing Truth and being Truth. Crossing this threshold means fully embodying one's Divine nature—not as an abstract ideal, but as a lived reality.

This is the final frontier of the Christos Revolution.

The invitation is clear:

Will we embody the Christos—not as a distant ideal, but as the breath in our lungs, the fire in our hearts, and the very essence of our Being?

Section VIII: The New World: A Christos-Aligned Reality

A world reborn in Christos Consciousness is not a distant dream—it is an inevitable emergence. As more individuals awaken and embody Divine intelligence, a new reality takes form—one guided not by coercion, control, or scarcity, but by Life's intelligence and higher Truth.

A World Guided by Life's Intelligence and Higher Truth

The systems of the old world—built on fear, separation, and domination—are dissolving under the weight of their own incoherence. The new world is not something we force into existence; it manifests organically when enough beings align with Truth. This reality is governed by:

- **Divine Wisdom** - A recognition that the highest intelligence is already woven into the fabric of Life itself.

- **Natural Law** - A return to the self-organizing principles that sustain harmony in all of Creation.

- **Sovereignty & Unity** - A paradox where each being stands in their full Divine power while simultaneously recognizing their interconnection with all of Life.

The Phoenix Rising: Humanity Reborn into Higher Awareness

Humanity stands at the precipice of transformation. Like the Phoenix, we are undergoing a necessary immolation—a sacred fire that consumes the old so that something higher may emerge. The structures, paradigms, and beliefs that have bound us in limitation are dissolving, not as an end, but as the birth pains of something new. This is not destruction for destruction's sake—it is a necessary purification, an alchemical process that allows the new to emerge.

This rebirth is not for an elite few—it is open to all who choose it. The Christos path is not about waiting for a savior or an external force to bring change—it is about becoming the architects of the new world by mastering the architecture of our own Being. As within, so without.

Beyond Utopian Idealism: The Inevitability of Emergence

Skeptics may dismiss the vision of a Christos-aligned world as utopian idealism, yet this emergence is not wishful thinking—it is the natural progression of consciousness. Evolution has always moved toward greater complexity, coherence, and intelligence. Just as the caterpillar cannot remain forever in its cocoon, humanity cannot remain trapped in lower states of awareness indefinitely.

The Christos Revolution does not need permission from outdated institutions or power structures. It does not require the approval of the masses. It only requires a critical mass of awakened beings, and from there, the rest will follow. As consciousness expands, the old world naturally fades, making way for the new.

The Christos Revolution is Already Happening

It does not begin tomorrow. It does not depend on external events. It is already happening—one awakened Soul at a time.

Every individual who chooses to live in alignment with Truth accelerates the shift. Every act of Love, every expression of Divine Will, and every moment of unwavering

Presence is a thread in the grand tapestry of the new world being woven into existence.

The only question that remains is:

Will we rise as the Phoenix, embracing the sacred fire of transformation? Or will we remain among the ashes, grasping at the remnants of a world that was never meant to last?

Section IX: Call to Action: Answering the Call

The Christos Revolution is not a prophecy of the future—it is unfolding now. It is not something we wait for, nor is it dependent on external circumstances. It is already in motion, manifesting through every awakened Soul that dares to embody Divine Truth in the present moment.

The Revolution is Here, Now

Many seek change outside of themselves, believing transformation will come from new systems, leaders, or technologies. But the Christos Revolution does not begin out there—it begins within. The unraveling of the old world is not just a collapse of external institutions; it is the dissolution of inner Falsehoods, the release of conditioned limitations, and the emergence of authentic Divine awareness within each of us.

Every Soul that steps into its true nature accelerates the revolution. The more we embody Christos, the more we shift the morphogenetic field of humanity. The tipping point is not determined by numbers alone—it is determined by frequency, depth, and coherence of Divine embodiment. This is because consciousness operates on a logarithmic scale[1], meaning those at higher octaves of consciousness have an exponentially greater influence on the morphogenetic field of human consciousness than those at lower octaves. Critical mass then is stacked very favorably compared to needing the reach the tipping point by quantity of people only.

Will You Recognize the Christos Within and Participate?

The Christos Revolution does not ask for followers—it calls forth sovereign creators willing to walk the path of initiation. To participate in this revolution is not to pledge

_____

[1] E.g. similarly to how we measure earthquakes on the Richter scale which is based on Log base 10, meaning every increase in scale increases the magnitude exponentially.

allegiance to an ideology but to commit to the inner alchemy of transformation. It is an invitation to:

- **Reclaim Divine Sovereignty** – To recognize that Truth is not dictated by external forces but revealed through direct communion with the Divine within.

- **Act in Love and Integrity** – To embody Christ Consciousness in every thought, word, and deed, bringing coherence into the world through our own Being.

- **Stand Unshaken in Truth** – To no longer be swayed by illusion, manipulation, or fear, but to remain rooted in the knowing that Christos is who we are.

The Necessity of True Spiritual Discernment

As Epictetus wisely said, *'A man cannot learn what he thinks he already knows.'* The greatest barrier to true transformation is the illusion that we have already arrived. The egoic Mind clings to certainty, convincing us that we see reality clearly when, in Truth, we often remain bound by unconscious filters of judgment, duality, and self-righteousness.

If we still operate at the level of partisanship in politics, if we continue to judge events, people, or ideologies as *'good'* or *'bad,'* *'right'* or *'wrong,'* then we have not yet risen into the Christos archetype. The Christos does not deny Truth—it sees all things *as they are*—but it also transcends the duality that keeps humanity bound in cycles of conflict and separation.

True spiritual discernment requires deep humility. It demands that we question our own perceptions, that we examine whether we are truly seeing from the lens of Christos or from the conditioning of our ego. Are we capable of looking at the most atrocious and seemingly 'evil' actors in this world through the lens of love and compassion? Not to condone their actions, but to see them in Truth—to recognize that their deeds, as misguided as they may be, are an expression of their own level of consciousness.

To embody Christos is to see even the darkest aspects of humanity as part of the collective evolutionary journey. The external world is always a reflection of our collective level of consciousness. If we cannot love the world as it is—even in its darkness—we are not yet embodying the Christos fully. Love does not mean passivity; it does not mean enabling corruption or ignoring injustice. It means seeing with clarity, acting with wisdom, and transforming reality not through opposition, but through transcendence.

The Unraveling of the Universe Begins Within You

Every great transformation starts within the individual before it ripples outward into the collective. The Christos Revolution is no different. It is not about fixing the world—it is about becoming the world we wish to see.

When you recognize the Christos within, you will see it in all things. When you walk as a fully embodied expression of Divine intelligence, you shift the very fabric of existence itself.

At one level, this Manifesto is merely an arrangement of words—translating observations into concepts that can be intellectually analyzed. But at this level, it will do little—because the world is already drowning in information. Lack of information was never the problem.

Yet on a deeper level, this Manifesto is coded as a Truth serum—one that activates only in those truly ready to embark on their Path of Initiation. This code is not found in the words themselves, but in the intelligence woven between them. Just as music is not in the notes, but in the silence between them—so too does Truth emerge from the white space between these words.

There is nothing you can do to read this Manifesto in this way, there's no intellectual exercise to engage in as universal Truth lives far beyond the limitations of logic and reason. Truth simply is—and when it touches us, we are forever changed in ways beyond logic or reason. So too with the encoded Truth in this Manifesto—when it reaches you, nothing will ever look the same again.

There is nothing left to wait for. No savior is coming. The only question that remains is:

If you knew the Truth, would you dare to live it?

In every Crucible, there's a choice that must be made.

THE CHRISTOS REVOLUTION: THE UNRAVELING OF THE UNIVERSE WITHIN

EXECUTIVE SUMMARY

Why Should You Read This Chapter?

This chapter is the culmination of everything that has been explored throughout this Manifesto. It is not merely an intellectual conclusion but a spiritual transmission, an invitation to transformation. The Christos Revolution is not an external event, nor is it a doctrine to be followed—it is an inner revolution, a return to the highest expression of human potential through divine embodiment. This chapter unravels the layers of illusion that have kept humanity bound in separation, suffering, and limitation, revealing the profound Truth that awakening is not something we wait for—it is something we choose to embody, here and now.

The Christos path is one of initiation, responsibility, and sovereignty. To walk this path is to dissolve the false self, to see beyond duality, and to recognize that our inner world shapes the outer world. It requires us to transcend our conditioned beliefs, including the very notions of "good" and "evil," and instead see all of reality through the lens of Love+Truth. This chapter calls upon those who are ready to rise beyond the limitations of the old world, to step into a higher octave of consciousness, and to become the architects of the new world—not through force or ideology, but through the embodiment of divine intelligence.

This is not an abstract philosophy—it is a call to action. If you have ever felt the pull toward something greater, if you sense that the world is shifting and something within you is awakening, then this chapter will resonate at the deepest level of your Being. The Christos Revolution is already underway. The only question that remains is: If you knew the Truth, would you dare to live it?

Executive Summary: Key Takeaways

- **Christos Consciousness is not a belief system but an embodied state of Divine Intelligence.** It is the highest expression of human potential, accessible to those who actively walk the path of inner transformation.

- **The Christos Revolution is not an external movement—it is an inner awakening.** This revolution unfolds within individuals first, then ripples outward into the collective.

- **Spiritual initiation is a process of reclamation, not submission.** Unlike religious initiation, which demands surrender to external authority, the Christos path is about reclaiming sovereignty and recognizing the Divine within.

- **Suffering is often the catalyst for awakening.** The Dark Night of the Soul is an essential initiation that dissolves the false self, leading to spiritual rebirth.

- **The illusion of separation keeps humanity in suffering.** As long as we judge reality through the dualistic lens of "good" vs. "evil," we remain bound in limitation. Christos Consciousness transcends these polarities.

- **Higher consciousness is not attained through intellectual knowledge but through embodiment.** Understanding spiritual principles is not enough—one must live them fully.

- **The Christos path demands spiritual discernment.** The ego often convinces us that we have "arrived," yet true awakening requires radical honesty about where we truly stand in our evolution.

- **Love+Truth is the lens through which the Christos sees all things.** This does not mean condoning or excusing darkness—it means seeing it for what it is while holding the highest perspective of evolution.

- **The Christos Revolution dismantles false systems through transcendence, not resistance.** When enough individuals awaken and withdraw their energy from incoherent structures, those structures collapse naturally.

- **The New World is not a utopian fantasy but an inevitable emergence.** As consciousness ascends, the false world dissolves, making way for a reality governed by higher intelligence and Natural law.

- **No savior is coming.** The Christos path is about recognizing that no external force will rescue humanity—we are the ones who must rise.

- **The revolution is already underway—one awakened Soul at a time.** The only question that remains is: If you knew the Truth, would you dare to live it?

CHAPTER 21

A NEW EARTH OF WONDER AND BEAUTY ENVISIONED

The Dawn of a New World

There comes a moment in the arc of history when the old must die,
not as pointless tragedy, but out of celestial necessity—
for from its ashes, something is poised to rise.

We are standing at the threshold.
One world is crumbling, its foundations built on fear, scarcity, and control.
Another world emerging—rooted in Truth, harmony, and the intelligence of Life itself.

This is not a future to be waited for.
It is a choice to be made. A path to be walked.
The architects of this new world are not leaders or institutions,
but sovereign Souls who dare to remember.

To remember that true freedom is not granted,
it must be claimed.
That true abundance is not given,
it must be actualized.
That beauty is not an indulgence,
it is the very signature of the Divine.

This new world is not a daydream or abstraction,
it is already here—waiting for those with the courage to see it,
to step into it,
to become it.

The old world is burning.
The Phoenix is arising.
The question remains:

What will you choose?

Section I: The Grand Odyssey of Human Civilization & Evolutionary Inflection Points

History is not a linear march toward progress, as many have been led to believe. It is a vast, cyclical odyssey—one that has witnessed the rise and fall of countless civilizations, each reaching its moment of greatness, stagnation, and eventual decline. Across time, the same pattern emerges: flourishing abundance, wisdom, and enlightenment, followed by eras of corruption, decay, and collapse. We have seen it in the ascent and ruin of Rome, the lost grandeur of Atlantis, the fall of the Mayan empire, and the long-buried civilizations hidden beneath oceans and deserts.

But this time, something is different. Humanity has arrived at an evolutionary inflection point—a moment unlike any before, where we are no longer bound to repeat the past. For the first time in recorded history, we hold the power to break the ancient cycle of creation and destruction—to rise rather than fall, to transcend rather than decay.

This transformation is not being engineered by human hands alone. A higher order intelligence is already orchestrating this shift. The old world is crumbling—not by chance, but because it is no longer in resonance with the intelligence of Life itself. In accordance with Natural and Cosmic law, that which is incoherent cannot be sustained.

When a critical mass of human consciousness is reached, the intelligence of Life will take over. Just as nature regenerates after a cataclysm—whether an ice age, a volcanic eruption, or a hurricane—so too will humanity's transition into the New Earth emerge organically, not by force or centralized control. Forests reclaim themselves when left untended, rivers carve new paths, and Life always finds a way. So it will be with us.

This is not about imposing a system or a blueprint. It is about alignment with the greater current of Life itself—a current already flowing toward regeneration, coherence, and expansion.

Yet, the question remains: Will we rise to meet this inflection point, or will we allow history to repeat itself once more? Will we recognize the sacred responsibility of this moment, or will we cling to the past, afraid to step into the unknown?

The choice is ours. But make no mistake—this is The Great Inflection Point, the Crucible of our epoch. The opening stands before us, the future unwritten.

Will we transcend the past, or repeat it?

Section II: The Phoenix Moment: Embracing Collapse as the Dawn of Mankind's Rebirth

The world we have known is unraveling before our eyes. Institutions once thought unshakable are collapsing under the weight of their own corruption. Systems built on control, scarcity, and fear are crumbling—not due to mere mismanagement or external forces, but because they were never in harmony with the intelligence of Life itself.

Yet, this collapse is not a tragedy. It is a necessary clearing. The end of an era is not the end of existence. Just as a forest fire sweeps through the land, consuming deadwood to make way for new Life, so too is this global upheaval a catalyst for renewal. The seeds of rebirth are already present within the ashes of disorder.

And death itself is not the end of Life—it is the birth of new Life. This Universe is inherently syntropic—constantly regenerating, creating, and evolving. What we perceive as destruction is only the visible half of the equation; the unseen forces of renewal are already at work. Just as the tides of creation and dissolution shape the Cosmos, so too do they shape civilizations.

What we are witnessing is not the death of Mankind—it is the contractions of a new birth. A labor, painful yet sacred, heralding the arrival of something profoundly greater.

The discomfort, the uncertainty, the chaos—these are not omens of doom; they are the birth pains of an emerging world. And like any birth, it is raw, intense, and unpredictable. It is messy. It is chaotic. It is real. It does not conform to human timetables or expectations—it follows a deeper rhythm, the rhythm of Life itself.

And so, we stand at the threshold. Do we cling to the decayed structures of the past, resisting the inevitable? Or do we surrender to the process, trusting that something far more beautiful is being born?

Every civilization that lost its way has met its collapse. But this time, something is different. Humanity has an unprecedented opportunity—to awaken, to shift from unconscious destruction to conscious rebirth.

We are not merely passengers in this transition—we are the midwives of the New Earth.

The question before us is no longer whether the old world will fall. That is already happening. The real question is:

Will we have the courage to embrace what is coming next?

This is our Phoenix Moment—the fire that purifies, the ashes from which we now have the choice to rise.

Section III: A Civilization Rooted in Natural and Cosmic Law

Imagine a world where everything flows in effortless harmony—not because of rigid control mechanisms or imposed order, but because it aligns with the intrinsic intelligence of Life itself. A world where governance, economics, and technology are not weights imposed upon humanity, but natural expressions of the same universal principles that guide the rivers, the stars, and the unfolding of a flower.

This is not a fantastical utopia, nor is it a futurist's dream. It is simply a return to coherence. The old world fractured itself by severing its connection to these higher-order laws—forcing order through coercion rather than allowing natural harmony to emerge. In the New Earth, we no longer fight against Life—we move with it.

Economics will shift from extraction and hoarding to regeneration and circulation. The mindset of scarcity will dissolve—not through forced redistribution, but through the recognition that true wealth is holistic, expansive, and self-renewing. Abundance is not a finite resource—it is a function of creative intelligence.

Technology will no longer be wielded as a tool of dominance but will be designed to serve humanity—to enhance and integrate with Life itself. Instead of lifeless mega-cities severed from nature, human habitation will be designed in harmony with the living world—our architecture, infrastructure, and urban planning mirroring the intelligence of forests, rivers, and ecosystems.

Medicine and healing will no longer be industries of control, profiting from sickness and dependency. Instead, they will return to their true purpose—restoring coherence to the body, Mind, and Spirit. The highest form of healing is not found in external interventions alone, but in alignment with natural rhythms—nutrition, movement, breath, sunlight, water, emotional balance, and spiritual awareness. The New Earth will honor these Truths, replacing suppression with restoration, dependency with sovereignty.

This shift is not imposed. It is not a forced plan or ideology. It emerges organically, like a garden reclaiming itself when left untended. Life always seeks harmony—it is only human ignorance that has obstructed it.

The future is regenerative—a realignment with the intelligence of Life. And when we align, Life itself will take care of the rest.

Section IV: The Sacred Reunion: Restoring Harmony Between the Masculine & Feminine

For too long, the world has been trapped in disharmony—caught in an illusion that pits the Masculine and Feminine forces against one another. The old world distorted these primordial energies, elevating one while suppressing the other, leading to cycles of oppression, imbalance, and fragmentation.

Yet, these forces were never meant to be adversaries. They are the twin pillars of Creation itself—the active and the receptive, the structured and the flowing, the visionary and the nurturing. When they are in harmony, all of Life flourishes.

The New Earth is not about the dominance of one force over the other—it is about the reunion of both in their highest expression. This is not about gender, but about restoring the cosmic dance of these energies within individuals, relationships, leadership, and civilization itself.

- When the Masculine is wise, it does not abuse force or dominate—it protects and builds with integrity.

- When the Feminine is empowered, it does not submit—it creates, inspires, and gives Life to new realities.

- True power is not control—it is presence in full awareness.

- True wisdom is not passivity—it is knowing when to flow and when to act.

In the New Earth, we will see this balance reflected in every aspect of existence:

- Leadership that stewards rather than dictates.

- Business that integrates intuition with logic, ethics with ambition.

- Education that cultivates both structure and creativity.

- Families and communities where the dance of Masculine and Feminine energies fosters harmony, rather than conflict.

This is the Sacred Reunion—the restoration of coherence between these forces. And with this reunion comes the rebirth of a civilization that moves not in opposition to itself, but in union with the very forces that give rise to Life.

Where there was once division, there will be unity.
Where there was once suppression, there will be sovereignty.
Where there was once distortion, there will be coherence.

The New Earth is built upon this Sacred Reunion—and from it, a world of wonder will emerge.

Section V: A Thriving Society of Unity, Dignity, Merit, & Unfettered Expression

The New Earth is a world where every individual is honored for their inherent dignity, valued for their unique contribution, and free to express their Truth without fear. Here, identity is not a shackle but a canvas—a reflection of one's essence, rather than a source of division. No longer will people be categorized, limited, or judged by race, gender, age, or background. Instead, they will be seen and celebrated for their merit, character, and the value they bring to the whole.

This is a world where freedom of thought and expression is absolute—where no ideology, no authority, and no system dictates what one can say, believe, or explore. The days of censorship, social policing, and ideological coercion will be over. In the New Earth, Truth is not manufactured or imposed—it is discovered, debated, and refined through the free exchange of ideas.

It is a world where elders are honored as the wisdom keepers of civilization, not discarded into isolation. No longer will they be cast aside in sterile nursing homes, forgotten by the very society they helped build. Instead, they will be reintegrated into the fabric of Life, revered as mentors, storytellers, and guides, holding a sacred place in the collective evolution of the generations that follow.

But this is not a world of forced equality, nor the artificial leveling of outcomes. True equality is not sameness—it is the freedom for all to rise to their highest potential. It is a true meritocracy, where effort, wisdom, and integrity pave the way, not inherited privilege or arbitrary status. In this world, the content of one's character is what matters most, and every individual has the right to pursue greatness, to express themselves fully, and to walk their own unique path.

At the same time, individuals in this New Earth embrace a deep sense of duty and responsibility toward co-creating the world that allows them to thrive. The fragmented, hyper-individualistic culture will give way to a commonwealth of purpose—not by force, but by the recognition that humanity flourishes together.

Yet, paradoxically, societal pressures for homogeneity and uniformity will fade, making room for a celebration of our individual uniqueness within the collective. Nature thrives on diversity—its health, resilience, and beauty increase when it follows its own true nature. Conversely, uniformity depletes, weakens, and diminishes Life. The New Earth will reflect this wisdom:

- A world where dignity is not a privilege, but a birthright.

- A world where individual expression is not muted or censored but celebrated.

- A world where humanity stands in unison, not divided.

- A world where Nature is consciously honored and revered, not unconsciously exploited.

This is the foundation of a thriving civilization—one where every Soul is seen, valued, and empowered to become all they are meant to be.

Section VI: Regenerative Prosperity – Co-Creating True Wealth and Abundance

Prosperity is not the accumulation of money in offshore bank accounts. It is not hoarding, nor is it control. True wealth is the ability to create, to give, and to uplift all aspects of Life itself. It is holistic, extending beyond material riches to the well-being of people, communities, and the planet.

In the old world, prosperity was built upon artificial scarcity and extraction—designed to benefit the few at the expense of the many. It was a system driven by competition, short-term profit, and monopolization. But in the New Earth, this paradigm dissolves. A regenerative economy emerges—one that does not deplete but replenishes, that does not enslave but empowers.

This new prosperity is not dictated by centralized institutions but arises naturally through human ingenuity, collaboration, and innovation. It is not built on government decrees or corporate mandates but founded upon the timeless principles of reciprocity, value creation, and symbiosis with Life itself.

- Entrepreneurship and human creativity will drive prosperity—not financial manipulation or monopolization.

- Wealth will be seen as a flowing river, not a stagnant pond—designed to circulate, uplift, and expand the Commons rather than be hoarded in vaults.

- Regenerative industries will replace extractive ones—businesses that heal the planet, not deplete it, will become the engines of prosperity.

- Financial success will be honored, but not worshipped. It will be understood that wealth is a tool, not an identity.

This is not about rejecting financial success—it is about redefining what success truly means. In the New Earth, wealth is not measured by how much one can take, but by how much one can generate, contribute, and share.

Because in this new paradigm, prosperity is not about mere survival—it is about flourishing. It is about creating a world where all can thrive, where abundance is cultivated, and where wealth is not a mechanism of power, but a force for Life.

Section VII: The Death of Artificial Scarcity & The Birth of Limitless Abundance

For too long, humanity has been shackled to the illusion of scarcity—taught to believe that resources are limited, that abundance must be hoarded, and that Life itself is a zero-sum game. This is a distortion—an artificial construct engineered to maintain control, suppress human potential, and keep entire populations locked in survival mode rather than creation.

But the Truth has always been in front of us: Life itself is inherently abundant.

- The sun does not ration its light.

- The ocean does not measure the waves it releases upon the shore.

- A tree does not withhold its fruit, nor does the Earth hesitate to bloom each season.

Scarcity is not a Natural law—it is a manufactured system. It exists not because resources are truly finite, but because they have been hoarded, controlled, and distributed based on profit rather than need.

As the New Earth emerges, these false constructs will dissolve. Human systems—economics, agriculture, energy, and technology—will be recalibrated to align with Natural law rather than fight against it.

- Energy will no longer be monopolized or rationed. Clean, decentralized, and limitless energy sources—already within our reach—will become the foundation of a thriving civilization.

- Food will not be controlled by corporations but cultivated in harmony with Nature. Regenerative agriculture, permaculture, and self-sustaining ecosystems will replace destructive industrial farming. Hunger will become an archaic relic of the past.

- Innovation and technology will no longer be weaponized for control but unleashed for collective flourishing. Knowledge, once hoarded for profit, will flow freely—not as a commodity, but as a birthright.

Abundance is not passive. It is not something we wait for—it is something we actively cultivate and co-create.

The moment we align with the intelligence of Life, we recognize that abundance is not about having more—it is about removing the barriers that prevent flow.

This is the death of artificial scarcity and the birth of a limitless world, where energy, knowledge, and resources are no longer shackled by control, but flow freely as Life intended.

And as abundance becomes the natural state of existence, humanity will finally shift from mere survival to expansion, creativity, and the unfolding of its limitless potential.

Section VIII: The End of War: A New Era of Global Peace

War has never been humanity's natural state. It is not an inevitability, nor is it woven into the essence of who we are. War has always been engineered—a construct of control, a game played by the powerful at the expense of the many. For millennia, civilizations have been led to believe that conflict is necessary, that survival demands violence, and that peace is an illusion too fragile to ever be sustained.

But these are the lies of a lower consciousness—manufactured to keep the world divided, distracted, and enslaved to fear.

In the New Earth, war is no longer a means of governance, commerce, or ideological enforcement. With the dissolution of artificial scarcity, the manufactured reasons for conflict disappear. Nations will no longer need to battle over resources when abundance flows freely. Societies will no longer be engineered toward division when the realization dawns that humanity is one. True power will no longer be measured by military might but by the ability to create, uplift, and harmonize.

Global relations will no longer be dictated by competition, fear, or zero-sum thinking. Instead, nations will flourish through collaboration and co-evolution—each contributing its unique gifts to the whole, rather than seeking conquest or dominance.

This is not a utopian fantasy. It is a shift in consciousness—one that recognizes that peace does not come from treaties, diplomatic agreements, or disarmament. Peace is a function of alignment with Life itself. When a civilization lives in harmony with Natural and Cosmic law, war becomes obsolete.

Imagine a world where:

- No child is raised with the expectation of war, and no generation is lost to battlefields.

- No economy is built on weapons and destruction, but on innovation and creation.

- National borders do not separate enemies, but neighbors who thrive together in celebration of the many unique patinas of human culture.

In the New Earth, conflict is not eradicated through force—it dissolves because its foundations no longer exist. Humanity will have no need to fight over what is abundant, nor will it seek power through conquest once it recognizes that its true power lies in creation.

True peace will not be enforced—it will be inevitable.

Section IX: The Sacred Restored: Beauty as the Language of God

In the New Earth, beauty is not a luxury or indulgence—it is the foundation of existence itself. It is not ornamentation, nor is it mere aesthetics. Beauty is the highest organizing principle of the Cosmos—the signature of the Divine, the language through which Life speaks.

In the old world, this Truth was forgotten. Sterility replaced reverence. Life was stripped of meaning, reduced to transactions, distractions, and artificial comforts. Cities became gray and soulless, architecture became brutal and uninspired, music lost its depth, art lost its Soul, and culture became an endless cycle of shock, vulgarity, and decay. A civilization that does not value beauty cannot sustain itself.

But the tide is turning. The New Earth restores the sacred—not through doctrine or dogma, but through the deep remembrance that Life itself is holy.

Every moment, every creation, every breath is an opportunity to engage with the Divine. This shift is not abstract—it is tangible. It manifests in:

- Architecture that breathes and inspires, mirroring the intelligence of forests, rivers, and celestial geometry.

- Music and art that uplift the Spirit, awakening the Soul rather than numbing it.

- Ritual, ceremony, and sacred traditions woven into daily Life—not as obligations, but as portals to deeper connection.

A civilization that restores beauty as its highest ideal restores its connection to the Divine Order itself.

To live in beauty is to live in alignment with the sacred.

And so, the New Earth will not be a place of sterility, vulgarity, or the grotesque. It will be a place of magnificence, wonder, and awe—an ongoing symphony of Creation.

Because beauty is not an indulgence. It is a divine responsibility.

Section X: Education as the Art of Thinking & Living Freely

The old education system was never designed to cultivate intelligence. It was built to manufacture obedience. Schools became factories, producing workers who could memorize facts, follow orders, and function within a system that required compliance, not creativity. Curiosity was stifled. Critical thinking was discouraged. The Mind was not trained to explore—it was conditioned to conform.

But in the New Earth, education is not a prison for the Mind—it is a liberation of the Soul. The purpose of learning is not to mold individuals into predefined roles but to awaken their innate genius. The emphasis shifts from memorization to mastery, from compliance to curiosity, from rigid instruction to self-driven exploration.

- Sovereign critical thinking will be developed from childhood—young minds will be encouraged to question, to challenge, to seek deeper Truths.

- Experiential learning will replace passive consumption—knowledge will be gained through real-world engagement, problem-solving, and hands-on discovery.

- Creative expression will be nurtured, not suppressed—art, music, philosophy, and storytelling will be as essential as mathematics and science.

- The wisdom of Life will be taught alongside intellectual pursuits—students will learn how to navigate emotions, relationships, purpose, and self-mastery.

The classroom will no longer be a sterile, lifeless box where information is spoon-fed in standardized doses. Education will become an adventure—rooted in Nature, experience, and the infinite potential of human imagination.

No longer will children be conditioned into dependency, trained to seek validation from external authorities. Instead, they will be empowered to think, to create, to lead, and to shape the world in their own unique way.

Because the true purpose of education is not to produce docile workers.

It is to cultivate free beings—sovereign, creative, fully alive, and equipped to navigate Life masterfully.

Section XI: Sovereignty & Mastery: The Liberation from Victim Consciousness

In the New Earth, sovereignty is not just a political ideal—it is recognized and revered as the Divine, unalienable birthright of every human being. It is the understanding that no external authority, institution, or leader holds dominion over one's Life. It is the reclamation of power from all the illusions that have kept humanity bound to fear, dependency, and the false belief that salvation comes from outside rather than from within.

For too long, societies have conditioned individuals to be subjects—to look to governments, corporations, and institutions for permission, validation, and rescue. People were taught to believe they were powerless, that they must submit to external structures in order to survive. This manufactured dependency created a world where victimhood became the default state, where blame replaced responsibility, and where sovereignty was traded for comfort.

But in the New Earth, this paradigm no longer holds. The shift is profound: every individual becomes the master of their own existence.

Sovereignty is not rebellion. It is not isolation. It is alignment with the inherent Truth that all power originates within.

This transformation is seen in every aspect of Life:

- People no longer seek external saviors—they recognize themselves as the creators of their own reality.

- Dependency on corrupt institutions dissolves—replaced by self-sufficiency, ingenuity, and collaborative creation.

- Blame fades as individuals take full ownership of their choices, actions, and destinies.

- Fear of the unknown is replaced by mastery—a profound understanding that Life is not something to be controlled, but something to be navigated with wisdom and awareness.

Sovereignty is the beginning. Mastery is the next step.

Mastery is not about control—it is about knowing when to act and when to surrender. It is about governing oneself with wisdom, discipline, and discernment. To be sovereign is not to act recklessly or in isolation, but to engage with Life from a place of true power—one that does not need to dominate or control, but simply is.

And so, in this reborn Earth, the age of victims and rulers comes to an end.

There are no more masters—only the mastery of self.
There is no more submission—only the embodiment of sovereign presence.

This is the liberation of humanity—the return to its Divine birthright.

Section XII: Architects of the New Earth: The Choice to Create or Perish

We stand at a crossroads unlike any before. The birth of the New Earth is now within reach—but it is not inevitable. History is littered with civilizations that approached the threshold of greatness, only to collapse under the weight of their own blindness, corruption, and disconnection from Life.

This time can be different.

For the first time, humanity possesses the awareness, the wisdom, and the technological capacity to consciously choose its future. Unlike past cycles, where civilizations rose and fell in unconscious repetition, we have the power to break the pattern—to rise rather than fall.

But the New Earth will not be built by governments, institutions, or centralized powers. It will not emerge through passive hope or wishful thinking. It will be built by those who dare to create, who refuse to wait, who refuse to comply with the dying remnants of the old world.

This is not a passive awakening—it is an active participation in Life itself.

- The architect who designs in harmony with Nature.

- The entrepreneur who pioneers regenerative industries instead of extractive empires.

- The teacher who ignites minds instead of suppressing curiosity.

- The artist who calls people back to wonder through beauty.

- The healer who restores coherence to the body, Mind, and Spirit.

- The leader who serves rather than rules.

- The sovereign Soul who embodies a new way of Being.

There will be no decree announcing the arrival of this world. It will not come by permission. It will not be handed to us.

The only access point is within.

It begins when we choose. It begins when we act.

Breath by breath.
Choice by choice.
Action by action.
Brick by brick.

There will be failure. There will be uncertainty. The process will be messy. But every masterful creation is born from chaos—and this will be humanity's greatest masterpiece.

In every Crucible, there is a reckoning:

Will we ascend like the Phoenix, forging a world of wonder and beauty? Or remain bound to the ashes of a dying past?

The New Earth is waiting—a chrysalis poised for emergence.

The question for Mankind is: Will we rise?

The only real question for you is: Will you rise?

CHAPTER 22

CLOSING REMARKS

To know that what you've written will be ridiculed—perhaps even violently opposed—is sobering. Yet, it requires little courage to simply write. To share it with the world, however, is an act of defiance against logic and reason. To give it away freely is to renounce even the smallest personal gain.

So, why bother?

History reveals an unmistakable pattern: the greatest Minds were rarely understood in their time. We revere them now, recognizing their brilliance, but in their day, most were mocked, ridiculed, and ostracized—or worse, as in the case of Socrates, who was condemned to drink hemlock.

I have often wondered—what compelled these men and women to share their Truth anyway? Was it courage? Bravery? Or was it hubris, even foolishness?

The answer I arrived at may not be the only one, but it resonates as Truth.

The politician, scholar, educator, activist, and even the rebel exists to reach, appeal to, and be understood by the masses.

The prophet, sage, mystic, seer, and true philosopher plant seeds so that, in time, the masses may come to understand.

"A society grows great when old men plant trees
in whose shade they shall never sit."
- Stoic proverb

I do not claim to know where this Manifesto will go or what may sprout from its seed. What I do know is that something deep within compelled me to write nearly the entirety of it in just under two weeks.

And I know I did not write this for myself. It must be made available—freely—so that its distribution is in no way encumbered by economics.

More importantly, by making it available, I will have imprinted its message into the morphogenetic field of human consciousness. In that sense, my most essential task is complete.

All that remains is to stand in its Truth. Not as a defender, repelling attacks, but as a beacon—drawing in pollinators to help impregnate human consciousness with the vision of a world that, in my own consciousness, already exists.

Already vibrant.

Already fully alive.

Whether I have spoken Truth, only time will tell.

Love+Truth,
Robert

TABLE OF RESOURCES: FURTHER EXPLORATION INTO THE CRUCIBLE MANIFESTO'S THEMES

This Table of Resources is not meant to be exhaustive, nor is it a definitive roadmap. It is merely a starting point—a curated collection of works that may serve as stepping stones on your own journey of discovery. True knowing does not come from intellectual understanding alone but from direct experience, deep inquiry, and synthesis. The only real path to wisdom is the one you forge yourself.

We stand on the shoulders of the greats—the mystics, philosophers, scientists, and visionaries who have illuminated the path of wisdom before us. Their enduring legacy is a gift, not to be followed blindly, but to be examined, wrestled with, and ultimately transmuted into our own direct knowing. Use this list not as an endpoint, but as an invitation to explore, challenge, and expand your own awareness.

1. Civilization, Collapse, and the Meta Crisis

Books

- *The Decline of the West* – Oswald Spengler
- *The Collapse of Complex Societies* – Joseph Tainter
- *The Lessons of History* – Will & Ariel Durant
- *The Fourth Turning* – William Strauss & Neil Howe
- *The Fate of Empires and Search for Survival* – Sir John Glubb
- *Critical Path* – R. Buckminster Fuller
- *The 100th Monkey* – Ken Keyes Jr.

Documentaries

- *Century of the Self* (2002) – Adam Curtis (BBC)
- *Collapse* (2009) – Michael Ruppert
- *HyperNormalisation* (2016) – Adam Curtis
- *Zeitgeist: The Movie* (2007) – Peter Joseph

Research Papers

- Tainter, Joseph. *Energy and the Evolution of Complexity*
- Bardi, Ugo. *The Seneca Effect: Why Growth is Slow but Collapse is Rapid*

2. Economic Manipulation & Debt-Based Systems

Books

- *Confessions of an Economic Hitman* – John Perkins
- *The Creature from Jekyll Island* – G. Edward Griffin
- *Debt: The First 5000 Years* – David Graeber
- *When Money Dies* – Adam Fergusson

Documentaries

- *The Money Masters* (1996) – History of central banking
- *Inside Job* (2010) – The financial collapse of 2008
- *Princes of the Yen* (2014) – The rise of central banking power

3. The War on Consciousness & Suppression of Truth

Books

- *The Perennial Philosophy* – Aldous Huxley
- *The Doors of Perception* – Aldous Huxley
- *The Master and His Emissary* – Iain McGilchrist
- *Wetiko: Healing the Mind-Virus That Plagues Our World* – Paul Levy
- *Initiation* – Elisabeth Haich

Documentaries

- *Unacknowledged* (2017) – Steven Greer
- *Thrive: What On Earth Will It Take?* (2011) – Foster Gamble

4. The Mechanistic Worldview vs. The Living Universe

Books

- *Science Set Free* – Rupert Sheldrake
- *The Tao of Physics* – Fritjof Capra
- *Biocentrism* – Robert Lanza
- *Man or Matter* – Ernst Lehrs
- *The Hidden Life of Trees* – Peter Wohlleben
- *Holism and Evolution* – Jan Smuts

Documentaries

- *Mindwalk* (1990) – Systems thinking and interconnected reality
- *An Ecology of Mind* (2010) – The Life of Gregory Bateson

5. The AI & Transhumanist Agenda

Books

- *The Age of Surveillance Capitalism* – Shoshana Zuboff
- *Scanned: Why AI Hasn't Made Healthcare Better* – Eric Topol
- *The Singularity is Near* – Ray Kurzweil
- *AI Superpowers* – Kai-Fu Lee

Documentaries

- *The Social Dilemma* (2020) – The dangers of AI-driven social manipulation
- *Transcendent Man* (2009) – The ideology behind transhumanism

6. Agriculture & Food Sources

Books

- *Steiner's Biodynamic Agriculture Lectures* – Rudolf Steiner
- *The Soil and Health* – Albert Howard
- *One-Straw Revolution* – Masanobu Fukuoka

- *Regenerative Agriculture* – Richard Perkins
- *Dirt: The Erosion of Civilizations* – David Montgomery

Documentaries

- *Kiss The Ground* (2020) – The importance of soil health
- *The Biggest Little Farm* (2018) – Regenerative farming
- *Food, Inc.* (2008) – The corruption of industrial agriculture
- *Cowspiracy* (2014) – The environmental impact of industrial farming

7. The Business of Sickness & Pharma

Books

- *Deadly Medicine and Organized Crime* – Peter Gøtzsche
- *Dissolving Illusions: Disease, Vaccines, and the Forgotten History* – Suzanne Humphries
- *The Case Against Sugar* – Gary Taubes
- *The Biology of Belief* – Bruce H. Lipton, Ph.D.

Documentaries

- *What the Health* (2017) – Processed food & disease industry
- *The Bleeding Edge* (2018) – Medical devices & corporate profit

8. The Control Grid & Manufactured Consent

Books

- *Propaganda* – Edward Bernays
- *Manufacturing Consent* – Noam Chomsky & Edward S. Herman
- *1984* – George Orwell
- *Brave New World* – Aldous Huxley

Documentaries

- *The Shock Doctrine* (2009) – Naomi Klein's work on crisis manipulation
- *They Live* (1988) – Allegorical critique of mass manipulation

9. Philosophical Insights on Governance & Society

Books

- *The Republic* – Plato
- *The Politics* – Aristotle
- *The Analects* – Confucius
- *Meditations* – Marcus Aurelius
- *On Liberty* – John Stuart Mill
- *The Tao Te Ching* – Laozi

10. Spirituality & Transcendence

Books

- *The Zohar* – Kabbalistic Wisdom
- *The Tao Te Ching* – Laozi
- *The Bhagavad Gita* – Hindu Scripture
- *The Kybalion* – The Three Initiates
- *The Creative Act* – Rick Rubin
- *Finite and Infinite Games* – James P. Carse
- *The Message of the Divine Iliad I & II* – Walter Russell
- *A Course in Miracles* – Helen Schucman
- *The Untethered Soul* – Michael Singer
- *The Gene Keys* – Richard Rudd
- *The I AM Discourses* – St. Germain
- *The Dhammapada* – Teachings of the Buddha
- *The Upanishads* – Ancient Hindu Philosophical Texts
- *The Gospel of Thomas* – Gnostic Teachings
- *The Hermetica* – Teachings of Hermes Trismegistus

- *Autobiography of a Yogi* – Paramahansa Yogananda
- *Meditations on the Tarot* – Anonymous
- *The Way of the Superior Man* – David Deida
- *The Essential Rumi* – Translations by Coleman Barks
- *The Red Book* – Carl Jung
- *Be Here Now* – Ram Dass
- *Power vs Force* – David R. Hawkins, M.D., Ph.D. (Book 1 of 9, whole series recommended)
- *The Gospel of Sri Ramakrishna* – Sri Ramakrishna
- *The Perennial Philosophy* – Aldous Huxley
- *The Secret Teachings of All Ages* – Manly P. Hall

Ancient Philosophers & Thinkers

- Plato
- Aristotle
- Socrates
- Pythagoras
- Lao Tzu
- Confucius
- Zhuangzi
- Heraclitus
- Marcus Aurelius
- Epictetus
- Seneca
- Cicero
- Plotinus

Spiritual Figures & Mystics

- Jesus Christ

- Buddha (Siddhartha Gautama)

- Krishna

- Rumi

- St. Germain

- Ralph Waldo Emerson

- Walt Whitman

- Meister Eckhart

- Teresa of Ávila

- St. John of the Cross

- Paramahansa Yogananda

- Sri Aurobindo

- Jiddu Krishnamurti

- Ramana Maharshi

- Mooji

- Swami Vivekananda

- The Baal Shem Tov

- Khalil Gibran

- Manly P. Hall

- Gurdjieff

- Nisargadatta Maharaj

- Alan Watts

- David Hawkins

Renaissance & Enlightenment Thinkers

- Leonardo da Vinci

- Niccolò Machiavelli

- Francis Bacon
- Baruch Spinoza
- René Descartes
- Isaac Newton
- Johann Wolfgang von Goethe
- Immanuel Kant
- Georg Wilhelm Friedrich Hegel
- Friedrich Nietzsche
- Arthur Schopenhauer
- William Blake
- Voltaire
- David Hume
- John Stuart Mill

Modern & Esoteric Thinkers

- Rudolf Steiner
- Walter Russell
- Buckminster Fuller
- Carl Jung
- Joseph Campbell
- Terence McKenna
- Rupert Sheldrake
- Paul Levy
- David Bohm
- Ken Wilber
- Aldous Huxley
- Alan Turing

- Nikola Tesla
- Michael Talbot
- Confucius
- James P. Carse
- Richard Rudd
- Eckhart Tolle
- Michael Singer
- Ram Dass
- Sri Ramakrishna
- G.I. Gurdjieff
- James Allen
- Kahlil Gibran
- Neville Goddard
- Leo Tolstoy
- Allan Watts
- Walter Russell
- Jiddhu Krisnamurti
- Mooji
- Terrance McKenna
- Paolo Coelho
- David Hawkins
- Annie Besant
- Helena Blavatsky

Historical Leaders with Philosophical Impact

- Alexander the Great
- Marcus Aurelius

- Mahatma Gandhi
- Martin Luther King Jr.
- Nelson Mandela
- John F. Kennedy

Scientists & Systems Thinkers

- F. Buckminster Fuller
- John Muir
- Albert Einstein
- David Bohm
- Werner Heisenberg
- Max Planck
- James Lovelock
- Ilya Prigogine
- Jan Smuts
- Fritjof Capra
- Robert Lanza
- Gregory Bateson
- Lynn Margulis
- Bruce H. Lipton, Ph. D.
- Zach Bush MD
- David R. Hawkins, M.D., Ph.D.
- Allan Savory